Applesoft BASIC Toolbox

Applesoft BASIC Toolbox

Larry G. Wintermeyer

Addison-Wesley Publishing Company

Reading, Massachusetts • Menlo Park, California
London • Amsterdam • Don Mills, Ontario • Sydney

Library of Congress Cataloging in Publication Data

Wintermeyer, Larry G.
  Applesoft Basic toolbox.

  (Addison-Wesley microcomputer books popular series)
  Includes indexes.
  1. Apple computer—Programming.   2. Basic (Computer
program language)   I. Title.   II. Series.
QA76.8.A66W56 1983   001.64'24   82-22710
ISBN 0-201-14775-0

Apple, Apple II, Apple IIe, and Applesoft BASIC are trademarks of Apple Computer, Inc.

ISBN 0-201-14775-0
ABCDEFGHIJ-HA-8987654

Contents

Section I   Using Applesoft BASIC

1.   Getting Started

This book is intended for use by either the beginning or the experienced programmer. Either person should find the material helpful in writing Applesoft programs.

For the beginning programmer the first half of the book includes detailed examples of each of the Applesoft instructions. Each instruction is explained using the format of

1. Instruction name
2. Instruction format
3. Examples of instruction code
4. Purpose of the instruction
5. Rules for use
6. Illustration of the rules (examples)

The instructions are presented in a sequence in which understanding of each new instruction is based on an understanding of the instructions already presented.

It is important for the beginning programmer to spend time going through the programs included with each instruction. The programs show more than just how to code each instruction. They show how the instruction is used in conjunction with other related instructions. They point out good and bad programming techniques. They provide a visual reenforcement by seeing the instructions in action.

The amount of time spent by the beginning programmer on the first half of the text will determine how easily the disk examples in the last half of the text will be understood.

Although an explanation is included with each program, the beginner should study the program code to obtain a better understanding of each instruction and coding style used. A book on programming cannot be read as a normal book would be read. The examples must be read and reviewed until the reader has a thorough understanding of what each instruction does.

The experienced programmer who knows BASIC but does not know Applesoft BASIC should go through the first half of the book looking specifically at the coding rules. By scanning the rules the experienced programmer will be able to identify differences between Applesoft and other BASIC languages.

Even the person who already knows Applesoft may want to go through the programs to check out the coding style of another programmer. The quickest way to learn programming is to study someone else's code and to extract the best from the examples of others.

For either the beginning or the experienced programmer, the first half of the book includes good examples of how each instruction is used, and the programs provide strong reenforcement of the rules for coding each instruction.

The second half of the book covers the instructions related to using various types of disk files. A simple name and address system is used to illustrate the coding logic for three access methods. Programs related to working with sequential files, random files, and index files are listed and explained.

The disk programs illustrate the logic for creating disk files, updating disk files, and inquiry/listing operations.

You may be overwhelmed by the size of some of these programs. But if each program is studied in small sections (called modules or routines), you will be surprised at how easy they are to understand. The first half of the book will come in handy as a reference guide as you study the disk programs. You may want to flowchart or draw a diagram tracing the logic of the more difficult parts of the disk examples.

The disk programs are intended to serve as models from which you can copy and build other disk oriented programs. The logic for these programs changes very little from application to application. The screen design, names of the variables, and amount of information processed vary, but the basic program structure remains the same.

Again, the purpose of the example disk programs is to serve as a model from which you may build your own program. Use the examples when writing disk programs which create, update, and work with disk files.

A Note on Redundance

The random example contains some redundant information which was presented in the sequential example, and the index example contains some redundant information from the random example. The redundance is intentional to allow each chapter to be used individually and to provide reenforcement to newer programmers.

If the narrative sounds too redundant and you feel you already have a complete understanding of the topic, skim the material until new information is encountered.

APPLE IIe Versus APPLE II+

The programs were written on the APPLE IIe but will run on either machine. To keep the programs compatible with the APPLE II+ none of the programs use lower case letters or use screens wider than 40 columns.

Both versions of the APPLE have a CONTROL key located at the left of the keyboard. On the APPLE IIe the word is spelled out, whereas on the APPLE II+ the word is abbreviated to CTRL. This book uses the complete word as it appears on the APPLE IIe.

2. DOS Control Commands

There are nine APPLE disk control commands with which you should be familiar.

These commands are

1. INITialize
2. SAVE
3. CATALOG
4. LOAD
5. RUN
6. RENAME
7. LOCK
8. UNLOCK
9. DELETE

There are several more DOS (Disk Operating System) commands which are used in special situations. The MONitor, NOMONitor, and MAXFILES commands are covered in the second half of the book along with the disk file examples. The commands EXEC, BSAVE, BLOAD, and BRUN are not covered in detail. They are explained briefly at the end of this chapter under the topic, Other DOS Commands. See the *APPLE DOS Manual* for greater detail.

With the exception of the MONitor, NOMONitor, and MAXFILES commands, each of the DOS commands has three optional parameters. In other words, there are three units of information which you may code depending on your needs. The parameters are separated by commas and follow the keywords SAVE, CATALOG, LOAD, RUN, RENAME, LOCK, UNLOCK, and DELETE.

The three optional parameters provide information on

1. Which slot the disk control card is in
2. Which of the two drives connected to the disk control card you want to use
3. The volume number (identification number) of the diskette you want to work with

Slot Number The APPLE has eight slots in which electric components may be connected to attach external devices such as disks, printers, monitors, data communication equipment, etc. Think of each slot as an electric wall outlet into which you can plug a computer device. The disk control card is placed in one of these slots and can control up to two disk drives. This book does not use the slot number option for the DOS commands.

If you have only one or two disk drives, the computer keeps track of which slot the disk control card is in.

If you have more than two disk drives attached to your computer, see the *APPLE DOS Manual* for information on the use of the slot parameter.

Drive Number   Each disk control card used with the APPLE computer can control two disk drives. If the system you are using has only one disk drive, then the computer keeps track of everything for you. Those of you who have more than one disk drive may tell the computer which of the two drives you wish to use by entering D1 or D2 following the disk commands. Make sure each of your disk drives is physically marked DRIVE 1 (D1) or DRIVE 2 (D2) so you can keep track of which label to use.

When you omit the D1 or D2 following a disk command the computer assumes you want to work with the last disk used. For example,

SAVE PROGRAM NAME

saves the program on the last disk used

SAVE PROGRAM NAME,D2

saves the program on disk drive 2 no matter which disk drive was previously used.

If you want to use a specific drive and you are not sure which of the two drives was used last, code a D1 or D2 to indicate which drive is to be accessed. It is better to be safe than sorry.

The terms *diskette, disk,* and *floppy disk* are all synonyms. The term *diskette* or *floppy disk* is normally shortened to *disk.*

Volume Number   Each disk has an identification number, which may range from 0 to 254. The volume number acts as a security measure to aid you in protecting information on your disk. The volume number is not required when working with the disk, but if you have only one drive and are switching disks in and out of that drive, you may want to get into the habit of using the volume number to make sure the computer is addressing the correct disk.

When the volume number is not given or a value of 0 is used, the computer carries out the action you have requested on the disk without checking the label.

SAVE PROGRAM NAME
SAVE PROGRAM NAME,V000

If the volume number is used, the number following the V must match the volume number of the disk in the drive or the computer gives you a **NO MATCH** error message and cancels the action you have requested.

SAVE PROGRAM NAME,V001

The slot number, drive number, and volume number are all optional parameters. When the optional parameters are used, they may occur in any sequence, but each number must be preceded by either an S for slot, D for drive, or V for volume. Do not use the slot option unless you have more than two drives and you know where the disk control cards are connected. If you give the computer a slot number or drive number that does not exist, it tries to use the nonexistent position, and the computer system locks up!

Now that I have you completely confused and afraid to use the instructions, read the next few pages and see how easy the instructions are to use.

The **INIT** Command

Command INIT program name,Snumber,Dnumber,Vnumber
It is important to remember that this command should not be used with any disk which contains programs or files you want to keep.

Example INIT HELLO,D1,V001
Initialize the disk in drive 1 with a start up program named HELLO and a volume number of 001.

Purpose The INIT command is used to format a new disk so it may be used with APPLE DOS.

Rules for Use 1. The program name parameter of the INIT command is required.
2. If no volume number is specified, a default value of 254 is used.
3. The drive number is optional but should be included if the system you are using has more than one disk drive.
4. This command reformats the disk and destroys any data which is on the disk.

Illustration of the Rules When you buy a blank disk you must use the INIT command to format the disk so it is compatible with APPLE's DOS. Since this command destroys all information on the disk, DO NOT USE IT on any disk which contains data you wish to keep.

Diskettes must be initialized with a start-up program. As an APPLE standard this program is normally called HELLO. The program can serve simply to identify the disk or may be the drive program for a turnkey system.

A turnkey system is a computer system which is designed so all the user has to do is insert a disk into drive 1, turn the computer on, and follow the directions.

The drive program or control program of a turnkey system determines the sequence in which other programs within the system are executed.

Whenever the APPLE is turned on, the computer automatically executes the start up program from the disk located in drive 1. The process of executing the start up program from drive 1 is called *booting*. Use the following procedure to initialize a disk and create a HELLO program.

The following example uses only a very simple start up program which displays the disk name and volume number. In the chapter on sequential disk operations, an example is provided of a more involved HELLO program.

1. Insert the blank disk into the drive you are going to use. If your system has more than one drive, open the doors on all the other drives. This eliminates the chance of destroying a good diskette.
2. Use the CATALOG command to ensure that the disk is actually blank. Key in the CATALOG command as shown below and press RETURN. The disk will whirl and make a loud noise, then the message I/O ERROR (Input/Output Error) will be displayed. If you don't receive the I/O error but get a listing of the disk catalog, then check to make sure you want to destroy this disk and lose all the programs and files which are currently on it. Enter

    CATALOG,D1 <RETURN>

    Substitute D2 for D1 if you are using the second disk drive.
3. If you are sure the disk is the one you wish to initialize, continue; otherwise take out the disk and start over.
4. Key in the following HELLO program.

```
NEW
HOME
1000 REMHELLO PROGRAM
1010 HOME
1020 PRINT "** WORK DISK FOR SAMPLE PROGRAMS **"
1030 PRINT "          VOLUME 001"
1040 END
```

You can change the disk title on line 1020 and the volume number on line 1030 to any message you would like.
5. Now are you ready? Enter

INIT HELLO,V001,Dnumber

Now press RETURN and wait for about 30 seconds until the disk stops spinning and the red light on the disk goes off.

6. When the disk stops and the red light goes off, enter

CATALOG <RETURN>

You will get a catalog listing of volume number 001 as shown in the following display:

```
DISK VOLUME 001

A 002 HELLO
```

The disk is now ready to store programs or data files.

To test the HELLO program, execute the following steps:

1. Place the newly initialized disk in drive 1.
2. Turn the computer off and then back on or enter

PR#6 <RETURN>

Entering PR#6 has the same effect as turning the computer off and then back on.

Unless the APPLE computer you are working with is one of the older models, the disk will whirl and the HELLO program will run.

After the HELLO program has executed, the screen will appear as shown in the following display:

```
** WORK DISK FOR SAMPLE PROGRAMS **
           VOLUME 001
```

Making Backup Copies

Rules to smile by:

1. Always keep a backup copy of your programs and data files.
2. Temporary backups may be kept on the same diskette.
3. Permanent backups should be kept on a separate disk and in a physical location separate from the original disk.

One of the first lessons you will learn is to always keep a backup copy of your work. Sooner or later you will experience the frustration of losing a file or program because of one of the following:

1. After spending time writing or changing a program, you forget to SAVE the program before turning off the computer.
2. While you are keying in a large program, power to the computer is lost, and you did not periodically SAVE your work.
3. You have been working on several programs, and without thinking (or checking) which program is currently in memory, you SAVE the program. Later you discover you SAVEd the program in memory under the same name which was used to SAVE a previous program. The earlier program is destroyed, and unless you have a backup copy you must rekey the old program. If you do not have a printed copy, you must rethink and recode the logic.
4. You have made some minor changes to one of your programs which works with a disk file. Since the changes were minor, you didn't test the program completely. Later you find that because of a program error, the data on the disk file you were using has been destroyed. If you do not have a backup copy of the data file, you must now spend hours keying in the data to recreate the file.
5. Your disk gets destroyed by spilled coffee, stray magnets, folding and mutilation, etc.
6. There are many other ways to lose programs and files. You will probably find some of your own unique methods. Please keep a backup copy of your work.

Creating Periodic Backup Copies

While working on a new program or making major changes to an old program, SAVE the program periodically, but use a new name each time. After you are done you can go back and delete the older versions of the program. In the example that follows the V stands for *version* and is followed by a number indicating the most recent version.

Example
SAVE program name V1   then 30 to 40 lines later
SAVE program name V2   then 30 to 40 lines later
SAVE program name V3

How to Make a Backup Copy of a Program

Making a backup copy of a program is easy. First, use the LOAD command to copy the program from the disk to the computer's memory. Second, use the SAVE command to transfer the program from memory to the new disk. This process works only for Integer BASIC and Applesoft BASIC programs. Text files and binary files cannot be copied using this method.

When saving the backup copy use the same program name but add the word BACKUP or COPY2 to it.

For single disk systems:

1. LOAD program name
2. Take out the original disk and replace it with the backup disk
3. SAVE program name BACKUP

For two disk systems:

1. LOAD program name,D1
2. SAVE program name BACKUP,D2

Making Backup Copies of Data Files or Large Numbers of Programs

If you want to make a copy of a data file (or what APPLE calls a text file), the system disk, which comes with the APPLE computer, contains a good copy program. The FID program (FIle Developer) can copy any type of file (Text, Applesoft BASIC, Integer BASIC, Binary) individually or as a group from one disk to another. If you have a copy of the system disk and *APPLE DOS Manual,* read the section in the manual on how to use the FID program. If you do not have a copy of the program or manual, find someone who does, and make it a point to learn how to use the FID program.

Making a Backup Copy of an Entire Diskette

If you want to make a copy of an entire disk, APPLE has a utility program named COPYA which will do the job. The term *utility program* refers to a program normally provided by the computer manufacturer which serves the common processing needs of persons using the computer. The COPYA program is one of the main utility programs you should know how to use. If you have a copy of the system disk and *APPLE DOS Manual,* use this program whenever you want to create a complete backup of a disk.

The **SAVE** Command

Command   SAVE program name,Snumber,Dnumber,Vnumber

Example   SAVE PAYROLL PROGRAM,D1,V001

Saves the program on disk volume 1, located in drive 1, under the name PAYROLL PROGRAM.

Purpose   The SAVE command is used to copy the program currently in memory to a disk and assign it a name.

Rules for Use

1. The SAVE command must be followed by the name you wish to assign to the program currently in memory.
2. The program name may be from 1 to 30 characters long. It must start with an alphabetic character. If the name is not unique, that is, if you use a name which already exists on the disk, then the old program is deleted and the new program stored under that name.
3. The slot, drive, and volume parameters following the keyword **SAVE** are optional and may occur in any sequence. If the optional parameters are used, each number must be preceded by either **S** for slot, **D** for drive, or **V** for volume. Each parameter must be separated by a comma.

When the drive number is not given, the computer places the program on the last drive used. If you wish to place the program on a specific drive, use either **D1** or **D2** to indicate which drive.

When the volume number is not given, the computer stores the program without checking the label of the disk. If the volume number is used, the number following the **V** must match the volume number of the disk or the program is not stored.

Illustration of the Rules   Key in the following program:

```
NEW
1000 HOME
1010 PRINT "SAVE COMMAND"
1020 PRINT "  1. GIVES PROGRAM A NAME"
1030 PRINT "  2. COPIES IT TO DISK SO THAT IT CAN"
1040 PRINT "     BE USED AGAIN."
1050 END
```

If you want to save the program on a disk other than the one which is currently in the drive you are using, switch the disks now, i.e., take out the disk you don't want to use, and put in the one onto which you want to copy the program.

Before entering the SAVE command, you must know which disk drive is going to be used when storing the program. If you only have one drive, you do not need to use D1, and don't try to use D2. Should you have two drives, decide which drive you want to write the program on. Use D1 for drive 1 or D2 for drive 2.

Now enter the following command with the correct number following the D. If you have only one drive, omit the comma and disk parameter.

SAVE DISK COMMANDS SAMPLE1,Dnumber <RETURN>

The disk will whirl for about 5 seconds and stop. If the cursor returns and a message has not appeared on the screen, you have now stored a program on the disk. Should you get an error message, make sure you have the correct diskette in the correct drive and try again.

To check your work and ensure that the program was written on the disk, see the CATALOG command in the following section.

The **CATALOG** Command

Command CATALOG Snumber,Dnumber,Vnumber

Example CATALOG,D1

Lists the programs and files which are on the disk located in drive 1.

Purpose The CATALOG command allows you to list on the screen the programs and files which are stored on a disk.

Rules for Use
1. The slot, drive, and volume parameters following the keyword CATALOG are optional and may occur in any sequence.
2. When the drive number is NOT SPECIFIED the computer lists the catalog or index of the disk which is in the last drive accessed. Use D1 or D2 to override the default option.
3. If the volume number is specified, the computer checks for a match. When the volume numbers do not match, the computer cancels the command and lets you put the correct disk in the drive. After the correct disk is in the drive, you must reenter the CATALOG command.

Illustration of the Rules

To see what files are on the disk, enter the following command:

CATALOG,Dnumber <RETURN>

The disk will whirl, and the program and file names will be listed on the screen. The terms *file* and *program* are synonyms when discussed in conjunction with the APPLE disk catalog. When there are more than 18 names on the disk, the screen fills up and stops so you may read the information. If the file is not in the group being displayed, press any symbol key, and the computer will show you more file names from the disk's catalog. Depending on how many files are on the disk, you may need to look through several screens before you find the right program name. A disk may contain up to 105 files.

Remember you are looking for the program named DISK COMMANDS SAMPLE1 which you just SAVEd on the disk. Since the program was just SAVEd, you might think it would be the last one listed in the CATALOG. This may or may not be the case, as DOS puts the name of the program in any available space. If you have been adding and deleting files from your disk, there will be gaps where names have been deleted. When you SAVE a program or create a data file, DOS puts the name in the first unused area of the catalog.

Did you find the program name?

If so, continue; if not, type in CATALOG <RETURN> to see the list again. If the program is not there, go back and start over with the SAVE command.

Did you notice that when you entered the CATALOG command the first line displayed gave the disk volume number? If you did not see the disk volume message enter the CATALOG command again. The first line will read

DISK VOLUME 001

Each line of the catalog listing consists of four parts. The first character of each line indicates whether the file or program is locked.

*A 023 LOCKED APPLESOFT PROGRAM
↑ Asterisk indicates file is locked

 T 015 UNLOCKED TEXT FILE
↑ Blank indicates file is unlocked

The second character of each line indicates the type of file or program format.

*A 011 RANDOM ADDRESS UPDATE PROGRAM
 ↑ An A indicates an Applesoft BASIC program

The following codes are used to represent the four types of disk files.

A: for Applesoft BASIC programs
I: for Integer BASIC programs
B: for Binary files
T: for Text files

The numbers next to the file name indicate how much room (in sectors) each file takes up on the diskette. Each disk sector contains 256 characters, and each disk has 496 sectors available for programs and files.

```
*A 003 program or file name
   ↑↑↑ Indicates that the program or file takes up 3 disk sectors
```

The following represents a sample CATALOG listing of disk 001.

```
DISK VOLUME 001

 A 003 HELLO
*T 018 LOCKED TEXT FILE 18 SECTORS
 I 020 UNLOCKED INTEGER BASIC PROGRAM
 B 027 UNLOCKED BINARY PROGRAM
```

The LOAD Command

Command LOAD program name,Snumber,Dnumber,Vnumber

Example LOAD PAYROLL PROGRAM,D1
The system locates the name PAYROLL PROGRAM on the disk in drive 1 and then LOADs the program into memory.

Purpose The LOAD command copies a program from the disk into memory. You normally use the LOAD command to retrieve a program from the disk in order to make changes or to review the code before running the program.

Rules for Use (Some of these rules should sound familiar.)

1. The program name must be spelled exactly as it was orginally recorded or the program is not loaded.

2. The slot, drive, and volume numbers following the program name are optional. If the slot, drive, or volume numbers are used, they may occur in any sequence.
3. When the drive number is not specified, the computer looks for the program on the last disk drive accessed.
4. When the volume number is specified, it must match the disk in the drive being referenced in order for the program to be loaded.

Illustration of the Rules

Load the program by entering

LOAD DISK COMMANDS SAMPLE1,Dnumber <RETURN>

Use of the comma and drive number is optional if the program is on the disk drive which was used last. Otherwise you must tell the computer on which drive the program is located.

The disk will whirl as the program is being loaded. The longer the program, the longer the disk will run.

If the cursor comes back on the screen and no error message has been displayed, then the program was successfully loaded. Now to convince yourself that the program is really there, enter

HOME <RETURN>
LIST   <RETURN>

What do you know! There it is! (I hope.)

If the computer beeps and displays the error message

FILE NOT FOUND

check that you spelled the name correctly.

If you spelled the name exactly as you did when you SAVEd the program, be sure you have the right disk in the correct drive. If you have done all this correctly, go back to the CATALOG command and find the name of the program. Recheck the name on the disk and make sure you have spelled it EXACTLY as it is shown on the catalog listing.

Before going on, see what happens when you do make a mistake.

Don't ever be afraid of making mistakes. Most programmers learn by trial and error. To err is human, to err perfectly takes a computer.

1. Misspell the name and see what happens. Enter

LOAD DISK COMMANDS SAMPLE 1 <RETURN>

Notice that there is a space between SAMPLE and 1. You will get the message

FILE NOT FOUND

2. Take out the disk and see what happens. Enter

LOAD DISK COMMANDS SAMPLE1 <RETURN>

In this case the spelling is correct but there is no disk from which to read the file. You will get the message

I/0 ERROR

3. If you have an extra disk, place it in the drive where the computer expects to find the program and see what happens. Enter

LOAD DISK COMMANDS SAMPLE1 <RETURN>

In this case the spelling is correct, but the disk being searched does not contain the program. You will get the message

FILE NOT FOUND

The **RUN** Command

Command RUN program name,Snumber,Dnumber,Vnumber (DOS format)
RUN (Applesoft format)

Example RUN PAYROLL PROGRAM,D1
The system locates the program named PAYROLL PROGRAM on the disk in drive 1, loads it into memory, and runs it.

Purpose The DOS version of the RUN command copies a program from the disk into memory and then starts executing it. If you want to execute a program without looking at or changing the code, use the RUN command.
The DOS RUN command both loads and executes the program, while the LOAD command shown previously only brings the program into memory.
The Applesoft version of the RUN command is used to execute the program currently in memory and does not load a program from the disk.

Rules for Use (The rules for Snumber, Dnumber, and Vnumber have been omitted; see the SAVE command.)

1. If the RUN command is used without any parameters, the program currently in memory is executed. RUN by itself is an Applesoft command and does not involve any disk operations.
2. If RUN is followed by a program name, the name must be spelled exactly as it was originally recorded or the program is not run.

Illustration of the Rules

If you have just LOADed a program, RUN it by entering

RUN <RETURN>

Otherwise, both load and run a program by entering

RUN DISK COMMANDS SAMPLE1 <RETURN>

(use drive number if needed).

After you have entered the RUN command, the screen will clear and the four lines of information from the program will be displayed (see sample screen). Remember, the program was written and saved in the SAVE command section.

```
SAVE COMMAND
  1. GIVES PROGRAM A NAME
  2. COPIES IT TO DISK SO THAT IT CAN
     BE USED AGAIN.
```

If the program did not work as expected, go back to the SAVE command and start over or attempt to correct the code and rerun the program.

The RENAME Command

Command RENAME current program name,new program name,Snumber,Dnumber, Vnumber

Example RENAME PAYROLL PROGRAM,PAYROLL PROG,D1
The system locates the name PAYROLL PROGRAM in the disk library and then changes it to PAYROLL PROG.

Purpose   The RENAME command can be used to change the names of either programs or files.

Rules For Use   (The rules for Snumber, Dnumber, and Vnumber have been omitted; see the SAVE command.)

1. The first name must be exactly the same as the current name on the disk.
2. The second parameter represents the new name for the program or file. The new name should not exist on the disk or else the renaming process causes two files with the same name to be on one diskette. If a disk contains more than one file with the same name, you can only access the first of the two files.

For the RENAME, LOCK, UNLOCK, and DELETE commands the terms *file* and *program* are synonomous. These four DOS commands treat text files the same as program files. Normally the term *file* is used to describe a text file, while the term *program* is used to describe a file of instructions.

Illustration   The name assigned to the program was fairly long. Let's give the program a shorter
of the Rules   name by entering

RENAME DISK COMMANDS SAMPLE1,DISK INST EX1 <RETURN>

(use drive number if required).
   The disk will whirl, and when the cursor returns, the name has been changed. If you get an error message such as FILE NOT FOUND check your work and try, try again.
   To see if the RENAME instruction worked, list the catalog by entering

CATALOG <RETURN>

The new name DISK INST EX1 will be somewhere in the catalog listing.

The **LOCK** Command

Command   LOCK program name,Snumber,Dnumber,Vnumber

Example   LOCK PAYROLL PROG,D1
   The system finds the program named PAYROLL PROG in the disk library (catalog) and flags the program as being protected.

Purpose   Programs: The LOCK command allows you to tag a program as protected, and the computer does not allow it to be DELETEd, or RENAMEd, or another program SAVEd under the same name.

Text Files: The LOCK command also allows you to tag a data file as protected, and the computer does not allow it to be DELETEd or RENAMEd. The computer also prevents a program from creating a new file with the same name or writing new records to the locked file. A text file which is locked can ONLY BE READ. If you try to write to a LOCKed file, the program is canceled and an error message is displayed.

Rules for Use   (The rules for Snumber, Dnumber, and Vnumber have been omitted; see the SAVE command.)

1.   The RUN, LOAD, and CATALOG commands are not affected by the LOCK command.
2.   The SAVE, RENAME, and DELETE commands cannot be used on a file or program name once it has been LOCKed.
3.   Before the SAVE, RENAME, or DELETE command can be used with a file or program name which is locked, the UNLOCK command must be used.

Illustration of the Rules   Let's pretend the program you are using is worth protecting. Lock it by entering

LOCK DISK INST EX1 <RETURN>

The disk will whirl, and the blinking cursor will appear with no messages displayed. If you get an error message, check the spelling, make sure you have the correct disk in the correct drive, and try again.

To check your work, use the CATALOG command to list the disk directory. You should get the following entry.

*A 002 DISK INST EX1
↑ Asterisk indicates locked Applesoft program

Now try to destroy the program by any of the following methods:

1.   SAVEing a program with the same name. Enter

SAVE DISK INST EX1 <RETURN>

You will get the following message:

FILE LOCKED

2. RENAMEing the program. Enter

RENAME DISK INST EX1,WILL NOT WORK

You will get the following message:

FILE LOCKED

3. DELETEing the program. Enter

DELETE DISK INST EX1

You will get the following message:

FILE LOCKED

In theory the only way to destroy a LOCKed program is to destroy the disk.

The **UNLOCK** Command

Command UNLOCK program name,Snumber,Dnumber,Vnumber

Example UNLOCK PAYROLL PROG,D1
The system finds the program in the disk library and then *removes* the flag indicating that it is protected.

Purpose The UNLOCK command allows you to change your mind and remove the protection provided by the LOCK command.

Rules for Use (The rules for Snumber, Dnumber, and Vnumber have been omitted; see the SAVE command.)

1. Think twice before you UNLOCK a file or program. Once the program is unlocked, it can be destroyed by accidentally saving a program under that same name or mistakenly deleting the program.
2. You can tell which files are unlocked by using the CATALOG command. If the file is locked there is an asterisk (*) at the far left of the screen. When no asterisk appears in front of the program or file name, the information is unprotected.

Illustration of the Rules The program you placed on the disk is not worth protecting. Use the UNLOCK command to remove the protection of the program so it may be deleted. Enter

UNLOCK DISK INST EX1 <RETURN>

Use the CATALOG command to check whether the asterisk was removed. Enter

CATALOG <RETURN>

The program name will be listed in the catalog without an asterisk in the leading character position.

 A 002 DISK INST EX1
↑ Blank character indicates file is not locked

The DELETE Command

Command DELETE program name,Snumber,Dnumber,Vnumber

Example DELETE PAYROLL PROG,D1

The system removes the program name from the disk library. The program is lost and the space it occupied freed.

Purpose The DELETE command allows you to remove currently unwanted programs or files from the disk. I stress *currently* because after you delete a program you may change your mind.

Rules For Use (The rules for Snumber, Dnumber, and Vnumber have been omitted; see the SAVE command.)

1. Make sure you want to delete the file or program before entering the command.
2. Spell the name correctly, and make sure you use the name of the program or file you intend to delete.
3. Double check. Think twice. Is there a backup copy? Are you sure you want to DELETE the file? If so, press RETURN.

Illustration
of the Rules

Since the program does not really do anything useful and you will not need it anymore, delete it by entering

DELETE DISK INST EX1 <RETURN>

To make sure the program has been deleted, use the CATALOG command. Enter

CATALOG <RETURN>

The name DISK INST EX1 should no longer be in the catalog listing.

Other DOS Commands

The following DOS commands are used in special situations. For further information on these commands, see the *APPLE DOS Manual*.

BSAVE f,Aa,Ln,Snumber,Dnumber,Vnumber

Where:

f = FILENAME
Aa = A is followed by the starting address in memory from which the data is to be copied
Ln = L is followed by a value indicating the number of bytes to be copied to the disk

The BSAVE command is used to create a disk file containing the contents of a specific area of memory. It can be used to save a high-resolution graphics picture or to save a machine language routine which has been POKEd into a specific memory location.

BLOAD f,Aa,Snumber,Dnumber,Vnumber

Where:

f = FILENAME
Aa = A is followed by the starting address in memory into which the data is to be copied

The BLOAD command is used to load a disk file into a specific area of memory. It can be used to load a high-resolution graphics picture into the first or second high-resolution screen area or to load a machine language routine which can later be executed by the CALL instruction.

BRUN f,Aa,Snumber,Dnumber,Vnumber

Where:

f = FILENAME
Aa = A is followed by the starting address in memory into which the data is to be copied

The BRUN command is used to load a disk file into a specific area of memory and then branch to that address to start execution of a machine language program.

EXEC filename

The EXECute command is used to run a text file consisting of DOS commands and lines of BASIC code. The commands in the text file operate as if they had been entered from the keyboard. Use of the EXEC and TEXT file allows a stream of programs and processing steps to be linked together in such a way that the operator need only know how to turn the computer on and enter data.

3. The HOME Instruction

Instruction   HOME

Purpose   The HOME instruction is used to clear the screen and position the cursor in the upper left hand corner of the screen.

Rules for Use   1.   The instruction may be used in either immediate execution mode or program execution mode. *Immediate execution mode* means the instruction is executed when the RETURN key is pressed. To enter an instruction in immediate execution mode, leave off the statement number.

HOME <RETURN>

The screen is cleared immediately upon pressing RETURN.

Use the HOME instruction in immediate execution mode to clear the screen and position the cursor when entering new programs.

2.   *Program execution mode* means the instruction is not executed until it is encountered during the execution of a program. Any statement which starts with a line number is only executed after a RUN command has been given.

NEW   <RETURN>
1000 HOME   <RETURN>
RUN   <RETURN>

The screen is not cleared until after the RUN command is entered.

Use the HOME instruction in the program execution mode to clear the screen and position the cursor during program execution.

3.   The HOME instruction has no effect on program or the contents of memory. Only the screen and cursor are affected by the instruction.

4.   The HOME instruction has no effect when writing data to a hard copy printer. The instruction is only used in conjunction with the display screen.

Illustration of the Rules   Key in the following program, or load and list the program by entering

LOAD HOME SAMPLE1 <RETURN>
LIST   <RETURN>

When keying in the program, remember to press RETURN after each line. Also, when keying in the REMarks instruction do not key a blank following the keyword REM. Applesoft will generate a blank for you when the program is listed.

```
NEW
HOME
1000 REMHOME SAMPLE1
1010 HOME : REMCLEARS SCREEN AT START OF PROGRAM
1020 PRINT "THE PURPOSE OF THE HOME INSTRUCTION"
1030 PRINT "IS TO:"
1040 PRINT "1. CLEAR THE SCREEN"
1050 PRINT "2. POSITION THE CURSOR"
1060 PRINT
1070 PRINT "PRESS ANY KEY AND WATCH THE HOME"
1080 PRINT "INSTRUCTION IN ACTION"
1090 GET X$: REMSTOPS PROGRAM UNTIL KEY PRESSED
1100 HOME: REMCLEARS SCREEN AT END
1110 END
```

NEW   Before keying in a new program, use the NEW instruction to clear the computer's memory. The computer should always be cleared before keying in a program.

     When LOADing or RUNning the program from disk, it is not necessary to use the NEW instruction since both commands automatically clear memory.

HOME   If you are keying in the program yourself, you can use the HOME instruction in immediate execution mode to clear the screen and position the cursor at the upper left hand corner.

1000   The first line of all programs in this text uses the REMarks instruction to give the name of the program. By following this standard you can list line 1000 after making changes and find out the name of the program in order to properly SAVE it on the disk.

1010   The second line of the program uses the HOME instruction in program execution mode to clear the screen and position the cursor at the upper left hand corner of the screen. The colon following the keyword HOME separates the HOME instruction from the REMarks instruction. REMarks is used in this example to document the program and indicate what the HOME instruction is to accomplish.

1020–1080   Lines 1020 through 1080 print a series of messages on the screen which tell what the HOME instruction does and request that you press a key in order to see the HOME instruction in action.

1090   The GET instruction accepts one character from the keyboard. It is used in this example to cause the computer to stop while you read the message. When you have read the message and responded by pressing any key, the computer continues to the next statement.

Note: To simplify the example the operator was allowed to press any symbolic key. In actual practice you should code your programs to ask for a specific response from the operator.

1100 After you have pressed a key, the computer executes the HOME instruction on line 1100. The instruction clears the screen at the end of the program and positions the cursor in the upper left hand corner.

1110 The END instruction stops execution of the program. Once the END instruction is encountered no further instructions are executed.

Exercise 1: The HOME Instruction in Program Execution Mode

1. After you have keyed in the program, enter

    HOME <RETURN>
    LIST   <RETURN>

    Check the listing against the sample listing. Make sure you didn't make any mistakes.
2. Once you are sure the program is keyed correctly, enter

    RUN

    (but don't press RETURN yet).
        Now watch the screen and see what happens when you press RETURN. The screen will clear because of the HOME instruction on line 1010:

    1010 HOME: REM CLEARS SCREEN AT START OF PROGRAM

    The information from the PRINT instructions will be displayed starting at the top of the screen. If you encounter a syntax error, correct the line in error and start over at step 1.
        A SYNTAX ERROR occurs when you key in an instruction without following the coding rules for that instruction.
        For example, if you misspell an instruction—HOEM instead of HOME— the machine cannot recognize the instruction and cancels the program. To let you know what went wrong, the computer displays the message SYNTAX ERROR along with the statement number which was in error.

3. After you have read the information on the screen, press any key and the HOME instruction on line 1100 will be executed. The screen will be cleared and the cursor repositioned.

Again, if you encountered a syntax error, correct the code and start over at step 1.

Exercise 2: The HOME Instruction in Immediate Execution Mode

1. List the program by entering

    LIST <RETURN>

2. At this point your screen will have the program displayed just as you entered it. Use the HOME instruction to clear the screen by entering

    HOME   <RETURN>

    (but don't press RETURN yet!). Now watch what happens to the screen when you press RETURN. The screen will be cleared, but the program will still be in the computer's memory.

3. To prove that the program is still there, enter

    LIST <RETURN>

    Just like magic the program will reappear. (If your magic fails start over by returning to the first page of the HOME instruction and trying again.)

4. The NEW Instruction

Instruction   NEW

Purpose   The NEW instruction is used to clear (erase) the current program in memory and ready the computer for a new program.

Note that you should always use the NEW instruction with care. Do not destroy a new program before SAVEing it on the disk.

Normally the very first line you enter before keying in a program is the NEW instruction. The instruction is executed immediately when you press RETURN and clears memory so you can enter a new program.

You do not see any change in the screen when entering the NEW instruction, but believe it: Any program in memory is gone. If you want to keep the program you have keyed in or keep a program you have made changes to, make sure you SAVE the program prior to entering the NEW instruction.

Unless you are sure of what you are doing, only use the NEW instruction in immediate execution mode. If the instruction is used in the program execution mode, the program is self-destructing (see Exercise 3).

Rules for Use   1.   The NEW instruction should only be used before entering a new program or, if you are sure of what you are doing, as the VERY LAST instruction of a program to erase memory.
2.   The NEW instruction clears the computer's memory but does not change anything displayed on the screen.
3.   If the NEW instruction is used during execution of the program it destroys the program.

Illustration of the Rules   Key in the following program. Remember to press RETURN after each of the entries.

```
NEW
HOME
1000 HOME
1010 REMA VERY SHORT SAMPLE PROGRAM
1020 END
```

Note: Do not key a blank between REM and A. Machine will insert a blank for you.

NEW   When you key in the NEW instruction without any statement number, memory is immediately cleared. The screen image remains unchanged.

HOME   When you key in the HOME instruction without any statement number, the screen is cleared and the cursor is positioned in the upper left hand corner of the screen. Memory remains unchanged.

1000   The first line of the program is the HOME instruction, which clears the screen and positions the cursor.

1010   The second instruction uses the REMarks instruction to tell you this is a very short program. (As if you could not tell.)

1020   The third and last instruction in the program ENDs the execution of the program.

Exercise 1: Mixing Lines of Code, or Why Use the NEW Instruction?

1.   To see the three lines of code you typed, enter

LIST <RETURN>

2.   Now let's assume you want to enter another program but forget to first use the NEW instruction to clear memory. Enter the following three lines:

1005 REMNEW LINE NUMBERS ARE MERGED IN WITH OLD LINE NUMBERS
1010 REMMATCHING LINE NUMBERS REPLACE OLD LINE NUMBERS
1015 REMTHE RESULT IS A MIX UP OF TWO PROGRAMS

3.   To see how these lines are treated, enter

LIST <RETURN>

You will see the following mixed lines of code:

```
1000 HOME
1005 REM NEW LINE NUMBERS ARE MERGED WITH OLD LINE NUMBERS
1010 REM MATCHING LINE NUMBERS REPLACE OLD LINE NUMBERS
1015 REM THE RESULT IS A MIX UP OF TWO PROGRAMS
1020 END
```

Notice that the new line numbers 1005 and 1015 are merged with the existing program, while the new line number 1010 replaces the previous line of code with the same number.

The example shows you why it is important to clear memory before entering a new program. If you do not clear memory, chances are very good the new program you key in will be merged with the previously used program, resulting in a mell-of-a-hess.

Exercise 2: The NEW Instruction in Immediate Execution Mode

1. Once more, the very first line entered before keying in a new program is the NEW instruction. The instruction is executed when you press RETURN and clears memory so you can enter a new program.

    The NEW instruction destroys the program in memory but does not change anything displayed on the screen. (But believe it: Any program in memory is gone. Make sure you SAVE your work before typing in NEW.)

    Let's start by clearing the screen and listing the current program in memory. Enter

    HOME <RETURN>
    LIST <RETURN>

    The screen should now contain the five lines previously entered:

    ```
    1000 HOME
    1005 REM NEW LINE NUMBERS ARE MERGED WITH OLD LINE NUMBERS
    1010 REM MATCHING LINE NUMBERS REPLACE OLD LINE NUMBERS
    1015 REM THE RESULT IS A MIX UP OF TWO PROGRAMS
    1020 END
    ```

2. Now to clear memory enter

    NEW <RETURN>

    The screen will not change, but the program you entered will be gone.

3. If you don't believe it, enter

    LIST <RETURN>

    Now see, I told you the program would be gone.

Exercise 3: The NEW Instruction in Program Execution Mode.

The NEW instruction should very seldom, if ever, be used in program execution mode. If the NEW instruction is used it will be the last instruction executed, since it erases the program.

Key in the following program, or load and list the program by entering

```
LOAD NEW SAMPLE2    <RETURN>
LIST                <RETURN>
```

```
NEW
HOME
1000 REMNEW SAMPLE2
1010 HOME : REMCLEARS SCREEN AT START
1020 PRINT "THE PURPOSE OF THE NEW INSTRUCTION"
1030 PRINT "IS TO:"
1040 PRINT "1. CLEAR THE COMPUTER MEMORY"
1050 PRINT "2. PREPARE THE COMPUTER FOR NEW PROGRAM"
1060 PRINT
1070 PRINT "PRESS ANY KEY AND WATCH THE NEW"
1080 PRINT "INSTRUCTION DESTROY THE COPY OF"
1090 PRINT "THIS PROGRAM."
1100 PRINT : PRINT
1110 PRINT "***********************************"
1120 PRINT "YOU ONLY GET TO WATCH THIS ONCE"
1130 PRINT "AS THIS PROGRAM WILL SELF DESTRUCT"
1140 GET X$: REMSTOPS PROGRAM UNTIL A KEY IS PRESSED
1150 HOME : REMCLEARS SCREEN AT END
1160 NEW : REMCLEARS MEMORY – USE WITH CARE
```

1. If you keyed in the program yourself, you may want to SAVE it on disk, as that was a lot of work for only one run. It is important to remember that THIS PROGRAM SELF-DESTRUCTS! To save the program enter

   SAVE NEW SAMPLE2 <RETURN>

2. Enter

   RUN

   (but don't press RETURN yet). Now watch what happens when you press RETURN.
   The screen will clear when the HOME instruction on line 1010 is executed. After the screen is cleared, lines 1020 through 1130 will PRINT a description of what the NEW instruction does and what the program will do.
3. After you have read the information, press any key. Allowing the operator to press any key is not a good programming technique. It is used here to keep the code short and simple. Later examples will show how to check for a specific response such as: C to continue, Q to quit, or a space for a general response.

Once a key is pressed the HOME instruction on line 1150 is executed, clearing the screen and repositioning the cursor to the upper left hand corner.

4. The NEW instruction on line 1160 clears the computer's memory and destroys the program you have just entered.

5. If you want to repeat the process, too bad; the program is gone. If you don't believe it enter

LIST <RETURN>

All you will see is a blank screen.

5.   The LIST Instruction

LIST: Format 1

Instruction   LIST (Format 1)

There are several formats used in conjunction with the LIST instruction. The first format allows you to LIST the entire program, while the other format allows you to LIST portions of the program.

Purpose   The LIST instruction provides a method of displaying an instruction or a group of instructions.

Rules for Use   1.   When the LIST instruction is entered, the program in memory is listed starting with the first statement and continuing until either the entire program is listed or the listing operation is interrupted by you.

    a.   To temporarily stop the listing, press CONTROL-S; i.e., press the CONTROL key and the S key at the same time. To continue the listing, press any key other than CONTROL-RESET. (Note: For APPLE II and APPLE II + users, the CONTROL key is labeled CTRL.)

    b.   To cancel the listing, press CONTROL-C; i.e., press the CONTROL key and the C key at the same time. This cancels the LIST instruction, and you may now enter other instructions.

  2.   A problem exists with the LIST instruction on some APPLE II and APPLE II + computers. If the listing operation goes to the end of the program, the next instruction you key in may be treated as an invalid entry. If you do allow the listing to go to the end, just press the RETURN key once to clear the computer before entering any further instructions.

Note: The computer lists the program at a rate faster than most people can follow. You may want to slow the computer down by using the SPEED instruction (see The SPEED Instruction, p. 49).

Illustration of the Rules

Key in the following program:

```
NEW
1000 REMLIST SAMPLE1
1010 HOME
1020 INPUT AANUMBER
1030 PRINT AANUMBER
1040 END
```

After entering the program, key in

LIST<RETURN>

If the cursor is in the middle of screen, the four statements will be listed starting at the current location of the cursor. If the cursor is at the bottom of the screen, each of the four statements will be listed on line 24. As each new statement is displayed, all previously displayed statements will be moved up one line. The upward movement of the lines is referred to as *scrolling*.

The program is too small to allow you to practice the use of the CONTROL-S and the CONTROL-C options, so add the following remarks to the end of the program, or load the program by entering

```
LOAD LIST SAMPLE1    <RETURN>
LIST                 <RETURN>
```

Note: If you get the message SYNTAX ERROR after entering the first instruction, just rekey the instruction and continue. Remember APPLE II and APPLE II + users sometimes get a syntax error on the first line entered after listing the entire program.

```
1050 REMQUICKEST FINGERS IN THE WEST
1060 REMREM STANDS FOR REMARKS
1070 REM
1080 REM
1090 REM
1100 REM
1110 REMAVERAGE FINGERS
1120 REM
1130 REM
1140 REM
1150 REM
1160 REMSLOW FINGERS
1170 REMDON'T GET IN GUN FIGHTS
1180 REM
1190 REM
1200 REM
1210 REM
1220 REM
1230 REMYOU NEED LOTS OF PRACTICE
1240 REM
1250 REMWHAT HAPPENED TO THE TOP LINE?
```

Now that all the instructions have been entered, run through the following exercises to practice the use of the LIST instruction.

Exercise 1: Using **CONTROL-S**

1. Enter

   LIST

   (but do not press RETURN yet).
2. With your left hand position one finger over the CONTROL key and one finger over the S key.
3. With your right hand press RETURN, and then see how quickly you can stop the listing by pressing CONTROL-S. Did the listing stop? If so, continue, if not, go back to step 1 of this exercise.
4. Once you have gotten the listing to stop, you can restart it by pressing almost any key. The most convenient key is the space bar.
5. Practice starting and stopping the listing by

   a. Entering

      LIST <RETURN>

   b. Pressing CONTROL-S to stop the listing and the space bar to start the listing again
   c. How many times can you start/stop the listing for the sample program?

0 = Very poor	1 = Poor	2 = Fair
3 = Good	4 = Very good	5 = I don't believe it

Exercise 2: Using CONTROL-C

1. Enter

   LIST

   (but do not press RETURN yet).
2. With your left hand position one finger over the CONTROL key and one finger over the C key.
3. With your right hand press RETURN, and see how quickly you can stop the listing by pressing CONTROL-C. Did it stop? If so, continue; if not, go back to step 1 of this exercise.

4. Now try to restart the listing by pressing any key. Remember that once the LIST instruction is canceled with the use of CONTROL-C, it cannot be restarted. If you want to temporarily stop the listing, use CONTROL-S. If you want to cancel the listing, use CONTROL-C.

LIST: Format 2

Instruction   LIST statement number
or LIST statement number,statement number
or LIST statement number-statement number
or LIST statement number,
or LIST statement number-

Sample

LIST 1000	List line 1000
LIST 1000,2000	List lines from 1000 through 2000
LIST 1000-2000	List lines from 1000 through 2000
LIST 2000,	List program starting at line 2000
LIST 2000-	List program starting at line 2000

Rules for Use

1. If only one statement number is used, only that statement is listed. If the statement number does not exist within the program, then nothing is displayed.
2. If a group of lines are to be displayed, the first statement number indicates the starting point for the LIST operation, while the second number indicates the ending point for the LIST operation. Neither statement number need exist within the program, but there must be some statements within the range of the two numbers for any instructions to be displayed.
3. If you wish to list the program starting at a certain instruction and continuing to the end of the program you may use a dash instead of a second statement number.
4. For Applesoft either the dash (-) or comma (,) may be used when listing segments of the program.
5. For group listings CONTROL-S and CONTROL-C may be used to interrupt the listing.

Illustration of the Rules   In all the following exercises the HOME instruction is entered prior to the listing operation. It is not necessary to always use the HOME instruction prior to listing part of a program. The HOME instruction is used in the examples so you always start off with a clear screen.

The following exercises assume the LIST program is still in memory. If the program is not currently in memory, reload the program by entering

LOAD LIST SAMPLE1

Exercise 3: Using LIST With an Existing Statement

1. Enter

    HOME   <RETURN>
    LIST 1030 <RETURN>

    Was the following instruction displayed?

    1030 PRINT AANUMBER

    If so, continue; if not, try again from step 1 of this exercise.
2. Try listing other single statements in the program by entering the LIST instruction followed by an existing line number.

Exercise 4: Using LIST With a Nonexistent Statement

1. Enter

    HOME   <RETURN>
    LIST 1035 <RETURN>

    Since there is no statement 1035, none will be listed.

Exercise 5: Using LIST With a Range of Statements

    LIST statement number,statement number
or LIST statement number-statement number

1. Enter

    HOME   <RETURN>
    LIST 1000,1040 <RETURN>

Were the following instructions displayed?

```
1000 REM LIST SAMPLE1
1010 HOME
1020 INPUT AANUMBER
1030 PRINT AANUMBER
1040 END
```

If so, continue; if not, try again from step 1 of this exercise.

2. Try listing other parts of the program by entering the LIST instruction followed by a range of statement numbers. Use either the comma or the dash to separate the two statement numbers.

Exercise 6: Using LIST With a Range of Nonexistent Statements

LIST statement number,statement number
or LIST statement number-statement number

1. Enter

   HOME   <RETURN>
   LIST 000,2000 <RETURN>

   Were all the program instructions displayed? If so, continue; if not, try again from step 1 of this exercise.

2. Enter

   LIST 1035,1095 <RETURN>

   The lines from 1040 to 1090 will be listed. When the numbers used in the list statement do not exist, the computer lists the statements within the numeric range.

3. Enter

   LIST 2000,3000 <RETURN>

   No instructions will be listed. Why?
   If you don't know why, LIST the entire program and check to see what the highest statement number is.

Exercise 7: LIST Statements From Any Point to the End of the Program.

LIST statement number-
or LIST statement number,

1. This time don't type in HOME. Leave all the information on the screen and see where it goes. Enter

   LIST 1035- <RETURN>

   The statements from 1040 to the end of the program will be listed. Notice that statement 1035 does not exist. Therefore, the computer starts the listing at the next higher statement number. The dash (-) following the statement number instructs the computer to list to the end of the program.

2. Enter

   LIST 1035, <RETURN>

   The same instructions will be listed. Applesoft allows you to use either the dash or the comma to separate statement numbers or to indicate a continued list operation. Some versions of BASIC do not accept the comma as a valid separator in the LIST operation.

6. The DEL Instruction

Instruction   Format 1: statement number or DEL statement number
Format 2: DEL statement number,statement number

There are two formats used in conjunction with the DELete instruction. The first format allows you to delete a single line, while the second format allows you to delete a group of lines.

Purpose   The DELete instruction provides a method of removing one or more statements from your program.

Rules for Use   1.   When entering the instruction think twice. Are you sure you want to delete the lines? Did you make a typing mistake? Check the first and the last number to make sure you entered them correctly. Press RETURN only after you are sure you want to delete the statement(s).

2.   When a range of line numbers is deleted, the two statement numbers must be separated by a comma. Unlike the LIST instruction which may use either a comma or a dash as a separator, the DELete instruction only recognizes the comma.

Right: DEL 1200,1300
Wrong: DEL 1200-1300

3.   Do not confuse the DELete instruction with the DELETE command. The DELete instruction is used to remove one or more lines from the program in memory and has no effect on the disk. The DELETE command erases an entire program from the disk and has no effect on the program in memory.

Illustration of the Rules   In order to see how to use the DELete instruction, key in 10 or more lines of code. (This do-nothing program is not included on the program disk.)

```
1000 REM DEL SAMPLE1
1010 REM
.... Add lines 1020 through 1070
1080 REM
1090 REM
```

Once the instructions have been entered, SAVE the code on the disk so it can be reused during the exercises that follow. Enter

```
SAVE DEL SAMPLE1 <RETURN>
```

After saving the program, enter the following instructions so that you can see the line numbers while running through the exercises. Enter

```
HOME <RETURN>
LIST   <RETURN>
```

Exercise 1: Deleting a Single Line

The easiest way to delete a single line is to simply enter the line number. Delete line 1000 by entering

```
1000 <RETURN>
```

By typing in the line number without anything following it, you tell the machine to delete that line.

Another way to delete just one line is to type in DEL followed by the line number. Delete line 1010 by entering

```
DEL 1010 <RETURN>
```

Now, to prove both lines are gone, try listing the deleted lines. Enter

```
LIST 1000-1010 <RETURN>
```

No statements were displayed. If you want a line back after it has been deleted, you must retype the line.

Exercise 2: Deleting Segments of Code

To delete more than one line, enter the DEL instruction followed by the starting and ending statement numbers to be deleted.

Delete lines 1020 though 1050 by entering

```
DEL 1020,1050 <RETURN>
```

The starting and ending statement numbers do not have to exist within the program. When nonexisting statement numbers are used, the lines between the two numbers are deleted. Delete the remaining code by entering a very low line number and a very large line number. Enter

DEL 1,32000 <RETURN>

Exercise 3: Common Mistakes Made When Using the DEL Instruction

For the DELete instruction you must use a comma as a field separator and must include the starting statement number.

Enter the following instructions and see what happens. Each should end with a SYNTAX ERROR.

Try to use the dash as a separator. Enter

DEL 1000-2000 <RETURN>

Try to delete from a specific line number to the end of the program. Enter

DEL ,2000 <RETURN>

Now to prove that the DELete instruction has no effect on the original copy of program, try the following instructions. Enter

LIST <RETURN>

to see that there is nothing left of the program that was in memory. Enter

LOAD DEL SAMPLE1 <RETURN>

to load the original copy from disk into memory. Enter

LIST <RETURN>

to see that the original copy is still intact.

7. The REM Instruction

Instruction   REM any group of symbols

Example   1000 REM PROGRAM NAME
1010 REM USE A REMARKS STATEMENT TO GIVE THE NAME
1020 REM OF THE PROGRAM.

Purpose   The REMarks instruction allows the programmer to include comments within the program to document what the code is supposed to accomplish or to make notes for later reference. The REMarks instruction can also be used to describe the meaning of short abbreviated variable names.

Rules for Use
1. The REM instruction can be used on a line by itself or following any instruction.
2. Once the REM instruction is used, no additional instructions can be coded for that line number.
3. Strong suggestions:
   a. Use the REMarks instruction while writing your program to document the logic. You will be surprised at how much it will help when you are trying to debug your program, especially if a few days have passed since you last worked on it.
   b. Put a data name dictionary at the end of your program defining each variable name and giving any additional information about the variable which will help clarify the program. (See the data name dictionary at the end of the REMarks program.)
4. For readability of your listing you may wish to limit remark entries to 22 characters per line number.
5. A large number of REMark entries within the code being executed will slow down the computer (somewhat). But think which is more important, your ability to understand and make changes to the program or the minor difference in execution speed.

Illustration of the Rules

Key in the following program, or load and list the program by entering

```
LOAD REM SAMPLE1
LIST
```

If you are keying in the program yourself, do not press the space bar after typing in REM. It will not mess up the operation of the program but will cause two spaces to print following the keyword REM instead of one.

The REM instruction generates a space automatically between the keyword REM and the first character typed. The space does not show up until the instruction is listed. If you type a space following the REM the listing will end up with two spaces, the one generated by the REM instruction and one entered by you.

Key in the example REM program exactly as shown.

If you key in any of the programs following this example you will have to remember NOT to key in the space following REM. To make the programs easier to read they are listed showing the generated space.

```
NEW
HOME
1000 REMREM SAMPLE1
1010 HOME
1020 INPUT "ENTER HOURS WORKED = ";AAHOURS
1030 INPUT "ENTER HOURLY WAGE  = ";ABWAGE
1040 ACGOSS = AAHOURS * ABWAGE: REMCALCULATES GROSS WAGE ONLY
1050 PRINT "TOTAL GROSS WAGE   = ";ACGOSS
1060 END
1070 REM1234567890123456789012
1080 REMDATA NAME DICTIONARY
1090 REMAAHOURS
1100 REM   NUMBER HOURS WORKED
1110 REMABWAGE
1120 REM   HOURLY WAGE
1130 REMACGOSS
1140 REM   GROSS WAGE = AAHOURS
1150 REM   * ABWAGE
1160 REM   ACGROSS CANNOT BE
1170 REM   USED BECAUSE "GR" IS
1180 REM   AN APPLESOFT RESERVE
1190 REM   WORD
```

The program is really too simple for such extensive remarks, but hopefully you will gain an idea of how to use the REM instruction to assist in documenting your program.

The program is set up to allow the operator to enter the number of hours worked and the hourly wage. After the two values are entered, the program computes and prints out the gross wage.

Rule 1. The REM instruction can be used on a line by itself or following an instruction.

1000 A standard practice you may wish to use is to enter a name or basic program description as the first line of code. Notice that no space is entered between REM and REM SAMPLE1. Later when the program is listed, the computer will insert a space for you.

1040 The REM instruction may be used on a line by itself as on line 1000, or it may be used following other instructions as shown on line 1040. A colon is used to separate multiple instructions on one line.

Rule 2. Once the REM instruction is used, no additional instructions may be coded for that line number.

Run the program by entering

RUN <RETURN>

The computer will clear the screen and display the message

ENTER HOURS WORKED = ?

In response to the question mark, enter

40 <RETURN>

Immediately after you press RETURN, the computer will display a second message asking you to enter the hourly wage. In response to the second message, enter

6.75 <RETURN>

The computer will then display the message

TOTAL GROSS WAGE   = 270

Did you see how the HOME instruction on line 1010 cleared the screen before executing the rest of the program? Let's see what happens if you change the program and put the HOME instruction after a REMarks entry. Key in the following two lines of code:

1000 REMREM SAMPLE1 : HOME <RETURN>
1010 <RETURN>

1000   When you type in a new line with the same number as an existing line, the new entry replaces the old entry. Typing in 1000 REM REM SAMPLE1 : HOME replaces 1000 REM REM SAMPLE1.

1010   By typing in a line number with no instruction following it, you are deleting the statement with the matching line number. Typing in 1010 deletes the instruction 1010 HOME.

    Now list the program and then run it again by entering

LIST <RETURN>
RUN <RETURN>

    What happened to the program listing which was on the screen?

    The screen did not clear prior to displaying the first message because the HOME instruction on line 1000 was taken as part of the REM instruction and not as an individual instruction. Remember, once the REMarks instruction is used, you must start a new line to enter instructions.

Incorrect: 1000 REMREM SAMPLE1 : HOME
Correct: 1000 REMREM SAMPLE1
              1010 HOME

1080–1180   Lines 1080 through 1180 show how you can use the REM instruction to document the data names used in a program. Applesoft allows you to use up to 238 characters in a name but only recognizes the first two characters. Since the computer only looks at the first two characters, I normally use a technique of assigning each variable name a unique two-character alphanumeric prefix followed by a descriptive name. By using a unique two-character prefix you are assured that the machine will not treat what you consider to be two variables as only one variable.

    The data name dictionary can give the name of the variable, a description of what the name stands for, and, if necessary, how the variable is used. Notice how the variable name starts immediately after the keyword REM but when the name is described, two spaces are used following REM. When you key in two blanks before describing the name, the first two letters of the variable name are easier to see. Remember Applesoft only recognizes the first two characters, and these two characters are what you should be concerned with.

    For readability of your listing, you may wish to limit remark entries to 22 characters per line number.

    When a program is keyed in, Applesoft uses all 40 columns of each line. However, when Applesoft lists a program, it reformats each line.

    The code looks fine while being entered but is harder to read when listed.

    When you limit your remarks to 22 characters, they are easier to read.

8.   The SPEED Instruction

Instruction   SPEED = number

Example   SPEED = 200
The speed at which I normally list programs.

Purpose   The SPEED instruction is used to slow the computer down. I have found the instruction helpful in two situations. First, when listing a program, you may use the speed instruction to slow down the rate at which the computer displays the instructions, making the code easier to read. Second, when writing programs which display information on the screen, you may use the SPEED instruction to slow down the rate at which the information is displayed. This may make it easier for the user to read the information and can produce a visual effect which catches the eye of the operator.

Rules for Use
1. The number used in conjunction with the SPEED instruction may range from 0 to 255. The slowest speed is 0, with increasing rates up to the normal speed of 255.
2. Once the speed is set to a rate other than 255, the computer remains at the slower rate until either another SPEED instruction is executed or the computer is RESET (turned off and then back on).
3. The SPEED instruction affects only the rate at which data is transmitted to the output devices (that includes the screen, printer, and disk drives).

Illustration of the Rules   Key in and run the following program, or run the program by entering

RUN SPEED SAMPLE1 <RETURN>

(Remember, if you are keying in the program, do not enter the space following the keyword REM.)

```
NEW
1000 REM SPEED SAMPLE1
1010 HOME
1020 REM 12345678901234567890012
1030 REM
1040 REM USE THE SPEED INST. TO
1050 REM SLOW DOWN THE COMPUTER
1060 REM TO HELP VIEW WHAT IS
1070 REM HAPPENING ON SCREEN.
1080 REM
1090 AANUMBER% = 255
1100 SPEED= AANUMBER%
1110 PRINT ">>>";
1120 AANUMBER% = AANUMBER% - 1
1130 IF AANUMBER% = 20 THEN PRINT: PRINT TAB(15)"SLOW ISN'T
     IT": PRINT
1140 IF AANUMBER% > -1 GOTO 1100
1150 SPEED= 255
1160 PRINT
1170 PRINT "THAT'S ALL FOLKS!"
1180 END
```

The program starts out displaying the *greater than* sign at a rate of 255 (fastest rate) and each time through the loop slows down by a value of 1 until the rate of 0 (slowest rate) is finally reached.

1090   The counter AANUMBER% is given a starting value of 255.

1100   Line 1100 sets the speed to the current value of AANUMBER%. The first time through the loop AANUMBER% contains 255. The second time through the loop AANUMBER% contains a value of 254. The third time through the loop AANUM-BER% contains a value of 253, etc. See line 1120, which subtracts 1 from AAN-UMBER% each time through the loop.

1110   This line prints the greater than signs, which soon fill the screen.

1120   The current value of AANUMBER% is decreased by 1 each time through the loop. Since AANUMBER% is used by the SPEED instruction on line 1100, the computer continues to slow down.

1130   The IF instruction was put in just for the fun of it. You need a break from the monotony of all the greater than signs.

1140   The IF instruction checks to see when AANUMBER% has reached a value of -1. When -1 is reached the program ends. Do not try to set the SPEED instruction to a value less than 0.

1150   The SPEED instruction resets the speed of the computer back to its normal level. If this instruction had not been included you would have had trouble continuing to use your system at a SPEED of 0.

Now that you have seen how the instruction works, let's look at the rules.

Rule 1.   The number used to set the SPEED instruction must range from 0 to 255.

Using the immediate execution mode, type in the following instruction and see what happens. Enter

SPEED = −1 <RETURN>

(remember in the immediate execution mode no statement numbers are used).

You will receive an

?ILLEGAL QUANTITY ERROR

message. The computer will not accept the value less than 0 for the SPEED instruction. Now try it again with SPEED = 256 and see what happens. You will get another ?ILLEGAL QUANTITY ERROR message.

Rule 2.   Once the speed is set to a rate other than 255, the computer remains at the slower rate until either another SPEED instruction is executed or the computer is RESET (turned off and then back on).

Reload the SPEED SAMPLE1 program by keying in

LOAD SPEED SAMPLE1 <RETURN>

Before running the program, read the following paragraph.

While the program is running, position your fingers over CONTROL-C. When the message SLOW ISN'T IT comes on, press the CONTROL-C. The computer will beep and indicate that a BREAK in the program has occurred. After you have used CONTROL-C to cancel the program, type in LIST and see how slowly the computer lists the program.

Now type in

```
RUN          <RETURN>
CONTROL-C              (while message is being displayed)
LIST         <RETURN> (after canceling the program)
```

To reset the speed enter

SPEED = 255

Rule 3 The SPEED instruction affects only the rate at which data is transmitted to the screen, printer, and disk drives.

Key in and run the following program, or run the program by entering

RUN SPEED SAMPLE2

```
NEW
1000 REM SPEED SAMPLE2
1010 HOME : SPEED= 255
1020 PRINT "PRESS ANY KEY AND SEE HOW FAST THE"
1030 PRINT "     COMPUTER COUNTS TO 100.": PRINT : GET X1$
1040 AACOUNTER = AACOUNTER + 1
1050 IF AACOUNTER < 100 GOTO 1040
1060 PRINT "DONE COUNTING TO 100": PRINT : PRINT
1070 SPEED= 0
1080 PRINT "PRESS ANY KEY AND SEE HOW FAST THE"
1090 PRINT "     COMPUTER COUNTS TO 100.": PRINT : GET X1$
1100 ABCOUNTER = ABCOUNTER + 1
1110 IF ABCOUNTER < 100 GOTO 1100
1120 PRINT "DONE COUNTING TO 100"
1130 SPEED= 255
1140 END
```

Did you notice that the computer took the same length of time to do the arithmetic and only the speed of the display was affected?

9. Assigning Variable Names

Format   String Names: AAname\$ Must end with dollar sign
                    Integer Names: AAname% Must end with percent sign
                    Real Names: AAname   Cannot end with \$ or % sign

Example   String Name: AANAME\$ = "JOHN JONES"
                    Integer Name: AANUMBER% = 45
                    Real Name: AANUMBER = 45.5

Rules for Use

1. Applesoft allows you to use up to 238 characters in a variable name but only recognizes the first two characters. That means you can use long names to describe variables, but Applesoft only recognizes the first two characters. The remaining characters serve only to document the program so you can remember how the variable is used.

2. Variable names must start with an alphabetic character.

3. A variable name may NOT contain embedded reserve words such as GOTO, PRINT, LIST, GET, PUT, NOT, OR, AND, etc.

4. Names ending with a dollar sign (\$) are treated as alphanumeric variables or *string variables*. String variables may contain any character, with each character taking 1 byte of memory.

5. Names ending with a percent sign (%) are treated as integer variables. Integer variables may only contain whole numbers between -32767 and $+32767$. The values are stored in binary taking up 2 bytes for each variable.

6. Names ending with characters other than a percent sign or a dollar sign are treated as real numbers. Real variables may contain any number from

   $-1000000000000000000000000000000000000000$ to
   $+1000000000000000000000000000000000000000.$

   Although the computer keeps track of the decimal to 38 places, only the nine most significant digits are stored in memory.

7. When real numbers have a fractional value between -.01 and .01 they are expressed in scientific notation.

Illustration of the Rules

The following illustrates the primary rules for assigning variable names.

Rule 1.

Only the first two characters of the variable name are recognized by Applesoft. Key in and run the following program, or run the program by entering

RUN NAMES SAMPLE1 <RETURN>

```
NEW
1000 REM NAMES SAMPLE1
1010 HOME
1020 REM
1030 COUNTER1 = 25
1040 COUNTER2 = 50
1050 PRINT "COUNTER 1 = ";COUNTER1
1060 PRINT "COUNTER 2 = ";COUNTER2
1070 END
```

The following will occur:

1030

Line 1030 sets COUNTER1 to a value of 25. As far as the computer is concerned, the instruction actually reads

1030 CO = 25

1040

COUNTER2 is set to a value of 50. Notice COUNTER1 and COUNTER2 both start with the same two characters. As far as the computer is concerned, the instruction actually reads

1040 CO = 50

1050

Line 1050 prints the current value in COUNTER1, which is 50. You might think the value should be 25, since line 1030 sets COUNTER1 equal to 25. But look at line 1040, which sets the field CO to a value of 50.

1060

Line 1060 prints the current value in COUNTER2, which is 50.

You consider COUNTER1 and COUNTER2 two distinct variables but both start with the same two characters. The computer treats these two names as one variable called CO.

To correct the program you have to start over with new variable names.

Key in and run the following program, or run the program by entering

RUN NAMES SAMPLE2 <RETURN>

```
NEW
1000 REM NAMES SAMPLE2
1010 HOME
1020 REM
1030 AACOUNTER1 = 25
1040 ABCOUNTER2 = 50
1050 PRINT "COUNTER 1 = ";AACOUNTER1
1060 PRINT "COUNTER 2 = ";ABCOUNTER2
1070 END
```

The following will occur:

1030   The variable AA is set to a starting value of 25.

1040   The variable AB is set to a starting value of 50.

1050   Line 1050 prints a descriptive heading followed by the current value in the variable AA.

1060   Line 1060 prints a descriptive heading followed by the current value in the variable AB.

Hopefully you see the importance of creating variable names in which the first two characters are unique.

The format used for this book consists of a two character prefix followed by a descriptive name. The two character prefix is normally assigned in an alphabetic sequence of AA, AB, AC, AD, AE, etc. The purpose of the two character prefix is to ensure that each variable name within the program is unique.

Rule 2.   Variable names must start with an alphabetic character.

If you attempt to use a name which starts with a number, Applesoft treats the number as a separate entry. Applesoft interprets the entry 1ABC as the number 1 followed by the variable ABC.

Rule 3.   The variable name may not contain embedded reserve words such as GOTO, PRINT, GET, LIST, PUT, NOT, OR, AND, etc.

A reserve word consists of any name which Applesoft uses as part of its instruction set. Since these words have a special meaning to the Applesoft interpreter, you can NEVER use any of the words as variable names or even have the words embedded within the names you create.

Key in the program shown below, or load and list the program by entering

```
LOAD NAMES SAMPLE3 <RETURN>
LIST                <RETURN>
```

```
NEW
1000 REM NAMES SAMPLE3
1010 HOME
1020 REM
1040 HAND$ = "LEFT"
1050 NORTH$ = "UP"
1060 FORTH = 4
1070 FIFTH = 5
1080 END
```

When you list the program you will find the following occurs:

1040 H AND $ = "LEFT"
The variable name HAND$ comes out H AND $ because AND is an Applesoft reserve word and cannot be part of a variable name.

1050 N OR TH$ = "UP"
The variable name NORTH$ comes out N OR TH$ because OR is an Applesoft reserve word and cannot be part of a variable name.

1060 F OR TH = 4
The variable name FORTH lists out as F OR TH because OR is an Applesoft reserve word and cannot be part of a variable name.

1070 F IF TH = 5
The variable FIFTH lists out as F IF TH because IF is an Applesoft reserve word and cannot be part of a variable name.

Attempt to run the program and see what occurs.

You will get a syntax error on line 1040. Since the variable name is broken into several parts, the instruction does not conform to any format that Applesoft can recognize. If Applesoft cannot interpret an instruction, it stops the program on that line of code and gives you the error message

SYNTAX ERROR ON LINE number

It is up to you to analyze why the syntax error occurred and to correct the problem.

In this case you have to create new variable names.

Before continuing you should make sure you understand the following definitions.

Variable: Field Name: Data Name: These terms are synonymous. They refer to the use of *symbolic names* (another synonym), to which the computer assigns an area of memory. When you use the symbolic name, the computer locates its memory address and uses the value in the area as directed by the instruction. For example,

AANUMBER = AANUMBER + 1

The computer locates the area of memory allocated to AANUMBER, increments the value in that area by 1, and then stores the new value back in the same area of memory.

Alphanumeric variable: String variable: An alphanumeric variable may contain any symbol you can key into the computer. The variable may contain both alphabetic and numeric symbols. For example

AASTREET$ = "123 FIRST STREET"

The variable AASTREET$ contains both numbers 123 and letters FIRST.

Constant: A constant is a self-defining term which remains the same during the execution of the program. For example, in the instruction

AANUMBER = AANUMBER + 1

The value 1 is a constant (not a symbolic name) and cannot be changed during execution of the program. There are two types of constants used in programming: numeric and alphanumeric. *Numeric constants* consist of the symbols plus (+), minus (−), 0 through 9, and the decimal point and are not enclosed within quotation marks. *Alphanumeric constants,* or string constants, consist of any character or group of characters enclosed within quotations marks "123 FIRST STREET".

Creating workable data names (variables) is not difficult.

1. Make up a meaningful name and assign it a two character prefix.
2. Check to see if you can recognize any embedded keywords. If you find an embedded keyword, change the characters to eliminate it, but try to keep a meaningful name.
3. As a sure check, code the name in a statement and LIST the statement. If the variable name is listed exactly as you typed it, then the name does not contain any embedded keywords. If the computer inserts blanks, you have used a reserve word and must try again.

Rule 4. Names ending with a dollar sign ($) are treated as alphanumeric variables, or string variables.

More rules for string variables:

a. String variables must end in a dollar sign.
b. Strings constants must be enclosed within quotation marks.
c. String variables cannot be used for arithmetic even if the variable contains only numeric characters.
d. When using the LET (=) instruction, string variables may only be used with other string variables or string constants.

Key in the following program and attempt to run it, or attempt to run the program by entering

RUN NAMES SAMPLE4 <RETURN>

```
NEW
1000 REM NAMES SAMPLE4
1010 HOME
1020 REM 123456789012345678912
1030 REM
1040 REM STRING VARIABLES CAN
1050 REM CONTAIN ANY CHARACTER
1060 AANAME$ = "ALPHANUMERIC STRINGS ARE ENCLOSED"
1070 ABNAME$ = "WITHIN QUOTES. "
1080 PRINT AANAME$
1090 PRINT ABNAME$
1100 REM
1110 REM CANNOT DO ARITHMETIC
1120 REM WITH STRING VARIABLES
1130 REM EVEN IF THEY CONTAIN
1140 REM NUMBERS
1150 ABNUMBER$ = "123.45"
1160 ABNUMBER$ = ABNUMBER$ + 1
1170 PRINT ABNUMBER$
1180 PRINT ABNAME$
1190 REM
1200 REM ONLY ALPHANUMERIC
1210 REM STRINGS CAN BE USED
1220 REM WITH STRING VARIABLES
1230 ACDTE$ = 103067
1240 ACDTE$ = "10/30/67"
1250 PRINT "ACDTE$ = ";ACDTE$
1260 END
```

The following will occur when you attempt to run the program:

1060–1090 The variables AANAME$ and ABNAME$ are set equal to the string constants following the equal sign. The contents of the two variables will be displayed by the PRINT instructions on lines 1080 and 1090.

Notice that the string names end in a dollar sign, the first two characters are different, and the alphanumeric constants are enclosed within quotation marks. The alphanumeric constant was divided into two parts so it could be displayed on two separate lines.

1150 The string variable ABNUMBER$ is set equal to the string constant "123.45". Since the number is enclosed within quotation marks, it is considered a string constant. The computer stores the value in character format, taking up 6 bytes of memory. By character format I mean that the symbols 1, 2, 3, point (.), 4, and 5 are stored using a binary pattern that the computer assigns to characters which are to be displayed or read from the keyboard. The binary pattern for printing the characters 123.45 is not the same as the binary pattern used by the computer for representing the number 123.45 in arithmetic operations. Since the string variable is stored in character format, the computer cannot use the variable for arithmetic operations.

Did you notice the variable ABNUMBER$ and ABNAME$ both start with the same two characters? Guess what happens to the old value in ABNAME$ when ABNUMBER$ is set equal to "123.45"? The old value is gone, and both ABNUM-BER$ and ABNAME$ refer to the value "123.45". Remember, you may think of the variables as two separate areas in memory, but since they start with the same two characters, the computer treats the two names as one variable called AB$.

Applesoft allows you to use names which start with the same two characters if the names represent different types of variables. That is, the names can start with the same two letters if one name represents a string name (AANAME$), one an integer name (AANAME%), and one a real name (AANAME).

1160   If you try to run the program, you will get the following error message for line 1160:

?TYPE MISMATCH ERROR IN 1160

The computer is trying to tell you it will not allow you to mix apples and oranges. You cannot add the numeric 1 to a string variable. In fact, you cannot do any arithmetic with string variables. To correct the program, delete the invalid line by entering

1160 <RETURN>

At this point the screen should contain the following lines:

```
ALPHANUMERIC STRINGS ARE ENCLOSED
WITHIN QUOTES.

?TYPE MISMATCH ERROR IN 1160
>1160
```

Now attempt to run the program again by entering

RUN <RETURN>

Don't worry if you get another error message. Keep reading.

1170–1180   Lines 1170 and 1180 are provided to show you that the computer treats the two names ABNAME$ and ABNUMBER$ as one variable. On your screen you should have four lines displayed followed by an error message. The first two lines show the contents of variables AANAME$ and ABNAME$ prior to line 1150. The second two lines show the contents of ABNUMBER$ and ABNAME$ after the execution of line 1150.

1230   On your second attempt to run the program you will get the following error message:

?TYPE MISMATCH ERROR IN 1230

Line 1230 causes the error message because in addition to not being able to do arithmetic with string variables you cannot set a string variable equal to a numeric constant. To correct the program delete the line by entering

1230 <RETURN>

At this point the screen should contain the following lines.

```
ALPHANUMERIC STRINGS ARE ENCLOSED
123.45
123.45

?TYPE MISMATCH ERROR IN 1230
>1230
```

Run the program again; this time you should not get any errors.

1240   The variable ACDTE$ is set equal to a string constant representing the date October 30, 1967. This is mainly just another example of working with strings; but do you know why the name ACDTE$ was used instead of ACDATE$?

If so, skip on to the next example; if not, key in the following:

NEW
HOME
1000 ACDATE$ = "10/30/67"
LIST

The computer separates ACDATE$ into ACD AT E$. The word AT is an Applesoft reserve word and cannot be used within variable names. To correct this and still have a fairly descriptive name, the A was dropped.

Rule 5. Names ending with a percent sign (%) are treated as integer variables. Integer variables may only contain whole numbers between -32767 and $+32767$.

Key in the following program and run it, or run the program by entering

RUN NAMES SAMPLE5 <RETURN>

```
NEW
1000 REM NAMES SAMPLE5
1010 REM 123456789012345789012
1020 HOME
1030 REM
1040 REM INTEGERS RANGE BETWEEN
1050 REM -32767 AND +32767
1060 REM
1070 AAMINUS% = - 32760
1080 ABPLUS% = + 32760
1090 PRINT "LOW VALUE","HIGH VALUE"
1100 AAMINUS% = AAMINUS% - 1
1110 ABPLUS% = ABPLUS% + 1
1120 PRINT AAMINUS%,ABPLUS%
1130 GOTO 1100
```

1070 The variable AAMINUS% is set to a starting value of -32760. Since the objective is to show you that integers cannot contain a number less than -32767, a number close to the limit was chosen so only a few lines would have to be displayed on the screen.

1080 The variable ABPLUS% is set to a starting value of $+32760$. Again, since the objective is to show you that integers cannot contain a number greater than 32767, a number close to the limit was chosen.

1100 The variable AAMINUS% is set equal to the current value of AAMINUS% minus 1. The first time through the instruction, AAMINUS% contains -32760 (see line 1070). After execution of the instruction, AAMINUS% contains -32761.

First pass: AAMINUS% $= -32760 - 1 = -32761$
Second pass: AAMINUS% $= -32761 - 1 = -32762$
Third pass: AAMINUS% $= -32762 - 1 = -32763$
etc. (see screen)

1110 The variable ABPLUS% is set equal to the current value of ABPLUS% plus 1. This is the same format as line 1100, except that instead of counting down with a negative 1, the computer is counting up with a positive 1.

1120 The PRINT instruction displays the contents of the variables AAMINUS% and ABPLUS%.

1130   The GOTO instruction tells the computer to go back to line 1100 and start over from that point.

The program continues counting (looping) until the variable AAMINUS% attempts to exceed the value of − 32767. Once − 32767 is exceeded, the computer displays the following error message:

?ILLEGAL QUANTITY ERROR IN 1100

So the rule for using an integer variable is: If there is a chance that the value will exceed + 32767 or − 32767, do not use an integer name.

Before leaving integer variables let's look at one more example of how integer variables work when used with real numbers or in arithmetic operations.

When an integer name is used to the left of the equal sign, the answer is truncated to a whole number and placed in the integer variable.

Key in the following program and run it, or run the program by entering

RUN NAMES SAMPLE6 <RETURN>

```
NEW
1000 REM NAMES SAMPLE6
1010 HOME
1020 REM
1030 REM 123456789012345678 9012
1040 REM IF INTEGER NAMES ARE
1050 REM USED TO THE LEFT OF
1060 REM EQUAL SIGN THE ANSWER
1070 REM WILL BE TRUNCATED TO
1080 REM A WHOLE NUMBER AND PUT
1090 REM INTO THE INTEGER FIELD
1100 REM
1110 AAWHOLE% = 1
1120 AAREAL = 1
1130 ABLINE% = 1
1140 REM
1150 PRINT "LINE" TAB( 8)"INTEGER" TAB( 20)"REAL"
1160 AAWHOLE% = 1.5 * AAWHOLE%
1170 AAREAL = 1.5 * AAREAL
1180 PRINT TAB( 2)ABLINE% TAB( 8)AAWHOLE% TAB( 20)AAREAL
1190 AAWHOLE% = AAWHOLE% + 1
1200 AAREAL = AAREAL + 1
1210 ABLINE% = ABLINE% + 1
1220 IF ABLINE% < 22 GOTO 1160
1230 END
```

1110–1130   The program begins by setting all three variables equal to 1. The variable AAWHOLE% is used to illustrate integers. The variable AAREAL is used to illustrate real numbers. And the variable ABLINE% is used to print a line number on the screen so you and I will have a common point of reference in the narrative which follows.

1150   This prints a heading at the top of the screen to identify each column of numbers.

1160   The current value in **AAWHOLE%** is multiplied by 1.5, and the answer is truncated to a whole number before being placed back into **AAWHOLE%**.

1170   The current value in **AAREAL** is multiplied by 1.5, and the answer is placed back into **AAREAL**.

1180   After the new values are computed, the three values are printed.

1190–1210   Just for the fun of it, all three variables are incremented by 1. There is really no point in incrementing **AAWHOLE%** and **AAREAL** other than to show you that real and integer numbers may be mixed on the right side of an equation.

1220   The IF instruction provides a way to stop the program. I have arbitrarily decided to stop the program when the value in **ABLINE%** becomes equal to 22 (close to a full screen).

   If you have not run the program, run it now and see if you get the same results as shown in the following screen:

LINE	INTEGER	REAL
1	1	1.5
2	3	3.75
3	6	7.125
4	10	12.1875
5	16	19.71125
6	25	31.171875
7	39	48.2578125
8	60	73.8867188
9	91	112.330078
10	138	169.995117
11	138	256.492676
12	313	386.239014
13	471	580.85852
14	708	872.787781
15	1063	1310.68167
16	1596	1967.52251
17	2395	2952.78376
18	3594	4430.67564
19	5392	6647.51346
20	8089	9972.77019
21	12135	14960.6553

The LINE numbers displayed on the screen are used in the following explanation. There are several points I would like you to understand about the numbers which have been displayed.

Line 1   LINE   INTEGER   REAL
            1   1   1.5

Integer numbers do not contain decimal positions. Real numbers may contain decimal positions.

Line 9   LINE   INTEGER   REAL
            9   91   112.330078

When printing numbers Applesoft does not automatically align the values printed according to decimal points.

For real numbers only the nine MOST SIGNIFICANT digits are kept. Notice that as the number of digits in front of the decimal increases, the number of digits behind the decimal decreases.

Line 13   LINE   INTEGER   REAL
           13   471   580.85852

Look closely at the real number. Only eight digits are printed. Applesoft automatically suppresses any leading or trailing zeros.

Rule 6.   Names which end in any character other than a percent sign or dollar sign are treated as real numbers. Real numeric variables may contain any number from

    − 1000000000000000000000000000000000000   to
    + 1000000000000000000000000000000000000.

Even though there are 38 zeros following the leading 1, the APPLE cannot actually store that many digits. The APPLE can store only the nine most significant digits, but keeps track of where the decimal is located, up to + 38 or − 38 positions.

Key in the following program and run it, or run the program by entering

RUN NAMES SAMPLE7 <RETURN>

Look over the code and try to get an idea of what each line does before reading the detailed explanation of each instruction.

```
NEW
1000 REM NAMES SAMPLE7
1010 HOME
1020 REM
1030 REM ONLY 9 SIGNIFICANT
1040 REM DIGITS ARE STORED FOR
1050 REM EITHER WHOLE OR
1060 REM FRACTIONAL NUMBERS.
1070 REM
1080 AAREAL = .999999999
1090 ABLINE% = 1
1100 PRINT "LINE" TAB( 8)"REAL"
1110 SPEED= 150
1120 PRINT ABLINE% TAB( 8)AAREAL
1130 AAREAL = AAREAL * 10
1140 ABLINE% = ABLINE% + 1
1150 GOTO 1120
1160 END
```

Since the program terminated with an error and the SPEED instruction is used within the program, enter the following instruction to get the computer back to its normal speedy self:

SPEED = 255 <RETURN>

1080 The field AAREAL is set equal to the fractional value .999999999. The number was chosen for a couple of reasons. First, it shows you that only the nine most significant digits are kept. Second, it shows you a problem with computers when you use binary arithmetic. When you do arithmetic with binary numbers, sometimes a small numeric error occurs. The error, which is common to all computers using binary arithmetic, is referred to as a *rounding error.*

1090 The variable ABLINE% is used as a counter to provide a line number for the information being displayed. Line 1090 assigns the variable an initial value of 1.

1100 This line prints the headings for the two variables to be displayed. The first column is a line number, which will provide you with a reference point in the following discussion. The second column shows the real number, which illustrates the rules being discussed.

1110 To make it easier for you to see the information as it is displayed on the screen, the SPEED instruction is used to slow down the computer. Since the program ends abnormally, you need to reset the SPEED.

1120 This line prints the current contents of ABLINE% and then tabs over to column 8 of the screen before printing the contents of AAREAL.

1130 Line 1130 gives a new value to the variable AAREAL. Each time the instruction is executed, the current value of AAREAL is multiplied by 10 and the new answer replaces the old value in AAREAL. Essentially, the decimal is moved one position to the right each time the instruction is executed.

1140 The instruction increments the line counter and places the new value back into the original variable.

1150 The GOTO instruction sends the logic back to line 1120, where the contents of the two fields ABLINE% and AAREAL are to be printed.

If you have not run the program, run it now and watch the values which are displayed. Since there are more than 24 lines to be displayed, not all the data will fit on the screen at one time.

The last of the screen appears as follows:

```
31      9.99999999E+29
32      9.99999999E+30
33      9.99999999E+31
34      9.99999999E+32
35      9.99999999E+33
36      9.99999999E+34
37      9.99999999E+35
38      9.99999999E+36
39      1E+38

?OVERFLOW ERROR IN 1140
```

Let's look at some of the lines displayed in more detail.

LINE	REAL
1	.999999999
2	10

When you run the program the first line prints out .999999999 as expected. The second line is supposed to display 10 * .999999999. The computer should display 9.99999999 but instead prints out 10. The computer circuitry decided the value is close enough to 10 and rounded it off. At line 14 you see that the computer changes its mind and brings back the 9s. These mistakes are called *rounding errors* and are caused because of the way the computer stores numbers.

LINE	REAL
9	100000000
10	1E + 09
11	1E + 10
12	1E + 11
13	1E + 12
14	9.99999999E + 12
15	9.99999999E + 13

Lines 9 and 10 show a change in the way the real number is displayed. Once the number of positions to the left or right of the decimal is greater than nine, the number is converted to scientific notation. When a number is displayed in scientific notation, the value is represented using the format of

*n.nnnnnnnn*E + *ee*

The numeric portion of the number is always displayed with one whole digit in front of the decimal followed by up to eight digits after the decimal.

The E always separates the number from the exponent and is followed by either a plus or minus sign. If a plus sign follows the E, then the decimal is to be moved to the right *ee* positions.

1E + 09	=	1000000000.
9.99999999E + 12	=	9999999990000.

Remember that the computer can store only the nine most significant digits.

If a minus sign follows the E, the decimal is moved to the left as indicated by the exponent *ee*.

1E − 09	=	.000000001
9.99999999E − 12	=	.000999999999

Look closely at the way the decimal moves:

9.99999999E + 12	=	9999999990000. (Results in 13 digits)
9.99999999E − 12	=	.000999999999 (Results in 12 digits)

The last few lines on the screen point out what happens when you exceed the limits of a real variable.

```
LINE      REAL
38        9.99999999E + 36
39        1E + 38
```

?OVERFLOW ERROR IN 1140

The computer can keep track of the decimal down to -38 positions or up to $+38$ positions. When you attempt to use a number larger than 38 decimal positions to the right or left, the program cancels with an overflow error message.

Run the program as many times as needed until you feel you understand that the computer

1. Only stores the nine most significant digits
2. Converts the number to scientific notation if it exceeds nine significant digits to the left or right of the decimal

Rule 7. When real numbers have a fractional value between $-.01$ and $+.01$, they are expressed in scientific notation.

You should already have a fairly good idea of what scientific notation is, but if you want to see how it is used with very small numbers or negative numbers, run the following program. Enter

RUN NAMES SAMPLE8 <RETURN>

```
NEW
1000 REM NAMES SAMPLE8
1010 HOME
1020 REM 1234567890123456789012
1030 REM
1040 REM NUMBERS BETWEEN -.01
1050 REM AND +.01 ARE SHOWN IN
1060 REM SCIENTIFIC NOTATION.
1070 REM
1080 AAPLUS = 1
1090 ABMINUS = - 1
1100 ACLINE% = 1
1110 PRINT "LINE" TAB( 8)"PLUS" TAB( 25)"MINUS"
1120 REM
1130 PRINT ACLINE% TAB( 8)AAPLUS TAB( 25)ABMINUS
1140 AAPLUS = AAPLUS * .1
1150 ABMINUS = ABMINUS * .1
1160 ACLINE% = ACLINE% + 1
1170 IF ACLINE < 21 GOTO 1130
1180 END
```

The program displays the following screen:

LINE	PLUS	MINUS
1	1	-1
2	.1	-.1
3	.01	-.01
4	1E-03	-1E-03
5	1E-04	-1E-04
6	1E-05	-1E-05
7	1E-06	-1E-06
8	1E-07	-1E-07
9	1E-08	-1E-08
10	1E-09	-1E-09
11	1E-10	-1E-10
12	1E-11	-1E-11
13	9.99999999E-13	-9.99999999E-13
14	9.99999999E-14	-9.99999999E-14
15	9.99999999E-15	-9.99999999E-15
16	9.99999999E-16	-9.99999999E-16
17	9.99999999E-17	-9.99999999E-17
18	9.99999999E-18	-9.99999999E-18
19	9.99999999E-19	-9.99999999E-19
20	9.99999999E-20	-9.99999999E-20

Lines 1 through 4 illustrate Rule 7:

LINE	PLUS	MINUS
1	1	-1
2	.1	-.1
3	.01	-.01
4	1E-03	-1E-03

The numbers 1, .1, and .01 are displayed correctly, but when the number becomes a decimal value between -.01 and +.01, the value is displayed in scientific notation.

The computer makes another rounding error between line 12 and line 13.

LINE	PLUS	MINUS
12	1E-11	-1E-11
13	9.99999999E-13	-9.99999999E-13

10.   The INPUT Instruction

INPUT: Format 1

Instruction   INPUT VN1,VN2,VN3,VN4,...
(where VN = Variable Name)

Example   INPUT AAEMPNUM%,ABEMPNAME$,ACHOURLYWAGE

The example INPUT instruction reads three values from the screen. The first value is a whole number (percent sign) representing the EMPloyee's NUMber. The second value is a string variable (dollar sign) and contains the EMPloyee's NAME. The third variable is a real number (no percent or dollar sign) and contains the HOURLY WAGE earned by the employee.

In response to the question mark displayed by the INPUT instruction, the operator keys in three variables as follows:

?1234,JOHN SMITH,5.75

The leading question mark is generated by the INPUT instruction. The whole number 1234 corresponds to the variable AAEMPNUM%. JOHN SMITH is a string value (alphanumeric value) matching the variable ABEMPNAME$. The value 5.75 is a real number corresponding to the variable ACHOURLYWAGE.

Purpose   This format of the INPUT instruction accepts one or more input values from the device being used for entering information (keyboard or disk).

INPUT: Format 2

Instruction   INPUT "string to be displayed";VN1,VN2,VN3, VN4,VN5,...
(where VN = Variable Name)

Example
INPUT "ENTER YOUR DATE OF BIRTH IN MM/DD/YY FORMAT ";AADTE$

The message ENTER YOUR DATE OF BIRTH IN MM/DD/YY FORMAT is displayed on the screen. The cursor ([) is positioned immediately following the message. In response, the operator keys in the date as requested. For example, 02/11/ 47 would be keyed in for February 11, 1947.

Purpose
The second format of the INPUT instruction combines the display feature of the PRINT instruction with the data entry operation of the INPUT instruction.

Rules for Use (General)
1. The keyword INPUT must be followed by one or more names.
2. The type of data keyed in must match the type of variable name defined; i.e., numeric characters for numeric variables and alphanumeric characters for string variables.
3. The number of variables keyed in must match the number of variables defined in the INPUT instruction.
4. When keying in the data, each variable must be separated by a comma. No variable may contain an embedded comma.
5. Only one string constant may be printed.
6. The string constant must be coded immediately after the keyword INPUT, and the constant must be followed by a semicolon.

Illustration of the Rules
The following illustrates the primary rules for the INPUT instruction.

Rule 1.
The keyword INPUT must be followed by one or more names.
Key in the following program:

```
NEW
1000 HOME
1010 INPUT AANUMBER
1020 PRINT AANUMBER
1030 END
```

After keying in the program run it, and enter the data as indicated below. Once you have entered RUN and pressed RETURN the following occurs.

1. A question mark appears in the upper left corner of the screen. The question mark is generated by the INPUT instruction unless the display option is used. The cursor ([) is positioned immediately following the question mark.

2. Since AANUMBER represents a real number, which may contain a decimal point use only the digits 0 through 9 and the decimal point, in response to the question mark. For example, key in any one of the following

   123
   or 123.45
   or 9876543.21

3. The number you key in will be displayed on the second line of the screen.

   In order to further understand the use of the INPUT instruction, run through the following exercises using the program just entered.

Exercise 1: Using the Plus Sign

1. Enter

   RUN   <RETURN>
   + 123.45 <RETURN>

2. Notice that when the number is displayed, the plus sign is not shown. Positive numbers are not shown with a sign.

Exercise 2: Using the Minus Sign

1. Enter

   RUN   <RETURN>
   − 123.45 <RETURN>

2. Notice that when the number is displayed, a leading minus sign is included. Applesoft recognizes either leading plus or minus signs but only prints negative signs.

Exercise 3: Suppression of Zeros

1. Enter

   RUN <RETURN>
   123.0 <RETURN>

2. Notice that the decimal and the 0 are not shown. Applesoft drops off nonsignificant digits. Nonsignificant digits consist of any leading or trailing zeros which are not needed for specification of a numeric value. For example, the number 000200.0300 has three leading nonsignificant zeros and two trailing nonsignificant zeros. The two zeros following the 2 and the one zero preceding the 3 are position holders and must be included to represent the number correctly. The number would print out as

200.03

Exercise 4: Entering a Value of Zero

1. Enter

RUN   <RETURN>
000.00 <RETURN>

2. Notice that for a value of zero, only one digit is printed no matter how many zeros were entered.

Try entering some numbers on your own until you are comfortable with how Applesoft treats numeric values entered with the INPUT instruction. Just enter RUN and then key in your number.

Rule 2. The type of data keyed in must match the type of name defined; i.e., numeric characters for numeric variables and alphanumeric characters for string variables.
Use the program you keyed in earlier to see what happens when you accidentally enter alphabetic data when the computer is expecting numeric data.

Exercise 5: Entering Alphabetic Data for Numeric Variables

1. Enter

RUN <RETURN>

2. A question mark will appear in the upper left corner. In response to the question mark, key in the value

ABC <RETURN>

3. The letters you key in will be rejected because the program is expecting a number to be entered. Applesoft will reject the letters and display the message

?REENTER

The program will continue to reject any nonnumeric value you key in.
4. Key in a valid number to end the program.

Now modify the program you have keyed in to accept a string value. This can be done by typing in the following two statements:

1010 INPUT AASTRING$
1020 PRINT AASTRING$

The two statements keyed in replace the previous statements with the same line numbers. To see that the changes were made correctly, type in

LIST <RETURN>

Exercise 6: Entering Alphanumeric Data

1. Enter

RUN <RETURN>

2. In response to the question mark, type in your name.
3. Notice that your name is printed exactly as you keyed it.

Exercise 7: Entering Numeric Values for String Variables

1. Enter

RUN   <RETURN>
+ 12.34 <RETURN>

2. Notice that the number is printed exactly as you keyed it (including the plus sign). Applesoft treats the value entered as a string (alphanumeric value) and not as a number. You cannot perform arithmetic operations with a string.

Exercise 8: Nonsignificant Digits in String Variables

1. Enter

    ```
    RUN        <RETURN>
    000200.0300 <RETURN>
    ```

2. Since the number is treated as a string variable, it will be printed exactly as you entered it with each character of the string taking up one memory location. Again, you cannot perform arithmetic operations with a string. String numeric values may be coverted to numeric format by using the VALue function (see p. 149).

Rule 3. The number of variables keyed in must match the number of variables defined on the INPUT instruction.
Key in the following program to be used with the exercises below.

```
NEW
1000 HOME
1010 INPUT AANUMBER,ABNUMBER,ACNUMBER
1020 PRINT AANUMBER,ABNUMBER,ACNUMBER
1030 END
```

Exercise 9: Entering Multiple Numeric INPUT Variables

1. Enter

    ```
    RUN        <RETURN>
    123,456,789 <RETURN>
    ```

2. Notice that after pressing return, all three numbers are displayed on one line with spaces separating each number. Applesoft automatically tabs to certain columns on the screen unless otherwise instructed.

Exercise 10: Entering Too Few Variables

1. Enter

    ```
    RUN <RETURN>
    ```

2. In response to the question mark, type in only two numbers separated by one comma. For example,

   123,456 <RETURN>

3. Notice that after pressing RETURN, a question mark appears on the next line, indicating that insufficient data was entered.

4. In response to the new question mark, type in

   789 <RETURN>

   Now all three numbers will be displayed.

Exercise 11: Entering Too Many Variables

1. Enter

   RUN <RETURN>

2. In response to the question mark, key in the following set of numbers:

   12,34,56,78 <RETURN>

3. Notice that the message EXTRA IGNORED is displayed, indicating that more variables were entered than requested. Only the first three values are displayed.

Exercise 12: Omitting a Variable

1. Enter

   RUN <RETURN>

2. In response to the question mark, type in the following numbers separated by two commas as shown

   123,,456 <RETURN>

3. Notice that after pressing RETURN three numbers are displayed. By using the two commas in a row, you accomplish the same thing as entering a 0 for the second variable (123,0,456).

Rule 4. When keying in the input, separate each variable with a comma. No variable may contain an embedded comma.

Key in the following program and use it for the exercises that follow:

```
NEW
1000 HOME
1010 INPUT AANUMBER,AASTRING$
1020 PRINT AANUMBER,AASTRING$
1030 END
```

Exercise 13: Entering Commas in Numeric Variables

1. Enter

   RUN   <RETURN>
   12,345.67,YEARLY SALARY <RETURN>

2. The message **EXTRA IGNORED** will be displayed, indicating that more variables were entered than requested. The comma in the number 12,345.67 is treated as a variable separator.

   When entering large numbers, do not key in commas.

3. Notice that since 345.67 followed the comma, it was treated as the second variable and placed in **AASTRING$**.

4. RUN the program again but this time enter the values correctly as

   12345.67,YEARLY SALARY <RETURN>

Exercise 14: Entering Commas in String Variables

1. Enter

   RUN   <RETURN>
   123,COLUMBUS, OHIO <RETURN>

2. Notice that the message **EXTRA IGNORED** is displayed, indicating that more variables were entered than requested. The comma after COLUMBUS was treated as a variable separator. The word OHIO was ignored.

3. RUN the program again, but this time enter the values without embedded commas. Type in

123,COLUMBUS OHIO <RETURN>

Rule 5. Only one string constant may be printed.
Key in the following program:

```
NEW
1000 HOME
1010 REM LINE 1020 CONTAINS AN ERROR
1020 INPUT "EMPLOYEE NUMBER";AAEMPNUM,"EMPLOYEE NAME";AAEMPN
     AME$
1030 PRINT "EMPLOYEE NUMBER = "AAEMPNUM
1040 PRINT "EMPLOYEE NAME    = "AAEMPNAME$
1050 END
```

After keying in the program, check your work, then enter RUN to test the program.
The following will occur:

1. You will get a syntax error on line 1020, indicating that the INPUT instruction is incorrectly formatted. The rule states that only one string constant may be displayed and it must precede all variable names. If you look at line 1020 you will see that the programmer tried to display two messages:

"EMPLOYEE NUMBER" and "EMPLOYEE NAME"

2. To correct the program, enter the following two lines of code:

```
1010 INPUT "EMPLOYEE NUMBER = ";AAEMPNUM
1020 INPUT "EMPLOYEE NAME    = ";AAEMPNAME$
```

3. Now that the program has been corrected, run it again.

4. The first line will be displayed, and the program will wait until you enter the employee number. After you enter the employee number, the second line will be displayed, and the computer will wait for you to enter the employee name. Once you have entered the number and name, lines 1030 and 1040 will display the two values.

When you use format 1 of the INPUT instruction, the computer displays a question mark. The question mark indicates to the computer operator that data is to be entered. When using format 2 of the INPUT instruction, the computer displays the message within quotes and does not display the question mark.

Format 1: INPUT AANUMBER   Displays as ?[
Format 2: INPUT "NUMBER = ";AANUMBER   Displays as NUMBER = [
The symbol [shows the position of the cursor.

When the programmers use the display option of the INPUT instruction, the person entering the data knows what to enter. By aligning the values to be entered and preceding them with an equal sign, the programmer improves readability of the data being entered.

Rule 6.   The string constant must be listed immediately after the keyword INPUT, and the constant must be followed by a semicolon.

This rule will not be discussed in detail. If you want to test it out on your own, make the following changes to the existing code and try to run the program.

First try

1010 INPUT "EMPLOYEE NUMBER = "AAEMPNUM

This change will result in a syntax error because the semicolon was left off following the constant.

Second try

1010 INPUT AAEMPNUM;" = EMPLOYEE NUMBER"

This change will result in a syntax error because the variable name is coded before the constant.

11.   The PRINT Instruction

Instruction   PRINT VN1,VN2,VN3,VN4,VN5,...
(where VN = Variable Name)

A comma, semicolon, TAB(number) function, or SPC(number) function may be used to separate the names. Each option results in different spacing.

Example   PRINT AAEMPNUMBER SPC(3) ABEMPNAME$ SPC(3) ACHOURSWORKED
Displays as

1234   YOUR NAME   40
  ↑↑↑   ↑↑↑   Three spaces between each variable

The PRINT instruction causes the value in each of the three variables to be displayed. The SPC(3) causes three blanks to be displayed between each variable.

Purpose   The PRINT instruction is used to display information on the CRT (Cathode Ray Tube) screen. The instruction is also used to transfer information from memory to the disk and printer.

Rules for Use   1.   The keyword PRINT may be followed by one or more variable names and/or constants.
2.   If a comma is used as a separator, default tab settings are used by the computer.
3.   If no symbol or a semicolon is used as a separator, no spacing occurs.
4.   If TAB(number) or SPC(number) functions are used, the computer tabs to the column indicated by the value within parentheses or spaces over the number of columns specified by the number within parentheses.
5.   When keying in the PRINT instruction, a question mark may be used in place of the word PRINT. The computer converts the question mark to the word

PRINT for you. This does not affect execution of your program but is simply a shorthand method of entering the word PRINT.

Illustration of the Rules   The following illustrates the primary rules for the PRINT instruction.

Rule 1.   The keyword PRINT may be followed by one or more variable names and/or constants. Key in and run the following program, or run the program by entering

RUN PRINT SAMPLE1

```
NEW
1000 REM PRINT SAMPLE1
1010 HOME
1020 PRINT "          1         2         3         4";
1030 PRINT "12345678901234567890123456789012345678 90"
1040 SPEED= 150
1050 PRINT "NUMBER = ",AANUMBER
1060 AANUMBER = AANUMBER + 1
1070 IF AANUMBER < 18 THEN 1050
1080 SPEED= 255
1090 END
```

After the program is run, the screen will appear as follows:

```
          1         2         3         4
12345678901234567890123456789012345678 90

NUMBER =        0
NUMBER =        1
NUMBER =        2
NUMBER =        3
NUMBER =        4
NUMBER =        5
NUMBER =        6
NUMBER =        7
NUMBER =        8
NUMBER =        9
NUMBER =        10
NUMBER =        11
NUMBER =        12
NUMBER =        13
NUMBER =        14
NUMBER =        15
NUMBER =        16
NUMBER =        17
```

1020–1030   Lines 1020 and 1030 display headings at the top of the screen so you can see which column the **TAB** operation has skipped to. The semicolon is required any time column 40 is used in a **PRINT** operation and single spacing is desired. If the semicolon had been omitted from line 1020, the headings would have been double spaced as follows:

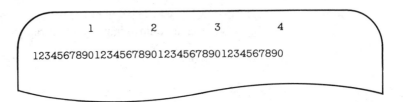

Anytime more than 40 characters are displayed, character 41 is printed in the first column of the next line.

Now comes the hard part: to explain where character 41 comes from and why it causes the machine to double space, when one would think it should single space.

Following each **PRINT** instruction which DOES NOT end with a semicolon is an invisible symbol called the *carriage return character.* When the display screen encounters the carriage return character, it automatically skips to the next line.

```
1030 PRINT "1234567890123456789012345678901234567890"
```
Invisible carriage return character ↑

If the computer has already printed the last visible character in column 40 of the first line, then the invisible carriage return character is printed in column 1 of the second line. Even though you cannot see it, it is there.

When the carriage return character is printed, it serves to terminate any additional printing for that line and positions the cursor at the start of the next line (line 3). The next **PRINT** instruction ends up printing the second line of heading on the third line of the screen.

With semicolon:

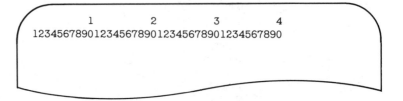

Without semicolon:

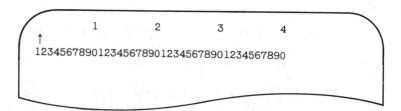

(Where the ↑ indicates the position of the invisible carriage return character.)

If you followed the explanation, fine; if not, just remember that when column 40 of the screen is used:

1. Ending with semicolon results in single spacing.
2. Not ending with a semicolon results in double spacing.

1040 The SPEED instruction is used to slow down the rate at which data is printed on the screen. This makes it easier for you to follow what is being displayed on the screen.

1050 When the PRINT instruction is followed by a constant, "NUMBER = ", the string between the quotation marks is displayed on the screen exactly as coded. When the PRINT instruction is followed by a variable name, AANUMBER, the current value of that variable is printed. The first time line 1050 is executed, a value of 0 is printed for AANUMBER. This is because Applesoft sets all numeric variables to a value of 0 at the start of the program. The second time line 1050 is executed, a value of 1 is printed (see line 1060).

1060 The current value of AANUMBER is replaced with the sum of the current value of AANUMBER plus 1. After the first execution of line 1060, AANUMBER contains the value 1. Remember AANUMBER started off with a value of 0 so

```
AANUMBER      =   AANUMBER   +            1
New value (1)  =   Old value (0)   +   constant (1)
```

1070 The IF instruction tests the new value of AANUMBER to see if it is less than 18. When the statement is true, that is, the value in AANUMBER is less than 18, logic flow goes back to line 1050, where the PRINT instruction is executed again. This is called a program loop, as lines 1050, 1060, and 1070 are executed over and over until AANUMBER is equal to 18.

1080   After the program has completed its normal cycle (loop), the speed is reset to 255 so that any further operations are displayed at the normal speed.

Rule 2.   If a comma is used as a separator, default tab settings are used by the computer. The default tab settings for your APPLE are

```
              1              2            3            4
   1234567890123456  7890123456789012  34567890
   AREA111111111111  AREA222222222222  AREA3333
```

1.   First area = columns 01 to 16.
     The PRINT instruction starts in column 1.
2.   Second area = column 17 to 32.
     The first comma causes the computer to tab over to column 17 unless something has been printed in column 16. If data has already been printed in or past column 16, the comma causes a skip to the next tab position (column 33).
3.   Third area = column 33 to 40.
     The second comma causes the third value to be printed starting in column 33 unless something printed in columns 24 through 32.

   The purpose of the following program is to show you what the automatic tab functions are for and how the comma works when used with the PRINT instruction.
   Key in and run the following program, or run the program by entering

RUN PRINT SAMPLE2

```
NEW
1000 REM PRINT SAMPLE2
1010 HOME
1020 PRINT "          1          2          3          4";
1030 PRINT "1234567890123456789012345678901234567890"
1040 SPEED= 150
1050 PRINT "TAB1","TAB2","TAB3"
1060 SPEED= 255
1070 END
```

1050   The PRINT instruction displays the strings **TAB1**, **TAB2**, and **TAB3**. Since each string is separated by a comma, the computer uses the automatic tab function. The position at which the T prints represents the default tab position for your machine. The T in each word starts in columns 1, 17, and 33.

There are, however, disadvantages which limit the usefulness of the automatic tab function. The following program is provided to illustrate two of the problems. Key in and run the following program, or run the program by entering

RUN PRINT SAMPLE3

```
NEW
1000 REM PRINT SAMPLE3
1010 HOME
1020 PRINT "          1         2         3         4";
1030 PRINT "1234567890123456789012345678901234567890"
1040 SPEED= 200
1050 PRINT "FIRST","SECOND","THIRD","FOURTH","FIFTH"
1060 PRINT : PRINT
1070 PRINT "FIRST 1234567890","SECOND","THIRD","FOURTH","FIFTH"
1080 SPEED= 255
1090 END
```

After you run the program the screen will appear as follows:

```
          1         2         3         4
1234567890123456789012345678901234567890

FIRST           SECOND          THIRD
FOURTH          FIFTH


FIRST 1234567890                SECOND
THIRD           FOURTH          FIFTH
```

1050 The first PRINT instruction demonstrates the wraparound function of the automatic tab operation. The words FIRST, SECOND, and THIRD are printed on one line, while the words FOURTH and FIFTH are printed on the next line down. If the number of variables separated by commas exceeds the number of default tab settings, a new line is started. This can be an advantage or a disadvantage depending on how you design your program.

1070 The next PRINT instruction demonstrates how the default tab reacts when a value is printed which is longer than the area covered by the automatic tab function. Notice that the value we wanted to print at the SECOND position is printed in the third column, while the THIRD value is printed at the start of the next line. Anytime the area allotted by the automatic tab function is filled or exceeded, the computer automatically goes to the next tab location.

The automatic tab operation for the third area works a little differently in that the computer skips to the next line if any value is printed in columns 24 through 32.

Rule 3.   If a semicolon is used as a variable separator, no spacing occurs between variables or between separate PRINT instructions.

The following program shows several examples of the use of the comma and semicolon. It should give you a clear understanding of the difference between the two characters.

Key in and run the following program, or run the program by entering

RUN SEMICOLON SAMPLE1

```
NEW
1000 REM SEMICOLON SAMPLE1
1010 HOME
1020 PRINT "          1         2         3         4";
1030 PRINT "1234567890123456789012345678901234567890"
1040 SPEED= 200
1050 PRINT "ENTER YOUR NAME PLEASE"
1060 INPUT AANAME$
1070 PRINT
1080 PRINT "ENTER YOUR AGE PLEASE"
1090 INPUT ABAGE
1100 PRINT AANAME$,ABAGE
1110 PRINT
1120 PRINT AANAME$;ABAGE
1130 PRINT
1140 PRINT "NAME = ";AANAME$,"AGE = ";ABAGE
1150 PRINT
1160 PRINT "NAME = ";
1170 PRINT AANAME$
1180 PRINT 'AGE  = '
1190 PRINT ABAGE
1200 SPEED= 255
1210 END
```

For the name JOHN JONES the screen would appear as follows:

```
          1         2         3         4
1234567890123456789012345678901234567890

ENTER YOUR NAME PLEASE
?JOHN JONES

ENTER YOUR AGE PLEASE
?25

JOHN JONES      25

JOHN JONES25

NAME = JOHN JONES                AGE = 25


NAME = JOHN JONES
AGE = 25
```

1050–1060 The PRINT instruction gives you a prompt to let you know what to enter. The INPUT instruction causes a question mark to be displayed and waits until you have entered your name.

1070 The PRINT instruction by itself causes a blank line to be displayed and is one way to create double spacing.

1080–1090 The PRINT instruction prompts you to enter your age, while the INPUT instruction reads what is keyed.

1100 This PRINT instruction shows the difference between the automatic tab function and the semicolon. Depending on the length of your name, your age is printed in either the second or the third tab location.

1120 The PRINT instruction shows that NO positions are skipped when the semicolon is used to separate variable names or constants. Notice that your age follows immediately after the last character of your name. You normally would not print two variables this way because it makes the data difficult to read.

1140 This line provides another example of how to use the semicolon and comma when displaying constants and variable names. The semicolon is used to separate an identifying title from the variable name

"NAME = ";AANAME$

The instruction also shows the use of the comma as a separator to provide automatic tabulation between the name and age.

The semicolon may be used to separate constants and variable names as shown but is optional and serves only to make the instruction more readable. The instruction could have been written as

1040 PRINT "NAME = "AANAME$,"AGE = "ABAGE

Notice that in this case the semicolons are omitted between the constants and variables.

1160–1190 Lines 1160 through 1190 show that if a PRINT instruction ends with a semicolon, the next information displayed occurs on the same line following the last character printed. The semicolon suppresses starting a new line and suppresses repositioning the cursor.

Lines 1160 and 1170 cause one line to be printed.

NAME = JOHN JONES

Lines 1180 and 1190 use the same concept to print your age; they generate only one line.

AGE = 25

Since lines 1170 and 1190 do not end with a semicolon a new line is started following each PRINT instruction.

Rule 4 If TAB(number) or SPC(number) functions are used, the computer TABs to the column indicated by the value within parentheses or SPaCes over the number of columns specified by the number within parentheses.

The following program illustrates the difference between the TAB and the SPC functions.

Key in and run the following program, or run the program by entering

RUN TAB & SPC SAMPLE1

```
NEW
1000 REM TAB & SPC SAMPLE1
1010 HOME
1020 PRINT "          1         2         3         4";
1030 PRINT "12345678901234567890123456789012345678901234567890"
1040 SPEED= 100
1050 PRINT "COLUMN 1"; TAB( 10);"COLUMN 10"; TAB( 30);"COLUM
N 30"
1060 PRINT:PRINT
1070 PRINT "COLUMN 1"; SPC( 10);"COLUMN 19"; SPC( 30);"NEW L
INE, COLUMN 18"
1080 SPEED= 255
1090 END
```

When the program is run, the screen will appear as follows:

```
           1         2         3         4
  12345678901234567890123456789012345678901234567890

  COLUMN 1 COLUMN 10           COLUMN 30


  COLUMN 1            COLUMN 19
                 NEW LINE, COLUMN 18
```

1050 Line 1050 demonstrates how the TAB function of the PRINT instruction may be used to position data across the screen at fixed locations by printing the word COLUMN starting in column 1, column 10, and column 30.

The semicolons between each of the strings constants and the tab functions are are optional. The instruction may be coded without the semicolons as follows

PRINT "COLUMN 1" TAB(10) "COLUMN 10" TAB(30) "COLUMN 30"

1070 Line 1070 demonstrates how the SPC function may be used to skip a specific number of spaces.

Use of the SPC function does not cause the data to be printed in fixed columns on the screen unless all the variables printed are a fixed length.

The SPC function causes the computer to skip the number of print positions specified before continuing to display information. The position on the screen where the new information is displayed depends on where the last character of data was printed prior to the SPC operation.

Before going on to the next rule, let's look at two more programs using the TAB and SPC functions.

The first example shows the use of a variable name with the **TAB** function and the wraparound effect of printing past the end of a line.

Key in and run the following program, or run the program by entering

RUN TAB SAMPLE2

```
NEW
1000 REM TAB SAMPLE2
1010 HOME
1020 REM
1030 REM VALUE FOR TAB FUNCTION
1040 REM MUST BE BETWEEN 1 AND
1050 REM 40.
1060 REM
1070 SPEED= 175
1080 AANUMBER = 1
1090 PRINT TAB( AANUMBER);AANUMBER
1100 AANUMBER = AANUMBER + 1
1110 IF AANUMBER < 41 THEN 1090
1120 SPEED= 255
1130 END
```

After you run the program, the screen will appear as follows:

```
                    21
                     22
                      23
                       24
                        25
                         26
                          27
                           28
                            29
                             30
                              31
                               32
                                33
                                 34
                                  35
                                   36
                                    37
                                     38
                                      39

                                       4
      0
```

1090 This line shows how a variable may be used with the TAB function to change the position at which data is printed during each loop through the program.

Notice that statement number 1080 gives AANUMBER a starting value of 1, so when line 1090 is executed for the first time, the computer TABs to position 1.

Do not try to use a value of 0 or a value greater than 40 in the TAB instruction.

1100 This line adds 1 to the current value of AANUMBER each time it is executed.

1110 The IF on line 1110 tests to see if the program has reached the limit of 40, which is the maximum for setting the TAB function. If you try to TAB to a value greater than 40, an error occurs. If you want to see what happens, remove line 1110. Just type in the number 1110 and rerun the program.

Before you go on, notice what happens to the numbers printed on the last two lines. Since there is not enough room for the value to be printed on the current line, the computer prints the excess data on the next line starting at the leftmost position.

The last TAB example shows what happens when the program attempts to TAB to a specific column when that column has already been bypassed.

Key in and run the following program, or run the program by entering

RUN TAB SAMPLE3

```
NEW
1000 REM TAB SAMPLE3
1010 HOME
1020 REM
1030 PRINT "          1         2         3         4";
1040 PRINT "1234567890123456789012345678901234567890"
1050 SPEED= 255
1060 PRINT "DATA GOES PAST COLUMN TWENTY";TAB( 19);
1070 PRINT "TAB OPERATION WILL BE IGNORED"
1080 PRINT
1090 PRINT "NOTICE HOW THE DATA RAN TOGETHER"
1100 PRINT "NO TAB OCCURRED BETWEEN TWENTY AND TAB"
1110 SPEED= 255
1120 END
```

After the program is run, the screen will appear as follows:

```
          1         2         3         4
1234567890123456789012345678901234567890

DATA GOES PAST COLUMN TWENTYTAB OPERATIO
N WILL BE IGNORED
NOTICE HOW THE DATA RAN TOGETHER
NO TAB OCCURRED BETWEEN TWENTY AND TAB
```

1060–1070   When data has already been printed past the column indicated by the TAB operation, the TAB operation is ignored. Normally this is not a problem since you know how large the data is and set the TAB operation accordingly. But if you use the TAB function and it does not seem to work, check the length of the data already printed against the TAB setting.

Since the semicolon is used on line 1060 following the TAB operation, the next information printed (line 1070) follows immediately behind the information printed by line 1060.

12. The GOTO Instruction

Instruction   GOTO statement number

Example   1000 PRINT NUMBER
1010 IF NUMBER > 100 THEN END
1020 NUMBER = NUMBER + 1
1030 GOTO 1000

Purpose   The GOTO instruction is used to change the flow of instruction execution from the current location (line) to the line number specified by the GOTO instruction.

Rules for Use   1.   The statement number used in the GOTO instruction must exist within the program.
2.   The GOTO instruction is considered unconditional GOTO when used by itself and conditional when used as part of an IF instruction.

Illustration of the Rules   The following illustrates the primary rules for the GOTO instruction.

Rule 1.   The statement number used in the GOTO instruction must exist within the program. Key in the following program, or load and list the program by entering

LOAD GOTO SAMPLE1
LIST

```
NEW
1000 REM GOTO SAMPLE1
1010 HOME
1020 PRINT "THE GOTO INSTRUCTION ALLOWS YOU TO"
1030 PRINT "BRANCH BACKWARD OR FORWARD IN YOUR"
1040 PRINT "PROGRAM."
1050 GOTO 1021
```

After entering the program, type RUN to execute it. The following will occur:

1. Lines 1020, 1030, and 1040 will each display one line.
2. When line 1050 is encountered, the computer will display the following error message:

?UNDEF'D STATEMENT ERROR IN 1050

The machine gives you an error message because there is no statement numbered 1021.

To correct the program, enter

1050 GOTO 1020

Don't rerun the program yet! Read on.

Look over the logic and see what is going to happen.

First lines 1010, 1020, 1030, 1040, and 1050 will be executed. When the computer executes the GOTO instruction on line 1050 the logic cycle will go back to statement 1020 and continue at that point. How does this cycle of 1020, 1030, 1040, 1050, 1020, 1030, etc. stop? It doesn't. The program is in what is called an *endless loop*. The only way to stop it is to interrupt the program by keying CONTROL-C or CONTROL-RESET or by pulling the plug (although it won't hurt, please don't pull the plug).

Now, type in RUN and execute the program. Be prepared to press the CONTROL-C to stop the loop.

Rule 2. The GOTO instruction is considered unconditional when used by itself and conditional when used as part of an IF instruction.

Key in and run the following program, or run the program by entering

RUN GOTO SAMPLE2

```
NEW
1000 REM GOTO SAMPLE2
1010 HOME
1020 SPEED= 150
1030 COUNTER = 1
1040 PRINT "COUNTER = "COUNTER
1050 COUNTER = COUNTER + 1
1060 IF COUNTER > 20 GOTO 1080
1070 GOTO 1040
1080 SPEED= 255
1090 END
```

The program will display the following rather unexciting screen:

```
COUNTER = 1
COUNTER = 2
COUNTER = 3
COUNTER = 4
COUNTER = 5
COUNTER = 6
COUNTER = 7
COUNTER = 8
COUNTER = 9
COUNTER = 10
COUNTER = 11
COUNTER = 12
COUNTER = 13
COUNTER = 14
COUNTER = 15
COUNTER = 16
COUNTER = 17
COUNTER = 18
COUNTER = 19
COUNTER = 20
```

1030 The COUNTER is initialized to a starting value of 1. If a numeric variable is not given a starting value, Applesoft starts it off with a value of 0.

1040 The PRINT instruction displays the string "COUNTER = " on the screen followed by the current value of COUNTER. The first time through the loop, COUNTER has a value of 1; the second time the line is executed, a value of 2 is printed, and so forth.

1050 COUNTER is reset to the current value of COUNTER plus 1. Basically this is a method of counting on the computer.

1060 Line 1060 provides a sample of how to use the GOTO within an IF instruction to create a conditional branch instruction. The GOTO is also an example of a *forward* GOTO. If the statement is true, logic flow branches to line 1080 further down (forward) in the program.

For this program the IF instruction is used to provide a way to end the looping cycle. When COUNTER reaches a value of 21, a conditional branch transfers logic forward in the program to statement 1090, where the program ends.

1070   Line 1070 creates an unconditional branch backward to line 1040. Every time line 1070 is executed, logic flow loops back to line 1040 and starts executing the instructions sequentially from that point. Since this GOTO causes logic to branch back to an earlier statement, it is called a backwards GOTO.

    The only way to get around or past an unconditional branch is to use another GOTO instruction to change the flow of logic and bypass the unconditional GOTO (see line 1060).

1090   The END instruction is the last logical instruction to be executed. Once the END is encountered, no further instructions are executed by the computer. Control passes back to the computer operator (you).

    The following terms were used in the preceding narrative. Make sure you understand the terms and how they relate to the use of the GOTO instruction.

Unconditional GOTO: when a GOTO instruction is used by itself.

Conditional GOTO: when a GOTO instruction is used within an IF instruction.

Forward GOTO: when a GOTO is used to branch futher down in the program code.

Backward GOTO: when a GOTO is used to branch upward to an earlier instruction.

13. The ON GOTO Instruction

Instruction   ON number GOTO statement numbers

Example   1000 INPUT "ENTER NUMBER OF MONTH = ";MTH

1010 ON MTH GOTO 1040, 1050, 1060, 1070, 1080, 1090,
         1100, 1110, 1120, 1130, 1140, 1150
1020 REM MTH < 1 OR > 12
1030 PRINT "ERROR IN MONTH VALUE":END
1040 PRINT "JANUARY":END
1050 PRINT "FEBRUARY":END
1060 PRINT "MARCH":END
1070 PRINT "APRIL":END
1080 PRINT "MAY":END
1090 PRINT "JUNE":END
1100 PRINT "JULY":END
1110 PRINT "AUGUST":END
1120 PRINT "SEPTEMBER":END
1130 PRINT "OCTOBER":END
1140 PRINT "NOVEMBER":END
1150 PRINT "DECEMBER":END

If the value of MTH is 1, 2, 3, 4, 5, 6, 7, 8, 9, 10, 11, or 12, the ON GOTO instruction causes logic flow to branch and print the correct name of the month. If the value of MTH is less than 1, or greater than 12, an error message printed.

Purpose   The ON GOTO instruction is used to change the sequence of instruction execution based on the value of the number following the keyword ON. The instruction combines the IF and GOTO instructions into one statement.

Instead of having to code 12 IFs with 12 GOTOs,

```
IF MTH = 1 GOTO 1040
IF MTH = 2 GOTO 1050
IF MTH = 3 GOTO 1060
........
IF MTH = 12 GOTO 1150
```

you may code one instruction to test for all 12 values:

```
ON MTH GOTO 1040,1050,1060,1070,1080,1090,1100,1110, 1120,1130,1140,1150
```

Rules for Use

1. The statement numbers used with the ON GOTO instruction must exist within the program.
2. The name or equation following the keyword ON may be either an integer or a real value. If the variable contains a real value, any decimal positions are ignored.
3. The value of the number or arithmetic expression following the keyword ON must not be negative or exceed 255. If the value is outside the computer's allowable range, an error message is displayed and the program terminated.
4. Each statement number following the keyword GOTO corresponds to a test for the value of 1, 2, 3, 4, 5, etc.
5. If the number being evaluated is 0 or is greater than the number of statements listed, logic flow falls through the ON GOTO and continues with the next sequential statement.

Illustration of the Rules

Key in the following program, or load and list the program by entering

```
LOAD ON GOTO SAMPLE1
LIST
```

```
1000 REM ON GOTO SAMPLE1
1010 HOME
1020 VTAB 10
1030 PRINT "ENTER A NUMBER FROM 1 TO 10.": PRINT
1040 PRINT "ENTER 11 TO TERMINATE THE PROGRAM.": PRINT
1050 INPUT " = ";AANUMBER
1060 PRINT
1070 ON AANUMBER GOTO 1100,1120,1100,1120,1100,1120,1100,112
     0,1100,1120,1170
1080 PRINT "NUMBER NOT WITHIN SPECIFIED RANGE."
1090 GOTO 1130
1100 PRINT "YOU ENTERED AN ODD NUMBER."
```

```
1110 GOTO 1130
1120 PRINT "YOU ENTERED AN EVEN NUMBER."
1130 VTAB 23
1140 PRINT "PRESS ANY KEY TO CONTINUE.";
1150 GET X1$
1160 GOTO 1000
1170 HOME
1180 PRINT "THAT'S ALL FOLKS!"
1190 END
```

1000–1060 Lines 1000 through 1060 clear the screen, position the cursor, and display what the program expects the operator to do.

1070 Depending on the value entered by the operator, the **ON GOTO** instruction either branches to one of the 11 statement numbers or falls through to line 1080. If 1, 3, 5, 7, or 9 is entered, logic flow branches to line 1100. For the value 2, 4, 6, 8, or 10, logic flow branches to line 1120. If the operator enters an 11, logic flow branches to line 1170. Should the operator enter a value of 0 or a value from 12 to 255, logic flow falls through to line 1080.

Notice that the same statement number may be used in several different positions. In the example all the odd numbers are associated with statement 1100, and all the even numbers are associated with statement 1120.

1080–1090 Lines 1080 and 1090 display an error message and then return to the start of the program if a value of 0 or a value from 12 to 255 is entered.

1130–1160 After the appropriate message is displayed, the operator is given a chance to read the message and press a key. After any key is pressed, the program starts over and gives the operator another chance to enter a number.

To help illustrate the rules, use the program to carry out the following exercises.

Exercise 1: Entering Real Numbers

RUN the program and enter

4.5

The computer will truncate the .5 and treat the number as an integer value of 4. The message "YOU ENTERED AN EVEN NUMBER." will be printed. Press any key and continue to the next exercise.

Exercise 2: Entering Numbers Outside the Specified Range

The ON GOTO instruction is set up to handle the values from 1 to 11. Enter a value of 0 or a value from 12 to 255 and see what happens. Enter

12

Logic flow will fall through the ON GOTO instruction and execute line 1080, which displays the message

NUMBER NOT WITHIN SPECIFIED RANGE.

Press any key and continue to the next exercise.

Exercise 3: Entering Invalid Numbers

Entering a negative value or a value greater than 255 results in an error message and cancellation of the program. Enter −1. You will get the error message

?ILLEGAL QUANTITY ERROR IN statement number

To prevent this from happening, you should always precede each ON GOTO instruction with an IF instruction to make sure the value entered is within the expected range.

```
1050 INPUT ' = ';AANUMBER
1060 PRINT
1065 IF AANUMBER < 1 OR AANUMBER > 11 THEN
        print error message & start over
1070 ON AANUMBER GOTO ...
```

14. The END Instruction

Instruction END

Example 2000 PRINT "NORMAL END OF PROGRAM" : END
or
2000 END

Purpose The END instruction is used to terminate program execution. Once encountered, no further instructions are executed.

Rules for Use
1. The END instruction can be located on any line of the program as long as it is the last logical instruction executed.
2. More than one END instruction may be used in a program, but once one is encountered, no further instructions are executed.
3. The program may be continued by using the CONT instruction (see p. 228).

Illustration of the Rules Key in and run the following program, or run the program by entering

RUN END SAMPLE1

```
NEW
1000 REM END SAMPLE1
1010 HOME
1020 PRINT "ENTER A NUMBER BETWEEN 1 & 5"
1030 INPUT " = ";AANUMBER
1040 ON AANUMBER GOTO 1050,1070,1080,1090
1050 PRINT "BETWEEN 1 & 5 PLEASE"
1060 PRINT "PRESS ANY KEY AND TRY AGAIN":GET X$:GOTO 1000
1070 PRINT "END #2":END
1080 PRINT "END #3":END
1090 PRINT "END #4":END
```

1050–1060 The program is coded to accept only the numbers 2, 3, or 4 as acceptable entries. Any other number causes an error message to be displayed (line 1050) indicating that an invalid number was entered. Line 1060 displays an error message before branching back to line 1000 to allow you to enter the number correctly. The GET X$ instruction on line 1060 causes the computer to pause while you read the messages.

1070–1090   This is the objective of the program, the END instruction. Before executing the END instruction and stopping the program, a message is displayed indicating which logical END path was taken. Once the END instruction is executed, no further instructions are processed.

Did you notice that several instructions are coded on the same line, separated by a colon? This is common practice for experienced programmers because the computer can execute the code a little faster and the program takes less memory. The examples in the text limit the number of instructions entered on one line to make it easier to read and easier for the beginning programmer to follow. Advanced programmers may code as many instructions for one statement number as the program logic allows. The only physical limit is that each line entered cannot exceed 255 characters.

Some experienced programmers object to having more than one END instruction in a program. They believe all logic paths should come to a single common END. Let's change this program to conform to their standards by modifying lines 1070, 1080, and 1090 and adding a new line.

Key in the following code, LIST the program, and then RUN it.

```
1070 PRINT "END #2":GOTO 1100
1080 PRINT "END #3":GOTO 1100
1090 PRINT "END #4":GOTO 1100
1100 END
```

If you run the modified program, you cannot tell any difference between the two methods of coding. The only difference is the programmer's opinion about which is the most logical method of coding.

15.   The Screen Control Instructions

Instructions   VTAB number from 1 to 24
HTAB number from 1 to 40
NORMAL
INVERSE
FLASH

Purpose   The screen control instructions of VTAB, HTAB, NORMAL, INVERSE, and FLASH are used to position data and direct attention to specific areas of the screen.

Example   1000 INVERSE: PRINT "DARK LETTERS ON LIGHT BACKGROUND"
1010 FLASH: PRINT "ALTERNATING LIGHT AND DARK DISPLAY"
1020 NORMAL: PRINT "LIGHT LETTERS ON DARK BACKGROUND"
1030 VTAB 10: HTAB 20: PRINT "X": REM MIDDLE OF SCREEN

Rules for Use   1.   VTAB is used to position the cursor on any one of the vertical lines of the screen. The number following the VTAB instruction must be from 1 to 24, corresponding to the 24 lines on the screen. Any number outside this range results in the following error message:

?ILLEGAL QUANTITY ERROR

2.   HTAB is used to position the cursor at any one of the 40 positions on a line. The number following the HTAB instruction may range from 1 to 255. If a value greater than 40 is used, the cursor wraps around to the next line. For this book we will consider the HTAB to have a maximum value of 40, corresponding to the character position of each line. Any number less than 1 or greater than 255 results in the following error message:

?ILLEGAL QUANTITY ERROR

3.   NORMAL refers to the normal mode of using white characters on a black background (or green characters on a black background, depending on the type of screen you are using). The instruction is used following either a FLASH or an INVERSE operation to place the computer back into its NORMAL mode.

4. INVERSE refers to the use of black characters on a white background or (black characters on a green background). This format is commonly used to indicate error messages or to highlight data as it is being entered.

5. FLASH refers to the changing between NORMAL mode and INVERSE mode in a rapid manner. The screen shows the data in NORMAL format followed by the same data shown in INVERSE format. This rapid change causes a flashing image on the screen.

Illustration of the Rules

Let's start with some very simple examples to demonstrate the NORMAL and INVERSE instructions.

The first program illustrates how to use the INVERSE and NORMAL instructions. Key in and run the following program, or run the program by entering

RUN SCREEN SAMPLE1

```
NEW
1000 REM SCREEN SAMPLE1
1010 HOME
1020 SPEED= 150
1030 INVERSE
1040 FOR NUMBER = 0 TO 30
1050 PRINT TAB(40)" "
1060 NEXT
1070 NORMAL
1080 SPEED= 255
1090 PRINT "THAT'S ALL FOLKS!"
1100 END
```

For those of you who don't run the program, here is what it does. The screen clears and starts to display a solid white line. As the program continues, a solid white line is printed on every other line of the screen (horizontal prison bars). Once the screen is full, the program continues to display alternating white and black lines until 30 white lines have been displayed.

1020 The SPEED instruction slows down the output to the screen so you can watch the cursor move across the screen.

1030 The INVERSE instruction tells the computer that all further information displayed on the screen is to use black letters on a white background. Since this program is only printing blanks, each line displayed is entirely white.

1040 The FOR/NEXT instruction sets up a looping process. The FOR/NEXT loop causes 30 lines to be displayed on the screen. After the first 12 lines are displayed, the screen scrolls up one line at a time as each new line is displayed. Since the line displayed prints a character in column 40 and no ending semicolon is used, each PRINT instruction results in double spacing.

1050 The PRINT instruction TABs to position 40 and prints a single blank. To reach position 40 the computer prints a blank in every position up to column 40 and then prints the blank enclosed within quotes (" "). This operation causes the line to be cleared to spaces, and since the program is in the INVERSE mode, the spaces show up as a white line.

Are you ready for another try at the invisible carriage return character and why the screen double spaces?

Since the PRINT instruction does not end with a semicolon, the computer attaches a carriage return character to the information being displayed. When the carriage return character is displayed, the cursor is positioned to the first of the next line. You cannot see this character, but it is there and it is printed.

1050 PRINT TAB(40) " "   Invisible carriage-return character
                         ↑

The PRINT instruction puts a blank in column 40, and the invisible carriage return character in column 1 of the next line. Since the printing of the carriage return character causes the cursor to be repositioned to the next line, the net effect is double spacing on the screen. In the screen below, the ↑ shows where the carriage return is printed.

```
      – inverse line –
 ↑  = invisible carriage return character
      – inverse line –
 ↑  = invisible carriage return character
      – inverse line –
```

1060 The keyword NEXT forms the other half of the FOR/NEXT instruction. Each time the keyword NEXT is encountered, the variable listed in the FOR instruction is incremented. After the variable is incremented, it is tested against the limit specified in the FOR instruction. In this case if NUMBER is less than or equal to 30, the instructions between the keyword FOR and keyword NEXT are executed again. If NUMBER is greater than 30, logic falls through to line 1070.

1070 The computer is instructed to display all the information following this instruction in NORMAL mode. If the program does not reset the display to NORMAL, all information displayed after the end of the program is in the INVERSE mode.

1080   The SPEED is reset so your display screen operates at its normal fast pace after the program ends.

Now that you have seen the INVERSE instruction in action, change line 1030 by entering

1030 FLASH

Be ready to cover your eyes!
Enter

RUN <RETURN>

The FLASH instruction causes the computer to alternate between white letters on a black background and black letters on a white background. It is a very good way to get the operator's attention and to cause temporary blindness.

You have seen two short examples of INVERSE and FLASH; now let's look at a more complete program.

The following program uses the VTAB, HTAB, NORMAL, INVERSE, and FLASH instructions to show you how to highlight messages. The program is very simple. Its single purpose is to introduce the use of the screen instructions. The program requests that you enter a number greater than 1000, less than 32768, and divisible by 3.

1.   If you guess a number which is divisible by 3, the program displays a message in FLASH screen format.
2.   If your number is not divisible by 3, the program displays a message using INVERSE screen format.
3.   If you enter a number less than 1001, the computer displays an error message in INVERSE screen format.

To terminate the program enter 0 in response to the INPUT instruction.
Key in and run the following program, or run the program by entering

RUN SCREEN SAMPLE2

```
NEW
1000 REM SCREEN SAMPLE2
1010 HOME
1020 REM
1030 REM NORMAL, INVERSE, FLASH
1040 REM
1050 SPEED= 150
1060 PRINT "GUESS A NUMBER GREATER THAN 1000 AND": PRINT
1070 PRINT "   LESS THAN 32768 WHICH IS DIVISIBLE": PRINT
1080 PRINT "   BY 3"
1090 PRINT "KEY IN A VALUE OF ZERO TO QUIT"
1100 VTAB 15: HTAB 10
```

```
1110 INPUT "GUESS = ";AAGUESS
1120 IF AAGUESS = 0 THEN SPEED= 255: HOME : PRINT "THAT'S
     ALL FOLKS!" : END
1130 IF AAGUESS < 1001 OR AAGUESS > 32767 THEN 1400
1140 ABWHOLE% = AAGUESS / 3
1150 ACREAL = AAGUESS / 3
1160 ADDECIMAL = ACREAL - ABWHOLE%
1170 IF ADDECIMAL > 0 GOTO 1300
1180 REM ----------------------
1190 REM CORRECT NUMBER MESSAGE
1200 REM
1210 VTAB 20: HTAB 1: FLASH
1220 PRINT TAB( 35)" "
1230 PRINT "     G R E A T    G U E S S      "
1240 PRINT TAB( 35)" "
1250 GOSUB 1510: REM CLEAR MES
1260 GOTO 1100
1270 REM ----------------------
1280 REM INCORRECT GUESS MES
1290 REM
1300 VTAB 20: HTAB 1: INVERSE
1310 PRINT TAB( 39)" "
1320 PRINT "CANNOT DIVIDE";
1330 NORMAL
1340 PRINT " "AAGUESS" ";
1350 INVERSE
1360 PRINT TAB( 30)"BY 3       ";
1370 PRINT TAB( 39)" "
1380 GOSUB 1510: REM CLEAR MES
1390 GOTO 1100
1400 REM ----------------------
1410 REM OUTSIDE OF RANGE MES
1420 REM
1430 VTAB 20: HTAB 1: INVERSE
1440 PRINT TAB( 39)" "
1450 PRINT "   VALUE ENTERED < 1001 OR > 32767      "
1460 PRINT TAB( 39)" "
1470 GOSUB 1510: REM CLEAR MES
1480 GOTO 1100
1490 REM ----------------------
1500 REM SUBROUTINE TO CLEAR
1510 REM MESSAGE AREA
1520 REM
1530 NORMAL
1540 PRINT "PRESS ANY KEY TO TRY AGAIN"
1550 GET X$
1560 VTAB 20: HTAB 1
1570 FOR X = 1 TO 160: PRINT " ";: NEXT
1580 VTAB 15: HTAB 18: PRINT "          "
1590 RETURN
```

Run the program and enter several numbers to see what happens on the screen.
Use the following numbers to test and view each of the routines in the program.

1. Enter 1000 to test the out-of-range error routine.
2. Enter 1001 to test the not divisible by 3 error routine.
3. Enter 1002 to test the divisible by 3 message.

After you have seen the various messages, read through the explanation to see how the program skipped around on the screen.

1100 The VTAB instruction positions the cursor on the fifteenth line. The horizontal position of the cursor remain unchanged. That is, if the cursor is in column 20 before the VTAB, it is still in column 20 after the VTAB is executed, but on line 15.

The HTAB instruction is used to position the cursor at the tenth column on the current line.

1110 Since the cursor is positioned on line 15 in the tenth column, the message GUESS = is displayed starting at that point. The cursor blinks following the message GUESS = until you enter a number.

By using the VTAB and HTAB instructions, you can display data at various points on the screen, making it easier for the operator to read and input data.

1120 This group of instructions tests to see if you entered zero. Before the program is ended the speed is reset, the screen is cleared, and an ending message is displayed.

1130 Just to see if you can follow directions, the IF instruction tests whether the number entered is within the limits requested. This is called an *edit check*. The lower range is important only to this program, but the value of 32767 is significant. Since the program uses an integer variable in the calculation process, the value entered is tested to make sure it does not exceed the maximum integer value which can be stored by the computer. Remember, an integer variable cannot store a number greater than 32767 (see p. 53).

If you enter a number less than 1001 or greater than 32767, logic flow branches to line 1400, where a message is printed indicating the mistake.

1140 Applesoft does not have an instruction which provides the programmer with the remainder of an integer division operation. In order to know whether the value in AAGUESS is divisible by 3, you must divide by 3 and check the remainder. A remainder of 0 indicates that it is divisible by 3. Any other value indicates that the number is not divisible by 3. The first step in this process is to find the whole number of times 3 goes into AAGUESS. Line 1140 gives the integer answer to dividing GUESS by 3. Lines 1150, 1160, and 1170 complete the process by finding out if there is a remainder of 0. Notice that ABWHOLE% is an integer variable (ends with a percent sign). For example, in integer format, 1004 / 3 = 34, and 1005 / 3 = 35.

1150   The division operation finds out the number of times 3 goes into AAGUESS and the answer is stored in the real number format (includes decimal positions). For example, in real format, 1004 / 3 = 34.666667, and 1005 / 3 = 35.0000.

1160   When the integer portion of the answer is subtracted from the real portion, only the decimal value remains. If the decimal value is 0 the guess is divisible by 3. If the decimal portion of the answer is greater than 0 the guess is not divisible by 3. So for AAGUESS = 1004, 34.666667 − 34 = .666667, indicating that AAGUESS is not divisible by 3. If AAGUESS = 1005, 35.0 − 35 = .0, indicating that AAGUESS is divisible by 3.

1170   If the decimal portion of the answer is greater than 0, logic flow branches to line 1300, where a message indicating a bad guess is displayed. If ADDECIMAL is equal to 0, logic flow drops down to the next section of code which FLASHes a message indicating that you selected a number divisible by 3.

1180–1210   In this program all the messages in response to the INPUT operation are printed starting on line 20 of the screen. The VTAB 20 instruction positions the cursor on line 20 but does not change the horizontal position.

The HTAB 1 instruction positions the cursor to column 1 of the current line. At this point the HTAB instruction could be left out. On line 1110 you enter a number and press the RETURN key. When the RETURN key is pressed, the computer automatically positions the cursor to the first column of the next line. Since we want the cursor in column 1, the HTAB instruction is not really needed. It is coded in this example to help you remember that usually the VTAB and HTAB instructions are used together.

The FLASH instruction tells the computer that all further information displayed on the screen is to alternate between white letters on a black background and black letters on a white background.

I suggest a limited application of this instruction as it is hard on your eyes!

1220   This instruction prints a line of 35 blanks. Since the screen is in FLASH mode, the line alternates between an all white line and an all black line.

1230   The PRINT instruction displays the GREAT GUESS message. Since the computer is in FLASH mode, the message alternates in patterns of white and black.

1250   The GOSUB is a new instruction which will be covered later in greater detail. The instruction is somewhat like the GOTO instruction and causes the logic flow to branch to line 1510. But unlike the GOTO instruction, the GOSUB (GO TO SUBROUTINE) remembers where it branched from, and upon completing the subroutine returns to the instruction following the GOSUB (line 1260).

The term *subroutine, routine,* or *module* refers to a set of instructions which are independent of the main body of the program. The subroutine may be executed from many different parts of the program, saving the programmer from having to repeat coding at different locations of the program.

For this program there are three different messages to be displayed. After displaying each message, the computer pauses and lets the operator read the message. Once the operator has responded, the subroutine clears lines 20 through 23. Since the process is common to all three messages, the code for clearing the lines is written once and then executed in each routine by using the GOSUB instruction.

1260   After logic flow returns from the subroutine, the GOTO on line 1260 causes logic flow to branch back to line 1100, where another guess is accepted.

1270–1300   The INVERSE instruction tells the computer that all further information is to be displayed in black letters with a white background.

1310–1370   For this message the CANNOT DIVIDE and BY 3 parts of the line are printed in INVERSE mode, while the actual number guessed is printed in NORMAL mode. In order to change back and forth between NORMAL and INVERSE, each part of the line must be printed separately. Notice the semicolon at the end of lines 1320 and 1340.

The instruction 1340 PRINT "   "AAGUESS"   "; causes the value in AAGUESS to be printed in normal mode with two leading and two trailing blanks.

1380   Once the message has been displayed, logic flow branches to the subroutine, which is responsible for waiting for a response from the operator and clearing lines 20 to 23.

1390   After the subroutine has waited for a key to be pressed, cleared lines 20 to 23 of the screen, and returned, line 1390 causes logic flow to go back to line 1100, where another guess is accepted.

1490–1530   The subroutine starts off by setting the computer to the NORMAL display mode no matter what mode the computer is in prior to entering the subroutine.

1540   This is the common message for all three logic routes taken by the program: correct guess, incorrect guess, or error in number entered. By putting the code in a common subroutine, the programmer need only write it once.

1550   The GET instruction is used to cause the computer to wait until a key is pressed. After a key is pressed logic flow continues to the next line of code.

1560 The VTAB and HTAB instructions are used to position the cursor prior to clearing lines 20 through 23.

1570 The FOR/NEXT instruction is used in conjunction with the PRINT instruction to clear four lines starting at line 20. This is done by printing 160 spaces (160 characters/ 40 characters per line = 4 lines).

   This is not the best way to clear the lines, but it does produce a nice visual effect as the cursor moves from left to right across the screen.

1580 Before the subroutine returns to the main portion of the program, it clears the old guess. It does this by displaying ten spaces starting at the same position where the old guess was entered.

1590 This is the last instruction of the subroutine and indicates to RETURN to the instruction following the calling GOSUB. (The term calling GOSUB refers to the GOSUB which caused logic flow to brach to this routine.)

Methods of Clearing a Line

The following code represents four ways to blank out a line:

```
1.   PRINT "      <   40 blanks >              ";
2.   FOR NUMBER = 1 TO 40 : PRINT " "; : NEXT
3.   PRINT TAB(40)" ";
4.   CALL -868
```

PRINT "   < 40 blanks   >   ";

The first example requires the programmer to count over 40 spaces. This means the programmer must not only count correctly but must do all the work in writing out the blank line.

FOR NUMBER = 1 TO 40 : PRINT " "; : NEXT

The second method requires the computer to loop through the FOR/NEXT statement 40 times. This is easier on the programmer but makes the computer work harder. Don't forget the semicolon at the end of the PRINT instruction.

PRINT TAB(40)" ";

The third method lets the computer TAB over to column 40, eliminating the need to count the number of blanks or repeat the loop. As the computer TABs over to column 40, it uses blanks as a fill character, erasing the current characters on the line. When column 40 is reached, one blank is printed. This one blank is necessary to get the computer to TAB correctly. Notice that the statement ends with a semicolon. The semicolon is required or else two lines end up being used instead of one.

CALL −868

The fourth method shown uses a CALL instruction to clear the line. The CALL instruction is similar to the GOSUB instruction in that the CALL causes logic flow to branch to a machine language subroutine and then return after the subroutine is done. In this case the CALL executes a machine language subroutine starting at address −868. The machine language code is part of the APPLE's operating system.

This method is quick but presents several problems.

1. The CALL −868 clears the line to NORMAL mode. That is, the CALL blanks out the line in the black background mode. You may want to have the background displayed in either the INVERSE or the FLASH mode. For either of these two cases the CALL will not work.
2. The CALL instruction address works only on the APPLE computer. If your Applesoft program is to be converted to another computer, this instruction will have to be replaced.
3. The person reading the code may not understand the CALL instruction as easily as the PRINT TAB(40)" "; instruction. The PRINT instruction is easier to maintain and read than the CALL −868.

16.

The GOSUB/RETURN Instructions

Instructions   GOSUB statement number
RETURN

Example   1000 GOSUB 2000:REM FORMAT SCREEN
1010 ...

....

2000 REM FORMAT SCREEN ROUTINE
2010 ...

....

2100 RETURN

The GOSUB instruction branches to line 2000, where a subroutine clears and formats the screen. After the screen has been formatted, logic flow RETURNs to the instruction following the GOSUB. Since the REM instruction following the GOSUB is a nonexecutable instruction, logic flow continues to line 1010.

Purpose   1.   The GOSUB instruction allows the programmer to code a set of related instructions once and execute those instructions from many different points of the program.

   When this technique is used, the size of the program is reduced and the length of time the programmer spends coding is decreased.

   Also, some routines which are used in a program are common to other programs. Once the routine is coded as an independent module, it can be copied as needed from program to program.

   2.   The GOSUB instruction allows the programmer to break the program into smaller, more workable units, which are easy to understand and code. After coding each segment or *module*, the programmer may then use GOSUB instructions to execute the modules in a specific sequence.

   This is an important concept. Originally you benefit because it is simpler to code smaller program modules. Later, if you try to modify the program, you will find the smaller modules much easier to change.

Rules for Use   1.   Each routine executed by way of a GOSUB instruction must end with the RETURN instruction.

If you exit a routine without going through the RETURN instruction use the POP instruction (see p. 125) to remove the RETURN address from the GOSUB stack table.

2. GOSUBs may be nested (GOSUB within GOSUB within GOSUB). Each group of instructions, or routine, executed by way of the GOSUB instruction must end with a RETURN instruction. It is important that you make sure you always exit a routine by way of the RETURN instruction.

If you want to exit a routine without executing all the instructions within the routine, use a GOTO instruction to branch to the matching RETURN instruction for that routine. When you always use the matching RETURN to exit a module, the chain of GOSUBs is not broken.

```
1000 GOSUB 2000: REM EXECUTE SUBROUTINE
1010 ...
........
2000 REM SUBROUTINE
2010 ... instructions
2020 IF ... GOTO 2200: REM CONDITIONAL GOTO
2030 ... instructions you want to skip over
........
2200 RETURN
```

Illustration of the Rules

The following example does not process anything but shows how the GOSUB works and shows the basic program structure which can be used to develop any program. The program is broken down into four parts:

DRIVE ROUTINE	= Lines 1030 to 1100
BEGINNING ROUTINE	= Lines 1120 to 1180
MAIN ROUTINE	= Lines 1200 to 1250
ENDING ROUTINE	= Lines 1270 to 1320

Look over the listing and see if you can follow the lines indicating the sequence in which the instructions are executed.

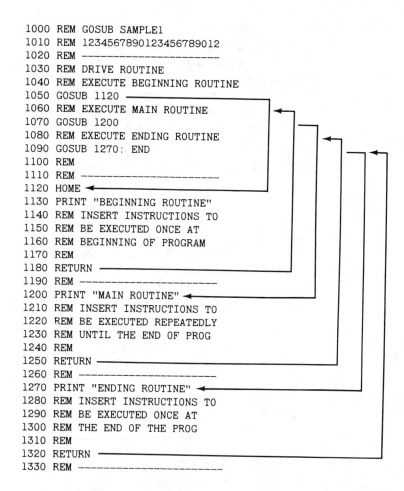

```
1000 REM GOSUB SAMPLE1
1010 REM 1234567890123456789012
1020 REM ------------------------
1030 REM DRIVE ROUTINE
1040 REM EXECUTE BEGINNING ROUTINE
1050 GOSUB 1120
1060 REM EXECUTE MAIN ROUTINE
1070 GOSUB 1200
1080 REM EXECUTE ENDING ROUTINE
1090 GOSUB 1270: END
1100 REM
1110 REM ------------------------
1120 HOME
1130 PRINT "BEGINNING ROUTINE"
1140 REM INSERT INSTRUCTIONS TO
1150 REM BE EXECUTED ONCE AT
1160 REM BEGINNING OF PROGRAM
1170 REM
1180 RETURN
1190 REM ------------------------
1200 PRINT "MAIN ROUTINE"
1210 REM INSERT INSTRUCTIONS TO
1220 REM BE EXECUTED REPEATEDLY
1230 REM UNTIL THE END OF PROG
1240 REM
1250 RETURN
1260 REM ------------------------
1270 PRINT "ENDING ROUTINE"
1280 REM INSERT INSTRUCTIONS TO
1290 REM BE EXECUTED ONCE AT
1300 REM THE END OF THE PROG
1310 REM
1320 RETURN
1330 REM ------------------------
```

When logic flow encounters line 1050, the GOSUB instruction causes the program to branch (GOTO) to line 1120. Before the computer branches, it stores the address of the next instruction (in this case line 1060) in a GOSUB stack table. When the computer encounters a RETURN instruction, it uses the address from the stack table as the RETURNing point.

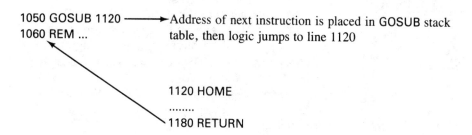

1050 GOSUB 1120 ———→ Address of next instruction is placed in GOSUB stack
1060 REM ...   table, then logic jumps to line 1120

1120 HOME
....
1180 RETURN

Once the RETURN is encountered, the computer returns to the address last placed in the GOSUB stack.

The computer stores the address of the next instruction in the stack table each time a GOSUB is executed. To make the sample easier to follow, statement numbers are used to represent the instruction address.

That is, when there is an instruction on the same line as the GOSUB, the computer stores the address of the instruction following the GOSUB.

```
2000 GOSUB 3000 : PRINT "STORES ADDRESS OF NEXT INSTRUCTION"
                  ↑  Stores address of PRINT instruction
```

To make the following explanation simpler each GOSUB is coded on a separate line, and line numbers are used in place of the return address.

But it is important that you understand that the GOSUB returns to the next sequential instruction and not to the next line number.

The GOSUB differs from the GOTO in that the GOTO does not cause the computer to save a return address. With the GOSUB the computer remembers where you want logic flow to return.

As indicated by the remarks in the BEGINNING ROUTINE, its purpose is to execute all the instructions which are necessary to get the program started. The beginning routine instructions are only executed once. After the RETURN instruction on line 1080 is executed, logic flow returns to line 1060 of the DRIVE ROUTINE.

When the computer returns to line 1060, logic flow continues down to line 1070, where the second GOSUB is executed.

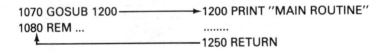

```
1070 GOSUB 1200 ─────────────→ 1200 PRINT "MAIN ROUTINE"
1080 REM ...                    ........
   ↑ ───────────────────────── 1250 RETURN
```

When the second GOSUB is executed, the computer stores statement number 1080 in the stack table and then branches to line 1200. After the instructions within the MAIN ROUTINE are executed and the RETURN instruction is encountered, logic flow returns to line 1080.

For this example the MAIN ROUTINE is only executed once. In a real situation you use a GOTO or FOR/NEXT instruction to repeat the MAIN ROUTINE until a condition exists which indicates ending the routine (such as reaching the end of the file). When the ending condition is encountered, logic flow is allowed to fall through to the RETURN instruction.

Once the computer is back in the DRIVE ROUTINE the GOSUB on line 1090 is executed, causing the computer to save the address of the END instruction in the stack table and then branch to line 1270.

```
1090 GOSUB 1270: END        1270  PRINT "ENDING ROUTINE"
                            ........
                            1320 RETURN
```

Once the RETURN instruction is executed, logic flow returns to the END next instruction following the GOSUB.

The purpose of the ENDING ROUTINE is to provide an area in which to locate instructions which are executed once prior to ending the program.

This structure of BEGINNING, MAIN, and ENDING ROUTINE is shown in more detail in the disk programs. Once you learn how to break a programming problem into units and code these units separately, your programs will be easier to write and easier to change.

Now run the program and see if the information displayed on the screen is what you expected.

The second GOSUB example is an extension of the first but demonstrates the use of nested GOSUBs (a GOSUB within a GOSUB).

For this example two additional routines have been added. To simplify the code, both routines display a single line indicating what they are suppose to do. In a complete program the instructions for formatting the screen would be coded in the first routine, and the instructions for reading the data would be coded in the second routine.

In order to give you a better idea of how the routines are repeated, a counter is used to cycle through the program five times.

Look over the following listing and see if you can follow the logic sequence, then run the program and watch the screen. Enter

RUN GOSUB SAMPLE2

```
1000 REM  GOSUB  SAMPLE2
1010 REM  12345678901234567890012
1020 REM  ---------------------
1030 REM  DRIVE ROUTINE
1040 REM  EXECUTE BEGINNING ROUTINE
1050 GOSUB 1120
1060 REM  EXECUTE MAIN ROUTINE
1070 GOSUB 1210
1080 REM  EXECUTE ENDING ROUTINE
1090 GOSUB 1300
1100 END
1110 REM  ---------------------
1120 HOME
1130 PRINT "BEGINNING ROUTINE"
1140 REM  INSERT INSTRUCTIONS TO
1150 REM  BE EXECUTED ONCE AT
1160 REM  BEGINNING OF PROGRAM
1170 REM
```

```
1180 LIMIT = 5
1190 RETURN
1200 REM ----------------------
1210 PRINT "MAIN ROUTINE"
1220 REM PRINT SCREEN ROUTINE
1230 GOSUB 1370
1240 REM READ SCREEN ROUTINE
1250 GOSUB 1420
1260 NUMBER = NUMBER + 1
1270 IF NUMBER < LIMIT THEN 1210
1280 RETURN
1290 REM ----------------------
1300 PRINT "ENDING ROUTINE"
1310 REM INSERT INSTRUCTIONS TO
1320 REM BE EXECUTED ONCE AT
1330 REM THE END OF THE PROG
1340 REM
1350 RETURN
1360 REM ----------------------
1370 PRINT "PRINT SCREEN ROUTINE"
1380 REM INSERT INSTRUCTIONS TO
1390 REM DISPLAY SCREEN
1400 RETURN
1410 REM ----------------------
1420 PRINT "READ SCREEN ROUTINE"
1430 REM INSERT INSTRUCTIONS TO
1440 REM READ DATA FROM SCREEN
1450 RETURN
1460 REM ----------------------
```

The DRIVE ROUTINE consists of basically the same code as in GOSUB SAMPLE1.

The BEGINNING ROUTINE consists of the same code but with one line added. Line 1180 sets the variable LIMIT to a starting value of 5.

The MAIN ROUTINE has been changed to show the use of nested GOSUB instructions.

The first GOSUB within the MAIN ROUTINE causes logic flow to branch to the PRINT SCREEN ROUTINE. Since the MAIN ROUTINE is executed by way of the GOSUB instruction on line 1070, the second GOSUB results in what is called a *nested* GOSUB, that is, the use of a GOSUB within a routine executed by way of a GOSUB.

When the first GOSUB is executed, Applesoft puts the address of the instruction to which it is suppose to return into the first location of a special table (called a *stack*).

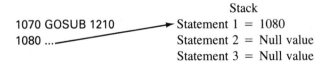

```
                                    Stack
1070 GOSUB 1210        ────►  Statement 1 = 1080
1080 ...────                   Statement 2 = Null value
                              Statement 3 = Null value
```

When the second GOSUB is executed, Applesoft puts the return address into the second location of the stack table. The stack table works using a LIFO sequence (Last In, First Out).

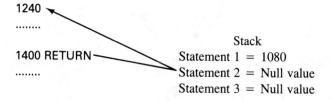

	Stack
1230 GOSUB 1370	Statement 1 = 1080
1240 ... ────────────►	Statement 2 = 1240
	Statement 3 = Null value

Applesoft continues to place return addresses at the end of the table each time a new GOSUB is encountered.

Each time a RETURN is encountered, the last entry placed in the table serves as the RETURN address. By using the LIFO method, Applesoft can continue to nest GOSUBs, and as long as you follow the rules, Applesoft returns to the correct instruction.

After execution of the RETURN on line 1400, Applesoft removes the statement number from the second entry of the table and branches back to that statement. After the second entry is removed, the stack table contains only the one statement number which is the return address for the MAIN ROUTINE.

```
1240 ◄
........
                                    Stack
1400 RETURN ──────────┐    Statement 1 = 1080
........               └──► Statement 2 = Null value
                           Statement 3 = Null value
```

When the GOSUB on line 1250 is executed, Applesoft places the address of the instruction following the GOSUB into the second location of the table.

	Stack
1250 GOSUB 1420	Statement 1 = 1080
1260 ... ────────────►	Statement 2 = 1260
	Statement 3 = Null value

When the RETURN on line 1450 is executed, the last address placed in the stack is removed and used as the returning point for logic flow.

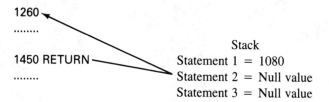

```
1260 ◄
........
                                    Stack
1450 RETURN ──────────┐    Statement 1 = 1080
........               └──► Statement 2 = Null value
                           Statement 3 = Null value
```

The process of inserting the return address and removing the return address continues through five loops of the MAIN ROUTINE. On the fifth time through, logic flow drops through the IF on line 1270 and encounters the RETURN at the end of the MAIN ROUTINE. At this point there is only one number in the stack table. The value is removed from the table and used as the return address.

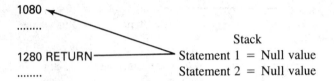

```
1080
........
                                    Stack
1280 RETURN                  Statement 1 = Null value
........                      Statement 2 = Null value
```

The next instruction to be executed is line 1080. When the GOSUB on line 1090 is executed, the return address of 1100 is placed in the stack, and then logic flow branches to line 1300. Upon completion of the ENDING ROUTINE, the return address is removed from the table, and logic flow ends on line 1100 with the END instruction.

17. The ON GOSUB Instruction

Instruction   ON number GOSUB statement numbers

Example   1000 INPUT "ENTER NUMBER OF MONTH = ";MTH
1010 IF MTH < 1 OR MTH > 12 THEN GOSUB 1160:GOTO 1030
1020 ON MTH GOSUB 1040,1050,1060,1070,1080,1090,1100,
        1110,1120,1130,1140,1150
1030 END
1040 PRINT "JANUARY":RETURN
1050 PRINT "FEBRUARY":RETURN
1060 PRINT "MARCH":RETURN
1070 PRINT "APRIL":RETURN
1080 PRINT "MAY":RETURN
1090 PRINT "JUNE":RETURN
1100 PRINT "JULY":RETURN
1110 PRINT "AUGUST":RETURN
1120 PRINT "SEPTEMBER":RETURN
1130 PRINT "OCTOBER":RETURN
1140 PRINT "NOVEMBER":RETURN
1150 PRINT "DECEMBER":RETURN
1160 PRINT "ERROR IN MONTH VALUE":RETURN

If the value of MTH is 1, 2, 3, 4, 5, 6, 7, 8, 9, 10, 11, or 12, the ON GOSUB instruction causes logic flow to branch and print the correct name of the month. If the value of MTH is less than 1 or greater than 12, line 1010 causes an error message to be printed. After the name of the month is printed, logic flow returns to line 1030, and the program ends.

Purpose   The ON GOSUB instruction is used to change the flow of instruction execution based on the value of the number following the keyword ON. The instruction combines the features of the IF and GOSUB instructions into one statement.

Instead of having to code 12 IFs with 12 GOSUBs,

```
IF MTH = 1 GOSUB 1040
IF MTH = 2 GOSUB 1050
IF MTH = 3 GOSUB 1060
........
IF MTH = 12 GOSUB 1150
```

you may code one statement to test for all 12 values:

```
ON MTH GOSUB 1040,1050,1060,1070,1080,1090,1100,1110,
        1120,1130,1140,1150
```

Rules for Use

1. The statement numbers used with the **ON GOSUB** instruction must exist within the program.
2. The name or equation following the keyword **ON** may be either an integer or a real value. If the variable contains a real value, any decimal positions are ignored.
3. The value of the number or arithmetic expression following the keyword **ON** must not be negative or exceed 255. If the value is outside the computer's allowable range, an error message is displayed and the program terminated.
4. Each statement number following the keyword **GOSUB** corresponds to a test for the value of 1, 2, 3, 4, 5, etc.
5. If the number being evaluated is 0 or is greater than the number of statements listed, logic flow falls through the **ON GOSUB** and continues with the next sequential statement.
6. Each routine executed using the **ON GOSUB** instruction must end with the **RETURN** instruction.

Illustration of the Rules

Key in the following program, or load and list the program by entering

```
LOAD ON GOSUB SAMPLE1
LIST
```

```
1000 REM ON GOSUB SAMPLE1
1010 HOME
1020 VTAB 10
1030 PRINT "ENTER A NUMBER FROM 1 TO 10.": PRINT
1040 PRINT "ENTER 11 TO TERMINATE THE PROGRAM.": PRINT
1050 INPUT " = ";AANUMBER
1060 PRINT
1070 IF AANUMBER < 1 OR AANUMBER > 11 THEN GOSUB 1130:GOTO 1 090
1080 ON AANUMBER GOSUB 1150,1170,1150,1170,1150,1170,1150,1170,
        1150,1170,1190
1090 VTAB 23
1100 PRINT "PRESS ANY KEY TO CONTINUE.";
1110 GET X1$
```

```
1120 GOTO 1000
1130 PRINT "NUMBER NOT WITHIN SPECIFIED RANGE."
1140 RETURN
1150 PRINT "YOU ENTERED AN ODD NUMBER."
1160 RETURN
1170 PRINT "YOU ENTERED AN EVEN NUMBER."
1180 RETURN
1190 HOME
1200 PRINT "THAT'S ALL FOLKS!"
1210 END
1220 REM DID NOT RETURN ON LAST GOSUB
```

1070   Before the **ON GOSUB** instruction is executed, the value entered is checked to see if it is within the specified range. To be on the safe side, precede each **ON GOSUB** and **ON GOTO** instruction with an **IF** instruction. When you test the value to be used prior to the **GOSUB** or **GOTO** operation, there is no chance for an illegal value to cause the program to abnormally terminate.

1080   Depending on the value entered by the operator, the **ON GOSUB** instruction branches to one of the 11 statement numbers. Since the **IF** instruction on line 1070 has already tested for any value outside the 11 numbers, the instruction is guaranteed a match. If 1, 3, 5, 7, or 9 is entered, logic flow branches to line 1150. For the value 2, 4, 6, 8, or 10, logic flow branches to line 1170. If the operator enters an 11, logic flow branches to line 1190.

    Notice that the same statement number may be used in several different positions. In the example all the odd numbers are associated with statement 1150, and all the even numbers are associated with statement 1170.

1090–1120   After the appropriate message is displayed, the operator is given a chance to read the message and press a key. After any key is pressed, the program starts over and gives the operator another chance to enter a number.

1190–1220   This section of code prints a message when an 11 is entered to terminate the program. Notice that when the program terminates, no **RETURN** is used. Since lines 1190 to 1220 are the last instructions to be executed by the program, the **RETURN** is omitted, and the program is terminated without returning to the calling **GOSUB**. Normally each **GOSUB** operation should have a matching **RETURN** instruction. Do not get into the practice of breaking the **GOSUB/RETURN** structure.

    To help illustrate the rules, run the program and enter the following values.

1.   Enter a real number with a decimal point, let's say 4.5. The computer will truncate the .5 and treat the number as an integer value of 4. The message **YOU ENTERED AN EVEN NUMBER.** will print out. Press any key to continue the program.

2. Enter a number outside the acceptable range, such as zero. Since zero is not within the range of the numbers requested, the IF instruction on line 1070 will intercept the number and branch to line 1130. The message NUMBER NOT WITHIN SPECIFIED RANGE. will be displayed. Press any key to continue the program.

3. Enter an odd or an even number within the acceptable range. If you enter an odd number, the ON GOSUB will cause logic flow to branch to statement 1150. If you enter an even number, the ON GOSUB will cause logic flow to branch to line 1170. In either case a message will be displayed, and logic flow will return to line 1090. Press any key to continue the program.

4. To terminate the program, enter 11. After terminating the program, delete line 1070 by entering

```
1070 <RETURN>
```

Run the program again and enter a negative value or a value greater than 255. Since the value was not checked prior to being used in the ON GOSUB instruction, the program will be terminated with an ILLEGAL QUANTITY error message.

Remember that when using either the ON GOSUB or the ON GOTO instructions, any negative number or value greater than 255 abnormally terminates the program.

18. The POP Instruction

Instruction POP

Example
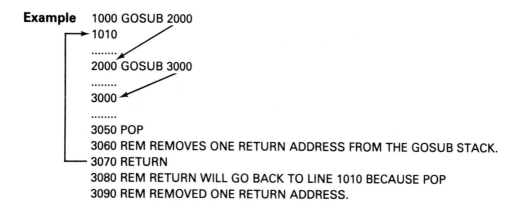
```
1000 GOSUB 2000
1010
........
2000 GOSUB 3000
........
3000
........
3050 POP
3060 REM REMOVES ONE RETURN ADDRESS FROM THE GOSUB STACK.
3070 RETURN
3080 REM RETURN WILL GO BACK TO LINE 1010 BECAUSE POP
3090 REM REMOVED ONE RETURN ADDRESS.
```

Purpose The POP instruction is used to remove the last instruction address placed in the GOSUB stack. If for some reason you DO NOT want to RETURN to the instruction following the calling GOSUB, the POP instruction can be used to remove the last return address placed in the GOSUB stack table.

Rules for Use
1. Prior to execution of a POP instruction, at least one GOSUB instruction must have been executed or the program ends with error code 22 (RETURN WITHOUT GOSUB).
2. After the POP instruction is executed, logic flow continues to the next instruction. No return or branching is associated with the POP instruction.

Illustration of the Rules For the following GOSUBs, three addresses are located in the GOSUB stack. To make the example easier to illustrate, statement numbers are used, but remember that the machine actually uses the address of the next instruction.

```
1000 GOSUB 2000                    Stack
1010 ........  ───────────────→ Statement 1 = 1010
2000 GOSUB 3000            ──→ Statement 2 = 2010
2010 ........               ──→ Statement 3 = 3010
3000 GOSUB 4000
3010 ........
4000 POP
4010 RETURN
```

The POP instruction on line 4000 removes the last address from the GOSUB stack, leaving only two return addresses:

Statement 1 = 1010
Statement 2 = 2010
Statement 3 = Cleared by POP

When the RETURN instruction on line 4010 is executed, program logic returns to statement 2010 since it is now the last address in the GOSUB stack.

19. The LET Instruction

Instruction LET variable name = $\begin{Bmatrix} \text{Formula} \\ \text{Variable} \\ \text{Constant} \end{Bmatrix}$

Example   LET A = B

Sets variable A equal to the value of B.

LET A$ = "ALPHA" + "NUMERIC"

Sets A$ equal to the value ALPHANUMERIC.

Purpose
1. To copy data from one variable to another.
2. To connect two or more strings into one string and store the results in the variable to the left of the equal sign.
3. To calculate a numeric value based on a formula and store the answer in the variable to the left of the equal sign.

   The LET instruction has many options. The discussion of the LET instruction is divided into four sections. Each subsection is divided further into a detailed explanation of each parameter and symbol to be used.

Rules for Use
1. General rules in using the LET instruction
   a. The keyword LET is optional in Applesoft.
   b. Only one variable name is allowed to the left of the equal sign.
   c. The type of variable to the left of the equal sign must match the type of value produced by the equation on the right side of the equal sign.
2. Numeric operations using the LET instruction
   a. + (plus) For addition
   b. − (minus) For subtraction or negation
   c. * (asterisk) For multiplication
   d. / (slash) For division
   e. ^ (caret) For exponentiation
   f. ( ) Left and right parentheses for sequence of execution

3. Numeric operations using the LET Applesoft functions

   Note: To help illustrate the formats of the various functions variable names are used. The names X and Y are used to show the location where either a numeric constant, numeric variable, or numeric equation must appear. The name A$ is used to show where either a string constant or string variable must appear.

a.	ABS(X)	References the absolute value of X
b.	ASC(A$)	References the ASCII (American Standard Code for Information Interchange) numeric value of the first character of the variable A$
c.	INT(X)	References the integer portion of the real number X
d.	LEN(A$)	References the number of characters in the variable A$
e.	RND(X)	Returns a random number based on the value of X
f.	SGN(X)	Returns a -1, 0, or $+1$ depending on the value of X
g.	VAL(A$)	References the numeric value of A$
h.	others SIN(X); COS(X); TAN(X); ATN(X); SQR(X); EXP(X); LOG(X)	

4. String operations using the LET string functions

a.	LEFT$(A$,X)	References the X leftmost characters of A$
b.	MID$(A$,X,Y)	References the middle of A$ starting at location X and continuing for Y characters
c.	RIGHT$(A$,X)	References the X rightmost characters of A$
d.	+	Can be used with string functions to **CONNECT** groups of alphanumeric characters together; the process of connecting two strings is called *concantenation*
e.	CHR$(X)	Returns the ASCII character corresponding to the numeric value of X
f.	STR$(X)	Returns the numeric value of X in string format

General Rules for Using the **LET** Instruction

1a. The keyword LET is optional in Applesoft.

1b. Only one variable name is allowed to the left of the equal sign.

1c. The type of variable name to the left of the equal sign must match the type of value produced by the equation on the right side of the equal sign.

Illustration of the Rules

Key in and run the program, or run the program by entering

RUN LET SAMPLE1

```
1000 REM LET SAMPLE1
1010 HOME
1020 REM
1030 REM FOR APPLESOFT "LET" IN
1040 REM THE LET INSTRUCTION IS
```

```
1050 REM OPTIONAL
1060 REM
1070 LET AANUMBER = 5
1080 ABNUMBER = 40
1090 ACNUMBER = ADNUMBER = AENUMBER = AANUMBER * ABNUMBER
1100 PRINT "AANUMBER = ";AANUMBER
1110 PRINT "ABNUMBER = ";ABNUMBER
1120 PRINT "ACNUMBER = ";ACNUMBER
1130 PRINT "ADNUMBER = ";ADNUMBER
1140 PRINT "AENUMBER = ";AENUMBER
1150 END
```

1070–1080 The first LET instruction shows the standard format with the keyword LET followed by the variable name to be changed, the equal sign, and the equation to be evaluated in developing the answer.

Except for statement 1070, none of the programs used in this book include the keyword LET.

Line 1070 sets AANUMBER equal to 5, while line 1080 sets ABNUMBER equal to 40.

1090 This line shows how you might mistakenly attempt to set several variables equal to the same value with a single LET instruction. Logically, the instruction is trying to set the variables ACNUMBER, ADNUMBER, and AENUMBER equal to the results of multiplying AANUMBER by ABNUMBER, but when the instruction is executed, Applesoft sets ALL variables to zero.

To correctly set all variables to the same value, use multiple LET instructions. First compute the answer, and then set the other variables equal to the results.

1090 ACNUMBER = AANUMBER * ABNUMBER: ADNUMBER = ACNUMBER:
AENUMBER = ACNUMBER

1100–1140 Lines 1100 through 1140 print the contents of each of the variables used in the example, proving that variables AC, AD, and AE were set to zero.

Rule 1c. The type of variable name to the left of the equal sign must match the results produced by the equation on the right side of the equal sign.

Example STRINGNAME\$ = STRING FUNCTION
REALNAME   = ANY ARITHMETIC OPERATION
INTEGERNAME% = ANY ARITHMETIC OPERATION to be truncated

Key in the following program, or load and list the program by entering

```
LOAD LET SAMPLE2
LIST

1000 REM LET SAMPLE2
1010 HOME
1020 REM CORRECT STR SAMPLES
1030 AASTRING$ = "APPLES"
1040 ABMTH$ = "SEPTEMBER"
1050 ACDTE$ = "12/28/81"
1060 REM
1070 REM INCORRECT STR SAMPLES
1080 ADVLUE$ = 1234
1090 AEDTE$ = 122881
1100 REM
1110 REM CORRECT REAL SAMPLES
1120 AANUMBER = 1234.56
1130 ABDTE = 122881
1140 REM
1150 REM INCORRECT REAL SAMPLES
1160 ACVLUE = "$123.45"
1170 ADDTE = 12/28/81
1180 REM
1190 REM CORRECT INT SAMPLES
1200 AANUMBER% = 1234
1210 ABDTE% = 1281:REM MONTH AND YEAR
1220 REM
1230 REM INCORRECT INT SAMPLES
1240 ACVLUE% = 123.45
1250 ADDTE% = 122881
1260 REM
1270 PRINT "AASTRING$ = "AASTRING$
1280 PRINT "ABMTH$    = "ABMTH$
1290 PRINT "ACDTE$    = "ACDTE$
1300 PRINT "AANUMBER  = "AANUMBER
1310 PRINT "ABDTE     = "ABDTE
1320 PRINT "ADDTE     = "ADDTE
1330 PRINT "AANUMBER% = "AANUMBER%
1340 PRINT "ABDTE%    = "ABDTE%
1350 PRINT "ACVLUE%   = "ACVLUE%
1360 END
```

1020–1060 String names are initialized to the value indicated by the alphanumeric string to the right of the equal sign. Alphanumeric constants (string constants) must be enclosed in quotation marks. Even if the value to be placed in a string variable consists of all numbers, the value must still be enclosed within quotation marks.

1070–1100 Lines 1080 and 1090 are examples of mismatch errors. Attempt to run the program and you will get the following message

?TYPE MISMATCH ERROR IN 1080

The computer is trying to tell you that you cannot mix variables. You cannot give an alphanumeric variable a numeric value or give a numeric variable an alphanumeric value.

Delete the lines in error by entering

```
DEL 1070,1100
LIST
```

1110–1140 Lines 1110 to 1140 provide correct examples of how to set a numeric variable to a numeric value. In this case the numeric variables and values represent what are called real numbers. The real number set includes whole numbers such as 23, 500, 1001, etc., as well as numbers with decimal portions such as .045, 12.45, 1001.15, etc. In other words, real numbers may or may not have a decimal portion whereas integers may only contain whole numbers. Most arithmetic is done with real numbers.

1150–1180 Lines 1150 to 1180 provide examples of incorrect attempts to set a numeric variable name equal to a specific value. In line 1160 there is another TYPE MISMATCH error: a numeric variable cannot be set equal to a string value enclosed within quotation marks.

In line 1170 the value to the right of the equal sign is not interpreted as a date but causes ADDTE to be set to a value of .00529101. The computer interprets the equation

```
ADDTE = 12 / 28 / 81
```

as 12 divided by 28 = .42857143 (see first slash), then .42857143 divided by 81 = .00529101 (see second slash).

This mistake does not result in a syntax error but does result in a logic error.

To eliminate these lines, enter

```
DEL 1150, 1180
LIST
```

1190–1220 Lines 1190 to 1220 provide correct examples of how to set an integer variable equal to an initial value. An integer variable is indicated by a percent sign used as the last character of the name. Integer variables may only contain positive or negative whole numbers. You may wonder why ABDTE% was set equal to a different date (value) than in previous examples. The largest whole number which can be stored in an integer variable is $(+, -)$ 32767. The numeric date 122881 used on lines 1050 and 1130 is too large and would result in an error message.

1230–1260 Line 1240 does not result in a syntax error but is logically incorrect. Applesoft sets

ACVLUE% equal to the integer portion of the real number 123.45. After execution of line 1240, ACVLUE% contains the whole number 123. If the programmer wants to truncate the decimal positions, this instruction is valid. If the programmer expects to keep the decimal positions, then a logic error has occurred.

Line 1250 shows what happens if you attempt to store a value larger then +32767 or smaller than −32767. If you try to run the program the following message is displayed

?ILLEGAL QUANTITY ERROR IN 1250

To delete this line enter

1250
LIST

At this point all the syntax errors should be out of the program. RUN the program and review the output to make sure you understand the following concepts:

STRING Variables

1. String variable names always end with a dollar sign.
2. String variables are always treated by the computer as alphanumeric even when they contain only numbers.
3. String constants MUST be enclosed within quotation marks.
4. String variables cannot be used in arithmetic operations.

REAL Variables

1. Real variable names end with either a numeric digit or with an alphabetic character (A1, A2, AB, AC, etc).
2. Real variables contain numeric values with possible decimal positions.
3. Real constants MUST NOT be enclosed within quotation marks and may or may not contain a decimal position (123 or 123.0).
4. Real variables can be used in any type of arithmetic operation.

INTEGER Variables

1. Integer variables always end with a percent sign.
2. Integer variables contain only whole numbers. No decimal positions can be stored.
3. Integer constants MUST NOT be enclosed within quotation marks.
4. Integer variables can be used in any type of arithmetic operation.

The LET Instruction / 133

Basic Numeric Operation in Applesoft

For numeric operations use the following symbols:

1. + For addition
2. − For subtraction
3. * For multiplication
4. / For division
5. ˆ For exponentiation
6. ( ) Left and right parentheses for sequence of execution

The examples of add, subtract, multiply and divide are very simple. You may want to look over the first four examples and execute only one before moving on to the example on exponentation.

Addition

To add, use the plus (+) sign. The following program asks you to input two numbers and then displays the two numbers and the answer in an equation format.

Key in and run the following program, or run the program by entering

RUN ADD SAMPLE1

```
NEW
1000 REM ADD SAMPLE1
1010 HOME
1020 REM
1030 REM + FOR ADDITION
1040 REM
1050 PRINT "ADD EXAMPLE +"
1060 PRINT
1070 INPUT "FIRST NUMBER = ";AANUMBER
1080 INPUT "SECOND NUMBER= ";ABNUMBER
1090 ACANSWER = AANUMBER + ABNUMBER
1100 PRINT:PRINT
1110 PRINT AANUMBER" + "ABNUMBER" = "ACANSWER
1120 END
```

1090 When using the LET instruction, each variable to the right side of the equal sign MUST be separated by an arithmetic symbol.

The value of the variable to the left of the equal sign is replaced by the new amount calculated on the right of the equal sign. Again, only one variable is allowed to the left of the equal sign.

In this case the number you enter for AANUMBER is added to the number entered for ABNUMBER and the results stored in ACANSWER.

Subtraction

To subtract use the minus (−) sign. The following program uses the same logic as the add example. If you decide to load the program, run it several times, entering various combinations of numbers so you get positive, negative, and zero results.

Key in and run the following program, or run the program by entering

RUN SUBTRACT SAMPLE1

Remember, once the program is loaded, you only need to key RUN and press RETURN to execute it again.

```
NEW
1000 REM SUBTRACT SAMPLE1
1010 HOME
1020 REM
1030 REM - FOR SUBTRACT
1040 REM
1050 PRINT "SUBTRACT EXAMPLE -"
1060 PRINT
1070 INPUT "FIRST NUMBER = ";AANUMBER
1080 INPUT "SECOND NUMBER= ";ABNUMBER
1090 ACANSWER = AANUMBER - ABNUMBER
1100 PRINT:PRINT
1110 PRINT AANUMBER" - "ABNUMBER" = "ACANSWER
1120 END
```

Multiplication

To multiply use the asterisk (*) character. Again, the following program follows the logic of the addition example. You may want to execute it to see how quickly you can exceed the limit of nine significant characters. Remember, the computer only stores the nine most significant digits. Multiply a five digit number by another five digit number and see if all the resulting digits are kept.

For example, try

55555 * 55555

You would expect

55555 * 55555 = 3086358025

But you will get

55555 * 55555 = 3.08635803E + 09

Key in and run the following program, or run the program by entering

RUN MULTIPLY SAMPLE1

```
NEW
1000 REM MULTIPLY SAMPLE1
1010 HOME
1020 REM
1030 REM * FOR MULTIPLY
1040 REM
1050 PRINT "MULTIPLY EXAMPLE *"
1060 PRINT
1070 INPUT "FIRST NUMBER = ";AANUMBER
1080 INPUT "SECOND NUMBER= ";ABNUMBER
1090 ACANSWER = AANUMBER * ABNUMBER
1100 PRINT:PRINT
1110 PRINT AANUMBER" * "ABNUMBER" = "ACANSWER
1120 END
```

Division

To divide use the slash (/) character. When dividing you must be careful to make sure that the divisor is not zero. The computer CANNOT divide by zero (nor can anyone else). Run the following sample, enter zero as the second number, and see what happens. Key in and run the following program, or run the program by entering

RUN DIVIDE SAMPLE1

```
NEW
1000 REM DIVIDE SAMPLE1
1010 HOME
1020 REM
1030 REM / FOR DIVISION
1040 REM
1050 PRINT "DIVIDE EXAMPLE /"
1060 PRINT
1070 INPUT "DIVIDEND     = ";AANUMBER
1080 INPUT "DIVISOR      = ";ABNUMBER
1090 ACANSWER = AANUMBER / ABNUMBER
1100 PRINT:PRINT
1110 PRINT AANUMBER" / "ABNUMBER" = "ACANSWER
1120 END
```

In order to avoid the division by zero error, you may want to use an IF instruction to check the value of a divisor prior to dividing.

1085 IF ABNUMBER = 0 THEN ACANSWER = 0: GOTO 1110

Exponentiation

To raise a number to a specific power (exponentiation), use the caret (^) character.

For the APPLE II and APPLE II +, the character is keyed as **SHIFT-N**, (see the symbol above the N key).

For the APPLE IIe, the symbol is the **SHIFT-6** key.

When using the exponentiation feature, it is very easy to exceed the limits of the computer. The first program follows the same format as the previous numeric examples.

Key in and run the following program, or run the program by entering

RUN EXPONENTIATION SAMPLE1

```
NEW
1000 REM EXPONENTIATION SAMPLE1
1010 HOME
1020 REM
1030 REM ^ FOR EXPONENTIATION
1040 REM
1050 PRINT "EXPONENTIATION EXAMPLE ^"
1060 PRINT
1070 INPUT "NUMBER      = ";AANUMBER
1080 INPUT "POWER       = ";ABNUMBER
1090 ACANSWER = AANUMBER ^ ABNUMBER
1100 PRINT:PRINT
1110 PRINT AANUMBER" ^ "ABNUMBER" = "ACANSWER
1120 END
```

The second exponentiation program prints out the powers of 2 until the limitations of the computer are exceeded. Since the program uses the **SPEED** instruction and ends in an error, you must reset the speed after program termination. Enter **SPEED** = 255 in response to the ending error message.

Key in and run the following program, or run the program by entering

RUN EXPONENTIATION SAMPLE2

```
NEW
1000 REM EXPONENTIATION SAMPLE2
1010 HOME
1020 REM
1030 REM PROGRAM WILL END IN
1040 REM ERROR AFTER 126 LOOPS.
1050 REM
1060 AANUMBER = 1
1070 ABNUMBER = 2 ^ AANUMBER
```

```
1080 PRINT " 2 TO THE POWER OF "AANUMBER" = "ABNUMBER
1090 AANUMBER = AANUMBER + 1
1100 GOTO 1070
```

1060 AANUMBER is set to an initial value of 1. The first time statement 1080 is executed, a value of 2 is printed. Each time through the loop, AANUMBER is incremented by 1 to continually increase the factor for exponentiation.

1070 The field ABNUMBER is set to 2 raised to the power indicated by the current value of AANUMBER. When AANUMBER gets to 127, the answer exceeds the limits of the computer and you get the following error message

?OVERFLOW ERROR IN 1080

Parentheses

Parentheses are used to override the standard sequence of arithmetic operations. The computer computes the answer to an equation by carrying out the individual arithmetic functions in the following order UNLESS PARENTHESES ARE USED.

1. Exponentiation is performed first if present. The computer scans the equation for the caret (^) starting at the left side of the equation and proceeding to the right.
2. Multiplication and division are performed next. The computer scans the equation from left to right looking for either an asterisk (*) or a slash (/). When either one is found the operation is carried out.
3. Addition and subtraction are performed last. The computer scans the equation from left to right looking for either a plus sign or a minus sign. When one is found, the operation is carried out.

When parentheses are used, the computer begins the sequence described above, scanning the innermost set of parentheses first. When ALL arithmetic operations are completed in the innermost parentheses, the next level of parentheses is scanned. The process continues from innermost parentheses to outermost parentheses until all the calculations are completed.

For example

GG = AA + BB * (CC / DD − EE) ^ FF

where

AA = 35, BB = 10, CC = 22, DD = 2, EE = 8, FF = 4

Answer

GG = 845

First, the innermost equation (CC / DD − EE) is solved. The value in CC is divided by DD (22 / 2 = 11). The value of EE is then subtracted from the quotient of the division operation (11 - 8 = 3).

Second, the result of the inner parentheses is carried to the power of FF (3 ^ 4 = 81). Remember, if no parentheses are present exponentiation is done first.

Third, the value in BB is multiplied by the value calculated to this point (10 * 81 = 810).

Last, the value in AA is added to the value calculated to this point, and the results stored in GG (35 + 810 = 845).

The variable GG ends up with a value of 845.

Example 1: Parentheses

The following example demonstrates the difference between using and not using parentheses.

Key in and run the following program, or run the program by entering

RUN PARENTHESES SAMPLE1

```
NEW
1000 REM PARENTHESES SAMPLE1
1010 HOME
1020 REM
1030 REM () FOR OVERRIDING SEQ
1040 REM    OF EXECUTION
1050 REM
1060 PRINT "PARENTHESES EXAMPLE"
1070 PRINT
1080 INPUT "FIRST NUMBER  = ";AANUMBER
1090 INPUT "SECOND NUMBER = ";ABNUMBER
1100 PRINT : PRINT
1110 PRINT "WITH PARENTHESES"
1120 ACANSWER = (AANUMBER + AANUMBER) * ABNUMBER - (ABNUMBER  /
     AANUMBER)
1130 PRINT "ANSWER = "ACANSWER
1140 PRINT : PRINT
1150 PRINT "WITHOUT PARENTHESES"
1160 ACANSWER = AANUMBER + AANUMBER * ABNUMBER - ABNUMBER /
     AANUMBER
1170 PRINT "ANSWER = "ACANSWER
1180 END
```

The statements 1120 and 1160 perform the same arithmetic operations but in different sequences.

Did you notice the difference when you ran the program? If not, run the program again to see how the use of parentheses changes the sequence in which the arithmetic operations are performed.

Arithmetic Functions in Applesoft

Applesoft has a set of predefined functions which allows the programmer to manipulate numeric variables, convert numbers stored in string format to numeric format, and perform the basic trigonometry operations.

These functons are listed below. The trigonometry functions are self explanatory (if you know trigonometry) and are not covered in detail. The other numeric functions are covered in alphabetic order.

1. ABS(X)   Returns the absolute value of X
2. ASC(A$)   Returns the ASCII numeric value of the first character of the variable A$
3. INT(X)   Returns the integer portion of the real number X
4. LEN(A$)   Returns the number of characters in the variable A$
5. RND(X)   Returns a random number based on the value of X
6. SGN(X)   Returns a value of -1, 0, or $+1$ depending on the value of X
7. VAL(A$)   Returns the numeric value of A$
8. Trigonometry and basic math functions

ATN (X) Used to retrieve the arctangent, in radians, of X
COS (X) Used to retrieve the cosine, in radians, of X
EXP (X) Used to retrieve e (2.718279) to the power of X
LOG (X) Used to retrieve the natural logarithm of X
SIN (X) Used to retrieve the sine, in radians, of X
SQR (X) Used to retrieve the square root of X
TAN (X) Used to retrieve the tangent, in radians, of X

ABS(X)

ABSolute is an Applesoft function which is used to convert numbers to their absolute value.

Rules for Use
1. The variable or expression used within the parentheses must be numeric.
2. If the value within the parentheses is negative, the sign is changed to positive. If the value within the parentheses is positive, the sign remains unchanged.

This function is very simple, and no program is provided. You may wish to test the instruction out in the immediate mode by keying in the following instructions:

PRINT "ABSOLUTE -123 = "ABS(-123) <RETURN>

displays as

ABSOLUTE − 123 = 123
PRINT "ABSOLUTE + 123 = "ABS(+ 123) <RETURN>

displays as

ABSOLUTE + 123 = 123

ASC(X$)

The American Standard Code for Information Interchange (ASCII) is the binary coding system used by the APPLE. The ASC function allows the program to convert a single ASCII symbol into its corresponding ASCII numeric value.

Example: Letter A = Numeric value of 65
Letter B = Numeric value of 66
(see Appendix A, p. 508)

The function has limited programming application but does come in handy when you need to know the numeric value of a specific key or combination of keys.

Rules for Use
1. The value within parentheses must be a string value.
2. If the string contains more than one character only the first character of the string is converted.
3. The ASCII code returned is from 0 to 127.

Key in and run the following program, or run the program by entering

RUN ASC SAMPLE1

```
NEW
1000 REM ASC SAMPLE1
1010 HOME
1020 REM
1030 PRINT "PRESS ANY KEY AND THE COMPUTER WILL"
1040 PRINT "SHOW YOU THE CORRESPONDING ASCII"
1050 PRINT "NUMERIC VALUE."
```

```
1060 PRINT
1070 PRINT "PRESS KEY   = ";
1080 GET X$
1090 PRINT X$
1100 AANUMBER = ASC (X$)
1110 PRINT "ASCII VALUE = "AANUMBER
1120 PRINT
1130 PRINT "PRESS  Q  TO QUIT"
1140 PRINT "PRESS ANY OTHER KEY TO CONTINUE"
1150 GET X$
1160 IF X$ < > "Q" GOTO 1000
1170 PRINT
1180 PRINT "THAT'S ALL FOLKS!"
1190 END
```

While running the program, press some of the control keys to see the corresponding numeric value. The numeric value for CONTROL-D is one that you should memorize, as it is used extensively when working with the disk I/O commands. The CONTROL-D combination of keys has an ASCII value of 4.

INT(X)

INTeger is an Applesoft function used to truncate the decimal portion of a real number.

Key in and run the following program, or run the program by entering

RUN INT SAMPLE1

```
NEW
1000 REM INT SAMPLE1
1010 HOME
1020 REM
1030 PRINT "ENTER A NUMBER WITH MORE THAN TWO"
1040 PRINT "DECIMAL POSITIONS.  EXAMPLE: 123.456"
1050 PRINT
1060 PRINT "THE PROGRAM WILL ROUND THE NUMBER"
1070 PRINT "TO TWO DECIMAL POSITIONS"
1080 PRINT
1090 INPUT "NUMBER=" AANUMBER
1100 ABNUMBER = (INT((AANUMBER + .005) * 100) / 100)
1110 PRINT "NUMBER=" ABNUMBER
1120 VTAB 15
1130 PRINT "PRESS  Q  TO QUIT"
1140 PRINT "PRESS ANY OTHER KEY TO CONTINUE"
1150 GET X$
1160 IF X$ <> "Q" GOTO 1000
1170 HOME
1180 PRINT "THAT'S ALL FOLKS!"
1190 END
```

1100 The innermost parenthesis is cleared by adding .005 to the value in AANUMBER. Once the value has been rounded, the number is shifted two decimal positions to the left by multiplying the intermediate result by 100. After the number has been shifted, the INTeger function truncates the decimal positions, and the decimal is shifted back to the right by dividing the value by 100.

For example if you enter 123.456, the following occurs:

1. 123.456 + .005 = 123.461
2. 123.461 * 100 = 12346.1
3. INT(12346.1) = 12346
4. 12346 / 100 = 123.46   Answer truncated and rounded

LEN(A$)

LENgth is a very handy function when working with I/O operations. The function works only with string variables and returns a value equal to the number of characters in the string variable.

Example PRINT "NAME IS " LEN(AANAME$) " CHARACTERS LONG"

where

AANAME$ = "JOHN DOE"

prints

NAME IS 8 CHARACTERS LONG

In the following example, the LENgth function is used to control the TAB operation. By using the length of each variable entered with the TAB operation, all the variables are aligned on the right (right justified) when PRINTed.

The program is set up to work with either integer numbers or real numbers, but no allowance has been made to align decimal points.

Key in and run the following program, or run the program by entering

RUN LEN SAMPLE1

```
NEW
1000 REM LEN SAMPLE1
1010 HOME
1020 REM
1030 INPUT "FIRST NUMBER  = ";AANUMBER
1040 INPUT "SECOND NUMBER = ";ABNUMBER
1050 ACANSWER = AANUMBER - ABNUMBER
1060 PRINT
```

```
1070 ADTBSET =  LEN ( STR$ (AANUMBER))
1080 AETBSET =  LEN ( STR$ (ABNUMBER))
1090 AFTBSET =  LEN ( STR$ (ACANSWER))
1100 PRINT TAB( 20 - ADTBSET)AANUMBER
1110 PRINT TAB( 20 - AETBSET - 2)"- "ABNUMBER
1120 PRINT TAB( 20 - AFTBSET - 2)"= "ACANSWER
1130 PRINT : PRINT
1140 PRINT "PRESS SPACE BAR TO REPEAT LOOP"
1150 PRINT "PRESS ANY OTHER KEY TO END PROGRAM"
1160 GET X$
1170 IF X$ = " " GOTO 1000
1180 HOME
1190 PRINT "THAT'S ALL FOLKS!"
1200 END
```

The program does the same as previous arithmetic examples, but when the output is printed the numbers are right justified (aligned on the right side).

1070–1090   Lines 1070 to 1090 compute the length of each of the variables entered. Later these lengths are used to TAB over the appropriate number of spaces. There are actually two functions being executed on each line. First, the number is converted to a string (see p. 153). The conversion is necessary because numbers are stored in a condensed form (binary) and the LENgth function only works on values stored in the string format (ASCII code). Second, the LENgth of the string is determined. The length includes the decimal point if present and the minus sign if present.

1100   Assume AANUMBER has a starting value of 123. The computer subtracts the length of AANUMBER from 20 (20 − 3 = 17). The first character of AANUMBER is printed in column 17, second character in column 18, and third character in column 19. The same process is used for lines 1110 and 1120.

1110   Again, to help explain the instruction, assume ABNUMBER has a starting value of 123. The computer subtracts the length of ABNUMBER from 20 to allow for the number of digits to be printed. The instruction also subtracts an additional 2 to allow for the two positions taken up by the minus sign and blank which precede the number (20 − 3 − 2 = 15).

```
Column 1234567890123456789
Line 1100 prints        123
Line 1110 prints      - 123
```

The minus sign prints in column 15. The space following the minus sign prints in column 16 with the number printing in columns 17 through 19.

1120   The answer in this case is 0 (123 − 123). Using the value of 0 the length of ACANSWER is 1 (length of a single 0). The computer subtracts 1 from 20 and also subtracts an additional 2 to allow for the two positions taken up by the equal sign and the space which precede the answer ($20 - 1 - 2 = 17$). The equal sign prints in column 17 with a space following in column 18. The 0 is right aligned in column 19.

```
Column 12345678901234567890123456789
Line 1100 prints          123
Line 1110 prints        - 123
Line 1120 prints        =   0
```

1130–1170 Lines 1130 to 1170 are used to allow you to repeat the program as many times as you want to see how the program right-aligns various numbers. Try entering combinations of positive and negative numbers and numbers with and without decimal points. When you want to quit, press any key except the space bar.

RND(X)

RaNDom is an Applesoft function which returns a random number. The type of value returned by the function varies with the value of the variable within the parentheses. The value within the parentheses is referred to as the seed.

The random number generator may be used in games to provide a means of selecting a logic path through the program which is not the same with each execution of the game.

In scientific or statistical applications, the RND function may be used to eliminate bias in data or to generate test data.

Rules for Use
1. The RND function does not actually generate a true random set of numbers. The same pattern is generated each time the machine is turned on. Within this fixed pattern the numbers are random.
2. RND(X) returns a value between 0 and 1. If you wish to have the number in larger units, multiply the function by a power of 10, for example,

   AARANDOM = INT(RND(X) * 10)

   produces numbers from 0 to 9.

   If you wish to have values from 0 to a specific number then multiply the random function by a value 1 greater than the maximun number you want returned. For example, to get a range from 0 to 6 multiply the random function by 7.

   AARANDOM = INT(RND(1) * 7)

3. If the value within parentheses (seed) is greater than 0 a random number is returned.

4. If the seed is 0, Applesoft returns the last random number generated. In other words RND(0) gives you the value from the last RND(X) instruction executed.
5. If the seed is negative, Applesoft returns a fixed sequence of numbers. The sequence generated depends on the value of the negative number. That is, for a −1 there is a fixed series of numbers generated, for a −2 there is a fixed series of numbers generated, etc.

Illustration of the Rules

The following illustrates the primary rules for the RND function.

Rule 1. The RND function returns a fixed pattern of numbers each time the computer is turned on.

Rule 2. The value returned by RND(X) is between 0 and 1.

Rule 3. A positive seed results in a random number.

If you do not have the program disk, key in and save the following program before continuing.

```
NEW
1000 REM RND SAMPLE1
1010 HOME
1020 REM
1030 PRINT "RANDOM NUMBER"
1040 SPEED = 100
1050 FOR AANUMBER = 1 TO 20
1060 PRINT RND(1)
1070 NEXT
1080 SPEED= 255
1090 PRINT "THAT'S ALL FOLKS!"
1100 END
```

SAVE RND SAMPLE1

Before running the program turn the computer off and then back on. After turning the computer on enter:

RUN RND SAMPLE1

The values generated will be equal to one of the following columns depending on which machine you are using.

```
        APPLE II                   APPLE IIe

        RANDOM NUMBER              RANDOM NUMBER
        .973136996                .281730746
        .103117626                .876072276
        .0177148333               .225704465
        .779343355                .403810008
        .551834438                .458575223
        .617419111                .290037373
        .960296981                .716005434
        .547150891                .78042385

        . . .                     . . .
```

Notice that all the numbers range between 0.000000000 and 1.000000000.

Now turn the computer off and then back on. After turning the computer on enter:

RUN RND SAMPLE1

You will get the same pattern as before.

Each time you run the program after turning the machine on you will get the same set of numbers.

Now run the program again, but without resetting the machine. Enter:

RUN

Each time you re-run the program you will obtain a different set of numbers. But, each time the computer is turned on, the pattern starts over with the same sequence of numbers being generated.

To overcome this problem execute the following subroutine before using the RND function.

```
5000 REM ---------------------
5010 REM RANDOM SUBROUTINE
5020 POKE - 16368,0:X1 = PEEK ( - 16384):R1 = PEEK (78):R2 =
PEEK (79): POKE 204,R1: POKE 205,R2
5030 RETURN
5040 REM ---------------------
```

The subroutine resets the memory addresses used by the computer to generate the random numbers. It only needs to be executed once after turning the computer on. To test the subroutine key in and save the following program.

```
NEW
1000 REM RND SAMPLE2
1010 HOME
1020 GOSUB 5000 : REM EXECUTE RANDOM SUBROUTINE
1030 PRINT "RANDOM NUMBER"
```

```
1040 SPEED = 100
1050 FOR AANUMBER = 1 TO 20
1060 PRINT RND(1)
1070 NEXT
1080 SPEED= 255
1090 PRINT "THAT'S ALL FOLKS!"
1100 END
5000 REM ----------------------
5010 REM RANDOM SUBROUTINE
5020 POKE - 16368,0:X1 = PEEK ( - 16384):R1 = PEEK (78):R2 =
PEEK (79): POKE 204,R1: POKE 205,R2
5030 RETURN
5040 REM ----------------------
```

SAVE RND SAMPLE2

To show you that the subroutine generates a different set of numbers each time
the machine is turned on, go through the same process of turning the machine off
and then back on. After turning the machine on enter:

RUN RND SAMPLE2

The numbers generated will not match the values displayed earlier.
Execute this subroutine once at the start of any program which uses the RND
function.

Rule 4. If the seed contains a value of 0, Applesoft returns the last random number generated.
In other words, RND(0) gives you the value from the last RND(X) instruction executed.
Key in and run the following program, or run the program by entering

RUN RND SAMPLE3

```
NEW
1000 REM RND SAMPLE3
1010 HOME
1020 REM
1030 PRINT "RANDOM # RND (1)" TAB( 20) "RANDOM # RND (0)"
1040 SPEED= 100
1050 FOR AANUMBER = 1 TO 20
1060 PRINT RND (1) TAB( 20) RND (0)
1070 NEXT
1080 SPEED= 255
1090 PRINT "THAT'S ALL FOLKS!"
1100 END
```

In this example two matching columns of numbers are printed. The first column
consists of a set of random numbers generated using a seed of 1. The second column
is an exact duplicate of the first column because the RND(0) function is used.

The use of the RND(0) function is somewhat limited, but you should know that it is available and how to code the instruction.

Rule 5. If a negative seed is used the RND function returns a fixed sequence of numbers. The sequence generated depends on the value of the negative number. That is, for a −1 there is a fixed series of numbers generated, for a −2 there is a fixed series of numbers generated, etc.

Key in and run the following program, or run the program by entering

RUN RND SAMPLE4

```
NEW
1000 REM RND SAMPLE4
1010 HOME
1020 REM
1030 SPEED= 150
1040 PRINT "RANDOM SERIES FOR -1"
1050 PRINT
1060 PRINT "FOR -1 SEED = "; RND (-1)
1070 FOR AANUMBER = 1 TO 8
1080 PRINT RND(+1)
1090 NEXT
1100 PRINT
1110 PRINT "FOR -1 SEED = ";RND (-1)
1120 FOR AANUMBER = 1 TO 8
1130 PRINT RND(+1)
1140 NEXT
1150 SPEED= 255
1160 END
```

After running the program, look at the first eight rows to see what numbers were generated. After you have looked at the first eight rows, compare the values to the second set of eight rows shown at the bottom of the screen. The two groups should be exactly alike.

Although the numbers for each negative value appear to be random, you get the same sequence each time you use a specific negative value as the seed.

Why would you want a fixed sequence of random numbers? When testing a program using the RND function you may want to use a negative number so you can generate a fixed set of values which will produce predictable results.

Since you know what the fixed set of numbers is going to be, you can check the results of your program to see if it executed correctly. Once your program works correctly with the fixed set of values, you can change the negative seed to a positive seed and use the random numbers generated.

SGN(X)

The SiGN function returns either −1, 0, or +1 depending on the value of the variable within the parentheses. The function has limited applications, but you should know that it is available and how it operates.

Key in and run the following program or run the program by entering

RUN SGN SAMPLE1

```
NEW
1000 REM SGN SAMPLE1
1010 HOME
1020 REM
1030 PRINT "ENTER ANY NUMBER": PRINT
1040 INPUT " = ";AANUMBER
1050 PRINT
1060 ABNUMBER = SGN (AANUMBER)
1070 ABNUMBER = ABNUMBER + 1
1080 ON ABNUMBER GOTO 1110, 1130
1090 PRINT "NUMBER WAS NEGATIVE"
1100 GOTO 1150
1110 PRINT "NUMBER WAS ZERO"
1120 GOTO 1150
1130 PRINT "NUMBER WAS POSITIVE"
1140 GOTO 1150
1150 PRINT : PRINT
1160 PRINT "PRESS SPACE BAR TO REPEAT LOOP"
1170 PRINT "PRESS ANY OTHER KEY TO END PROGRAM"
1180 GET X$
1190 IF X$ = " " GOTO 1000
1200 HOME
1210 PRINT "THAT'S ALL FOLKS!"
1220 END
```

1060 The variable ABNUMBER is set to -1, 0, or $+1$ depending on the value you enter. If you enter a negative number, ABNUMBER is set to -1; 0 sets ABNUMBER to 0; a positive number sets ABNUMBER to $+1$. The function SGN only returns one of these three values. The program uses the SGN function to determine the sign of the number you enter and then branches to print the appropriate message.

1070 The value in ABNUMBER is increased by 1 so the ON count GOTO instruction can be used. After 1 is added to ABNUMBER, the possible values are 0, 1, and 2.

1080 Since the value returned by the SGN function is increased by 1, the computer falls through to line 1090 for a negative number, branches to line 1110 for a value of 0, or branches to line 1130 for a positive value.

VAL(X$)

The VALue function is used to convert a string variable into numeric format so the number can be used in arithmetic operations.

Rules for Use
1. The value within parentheses must be a string.
2. The computer returns a numeric value equal to the value of the numbers present at the start of the string. If the string contains nonnumeric characters, only the leading numeric characters are used to determine the value returned. The computer recognizes leading plus and minus signs as being part of the numeric character set.
3. If the first symbol is a nonnumeric character, the computer returns a value of zero.

Illustration of the Rules

Key in and run the following program or run the program by entering

RUN VAL SAMPLE1

```
1000 REM VAL SAMPLE1
1010 HOME
1020 REM
1030 PRINT "ENTER NUMBERS AND LETTERS IN ANY"
1040 PRINT "COMBINATION."
1050 PRINT
1060 PRINT "THE COMPUTER WILL REPLY WITH THE"
1070 PRINT "NUMBERS YOU ENTERED UP TO THE FIRST"
1080 PRINT "NONNUMERIC CHARACTER."
1090 PRINT
1100 PRINT "IF THE FIRST CHARACTER YOU ENTER"
1110 PRINT "IS NONNUMERIC A ZERO VALUE IS RETURNED."
1120 PRINT
1130 INPUT "ENTER VALUE = ";AASTRING$
1140 PRINT
1150 AANUMBER = VAL (AASTRING$)
1160 PRINT "LEADING NUMBER WAS: "AANUMBER
1170 PRINT
1180 PRINT "PRESS  Q  TO QUIT"
1190 PRINT "PRESS ANY OTHER KEY TO TRY AGAIN"
1200 GET Q$
1210 IF Q$ < > "Q" GOTO 1000
1220 HOME
1230 PRINT "THAT'S ALL FOLKS!"
1240 END
```

While running the program enter some of the following values:

123ABC456	Returns a value of 123
− 123ABC456	Returns a value of − 123
ABC − 123DEF	Returns a value of 0

1130 The value you enter is stored as an alphanumeric string (see dollar sign on AASTRING$). Each character you enter takes one byte in memory.

1150   The VAL function is used to convert the string of characters you enter into a numeric value. Leading plus or minus signs are interpreted correctly.

You should get in the practice of always using string variables with the INPUT instruction and then converting the strings to numbers by using the VAL function. By following this practice you can keep the program from being canceled when the operator accidently presses a nonnumeric key while entering a numeric value. But using string names with the INPUT instruction does not correct the operator's mistake. If the operator enters 123.A5 instead of 123.45 the VAL function returns a numeric value of 123, not 123.45. The use of string variables only prevents the program from being canceled, it is not a substitute for editing (checking) the values entered by the operator.

String Functions in Applesoft

When you work with string variables (alphanumeric data), it is often necessary to break the data into parts. The LEFT$, MID$, and RIGHT$ functions are Applesoft's way of manipulating string values.

Note: The following examples contain variable names which are completely spelled out. Some of these names contain embedded Applesoft keywords and will not work if used in a program. They are spelled out in the examples to help you understand the instructions.

LEFT$(variable$,number)

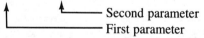
Second parameter
First parameter

The LEFT$ function allows the program to reference the leftmost characters of the variable indicated by the first parameter. The number of characters to be referenced is indicated by the number in the second parameter.

Example   MONTH$ = LEFT$(DATE$,2)

The variable MONTH$ is set equal to the left two positions of the DATE$. If DATE$ = "013182", then MONTH$ = "01".

MID$(variable$,starting character,number of characters)

The MID$ function allows the program to reference any part of a variable. The variable name to be referenced is placed in the first of the three parameters. The second parameter indicates the starting position. The third parameter indicates how many characters are to be referenced.

Example   DAY$ = MID$(DATE$,3,2)

The variable DAY$ is set equal to the characters within the DATE$ starting with the third character and continuing for two positions. If DATE$ = "013182", then DAY$ = "31".

RIGHT$(variable$,number)

The RIGHT$ function allows the program to reference the rightmost portion of a variable. The variable name to be referenced is placed in the first parameter. The second parameter indicates how many positions of the variable are to be used.

Example   YEAR$ = RIGHT$(DATE$,2)

The variable YEAR$ is set equal to the rightmost two characters of the DATE$. If DATE$ = "013182", then YEAR$ = "82".

Plus Sign (+)

The plus sign can be used with string functions to CONNECT, NOT ADD, groups of alphanumeric characters together.

Example   DATE$ = MONTH$ + DAY$ + YEAR$

The variable DATE$ is set equal to the combined characters of MONTH$, DAY$, and YEAR$. If MONTH$ = "01", DAY$ = "31", and YEAR$ = "82", then DATE$ would equal "013182".

CHR$(number)

The CHR$ (CHaRacter) function has a somewhat limited application and requires understanding of how characters are stored in the computer. The CHR$ function returns the ASCII character corresponding to the numeric value within the parentheses (see Appendix A, p. 508).

Example

```
1000 D$ = CHR$(4)
1010 REM RETURNS THE CHARACTER CORRESPONDING TO THE
1020 REM CONTROL-D KEY.  THIS SYMBOL IS USED WHEN READING
1030 REM DATA FROM THE DISK OR WRITING INFORMATION
1040 REM TO THE DISK.
```

```
1000 L$ = CHR$(12)
1010 REM RETURNS THE CHARACTER CORRESPONDING TO THE
1020 REM CONTROL-L KEY.  THIS SYMBOL IS USED WITH PRINTER
1030 REM TO POSITION THE PAPER AT THE TOP-OF-PAGE.
```

STR$(number)

The STR$ (STRing) function converts numbers to string format (each symbol takes up one byte). This is helpful when printing numbers or writing numbers to disk.

Example
```
WAGE = 15000
WAGE$ = STR$(WAGE)
```

The variable WAGE contains a numeric value of 15000 and can be used in arithmetic operations. The variable WAGE$ contains the same characters but is stored by the computer in string format (one symbol, 1 byte).

LEFT$(variable$,number) Function

Rules for Use
1. The first parameter must be a string.
2. The second parameter must have a value greater than 0 and less than 256.

To illustrate how the LEFT$ works, the following program asks you to type in your name. After you have typed in your name and pressed RETURN, the computer slowly prints the name using a pattern consisting of the first character, then the first two characters, then the first three characters, etc.

Key in and run the following program, or run the program by entering

RUN LEFT$ SAMPLE1

```
NEW
1000 REM LEFT$ SAMPLE1
1010 HOME
1020 SPEED= 100
1030 PRINT "ENTER YOUR FULL NAME"
1040 INPUT AANAME$
1050 HOME
1060 FOR ABNUMBER = 1 TO LEN (AANAME$)
1070 PRINT LEFT$(AANAME$,ABNUMBER)
1080 NEXT
1090 PRINT
1100 PRINT "THAT'S ALL FOLKS!"
1110 SPEED= 255
1120 END
```

The screen below shows the output for JOHN JONES. The caret (ˆ) symbol is used to represent a blank when the printing of a blank might not be immediately obvious (see fifth line down).

```
J
JO
JOH
JOHN
JOHNˆ
JOHN J
JOHN JO
JOHN JON
JOHN JONE
JOHN JONES

THAT'S ALL FOLKS!
```

1060–1080   The FOR instruction will not be covered in detail until later. A brief explanation is provided now to help you understand the program.

The LENgth function allows the programmer to ask the computer how many characters are in a string. The keyword LENgth is followed by a string name within parentheses. The computer calculates the length of the string and substitutes the value in the position of the LEN function.

```
1060 FOR ABNUMBER = 1 TO LEN(AANAME$)
...    Instructions
1080 NEXT
```

The FOR instruction causes the program to repeat all the instructions between the keyword FOR and the keyword NEXT until the value in ABNUMBER is greater than the LENgth of the variable AANAME$.

For example, if you enter JOHN JONES, the variable AANAME$ is 10 characters long. This means line 1070 is executed 10 times. The FOR instruction automatically adds 1 to the variable ABNUMBER each time the keyword NEXT is encountered. At the end of the tenth execution, the loop is broken, and program flow continues to the statement following the keyword NEXT.

1070   The PRINT instruction displays the LEFT$ portion of AANAME$. The number of characters displayed depends on the value in ABNUMBER. Since the value in ABNUMBER varies each time line 1080 is executed, you see your name printed starting with the first character and continuing until your entire name is printed.

MID$(variable$,starting character,number of characters)

This MIDdle function allows you to access the middle or any part of a string variable.

Rules for Use
1. The first parameter must be a string.
2. The second parameter must have a value greater than 0 and less than 256.
3. The third parameter must have a value from 0 to 255. Notice this operand may contain a value of 0.

Key in and run the following program or run the program by entering

RUN MID$ SAMPLE1

```
NEW
1000 REM MID$ SAMPLE1
1010 HOME
1020 REM
1030 REM TAB IN PRINT STATEMENT
1040 REM MAY NOT BE AN INTEGER OR
1050 REM ZERO VALUE.
1060 REM
1070 REM STARTING LOCATION FOR
1080 REM MID$, LEFT$, & RIGHT$
1090 REM CAN NOT BE ZERO.
1100 REM
1110 SPEED= 100
1120 PRINT "ENTER YOUR FULL NAME"
1130 INPUT AANAME$
1140 HOME
1150 ABNUMBER = 1
1160 ACSIZE = LEN (AANAME$)
1170 ADHALF = ACSIZE / 2
1180 AENUMBER = 1
1190 PRINT TAB(ABNUMBER) MID$ (AANAME$,ABNUMBER,ACSIZE -
     ABNUMBER - ABNUMBER + 2)
1200 ABNUMBER = ABNUMBER + AENUMBER
1210 IF ABNUMBER > ADHALF THEN AENUMBER = - 1
1220 IF ABNUMBER > 0 GOTO 1190
1230 PRINT
1240 PRINT "THAT'S ALL FOLKS!"
1250 SPEED= 255
1260 END
```

Before reading what each line of the program does, run the program to see the output. The program requests that you enter your name, and then program logic prints it out in an hourglass format.

For the name JOHN JONES the screen would appear as follows:

```
JOHN JONES
 OHN JONE
  HN JON
   N JO
    J
   N JO
  HN JON
 OHN JONE
JOHN JONES
```

Did you get your name in an hourglass format as shown in the sample screen? If not, check the program for typing errors and try again.

1020–1100 Lines 1020 to 1100 show a technique you may want to copy. As you learn by trial and error, you may want to make notes in the program so you remember things which work or do not work.

1150 The variable ABNUMBER is used to control how many characters of your name are to be printed, where the portion of your name starts printing, and when the program ends.

The variable ABNUMBER is initialized to a starting value of $+1$. Later ABNUMBER is incremented, causing the value to increase until it reaches a point equal to $\frac{1}{2}$ the total number of characters in your name. When it is equal to $\frac{1}{2}$ of the number of characters in your name, then the value decreases by 1 down to 0. When ABNUMBER reaches 0 the program ends.

1160 The variable ACSIZE is set equal to the LENgth of your name. This value is used in conjunction with ABNUMBER to determine how many characters of your name are printed.

1170 The variable ADHALF is used to determine when the lines being displayed have shortened to the halfway point of your name and should start lengthening back to the full name.

1180 The variable AENUMBER starts with a value of $+1$. The value of AENUMBER is added to ABNUMBER each time through the main loop to control the position on the line where the characters are printed (see line 1200). When the value of ABNUMBER becomes greater than $\frac{1}{2}$ the size of your name, AENUMBER is reset to a value of -1 (see line 1210).

1190 The program was developed to illustrate how the MID$ instruction works. So we are now at the instruction which is the key to the program's operation. The MID$ function allows you to reference a MIDdle portion of the string variable indicated by the first operand, AANAME$. The starting location is indicated by the second operand, ABNUMBER. The third operand indicates the number of characters, including the starting location, which are to be referenced. In this example the third operand consists of the formula

(ACSIZE - ABNUMBER - ABNUMBER + 2)

To help illustrate how the instruction works, let's work through an example using the formula with the name JOHN D. SMITH. For this name the value in ACSIZE is 13.

First Line For the first line ABNUMBER contains a value of 1 so the results are

	ACSIZE	–	ABNUMBER	–	A BNUMBER	+ 2
Number of characters =	13	–	1	–	1	+ 2
Answer = 13 characters						

By adding the 2 you offset the starting value of 1 in ABNUMBER and end up displaying the entire name on the first and last line.

JOHN D. SMITH

Second Line: For the second time through the loop, ABNUMBER contains a value of 2, so the results are

	ACSIZE	–	ABNUMBER	–	ABNUMBER	+ 2
Number of characters =	13	–	2	–	2	+ 2
Answer = 11 characters						

The middle 11 characters of the name are printed, with the screen now showing two lines:

JOHN D. SMITH
OHN D. SMIT

Seventh Line For the seventh time through the loop ABNUMBER will contain a value of 7, so the results are

	ACSIZE	–	ABNUMBER	–	ABNUMBER	+ 2
Number of characters =	13	–	7	–	7	+ 2
Answer = 1 character						

In this case if the 2 had not been added, the answer would have been − 1, and the program would have been canceled since the third parameter of the MID$ function cannot be negative. By adding the + 2 we eliminate the chance of having a negative value.

The seven printed lines appear as follows—a caret symbol (^) is used to show blank positions which may not be obvious to the reader.

```
JOHN D. SMITH
 OHN D. SMIT
  HN D. SMI
   N D. SM
    ^D. S
     .^
     .
```

If you can think of a better way to achieve the same results, try it. That's part of the game of programming.

1200 The current value of ABNUMBER is incremented or decremented depending on whether AENUMBER contains + 1 or − 1.

1210 When the value in ABNUMBER is greater than ADHALF, the variable AENUMBER is set to − 1. For those of you who try to make the program more readable by saying equal to instead of greater than, remember that ABNUMBER is counting in whole numbers, while ADHALF may contain a .5 because of an odd number of characters in a name. The program would not work with an equal test if the name contained an odd number of characters.

Be careful when comparing variables and using the equal sign.

1220 If the value of ABNUMBER is greater than 0, the program has not completed all the necessary loops, and logic flow returns to statement 1190. When ABNUMBER reaches a value of 0, logic flow drops through the IF, and the program ends.

RIGHT$(variable$,number)

Rules for Use
1. The first parameter must be a string.
2. The second parameter must have a value greater than 0 and less than 256.

The RIGHT$ function allows you to access any portion of a string starting from the right side of the variable.

The program that follows asks you to enter your name and then prints the name starting with the rightmost characters. The name is printed in a pattern consisting of the rightmost character, then the two rightmost characters, and then the three rightmost characters, etc.

Key in and run the following program, or run the program by entering

RUN RIGHT$ SAMPLE1

```
NEW
1000 REM RIGHT$ SAMPLE1
1010 HOME
1020 SPEED= 100
1030 PRINT "ENTER YOUR FULL NAME"
1040 INPUT AANAME$
1050 HOME
1060 FOR ABNUMBER = 1 TO LEN (AANAME$)
1070 PRINT TAB( LEN (AANAME$) - ABNUMBER + 1) RIGHT$ (AANAME$,
     ABNUMBER)
1080 NEXT
1090 PRINT
1100 PRINT "THAT'S ALL FOLKS!"
1110 SPEED= 255
1120 END
```

Before reading what each line of the program does, run the program to see the output. You will have to enter your name when the program requests it. The screen below shows the output for JOHN D. SMITH.

```
              H
             TH
            ITH
           MITH
          SMITH
         ˆSMITH
        . SMITH
      D. SMITH
     ˆD. SMITH
    N D. SMITH
   HN D. SMITH
  OHN D. SMITH
 JOHN D. SMITH
```

When you ran the program, did your name print out in the same pattern as that of Mr. SMITH? If so, continue; if not, debug what you keyed in and try again

1060–1080 The FOR/NEXT instruction sets up a loop which is executed repeatedly until the value in ABNUMBER is greater than the LENgth of the name you keyed in.

1070   The PRINT instruction consists of two parts. The first part TABs to the correct spot so the characters to be printed are aligned correctly starting from the right side. The position is computed by subtracting the number of characters which will be printed (ABNUMBER) from the LENgth of the name. For the very first time through the loop, the subtraction results in a value of 0. Since the value portion of the TAB operation cannot contain a 0, a +1 is added to correct for this condition.

The second part prints the results of the RIGHT$ function. The number of positions printed is indicated by the value of ABNUMBER. Since the ABNUMBER ranges from 1 to the number of characters in your name, the program prints one line for each character in your name. Each line printed displays an increasing portion of your name until the entire name is displayed.

Using the **STRING$** Functions Together: **LEFT$, MID$,** and **RIGHT$**

In the following example, the three string functions are used to convert a date entered in YY/MM/DD format to MM/DD/YY format.

Before running the program look over the code to see if you can follow the logic and predict what will happen.

Key in the program or load and list the program by entering

```
LOAD STRING FUNCTIONS SAMPLE1
LIST
```

```
NEW
1000 REM STRING FUNCTIONS SAMPLE1
1010 HOME
1020 REM
1030 REM PROG TO CONVERT DATE
1040 REM FROM YY/MM/DD FORMAT
1050 REM TO MM/DD/YY FORMAT
1060 REM
1070 PRINT "ENTER ANY DATE IN YY/MM/DD FORMAT"
1080 INPUT AADTE$
1090 ABMTH$ = MID$ (AADTE$,4,2)
1100 ACDAY$ = RIGHT$ (AADTE$,2)
1110 ADYEAR$ = LEFT$ (AADTE$,2)
1120 IF ABMTH$ < "01" OR ABMTH$ > "12" GOTO 1260
1130 IF ACDAY$ < "01" OR ACDAY$ > "31" GOTO 1260
1140 IF ADYEAR$ < "00" OR ADYEAR$ > "99" GOTO 1260
1150 AEDTE$ = ABMTH$ + "/" + ACDAY$ + "/" + ADYEAR$
1160 HOME
1170 PRINT "PROGRAM CONVERTED DATE FROM YY/MM/DD"
1180 PRINT TAB(27)"TO MM/DD/YY"
1190 PRINT
1200 PRINT "ADDTE$   = "AADTE$
1210 PRINT "ABMTH$   = "ABMTH$
1220 PRINT "ACDAY$   = "ACDAY$
1230 PRINT "ADYEAR$  = "ADYEAR$
```

```
1240 PRINT "AEDTE$  = "AEDTE$
1250 END
1260 INVERSE
1270 PRINT "DATE MUST BE IN YY/MM/DD FORMAT"
1280 PRINT "PRESS ANY KEY AND TRY AGAIN"
1290 NORMAL
1300 GET X$
1310 GOTO 1000
```

1090–1110   Lines 1090 through 1110 break the data entered into smaller parts and assign more descriptive names. If you are going to reference part of the variable only once, there is no need to assign it a separate name. For example, if you were not going to edit (check) the date entered, you could code one line to rearrange the date:

AEDTE$ = MID$(AADTE$,4,2) + "/" + RIGHT$(AADTE$,2) +
         "/" + LEFT$(AADTE$,2)

If you are going to use a portion of a variable more than once, you should assign it a more descriptive name. By assigning it a more descriptive name, you make the code easier to read and increase the execution speed of the computer. The computer can interpret a single name faster than it can analyze the MID$, RIGHT$, or LEFT$ functions.

1120–1140   Lines 1120 through 1140 check (edit) the data to see that what is entered conforms to what is requested. This is not a complete edit, as ACDAY$ is only checked for less than 01 or greater than 31. No consideration is given to which month the days correspond to. If any of the three variables are in error, logic branches to line 1270, where an error message is displayed prior to restarting the program.

There is a specific reason for using string values in the edit checks rather than converting the data entered to numeric format by use of the VALue function. If 1A1BAA were entered and the VALue function used in the edit check, the machine would not catch the data entry error.

VAL(ABMTH$)	would result in 1 with letter ignored
VAL(ACDAY$)	would result in 1 with letter ignored
VAL(ADYEAR$)	would result in 00 with both letters ignored

1150   This line rearranges the information into MM/DD/YY format. The plus sign is the only connector allowed when working with strings. The sign is interpreted by the computer as meaning 'connect these alphanumeric values'. The computer does NOT add the strings, but only connects two or more variables into a larger single variable.

1260–1310   Lines 1260 through 1310 make up an error routine. If you enter a date which does not pass the edit instructions on lines 1120, 1130, or 1140, the program branches to this routine.

Now, hopefully, you have a basic understanding of what the program is doing. Go through the following exercises and study the logic flow through the program.

Exercise 1: Entering an Incorrect Date

Run the program, and in response to the input message, enter an incorrect date, such as

AA/AA/AA

You will receive an error message shown in the bright inverse format.

After you have seen enough of the error message, press any key, and this time enter what you think is a valid date, such as

81/12/30

Exercise 2: Entering a Logically Incorrect Date

Enter a date which is logically incorrect but which will pass the limited edit tests, such as 81/02/30. You and I know there is no February 30, but the computer does not catch this error because it is not programmed to do so.

CHR$(X) Function

The CHaRacter function returns the ASCII character corresponding to the numeric code indicated by the variable within parentheses (see Appendix A, p. 508). For example,

```
LETTER$ = CHR$(65): REM PLACES A 'A' IN THE LETTER$
LETTER$ = CHR$(66): REM PLACES A 'B' IN THE LETTER$
LETTER$ = CHR$(67): REM PLACES A 'C' IN THE LETTER$
```

The ASCII value for the letter A is the number 65. The ASCII value for the letter B is 66, and C is 67. Any number between 0 and 127 has a corresponding ASCII symbol. The symbol may be an upper case letter, a lower case letter, a number, or a control symbol used in data communications.

The following program displays the numbers between 0 and 127 with their matching ASCII printable character set. The ASCII code runs from 0 to 127, but unless you have an APPLE IIe or additional hardware on your APPLE II, the lower case characters (values above 95) will be repeated as upper case. Also, you may be surprised at the first screen displayed, because the numbers between 0 and 32 do not have a matching printable character. The numbers between 0 and 32 are used for control functions (operations for controlling the computer).

Key in and run the following program, or run the program by entering

RUN CHR$ SAMPLE1

```
NEW
1000 REM CHR$ SAMPLE1
1010 REM ASCII NUMERIC VALUES
1020 HOME
1030 REM
1040 REM ASCII CHARACTERS FOR
1050 REM NUMBER 10 & 13 ARE
1060 REM NOT DISPLAYED AS THEY
1070 REM CAUSE THE SCREEN TO
1080 REM SKIP EXTRA LINES.
1090 REM
1100 REM ASCII CHARACTER FOR
1110 REM MAKING THE SOUND IS
1120 REM NUMBER 7.
1130 REM
1140 PRINT "NUMBER = SYMBOL     NUMBER = SYMBOL"
1150 AANUMBER = 2
1160 FOR ABNUMBER = 1 TO 32
1170 HTAB (AANUMBER)
1180 IF ACNUMBER = 10 OR ACNUMBER = 13 THEN PRINT ACNUMBER:
GOTO 1200
1190 PRINT ACNUMBER TAB(AANUMBER + 11) CHR$ (ACNUMBER)
1200 ACNUMBER = ACNUMBER + 1
1210 IF ABNUMBER = 16 THEN VTAB 2:AANUMBER = AANUMBER + 20
1220 NEXT
1230 IF ACNUMBER > 127 GOTO 1280
1240 PRINT
1250 PRINT "PRESS ANY KEY TO SEE REMAINING SYMBOLS"
1260 GET X$
1270 GOTO 1000
1280 PRINT
1290 PRINT "THAT'S ALL FOLKS!"
1300 END
```

Before reading what each line of the program does, run the program to get a basic idea of what is displayed. The program displays four screen images. At the end of the first three displays, you need to press a key to get the program to continue.

Each screen shows a set of numbers and the matching ASCII printable characters. On the first screen you cannot see the characters printed. The numbers from 0 to 31 are used for **CONTROL** functions and are not printable. The second screen shows the numeric value of the special symbols and numeric keys. The third screen shows the numeric value of each of the upper case letters.

The fourth screen repeats the special symbols and numeric values unless you have an APPLE IIe or your APPLE is equipped to recognize the lower case letters. The APPLE II and APPLE II+ use only the first 96 bit patterns to represent control functions, special symbols, numbers, and upper case letters.

1180 Some of the ASCII codes below 32 are used to control the functions of the display screen and other devices. If the ASCII code for 10 or 13 is displayed, it causes the screen to skip extra lines. To prevent this, the IF instruction tests for these values and displays the numbers 10 and 13 but not the corresponding ASCII character.

1190 Line 1190 is the key to the whole program. It uses the CHR$ function to convert the numeric value of ACNUMBER to the related ASCII code. Since ACNUMBER varies from 0 to 127 as the program is executed, all the 128 combinations of the ASCII code are converted and displayed.

1210 This IF test is to see if all the values for the first column have been printed. If the first column has been displayed, then the second column is started. Before the second column is started, the cursor is repositioned by use of the VTAB instruction. The VTAB instruction moves the cursor back up to the second line of the screen. Next, 20 is added to AANUMBER so that the cursor will be tabbed over to column 22 the next time line 1170 is executed.

Normally you use the CHR$ function when working with the disk or the printer, or any time you are defining control characters within your program. That is, any time you need to use a symbol which is keyed by pressing the CONTROL key and another key at the same time, you should use the CHR$ function to define that character. Do not include CONTROL key symbols within the text of your programs.

For example, when you define control characters to use with the disk or printer, define the special characters with the CHR$ function.

To define a CONTROL-D for use when working with disk files.

```
Wrong:   D$ = "":REM CONTROL-D BETWEEN QUOTES.
Right:   D$ = CHR$(4):REM CONTROL-D
```

To define a CONTROL-L for use when working with printers.

```
Wrong:   L$ = "":REM CONTROL-L BETWEEN QUOTES.
Right:   L$ = CHR$(12): REM CONTROL-L
```

There are two reasons for using the CHR$ function instead of keying in the special character.

1. If you key in the control character, it does not show up on the screen, and you cannot be sure you entered it correctly. Notice that in the examples above you cannot see the CONTROL-D or the CONTROL-L because they are not printable characters.
2. If you try to run a listing of a program on a printer and special control characters are used in the program, the actions taken by the printer may be very surprising. The printer will be funny to watch, but your listing will most likely be unreadable.

A more complete example of the CHR$ function is given with the sample disk programs.

STR$(X) Function

The STRing function converts the number enclosed within parentheses from a numeric format to an alphanumeric format.

Key in and run the following program, or run the program by entering

RUN STR$ SAMPLE1

```
NEW
1000 REM STR$ SAMPLE1
1010 HOME
1020 REM
1030 REM STR$ CONVERTS NUMERIC
1040 REM VALUE TO STRING FORMAT
1050 AANUMBER = 1.00
1060 PRINT "NUMBER","STRING"
1070 PRINT
1080 FOR ABNUMBER = 1 TO 20
1090 PRINT AANUMBER,STR$ (AANUMBER)
1100 AANUMBER = AANUMBER + .1
1110 NEXT
1120 END
```

The program counts from 1 to 2.9 in increments of .1. The left column contains the numeric version, while the right column contains the string version. The first part of the screen appears as follows:

NUMBER	STRING
1	1
1.1	1.1
1.2	1.2
1.3	1.3
1.4	1.4
1.5	1.5
1.6	1.6
1.7	1.7

Do you see any difference?

Even though the values in the two columns look exactly alike when printed, they are not stored in the computer in the same format. Remember you can do arithmetic with numeric variables but CANNOT do arithmetic with string variables.

Let's look at a second example, which shows a practical application of this STR$ function.

Applesoft has no easy way to align decimal points when printing numbers. If the numbers being printed do not contain exactly the same number of digits to the left and right of the decimal, then the decimals are not aligned correctly.

For example: Should Print as	Print as
123.45	123.45
23.40	23.4
.50	.5
1.00	1

The following program contains a subroutine which converts a number from numeric format to string format in order align the decimals.

Before looking at the program let's consider the four possible situations the subroutine must handle in order to align the the decimal positions.

1. A whole number is entered with no significant digits following the decimal. The subroutine must add a decimal and two zeros.

Example   Enter 12345, 12345.0, or 12345.00
Computer prints as 12345
Subroutine prints as 12345.00

2. A number is entered with just one decimal position. The subroutine must add a trailing 0.

Example   Enter 12345.6 or 12345.60
Computer prints as 12345.6
Subroutine prints as 12345.60

3. A number is entered with two decimal positions, and no trailing zeros are needed.

Example   Enter 12345.67
Computer prints as 12345.67
Subroutine prints as 12345.67

4. A number is entered with three or more decimal positions, and the extra decimal positions need to be truncated.

Example   Enter 12345.6789
Computer prints as 12345.6789
Subroutine prints as 12345.68

To see the subroutine in action, key in and run the following program, or run the program by entering

RUN STR$ SAMPLE2

```
NEW
1000 REM STR$ SAMPLE2
1010 REM ----------------------
1020 HOME
1030 REM
1040 REM THE PROGRAM EDITS NUMBERS ENTERED TO PRINT OUT DECIMAL
     ALIGNED.
1050 REM
1060 REM EACH NUMBER IS TRUNCATED OR EXTENDED TO TWO DECIMAL
     POSITIONS.
1070 REM
1080 REM THE NUMBER RETURNED BY THE SUBROUTINE IS 11 CHARACTERS
     LONG.
1090 REM
1100 PRINT "ENTER NUMBER < THAN OR = TO 9999999.98"
1110 VTAB 3: CALL -958
1120 INPUT " = ";AANUMBER
1130 GOSUB 1230
1140 PRINT
1150 PRINT "ANSWER = '"ABNUMBER$"'"
1160 PRINT
1170 PRINT "PRESS  Q  TO QUIT"
1180 PRINT "PRESS ANY OTHER KEY TO CONTINUE"
1190 GET X$
1200 IF X$ = "Q" THEN HOME : PRINT "THAT'S ALL FOLKS!": END
1210 GOTO 1110
1220 REM ----------------------
1230 REM EDIT NUMBER SUBROUTINE
1240 ABNUMBER = AANUMBER + .005
1250 ABNUMBER$ = RIGHT$ ("            " + STR$ ( INT (ABNUMBER
     * 100) / 100),11)
1260 IF MID$ (ABNUMBER$,9,1) = "." THEN 1290
1270 IF MID$ (ABNUMBER$,10,1) = "." THEN ABNUMBER$ = RIGHT$
     (ABNUMBER$ + "0",11): GOTO 1290
1280 ABNUMBER$ = RIGHT$ (ABNUMBER$ + ".00",11)
1290 RETURN
1300 REM ----------------------
```

The subroutine uses three variables.

AANUMBER = The number to be converted. The value to be converted is placed in AANUMBER before executing the subroutine.

ABNUMBER = A work variable used by the subroutine so the original value of AANUMBER is not destroyed.

ABNUMBER$ = The 11 byte, two decimal string answer returned by the subroutine.

1100–1130 Line 1100 prints the headings for the screen. After the message is displayed, statement 1110 positions the cursor on the third line and clears the remainder of the screen. The instruction CALL −958 calls a prewritten APPLE machine language subroutine at address −958 which clears the screen from the current cursor position to the end of the screen.

Two call addresses you may want to remember are

CALL −868   Clears to the end of the line
CALL −958   Clears to the end of the screen

(See the CALL instruction for additional addresses of machine languages subroutines.)

After the lower portion of the screen has been cleared, you are asked to enter a number (line 1120). Once you have entered a number and pressed RETURN, logic flow branches to the subroutine to convert the number you entered into string format.

1150   After the number is converted, line 1150 prints the results. Notice the use of double and single quotes to highlight the answer.

1240   The first line of the subroutine adds .005 to the number in order to round it up or down as needed. Now what did I mean by 'round up or down'? If you enter a negative value, it should be rounded down. A positive value should be rounded up, and a value of 0 should not be rounded.

Let's look at what happens for each situation.

Why the program adds .005 to a negative number in order to round down is the hardest to explain. To start with you must know that the INTeger function automatically changes negative values to the next lower negative whole number when truncating decimals (something the manuals don't say even in fine print).

INT (−1.0)   Gives a value of −1
INT (−1.1)   Gives a value of −2
INT (−1.9)   Gives a value of −2

Notice the INTeger function is NOT rounding. It is changing the negative value to the next lower whole number.

To compensate for this automatic change in negative values, a positive .5 is added (for this example only, the subroutine uses .005 to round to the correct cent).

INT (−1.0 + .5) = (−0.5)   Gives a value of −1
INT (−1.1 + .5) = (−0.6)   Gives a value of −1
INT (−1.9 + .5) = (−1.4)   Gives a value of −2

Hopefully you follow the logic of how adding a positive number causes the negative value to be rounded correctly. If not, just use the subroutine with the knowledge it works with negative numbers.

If you enter a value of 0, a .5 is still added but is truncated later when the value is converted to a string.

INT (0.0 + .5) = (0.5)   Gives a value of 0

If you entered a positive value, then the number is rounded up by adding .5.

INT (1.0 + .5) = (1.5)   Gives a value of 1
INT (1.9 + .5) = (2.4)   Gives a value of 2

1250–1280   Now for the big one! Once the number has been rounded, any excess decimal positions must be truncated. Line 1250 converts the number to a string and truncates any excess decimal positions which might exist. To see how the instruction works, let's take it in parts.

(INT (ABNUMBER * 100) / 100)

First, the function in the inner parentheses multiplies the number entered by 100, moving the decimal two positions to the right. After the decimal has been moved to the right, the INTeger function is used to drop off any excess decimal positions. Once the decimal positions have been dropped, the decimal point is moved back to the left by dividing the number by 100. For example:

Multiply: 12345.6789 * 100 = 1234567.89
INteger: 1234567
Divide: 12345.67

RIGHT$ ('   ' + STR$ (INT (ABNUMBER * 100) / 100),11)

After any excess decimal positions have been truncated, the STRing function converts the number into alphanumeric form. The value is now in string format and takes up 11 bytes of memory.

Unfortunately, the conversion process does not ensure that there are two decimal positions. Any nonsignificant digits (trailing zeros) are truncated by Applesoft. If the decimal portion of the number is 0 (.00) or contains only a single digit (.n0), the trailing zeros are dropped.

To overcome the problem, lines 1260 though 1280 test to see where the decimal point is located and adds on one or two ending zeros as required.

Keep this subroutine in mind. Anytime you need a routine to print numbers with decimal alignment, here is a solution.

If you decide to use the subroutine, you may want to change the variable name prefixes from AA, AB, and AB$ to some other characters so the names do not conflict with variable names within your program.

20. The IF Instruction

Instruction   (Simple IF Format)

$$IF \begin{Bmatrix} \text{constant} \\ \text{variable name} \\ \text{expression} \end{Bmatrix} \begin{Bmatrix} \text{relationship} \\ \text{indicator} \end{Bmatrix} \begin{Bmatrix} \text{constant} \\ \text{variable name} \\ \text{expression} \end{Bmatrix}$$

$$\begin{Bmatrix} \text{THEN} \\ \text{GOTO} \end{Bmatrix} \begin{Bmatrix} \text{statement(s)} \\ \text{statement number} \end{Bmatrix}$$

Example   IF AGE > 21 THEN PRINT "OF VOTING AGE"

Purpose   To allow the programmer to ask questions and thereby take different logical paths through the program.

Rules for Use
1. The value of the first operand is compared with the value of the second operand. If the question is true, the computer executes the instructions following the keyword THEN. If the question is false, all instructions included with the IF are skipped.
2. The allowable relationship indicators are:
   a. < for A LESS THAN B
   b. > for A GREATER THAN B
   c. = for A EQUAL TO B
   d. <> for A NOT EQUAL TO B
   e. <= for A LESS THAN OR EQUAL TO B
   f. => for A EQUAL TO OR GREATER THAN B
3. The value preceding the relationship indicator must be of the same type as the value following the relationship indicator (numeric to numeric; string to string).
4. If the GOTO statement is the only instruction following the IF, then either the keyword GOTO or THEN may be used.
   For example,

   IF A > B GOTO 1000

may also be worded as

IF A > B THEN 1000

Illustration of the Rules   If you have been reading the text from the start, you have seen the IF instruction used in most of the examples, but let's look at a few programs in which various combinations of the simple IF format are used.

Key in and run the following program, or run the program by entering

RUN IF SAMPLE1

```
1000 REM IF SAMPLE1
1010 HOME
1020 SPEED= 150
1030 PRINT "ENTER TWO NUMBERS AND THE COMPUTER"
1040 PRINT "WILL TELL YOU WHICH IS THE LARGEST"
1050 PRINT
1060 INPUT "FIRST NUMBER  = ";AANUMBER$: AANUMBER =
     VAL (AANUMBER$)
1070 INPUT "SECOND NUMBER = ";ABNUMBER$: ABNUMBER = VAL
     (ABNUMBER$)
1080 PRINT
1090 IF AANUMBER > ABNUMBER THEN PRINT "THE FIRST NUMBER IS
     GREATER THAN THE ": PRINT "SECOND NUMBER.": GOTO 1120
1100 IF AANUMBER = ABNUMBER THEN PRINT "THE FIRST NUMBER IS
     EQUAL TO THE": PRINT "SECOND NUMBER.": GOTO 1120
1110 PRINT "THE FIRST NUMBER IS LESS THAN THE": PRINT "SECOND
     NUMBER."
1120 PRINT
1130 PRINT "PRESS  Q  TO QUIT."
1140 PRINT "PRESS  C  TO CONTINUE.";
1150 GET X1$
1160 IF X1$ = "C" THEN 1000
1170 IF X1$ <> "Q" THEN 1150
1180 PRINT
1190 PRINT "THAT'S ALL FOLKS!"
1200 SPEED= 255
1210 END
```

The first program is super simple but does show several examples of the basic format of the IF instruction.

1060–1070   Lines 1060 and 1070 allow the operator to enter the two numbers to be compared. The numbers are entered in string format and converted to numeric format in order to avoid REENTER errors should the operator enter a value which contains a non-numeric character.

1090   The first IF compares the two input variables to see whether AANUMBER is greater than ABNUMBER. If the statement is true, all instructions on line 1090 following the keyword THEN are executed. If the statement is false, all instructions on line 1090 following the keyword THEN are skipped, and logic flow continues to the line 1100.

Following the IF clause the keyword THEN is used as a separator between the conditional test and the instructions to be executed. For all instructions following the keyword THEN, a colon (:) is used as a separator. Again, notice that each statement is separated by a colon. The computer requires the word THEN and the colons to be able to tell where one instruction stops and the next one starts.

1100–1110   The second IF instruction uses the same format as the first IF, but tests for an EQUAL TO condition.

If the statement is true, the appropriate message is displayed. If the statement is false, logic flow continues to line 1110.

Notice that for the last condition, LESS THAN, no IF is needed. Since the tests for GREATER THAN and EQUAL TO have already been made, this leaves the LESS THAN condition as the only possibility.

1120–1170   Lines 1120 through 1170 cause the program to pause and wait for the operator to enter either a C to continue or a Q to quit. If any key other than C or Q is pressed, the program ignores the entry and waits until one of the correct characters is entered.

The GET instruction accepts one character from the keyboard. The symbol is placed in the string variable called X1$. The value in X1$ is tested to see if the program is to continue or quit.

There are three points to consider relating to the use of strings in an IF instruction.

1.   String variables are compared bit by bit.
2.   String constants are enclosed between quotation marks, and therefore use of quotation marks within the string requires special handling.
3.   You should always compare equal size strings.

First, strings are compared by bit pattern on a logical basis. For example, if the letter A is compared to the letter Q, the following bit patterns would be used:

A = 1000001
Q = 1010001

The bit pattern of A is less than the bit pattern of Q. Notice the third bit from the left. A contains a 0 bit, while Q contains a 1 bit, making it greater.

Second, the first operand is a string name X1$ while the last operand is a constant with a value of Q. Constants can be used in either the first or the second operand. Numeric constants may consist of any numeric equation. Alphanumeric constants may consist of any of the 128 different bit patterns which can be stored by the computer.

Since the quotation mark is used to indicate the start and end of a string constant, there is a problem in including quotation marks within the constant. If you want to use a quote between quotation marks you must key two quotation marks for every quote you want to appear. For example,

PRINT """"TWO QUOTES = 1"""""

prints as

"TWO QUOTES = 1 "

The outside set of quotes defined the string constant, the two quotes immediately following and preceding the outside quotes are treated as a single set of quotes.

Third, the strings must be of equal length in order for a valid comparison to be made. For example if "ABC" were compared with "ABC ", the longer string would be greater than the shorter string even though they contain the same leading characters. The APPLE does not recognize trailing blanks as being neutral characters.

Notice on line 1170 that two relational indicators (< >) are used. The IF instruction tests for both a LESS THAN condition and a GREATER THAN condition. If either condition exists, logic flow branches to line 1150 and waits for the operator to enter an acceptable character.

With Applesoft, instead of saying NOT >, NOT <, or NOT =, the condition is worded in a positive format using the two symbols corresponding to the NOT test.

NOT > same as < =
NOT < same as = >
NOT = same as < >

The next example is rather long for what it is intended to accomplish. The example shows the comparison of numeric variables, numeric constants, and numeric expressions.

Key in and run the following program, or run the program by entering

RUN IF SAMPLE2

```
NEW
1000 REM IF SAMPLE2
1010 HOME
1020 SPEED= 150
1030 PRINT "1. IF NUMERIC VARIABLE <=> CONSTANT"
1040 PRINT
1050 INPUT "ENTER ANY NUMBER = ";AANUMBER
1060 IF AANUMBER > 25 THEN PRINT AANUMBER" GREATER THAN CONSTANT
       25": GOTO 1090
1070 IF AANUMBER = 25 THEN PRINT AANUMBER" EQUAL TO
       CONSTANT 25":
       GOTO 1090
```

```
1080 PRINT AANUMBER" LESS THAN CONSTANT 25"
1090 PRINT
1100 PRINT
1110 PRINT "2. IF VARIABLE NAME <=> VARIABLE NAME"
1120 PRINT
1130 INPUT "ENTER ANY NUMBER = ";ABNUMBER
1140 IF AANUMBER > ABNUMBER THEN PRINT "FIRST NUMBER
     "AANUMBER " IS GREATER THAN SECOND": PRINT "NUMBER
     "ABNUMBER:GOTO 1170
1150 IF AANUMBER = ABNUMBER THEN PRINT "FIRST NUMBER
     "AANUMBER " IS EQUAL TO SECOND":PRINT "NUMBER
     "ABNUMBER: GOTO1170
1160 PRINT "FIRST NUMBER "AANUMBER" IS LESS THAN SECOND": PRINT
     "NUMBER ":ABNUMBER
1170 PRINT : PRINT
1180 PRINT "3. IF EXPRESSION <=> EXPRESSION"
1190 PRINT
1200 INPUT "ENTER ANY NUMBER = ";ACNUMBER
1210 IF AANUMBER * ABNUMBER > AANUMBER + ABNUMBER *
     ACNUMBERTHEN PRINT  AANUMBER" * "ABNUMBER" > "AANUMBER" +
     "ABNUMBER" * " ACNUMBER: GOTO 1240
1220 IF AANUMBER * ABNUMBER = AANUMBER + ABNUMBER * ACNUMBER
     THEN PRINT AANUMBER" * "ABNUMBER" = "AANUMBER" +
     "ABNUMBER" * " ACNUMBER: GOTO 1240
1230 PRINT AANUMBER" * "ABNUMBER" < "AANUMBER" + "ABNUMBER"
     * " ACNUMBER
1240 PRINT : PRINT
1250 PRINT "THAT'S ALL FOLKS!"
1260 SPEED= 255
1270 END
```

The first sequence of instructions requests you to enter a number which will be compared to a numeric constant of 25.

1060–1080 When using numeric constants, no quotation marks are used. The numeric constant may contain any numeric symbol along with a leading plus or minus sign. Common sense indicates that if an integer name is used, the constant value should not have a decimal point. For example, do not use IF AANUMBER% = 12.34 since there is no way the integer variable can contain a decimal value. Also, numeric constants CANNOT be compared to string variables unless the STR$ or VAL functions are used to make the two variables of the same type.

The program is not very functional but does provide an example of mixing variables within the IF instruction. Line 1130 asks you to enter a second number. The number is compared with the first number and an appropriate message printed.

1140–1160 The IF instructions on line 1140 and 1150 show how to compare two numeric variables. Normally you do not want to mix the types of numeric variables. Integer variables should only be compared with other integer variables and real values should only be compared with other real values.

1210–1230 The last group of instructions shows how an arithmetic expression can be used within the IF instruction. An arithmetic expression may be compared with another arithmetic expression, a numeric variable, or numeric constant.

From an efficiency standpoint, you should not code an equation twice as done for lines 1210 and 1220. The computer has to calculate the values twice, and if the program were to be changed, the programmer would have to remember to change both statements. Whenever the results of an arithmetic expression are used more than once, calculate the value and give it a variable name.

The third example shows how the word NOT can be used preceding the first operand of the IF instruction to reverse the meaning of the question. I would suggest that you do not use negative questions. It is harder for the person reading the code to follow the logic and make coding changes.

Key in and run the following program, or run the program by entering

RUN IF SAMPLE3

```
1000 REM IF SAMPLE3
1010 HOME
1020 SPEED= 150
1030 PRINT "THE WORD NOT CAN BE USED PRECEDING"
1040 PRINT "THE IF CLAUSE TO REVERSE THE RESULTS"
1050 PRINT "OF THE CONDITIONAL TEST."
1060 PRINT : PRINT
1070 PRINT "NOT (A>B) = LESS THAN OR EQUAL TO"
1080 PRINT "NOT (A=B) = LESS THAN OR GREATER THAN"
1090 PRINT "NOT (A<B) = GREATER THAN OR EQUAL TO"
1100 PRINT : PRINT
1110 INPUT "ENTER FIRST NUMBER  ";AANUMBER
1120 INPUT "ENTER SECOND NUMBER ";ABNUMBER
1130 PRINT
1140 IF NOT (AANUMBER > ABNUMBER) THEN PRINT "FIRST NUMBER =
     OR < SECOND NUMBER": GOTO 1170
1150 IF NOT (AANUMBER = ABNUMBER) THEN PRINT "FIRST NUMBER <
     OR > SECOND NUMBER": GOTO 1170
1160 PRINT "FIRST NUMBER = OR > SECOND NUMBER"
1170 PRINT TAB( 5)AANUMBER TAB( 25)ABNUMBER
1180 PRINT : PRINT
1190 PRINT "PRESS  Q  TO QUIT"
1200 PRINT "PRESS ANY OTHER KEY TO TRY AGAIN"
1210 GET Q$
1220 IF NOT (Q$ = "Q") THEN 1000
1230 PRINT
1240 PRINT "THAT'S ALL FOLKS!"
1250 SPEED= 255
1260 END
```

1070–1090 Lines 1070 through 1090 display some variations on the use of the NOT. You should look at these lines and see if you follow how the computer interprets the use of the NOT for each example.

1140–1160 Lines 1140 through 1160 compare the values and display the related message. Notice that the NOT precedes the test and the entire test MUST be within parentheses.

1210–1220 Line 1220 shows one more example of how the NOT may be used to change the interpretation of the equal sign. If the value in Q\$ is less than or greater than Q, logic flow branches to statement number 1000

Instruction (Compound IF format)

$$\text{IF question 1} \begin{Bmatrix} \text{AND} \\ \text{OR} \end{Bmatrix} \text{question 2}$$

$$\begin{Bmatrix} \text{THEN} \\ \text{GOTO} \end{Bmatrix} \begin{Bmatrix} \text{basic statements} \\ \text{statement number} \end{Bmatrix}$$

Rules for Use
1. Two or more simple "questions" may be combined by using AND or OR.
    a. If AND is used to connect two or more simple questions all the questions must be true for the compound question to be considered true.
    b. If OR is used to connect two or more simple questions, only one of the simple questions needs to be true for the compound question to be true.
    c. When both AND and OR are used to connect simple questions the AND takes precedence, tying the two questions together and treating them as one statement. Any statement following an OR is treated independently of the other statements.
        For example,

        IF A > B AND A > C OR B = C THEN ...

        The IF question is considered true only if A is greater than both B and C, or B is equal to C. The AND between the first two questions combines the two clauses. The OR indicates that one should consider the last question independent of any prior question.
2. Whenever the AND and the OR are used together, parentheses may be used to override the default relationships of the AND and OR connectors.

Illustration of the Rules
1a. If AND is used to connect two or more simple questions, all the questions must be true for the compound question to be considered true.

IF GRADEPOINT < 2.0 AND HOURSEARNED < 10 AND PROBATION\$ = "YES" THEN PRINT "TERMINATE STUDENT"

In this statement all the individual questions must be true in order for the message TERMINATE STUDENT to be printed. The grade point average must be less than 2.0, the hours earned by the student must be less than 10, and the student must currently be on probation. If any one of the three questions is false, the entire IF is considered false, and the message is not printed. Notice that both numeric variables and string variables are combined in the question, but numeric variables are still compared with numeric constants and string variables are still compared with string constants.

1b. If OR is used to connect two or more simple questions, only one of the simple questions needs to be true for the compound question to be true.

IF GRADEPOINT < 2.0 OR HOURSEARNED < 10 OR PROBATION$ = "YES" THEN PRINT "TERMINATE STUDENT"

In the above IF only one of the individual questions need be true in order for the message TERMINATE STUDENT to be printed. The grade point average may be less than 2.0, or the hours earned by the student may be less than 10, or the student may currently be on probation. If any one of the three questions is true, the IF is considered true, and the message is printed. If all the statements are false, the message is not printed.

1c. When both AND and OR are used to connect simple questions within one IF, the AND takes precedence, tying the two questions together and treating them as one statement. Any statement following an OR is treated independently of the other statements.

IF GRADEPOINT < 2.0 AND HOURSEARNED < 10 OR PROBATION$ = "YES" THEN PRINT "TERMINATE STUDENT"

There are two ways that the message can be printed. If the grade point average is less than 2.0 and the hours earned are less than 10, the message is printed. The message is also printed if the student is on probation. Notice that the AND is the stronger of the connectors and ties the first two questions together. The question following the OR is considered independently of the first two questions.

2. Whenever the AND and the OR are used together, parentheses may be used to override the default relationships of the AND and OR connectors.

IF GRADEPOINT < 2.0 AND (HOURSEARNED < 10 OR PROBATION$ = "YES") THEN PRINT "TERMINATE STUDENT"

For this example parentheses are used to change the way in which the machine examines the question. For this version of the question, there are several ways the message can be printed. First, the grade point must be less than 2.0 for the computer to consider either of the last two questions.

Only if the grade point average is less than 2.0 does the machine check the hours earned to see if they are less than 10. If the hours are less than 10, the message is printed without considering the value of probation. If the hours earned are NOT less than 10, the computer checks the value in probation for a YES. If probation contains YES the message is printed.

If both the last two questions are false, the message is not printed.

When parentheses are used, the AND is tied to both questions within the parentheses. The same statement could be written without parentheses as follows:

```
IF GRADEPOINT < 2.0 AND HOURSEARNED < 10 OR
   GRADEPOINT < 2.0 AND PROBATION$ = "YES"
   THEN PRINT "TERMINATE STUDENT"
```

21. The FOR/NEXT Instruction

Instruction FOR number1 = parameter1 TO parameter2 STEP parameter3
... instructions to be executed ...
NEXT number1

Where

1. Number1 is a numeric variable which serves as a counter during execution of the FOR/NEXT loop.

    The variable starts with the value indicated by parameter1 and is incremented by the value of parameter3 each time the keyword NEXT is encountered.

    When the value in number1 is less than or equal to the value in parameter2, logic flow automatically branches back to the FOR instruction and executes the instructions between the FOR and the NEXT instruction again. (An exception to this statement is given in Example 2.)

    When the value in number1 exceeds the value in parameter2, the FOR/NEXT loop ends, and the instructions following the keyword NEXT are executed.

2. Parameter1 is the starting value placed in number1 each time the FOR instruction is encountered in the logic flow of the program.

3. Parameter2 is the comparison value which indicates when to stop the FOR/NEXT loop. When the value of number1 is greater than the value of parameter2, the FOR/NEXT cycle is broken, and logic flows to the instruction following the keyword NEXT.

    Note: Since number1 is not compared with parameter2 until the keyword NEXT is encountered, the instructions between the FOR and the NEXT are executed at least once.

4. Parameter3 is AN OPTIONAL NUMBER which indicates the value to be added to number1 each time the keyword NEXT is encountered. The value may be positive or negative and affects how many times the FOR/NEXT instructions are executed. The default value is 1.

Example 1. Counting from 1 to 10 (STEP 1 is optional):

```
1000 FOR N1 = 1 TO 10 STEP 1
1010 PRINT N1
1020 NEXT
```

The example FOR/NEXT loop is executed 10 times, printing out the numbers 1, 2, 3, 4, 5, 6, 7, 8, 9, and 10.

2. Counting backward from 10 to 1:

```
1000 FOR N1 = 10 TO 1 STEP − 1
1010 PRINT N1
1020 NEXT
```

The example FOR/NEXT loop is executed 10 times, printing out the numbers 10, 9, 8, 7, 6, 5, 4, 3, 2, and 1.

Purpose   The FOR/NEXT instruction allows the programmer to set up a repetitive loop in which the FOR indicates the start of the loop and the NEXT indicates the end of the loop.

Rules for Use
1. In Applesoft the variable used as a counter (number1) must be a real number.
2. Parameters 1, 2, and 3 may be real numbers, integers, or equations.
3. The variables represented by number1 and parameter2 may vary during execution of the FOR/NEXT instructions. Once the FOR instruction has started, changing the values of number1 and parameter2 affects the number of times the instructions within the FOR/NEXT loop are executed.

    The values represented by parameter1 and parameter3 are used to initialize the counter and to give an incrementing value. Once the FOR instruction has started, changing the values for parameter1 or parameter3 does not change the number of times the instruction executes.
4. Since the comparison between the counter (number1) and the limit (parameter2) is not made until the keyword NEXT is encountered, the instructions between the FOR and NEXT are executed at least once.
5. The value following the keyword STEP (parameter3) may be either a positive or a negative number. If positive, the conditional test generated by the keyword NEXT tests for (number1 > parameter2). If negative, the conditional test generated by the keyword NEXT tests for (number1 < parameter2).

Illustration of the Rules   The following exercise shows the basic format of the FOR/NEXT loop with the variable AA used as the counter and numeric constants used for the first and the second parameter.

Exercise 1   Key in and run the following program:

```
NEW
HOME
```

```
1000 FOR AA = 1 TO 10
1010 PRINT "AA = "AA
1020 NEXT
1030 PRINT "FOR/NEXT INSTRUCTION DONE"
1040 END
```

The variable AA is set to 1 when line 1000 is encountered. After AA is set to the starting value, the instructions between the FOR and the NEXT are executed *at least once*.

When the keyword NEXT is encountered, the value in AA is incremented by the value following the keyword STEP or by 1 if no STEP value is specified. After AA is incremented, the new value of AA is tested against the limit of 10.

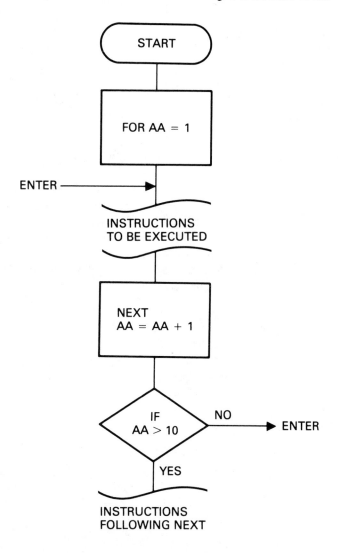

If the value of AA is greater than the 10, logic flow continues down to the next line (line 1030). If the value in AA is less than or equal to 10, logic flow branches back to the first instruction following the FOR instruction (line 1010). Each time the keyword NEXT is encountered, the value in AA is STEPed up by 1 and tested against 10.

For this example line 1010 is executed 10 times, after which line 1030 is executed, indicating the end of the FOR/NEXT instruction group.

The flowchart on the previous page shows the cycle of the FOR/NEXT instruction.

The second exercise shows that all the parameters in the FOR/NEXT instruction can be variables and the STEP value does not have to be 1 (notice DD = 2).

Exercise 2   Key in and run the following program:

```
NEW
HOME
1000 BB = 1: CC = 10: DD = 2
1010 FOR AA = BB TO CC STEP DD
1020 PRINT "AA = "AA
1030 NEXT
1040 PRINT "FOR/NEXT INSTRUCTION DONE"
1050 END
```

The variables BB, CC, and DD are set to their starting value by line 1000. When the FOR/NEXT instruction is first encountered, the variable AA is set to the current value of BB. The FOR/NEXT loop continues until the value in AA is greater than the value in CC. Each time the keyword NEXT is encountered, AA is incremented by the current value of DD (in this case 2).

The loop is executed five times (AA = 1; AA = 3; AA = 5; AA = 7; AA = 9). When AA reaches a value of 11, the loop is terminated, since 11 is greater than the current value of CC.

Exercise 3   In the third exercise, a negative value is used to decrement the starting value of the FOR/NEXT instruction.

Key in and run the following program:

```
NEW
HOME
1000 BB = 10: CC = 1: DD = - 1
1010 FOR AA = BB TO CC STEP DD
1020 PRINT "AA = "AA
1030 NEXT
1040 PRINT "FOR/NEXT INSTRUCTION DONE"
1050 END
```

The variable AA starts off with a value of 10. Each time through the FOR/NEXT loop a negative 1 is added to AA causing the value in AA to decrease in increments of 1(10,9,8,7,6,5,4,3,2,1). When the value in AA is LESS THAN the value in CC, the FOR/NEXT loop is terminated.

Since a negative value is used to decrement the counter, the computer tests for a LESS THAN condition to indicate termination of the FOR/NEXT loop.

Nested FOR/NEXT Instructions

Sometimes you want to use a FOR/NEXT instruction within another FOR/NEXT instruction. The use of loops within loops is referred to as nested loops or nested FOR/NEXT instructions.

Rules for Use
1. When you nest FOR/NEXT instructions, the inner FOR/NEXT instruction MUST be contained entirely within the outer FOR/NEXT instruction.

Right

```
FOR AA = 1 TO 20
instructions
    FOR BB = 1 TO 30
    instructions
    NEXT BB
instructions
NEXT AA
```

Wrong

```
FOR AA = 1 TO 20
instructions
    FOR BB = 1 TO 30
    instructions
    NEXT AA
instructions
NEXT BB
```

To help you read the nested FOR/NEXT instructions, the inner sets are indented. Unfortunately, Applesoft suppresses leading spaces, so using spaces to indent does not work. Some programmers use colons to show indentation (see example program which follows).

2. Although it is not required by Applesoft, the variable may be included with the NEXT instruction to help the programmer remember which variable is being used. The APPLE always matches the inner FOR with the inner NEXT.

3. Values for the inner set of FOR/NEXT instructions are reset each time an outer FOR/NEXT causes them to be executed again. That is, each time an inner FOR/NEXT sequence is completed and the outer FOR/NEXT instruction causes the inner group to be executed again, values for the inner FOR/NEXT are reset.

4. Nested FOR/NEXT loops should always exit by way of the keyword NEXT. That is, you should not terminate a FOR/NEXT loop by branching around the NEXT

instruction. Terminating the FOR/NEXT loop without going through the NEXT instruction may or may not cause problems in your program depending on the logic sequence and the statements being used.

The following program shows three levels of nested FOR/NEXT instructions. It prints nine random numbers on the screen in the same location, giving the appearance of a slot machine.

After the ninth number is printed, the computer skips to the next column on the screen and starts printing nine more random numbers. When one entire line is full, the program skips to the next line and starts the whole process over.

The program takes 4 or 5 minutes to completely fill the screen. After the first few lines, you may want to press CONTROL-C to cancel the program.

You should look at line 1090 carefully to see how the counters are used as part of the VTAB and HTAB instructions.

Key in and run the following program, or run the program by entering

RUN FOR NEXT SAMPLE2

```
NEW
1000 REM FOR NEXT SAMPLE2
1010 HOME
1020 REM
1030 REM NESTED FOR NEXT
1040 REM STATEMENTS.
1050 REM
1060 FOR A1 = 1 TO 24
1070 :: FOR A2 = 1 TO 40
1080 :::: FOR A3 = 1 TO 9
1090 :::::: VTAB A1 : HTAB A2
1100 :::::: A4 = RND (A3)
1110 :::::: PRINT INT (A4 * 10);
1120 ::::NEXT A3
1130 ::NEXT A2
1140 NEXT A1
1150 END
```

1060 The first FOR/NEXT instruction sets up the outermost loop, which corresponds to the 24 lines on the screen. The outermost loop is executed 24 times.

1070 The second FOR/NEXT instruction sets up the middle loop, which corresponds to the number of characters on a line. The middle loop is executed 960 times, once for each character position on the line times the number of lines on the screen (24 * 40 = 960).

1080 The third FOR/NEXT instruction sets up the innermost loop, which causes nine random numbers to be printed in the same character position on the screen. When the numbers are printed in the same screen position, they appear to be rotating like the symbols on slot machines. When random digits are used, there is no pattern to the numbers printed on the screen.

You may want to use this technique in developing games or creating various visual effects on the screen.

The innermost loop is executed 8,640 times (24 * 40 * 9 = 8,640).

1090 The VTAB instruction positions the cursor to the current value of A1. Since A1 is the counter corresponding to lines 1 through 24, the VTAB positions the cursor each time the innermost loop is executed.

The HTAB instruction positions the cursor to the current value of A2. Since A2 is the counter corresponding to columns 1 through 40, the HTAB positions the cursor at the column to be used each time the inner loop is executed. Since the value in A2 remains the same during execution of the inner loop, the cursor stays in the same print position and displays nine random numbers. Each time the middle loop is executed, the value of A2 is changed and the cursor is moved one column to the right.

Each time the outer loop increments A1, the middle loop resets A2 to a starting value of 1, causing the cursor to be repositioned to the first column.

1100 Using the current value of A3 as a seed for the RND function, a random number is generated and placed in the variable A4. Random values consist of nine digit numbers between .000000000 and 1.0.

1110 The random number A4 is multiplied by 10 to shift the decimal one position to the right. After the multiplication, the numbers range from 0.00000000 to 9.99999999. When the INT function is used, the decimal positions are truncated, resulting in a number ranging from 0 to 9.

1120 This is the matching NEXT instruction for the innermost FOR instruction. In Applesoft the variable following the keyword NEXT is optional. When working with single FOR/NEXT loops the variable is normally left off. When working with nested FOR/NEXT loops the variable is normally included to help clarify which counter is being varied. Including the variable name as part of the NEXT instruction does slow down the execution speed of the FOR/NEXT instruction.

1130 This is the matching NEXT instruction for the middle FOR instruction. Each time the instruction is encountered, A2 is incremented by 1 and the resulting value is tested to see if it is greater than 40.

1140 This is the matching NEXT instruction for the outermost FOR instruction. Each time this instruction is encountered, A1 is increased by 1 and the resulting value is tested to see if it is greater than 24. When a value of 25 is reached, the program ends.

22. The Screen Editing Functions

When you want to make changes to a program, you have two ways in which to modify statements.

1. Retype the entire statement.
2. List the statement and use the screen editing keys to modify the statement.

There are 10 keys with which you must be familiar when editing Applesoft statements. The keys include the following:

1. ESC key, the key pressed prior to any cursor movement using the A, B, C, D, J, K, I, and M keys.

After the ESC key is pressed, the letters A, B, C and D are used to move the cursor one position. After any of the four keys is pressed, the computer automatically exits edit mode and returns to normal data entry format.

2. A moves the cursor one column to the left.
3. B moves the cursor one column to the right.
4. C moves the cursor up one row.
5. D moves the cursor down one row.

After the ESC key is pressed, the letters J, K, I, and M may be keyed repeatedly to move the cursor. To break out of the edit mode and return to normal data entry format, press any key other than J, K, I, or M. APPLE IIe users should not press the arrow keys to attempt to break out of the edit mode. Use the space bar or some other symbol key.

6. J moves the cursor to the left.
7. K moves the cursor to the right.
8. I moves the cursor up.
9. M moves the cursor down.

While changing a line, if you decide the changes should not be included in the program, press the CONTROL and X keys at the same time to cancel the current line being entered.

10. CONTROL-X deletes the line *currently being entered.*

Applesoft provides for full screen editing to make changes to the program. That is, by using the J, K, I, and M keys you can move the cursor around on the screen without destroying the data on the screen. Once the cursor is positioned to the statement you wish to edit, you may press a key to break the cursor movement function and proceed to change, insert, or delete characters.

Making changes to statements which contain information between quotation marks is rather involved. Editing the REMarks instruction can also be difficult. To start off, let's see how to change, insert, and delete characters from a simple LET instruction.

Enter the following instructions:

```
NEW
HOME
1000 LET NUMBER = NUMBER + 1
```

Let's assume you want to change the word NUMBER to N1. The following steps allow you to change the U to a 1 and delete the unwanted characters.

1. List the instruction you wish to edit.

```
LIST 1000 <RETURN>
```

The line will be listed out as

```
1000 LET NUMBER = NUMBER + 1
```

↑ The cursor will be positioned in the second column two or three lines below the instruction listed. The line position will vary depending on the length and type of instruction listed.

2. Press the ESC key. The ESC key tells the computer to enter edit mode so you can use the J, K, I, and M keys to move the cursor.

3. Press the I key two times to position the cursor over the 0 in the second column of the statement number.

```
1000 LET NUMBER = NUMBER + 1
 ↑ Cursor should be over the 0
```

4. Press the J key one time to move the cursor over to the start of the statement number.

```
1000 LET NUMBER = NUMBER + 1
↑ Cursor should be over the 1
```

Note: All the characters passed over while in edit mode are ignored. That is, the characters passed over using the J, K, I, and M keys are NOT included in the statement.

5. Press the space bar and the cursor will not move, but the movement function associated with the edit keys will be broken. Now press the right arrow key until the cursor is positioned over the U in NUMBER.

```
1000 LET NUMBER = NUMBER + 1
          ↑ Cursor should be over the U
```

6. Key in the number 1 and press the space bar four times. By entering 1 and the blanks, you have changed the variable NUMBER to N1. Now move the cursor over to the next U by using the right arrow key. All the characters passed over with the arrow key are included in the statement just as if you had retyped them.

Repeat the process of entering a 1 followed by four spaces. After changing the second variable, use the right arrow key to move the cursor over the + 1.

```
1000 LET N1     = N1      + 1 [
                          ↑ Cursor should be over the blank following
                            the 1.
```

7. Now press RETURN to complete the process. To make sure the change was made correctly LIST the statement. Line 1000 should appear as

```
1000 LET N1 = N1 + 1
```

You have now been through the process of changing and deleting characters. To change characters, type the new characters over the old. To delete characters, use the space bar to blank them out. Applesoft automatically reformats the lines after the RETURN key is pressed.

For the sake of the example, let's say you have changed your mind after pressing RETURN and want to change N1 back to NUMBER. This requires you to insert the value UMBER in place of the 1.

To insert characters into the line use the following steps:

1. List the instruction to be changed:

```
LIST 1000
```

2. Position the cursor by using the ESC, I, and J keys. Press the ESC key once. Press the I key two times to position the cursor at the second column of the statement number. Press the J key once to position the cursor at the first column of the statement number.

3. Press the space bar to break the edit function.

4. Using the right arrow key, move the cursor over the characters to the 1 in N1.

1000 LET N1 = N1 + 1
       ↑ Cursor should be over the 1

5. Press the ESC key once to enter edit mode. Press the I key to move the cursor up one line. Press the space bar once to break out of the edit mode and then enter the letter U. Now finish the word by entering the letters MBER. The screen should appear as shown below, with the cursor following the letter R.

      UMBER [Cursor should be after R
1000 LET N1 = N1 + 1

6. The cursor needs to be moved back to the blank following the number 1. To move the cursor, press the ESC key once, press the M key to move the cursor down one line, and press the J key until the cursor is back to the blank following the number 1.

      UMBER
1000 LET N1 = N1 + 1
       ↑ Cursor should be here

7. Since the number 1 is to be deleted, we do not want to include it in the data to be kept. Press the space bar one time to break out of edit mode and the right arrow key four times to move the cursor to the second 1.

      UMBER
1000 LET N1 = N1 + 1
       ↑ Cursor should be here

8. Now you need to repeat the process done earlier to enter the UMBER. Go back to step 5 and repeat the process. When you finish step 6, the screen should appear as shown below, and the cursor should be positioned at the blank following the second 1.

      UMBERUMBER
1000 LET N1 = N1 + 1
       ↑ Cursor should be here

9. Finish the editing process by pressing the space bar and then using the right arrow key to move the cursor over the + 1. You must move the cursor to the end of the line in order to include the remainder of the statement. After positioning the cursor, press the RETURN key to enter the statement. To check your work, list the statement. The newly edited instruction should appear as

1000 LET NUMBER = NUMBER + 1

If you do not get the same answer, rekey the instruction and start over from scratch. This is a lot of work to edit such a small statement, but the knowledge of how to use the edit function will be invaluable when working with long statements.

You now know how to change, insert, and delete characters on a simple LET instruction by using the editing keys to move the cursor around. You should practice the editing operation until it becomes second nature to you.

Editing Statements Which Contain Values Within Quotes

When editing statements which contain information within quotation marks, you must be careful because of the margins generated by Applesoft. For example if you key in

1000 PRINT "1 PRESS THE ESCAPE KEY"

and list the instruction, Applesoft breaks the instruction up and list it on two separate lines as follows:

```
1000 PRINT "1 PRESS THE ESCAPE K
EY"
```

Applesoft breaks the line between the letters K and EY because the line extends past the margin Applesoft uses for displaying instructions. The margin is between the thirtieth and the fortieth column. Whether or not the break occurs depends on whether key words or programmer supplied information is encountered in this area.

For the sake of the example, let's change the statement to read

1000 PRINT "1 PRESS THE ESCAPE KEY ONCE"

To add the new word, use the following steps:

1. List the instruction and move the cursor to the first position of the statement

by pressing ESC once, I three times, and J once. The cursor MUST be at the very beginning of the line over the first digit of the statement number.

2. Use the space bar to break out of edit mode and the right arrow key to move the cursor over to the space following the letter K.

```
1000   PRINT "1 PRESS THE ESCAPE K
EY"                                ↑ Cursor should be here
```

Do not move the cursor all the way across the margin following the letter K. Remember, using the right arrow key is just like retyping the symbols it passes over.

There are blanks between the K on the first line and the EY on the next line. If you use the arrow key to move the cursor over the blanks, they will be included as part of the statement because they are between quotation marks!

3. To get the cursor to the next line, first press the ESC key. Once in the edit mode, use the K key to position the cursor over the letter E. APPLE II and APPLE II+ users should press both the REPT and the K key to move the cursor.

```
1000   PRINT "1 PRESS THE ESCAPE K
EY"
↑ Cursor should be here
```

4. Once the cursor is over the E, press the space bar once to break out of edit mode and the right arrow key two times to move the cursor to the last quotation mark. With the cursor on the quotation mark, enter a space and ONCE". Do not forget the ending quotation mark. After entering a blank, the word ONCE, and a quotation mark, the screen should appear as follows:

```
1000   PRINT "1 PRESS THE ESCAPE K
EY ONCE"
            ↑ Cursor should be here
```

5. Press RETURN to enter the instruction, and then list the instruction to see if you entered it correctly.

Be careful when editing data enclosed within quotation marks.

Now that you know how to do it the hard way, you should know that there is a shorter, easier method.

The instruction POKE 33,33 places the number 33 (second operand) into memory location 33 (first operand). Memory location 33 indicates to the computer the number of columns used on the screen. By resetting the screen to 33 columns, you override the way in which Applesoft breaks up the instructions when they are displayed. Instead of being broken up between lines, the instructions are displayed without any breaks. Enter the following instruction, and follow through the steps to do the same edit as before. Enter

```
HOME
NEW
1000 PRINT "1 PRESS THE ESCAPE KEY"
```

1. After entering the instruction, key in the following three instructions.

```
HOME
POKE 33,33
LIST
```

   Although it is not required you should enter HOME prior to resetting the screen margins to clear the garbage out of the right margin.
   The screen will display the instruction using only the first 33 columns.

```
1000 PRINT "1 PRESS THE ESCAPE K
EY"
```

   To edit the statement, press the ESC key once. Use the I and J keys to position the cursor over the 1 in statement 1000. Once the cursor is positioned, use the space bar to break out of edit mode and the right arrow key to move the cursor to the last quotation mark. Watch closely as the cursor moves from column 33 to column 1. Since only 33 columns are being used, the cursor moves to the second line without any problem. With the cursor over the quotation mark, enter a space and ONCE". Do not forget the leading blank or trailing quotation mark.

2. After changing the statement, key in the following three instructions to reset the screen to 40 columns:

```
HOME                    HOME
POKE 33,40      or      TEXT
LIST                    LIST
```

   To reset the screen, use the POKE or the TEXT instruction. The POKE instruction places a value of 40 back in memory location 33. The TEXT instruction automatically sets the screen back to normal mode. After resetting the screen, LIST the statement to see if it was entered correctly. The screen should appear as follows:

```
1000   PRINT "1 PRESS THE ESCAPE K
EY ONCE"
```

POKE memory location 33 with the value 33 prior to editing any of the following:

1. A statement which has data within quotes
2. A REM instruction which extends beyond one line
3. A DATA instruction which extends beyond one line.

With some practice the whole process becomes easy—believe me, it does.

Just remember, if what you are editing is within quotation marks or is a REM instruction, do not use the arrow keys to move the cursor over the margins. Use the editing keys J, K, I,and M, or use the POKE instruction to change the margin settings.

When editing the REMarks instruction, you must be aware of the problems not only with margins but also with the generated blank following the keyword REM.

When you enter the REMarks instruction, it is normally keyed without a space following the keyword REM.

1000 REMGENERATES ONE BLANK

When you list the REMark statement, a blank is generated between the keyword REM and the first letter of the remarks.The blank causes a small problem when editing a REM instruction. If you edit the REM instruction and use the arrow keys to move the cursor over the blank following the keyword REM, the blank is included as part of the remarks entry. When the remarks instruction is listed, Applesoft generates a second blank to separate the keyword REM from the leading blank or what it considers the start of the remarks.

To prevent the extra blank from being generated, use the following procedure.

1. Key in the following statement and list it.

   1000 REMGENERATES ONE BLANK
   LIST

   The statement will be displayed as

   1000 REM GENERATES ONE BLANK

   Notice the blank inserted by the computer between the REM and GENERATES.
2. Press the ESC key and align the cursor over the first digit of the statement number by pressing I twice and J once.
3. Use the space bar to break out of edit mode and the right arrow to position the cursor over the letter R of REM.

4. Now type in a single space followed by the letters REM (REM).
5. The cursor should now be over the top of the G in GENERATES.
6. Use the right arrow and repeat key to move the cursor to the blank following the letter K, and press RETURN. Do not go past the end of the statement. Any blanks passed over by the cursor will be included in the REMarks statement whether or not you can see them.
7. List the line and you will see a single blank between the REM and the word GENERATES.

Editing Lines With Multiple Instructions

For most of the programs in this book each instruction is put on a line by itself to make the programs more readable and easier to follow. Applesoft executes faster and the programs take up less memory if several instructions are coded for one statement number. Because many programmers want efficiency in speed of execution and in memory usage, they code numerous instructions for one statement number. The technique makes the program run a little faster and take up less memory, but the technique does make it more difficult to read and modify the code.

Type in the line below, which shows four instructions for one statement number. The instructions are samples of how you might accumulate the total hours worked (TAHRSWK), total gross pay (TBGROSS), total net pay (TCNET), and total taxes (TDTAX). Remember, Applesoft only uses the first two characters of the name. This is the reason for the TA, TB, TC, and TD.

1000 TAHRSWK = TAHRSWK + AAHRSWK: TBGROSS = TBGROSS + ABGROSS: TCNET = TCNET + ACNET: TDTAX = TDTAX + ADTAX

Now LIST the instruction. It should appear as follows (notice the spaces within the variable names):

```
1000 TAHRSWK = TAHRSWK + AAHRSWK:
     TB GR OSS = TB GR OSS + AB GR
     OSS:TCNET = TCNET + ACNET:TD
     TAX = TDTAX + ADTAX
```

A statement such as this is where the editing feature really comes in handy. When we created the names TBGROSS and ABGROSS, we did not realize the names include the Applesoft command for GRaphics. The letters GR stand for low resolution graphics and make up an Applesoft reserve word, which can only be used as an instruction. We must correct the error by changing TBGROSS to TBSUM and ABGROSS to ABSUM.

Use the following steps to modify the statement:

1. List the statement.
2. Press the ESC key and move the cursor to the first position of the statement number. This should take five presses of the I key and one press of the J key.
3. Use the space bar to break out of edit mode and the right arrow key to position the cursor over the blank following the first TB. Do not worry about moving the cursor over the blank spaces in the margin. Type in SUM. The line should appear as

   ```
   TBSUM OSS = TB GR OSS + AB GR
         ↑ Cursor should be here
   ```

4. Using the space bar, blank out the letters OSS so that the line appears as

   ```
   TBSUM       = TB GR OSS + AB GR
          ↑ Cursor should be here
   ```

5. Using the right arrow key, move the cursor to the blank following the next TB and type in SUM. The line should appear as

   ```
   TBSUM       = TBSUM OSS + AB GR
                    ↑ Cursor should be here
   ```

6. Using the space bar, blank out the letters OSS. The line should appear as

   ```
   TBSUM       = TBSUM       + AB GR
                    ↑ Cursor should be here
   ```

7. Using the right arrow key, move the cursor to the blank following the AB and type in SUM. The line should appear as

   ```
   TBSUM       = TBSUM       + ABSUM
                         ↑ Cursor should be here
   ```

8. Using the right arrow key, move the cursor to the OSS on the next line and blank out the three characters by using the space bar. The two lines should appear as

   ```
   TBSUM       = TBSUM       + ABSUM
     :TCNET = TCNET + ACNET:TD
        ↑ Cursor should be here
   ```

9. Use the right arrow key to move the cursor to the end of the fourth line and press RETURN. Remember, you must go to the end of the statement prior to pressing RETURN.

10. List the line again to see if the information was entered correctly. The statement should appear as

```
1000 TAHRSWK = TAHRSWK + AAHRSWK:
     TBSUM = TBSUM + ABS UM: TCNE
     T = TCNET + ACNET:TDTAX = TD
     TAX + ADTAX
```

Look at the code closely. Do you notice another problem? The variable name ABSUM includes the Applesoft reserve word ABS (ABSolute) and therefore cannot be used. Give up and key in 1000 to delete the line.

Summary of Edit Keys and POKE Functions

1. ESC key   used to engage the edit keys
2. J   used to move the cursor to the left one column
3. K   used to move the cursor to the right one column
4. I   used to move the cursor up one row
5. M   used to move the cursor down one row
6. POKE 33,33   used to change the width of the screen to 33 columns prior to editing one or more lines.
7. POKE 33,40   used to change the width of the screen back or TEXT to 40 columns after the editing process is over.
8. PROBLEMS
   a. Most people have problems when learning how to edit variables when data is contained between quotation marks. Be careful not to include the blanks making up the margin.
   b. Be careful when editing the REMarks instruction.

23. The GET Instruction

Instruction   GET variable name

Example   GET ANSWER$ Retrieves a single string character
GET NUMBER   Retrieves a single numeric digit

Purpose   1.   To retrieve one keystroke from the keyboard.
2.   To save the operator from having to press the RETURN key when only one character of information is to be entered.
3.   To cause the program to stop until the operator is ready and presses a key.

Rules for Use   1.   Numeric variable names can only accept numeric values. String variable names can accept any key except CONTROL-RESET.
2.   The computer waits for a key to be pressed. Once a key is pressed, the computer continues processing. The operator does not need to press the RETURN key.
3.   If a key is pressed prior to execution of the GET instruction, the symbol is placed in the keyboard buffer (storage area). When the GET instruction is executed the character is retrieved from the single character buffer. If more than one key is pressed prior to execution of the GET instruction, only the last key pressed is accepted.
4.   The symbol entered by way of the GET instruction is not automatically displayed on the screen. If you want the symbol to appear on the screen, you must PRINT the symbol as part of your program logic.
5.   If your program is using both the GET instruction and DOS commands, you must cause a RETURN symbol (CHR$(13) to be PRINTed at some point between using the GET instruction and execution of a DOS command. The RETURN symbol is generated by any PRINT operation which does not end in a semicolon.

Illustration of the Rules   The same program is used to illustrate the first five rules. Rule 5 is not covered in this section but is covered in Section II, on disk file usage.
Key in and run the following program, or run the program by entering

RUN GET SAMPLE1

```
NEW
1000 REM GET SAMPLE1
1010 HOME
1020 SPEED= 150
1030 PRINT "PRESS ANY KEY OTHER THAN CONTROL-RESET"
1040 GET X$
1050 PRINT
1060 IF X$ < "!" OR X$ > "^" THEN 1090
1070 PRINT "YOU PRESSED THE "X$" KEY"
1080 GOTO 1110
1090 PRINT "YOU PRESSED AN UNPRINTABLE KEY"
1100 PRINT "THE ASC II VALUE FOR THE KEY IS " ASC (X$)
1110 PRINT : PRINT
1120 PRINT "NOW PRESS A NUMERIC KEY"
1130 GET AANUMBER
1140 PRINT
1150 PRINT "YOU KEYED THE NUMBER "AANUMBER
1160 PRINT : PRINT
1170 PRINT "THE NEXT GET INSTRUCTION IS CODED AS:"
1180 PRINT
1190 PRINT "     GET AANUMBER"
1200 PRINT
1210 PRINT "ATTEMPT TO ENTER A NONNUMERIC VALUE"
1220 PRINT "INTO THE NUMERIC FIELD."
1230 PRINT
1240 PRINT "THE PROGRAM WILL CANCEL WITH A SYNTAX"
1250 PRINT "ERROR."
1260 SPEED= 255
1270 GET AANUMBER
1280 PRINT "YOU ENTERED A NUMBER WHEN YOU WERE TO"
1290 PRINT "ENTER A NONNUMERIC VALUE.  TRY UNTIL"
1300 PRINT "YOU GET IT RIGHT."
1310 GOTO 1270
```

The program consists of three parts. The first part illustrates the use of the GET instruction with a string variable. The second illustrates the use of the GET with a numeric variable. The third illustrates what happens when a nonnumeric key is pressed for a numeric variable name and what happens when several keys are pressed prior to execution of the GET instruction.

1030 You may enter any key with the GET instruction except CONTROL-RESET. When CONTROL-RESET is pressed, it causes the computer to be reset, canceling your program.

1040 The variable following the GET instruction should *always* be a string variable. If you want a number entered, use a string variable, edit the the value entered, and convert the entry to a numeric value by using the VAL function.

```
1240  GET X$
1241  IF X$ < "0" OR X$ > "9" THEN GOTO error routine
1242  NUMBER = VAL(X$)
```

1060–1100 The value you enter is compared to the bit pattern of the first and last printable characters. If the key pressed is a nonprintable character, logic branches to line 1090 and prints an appropriate message. If the character is printable, logic falls through the IF and prints the character entered. Either way logic flow ends up at line 1110.

Did you that notice the character entered by the GET instruction on line 1040 is not printed until line 1070? Remember, a symbol entered by way of the GET instruction is not automatically printed. If you do not code an instruction to PRINT the symbol, it does not show up on the screen.

1110–1150 The GET instruction on line 1130 retrieves one numeric character. If you code a numeric name following the GET instruction, any key entered other than a numeric character causes the program to terminate and the message ?SYNTAX ERROR to be displayed.

1160–1270 In the third section of the program you see what happens when a nonnumeric value is entered in response to a GET instruction that uses a numeric variable name.

As indicated earlier, once you have pressed a nonnumeric character in response to a request for a numeric value, the computer immediately cancels the program and displays the message

?SYNTAX ERROR

To prevent this type of error from happening, always use a string variable with the GET instruction.

Exercise 1: Entering Characters

Enter

RUN <RETURN>

Follow the instructions displayed on the screen. The program will terminate with an error message if you follow the instructions correctly.

Exercise 2: Entering CONTROL-RESET

Enter

RUN <RETURN>

In response to the first message, press the CONTROL and RESET keys at the same time. The computer will beep and the program will be cancel.

CONTROL-RESET is the only key I have encountered which the GET instruction does not accept. You may want to use the following program to see if there are any other keys which cannot be used with the GET instruction.

```
1000 HOME: GET X1$: PRINT " = ("X1$")": GOTO 1000
```

Remember that some symbols such as CONTROL-C, CONTROL-S, CONTROL-D, etc. do not print.

Exercise 3: Entering a Character Into the Buffer

Before running the program again to illustrate Rule 4, modify the code by keying in

```
DEL 1120,1310 <RETURN>
```

The delete instruction will eliminate the last two GET instructions and leave only the first section of the program.

If you accidentally press a key before the computer executes the GET instruction, the last key pressed is kept in the keyboard's buffer (a memory area) and used as the input character for the GET instruction. If the operator correctly anticipates the character which is to be entered, processing can continue without any error. If the operator does not key in the correct response, hopefully the program edits the input and catches the error before continuing.

Now run the program again. As the program is printing out the message on line 1030, press several keys. When the computer finishes printing the message, the last character you press will automatically be accepted by line 1040 (GET instruction). Key in

```
RUN <RETURN>
```
(press several keys)

The last character pressed will be printed by line 1070. The other characters will be lost.

Using GET to Accept a Yes/No Response

One of the most common ways you will use the GET instruction is to accept a yes/no response or a continue/stop response. When using the GET instruction to accept a specific character you should test the symbol entered for each acceptable value. If an acceptable value is not entered, make the operator reenter the character.

The following lines show how to code a yes/no response using the GET instruction.

```
1000 HOME
1010 PRINT "PRESS   Y   FOR YES"
1020 PRINT "PRESS   N   FOR NO";
1030 GET X1$: PRINT X1$;
1040 IF X1$ = "Y" THEN 1090
1050 IF X1$ = "N" THEN 1110
1060 PRINT "PRESS ANY KEY AND TRY AGAIN!"
1070 GET X1$
1080 GOTO 1000
1090 REM INSTRUCTIONS FOR YES RESPONSE
1100 REM
1110 REM INSTRUCTIONS FOR NO  RESPONSE
1120 REM
```

The basic logic for accepting a response from the operator consists of the following steps:

1. Display the responses which are acceptable.
2. Use the GET instruction to retrieve the character and the PRINT instruction to display the character entered.
   Warning: Printing symbols on line 24 can cause problems. If a character is printed on line 24 and not followed by a semicolon, it causes the screen to scroll. If the operator presses the RETURN key in response to the GET instruction and the symbol is printed on line 24, the screen scrolls whether or not a semicolon is used. These problems can be eliminated by editing the values prior to printing or by not displaying responses on line 24.
3. Test the character entered for ALL the acceptable values. Do not test for one value and let program logic fall through for the other values as shown by the following code:

   ```
   1030 GET X1$: PRINT X1$;
   1040 IF X1$ = "N" THEN 1110
   1050 REM FALL THROUGH FOR YES RESPONSE
   1060 REM
   1070 REM INSTRUCTIONS FOR NO RESPONSE
   ```

4. If no acceptable value is entered, let the operator know by having the program display an error message. Have the program wait for the operator to read the message and then start the process over.

24. The DIM Instruction

Instruction DIM NAME(number,number,number,...)

Note: Although the DIMension instruction may be used to define multiple arrays, this book only illustrates single entry arrays. Multiple levels are defined when more than one number (called a subscript) is used within parentheses.

Single dimension: DIM NAME(subscript1)
Double dimension: DIM NAME(subscript1,subscript2)
Triple dimension: DIM NAME(subscript1,subscript2, subscript3)

Arrays are also referred to as: tables, matrixes, and lists. For this book, the terms *array* or *table* will be used.

Example DIM MTHLYSALES(11)
....
FOR N1 = 0 TO 11
INPUT "MONTHLY SALES = "; MTHLYSALES(N1)
NEXT

The DIMension instruction creates 12 variables which are accessed by using the name MTHLYSALES followed by a number within parentheses. The subscript (number within parentheses) may range from 0 to 11. The FOR/NEXT instruction shows how you might vary the subscript in order to load a value into each of the 12 variables making up the table.

Purpose The DIMension instruction allows the programmer to define large groups of related variables with one general name. Each individual variable is then uniquely referenced by the number following the general name. Without the DIMension instruction many problems would be impossible to code.

Rules for Use 1. If a DIM instruction is used in the program to define an array, the DIM instruction must be executed once prior to any instruction which uses the array or else a REDIM'D ARRAY error occurs. (There is one exception, see Rule 5.)

BEGINNING ROUTINE	Put the DIM instruction at the start of the program in
DIM TABLE(100)	a segment of code which is executed only once.
....	
MAIN ROUTINE	Arrays are also referred to as tables, matrixes, and
....	lists.
TABLE (N1) = SALESIN	
....	

2. The maximum number of subscripts or levels is 88. I cannot imagine how anyone could come close to this limit.

TABLENAME (subscript1,subscript2,subscript3,subscript4,
    ...,subscript88)

Most programmers never get beyond three levels of subscripts:

TABLENAME (subscript1,subscript2,subscript3)

Do not confuse the maximum number of subscripts with the maximum number of array entries. The maximum number of array entries is limited only by the memory size of your computer.

3. Since the computer starts counting at 0, all DIMension definitions and subscripts are relative to 0.

DIM MTHLYSALES (11)	Defines 12 variables from 0 to 11
MTHLYSALES (0)	References the first entry in the array
MTHLYSALES (1)	References the second entry in the array
MTHLYSALES (11)	References the twelfth entry in the array

Because of the difference between the way humans count and the way computers count, many programmers ignore the first entry of a table, entry (0), and start with entry (1).

Even though the sample programs use entry (0) I would suggest that you define and access table entries in human terms.

In human terms the earlier example would be defined as:

DIM MTHLYSALES (12)

The DIMension instruction defines 12 variables from 1 to 12 (actually defines 13, from 0 to 12, but who cares?).

Use 1 as the starting point for accessing the table.

MTHLYSALES(1) = 25000.00 : REM JANUARY SALES

4. Memory usage
   a. Integer array entry   2 bytes per entry
   b. Real array entries   5 bytes per entry
   c. String array entries   3 bytes per entry + length of the string

For more information on memory allocation and usage related to the DIM instruction, see the APPLE programming manuals.

5. If an array name is used in a program and no DIM instruction is specified for that name, Applesoft automatically generates 10 entries for the array. This means if you are going to use arrays with 10 or fewer entries, you do not have to define them with a DIM instruction.

Illustration of the Rules
The following program shows how to define, load, and sort an array with up to 100 entries. This program may be useful to you as a model if you plan to write any code which sequences data.

```
1000 REM DIM SAMPLE1
1010 HOME
1020 DIM NUMBER(99)
1030 REM ---------------------
1040 REM ENTER VALUES
1050 PRINT "ENTER FROM 2 TO 100 NUMBERS"
1060 PRINT
1070 PRINT "ENTER  Q  TO QUIT"
1080 VTAB 5: HTAB 1
1090 CALL - 958
1100 INPUT " = ";NUMBER$: NUMBER = VAL(NUMBER$)
1110 IF LEFT$(NUMBER$) = "Q" THEN 1160
1120 NUMBER(N1) = NUMBER
1130 N1 = N1 + 1
1140 IF N1 > 99 THEN 1160
1150 GOTO 1080
1160 REM ---------------------
1170 REM REPLACEMENT SORT
1180 HOME
1190 PRINT "SORTING NUMBERS": PRINT
1200 PRINT "THE LENGTH OF TIME DEPENDS ON THE": PRINT
1210 PRINT "NUMBER OF VALUES ENTERED."
1220 N3 = N1 - 1
1230 FOR N1 = 0 TO N3 - 1
1240 FOR N2 = N1 + 1 TO N3
1250 IF NUMBER(N1) < = NUMBER(N2) THEN 1290
1260 NUMBER = NUMBER(N1)
1270 NUMBER(N1) = NUMBER(N2)
1280 NUMBER(N2) = NUMBER
1290 NEXT
1300 NEXT
1310 REM ---------------------
1320 REM PRINT NUMBERS
1330 N2 = 0
```

```
1340 HOME
1350 FOR N1 = O TO N3
1360 PRINT NUMBER(N1)
1370 N2 = N2 + 1
1380 IF N2 < 20 THEN 1430
1390 PRINT "PRESS ANY KEY TO CONTINUE"
1400 GET X1$
1410 N2 = 0
1420 HOME
1430 NEXT
1440 PRINT "THAT'S ALL FOLKS!"
1450 END
```

1000–1020 The DIM instruction defines a table of 100 elements with the general name of NUMBER. In order to work with any one of the 100 elements, the label NUMBER must be followed by either a number or a variable ranging from 0 to 99.

1030–1150 Lines 1030 through 1150 are responsible for accepting up to 100 numbers from the operator. The input operation is terminated when the operator has entered 100 numbers or has entered a Q. The CALL – 958 instruction is used to clear the lower portion of the screen after each entry. The CALL instruction is used to clear the screen rather than clearing just one line, since mistakes made by the operator during the entry process can result in the computer's displaying messages on several lines.

1120–1130 You should look closely at lines 1120 and 1130. Since N1 starts off with a value of 0 the first time though the loop, the first number entered is placed in the area NUMBER(0). After each number is placed in the table, the value of N1 is incremented to point to the next available table location.

1160 REM ----------------------
1170 REM REPLACEMENT SORT
....
1220 N3 = N1 − 1
1230 FOR N1 = 0 TO N3 − 1
1240   FOR N2 = N1 + 1 TO N3
1250   IF NUMBER(N1) < = NUMBER(N2) THEN 1290
1260   NUMBER = NUMBER(N1)
1270   NUMBER(N1) = NUMBER(N2)
1280   NUMBER(N2) = NUMBER
1290   NEXT
1300 NEXT

Basically the sort consists of two FOR/NEXT loops. The inner loop is responsible for doing the comparisons and switching the variables, while the outer loop resets the counters and determines how many times the inner loop is executed.

To help explain the logic, let's use the following table values:

```
              Value
NUMBER (0) = 00123
NUMBER (1) = 09876
NUMBER (2) = 00001
NUMBER (3) = 00022
```

1220 N3 = N1 - 1

At the time the sort routine is entered, N1 is 1 greater than the number of entries loaded into the table. Line 1220 sets N3 equal to the exact number of values entered. The value in N3 is used during the sort process to limit the number of comparisons which must be done in order to sequence the numbers. For the data in this example, the value of N3 is equal to 3. Remember, all the subscripts are relative to 0 so the value of 3 indicates that four numbers were entered.

The last sentence emphasizes why many programmers ignore entry 0 when using tables.

1230–1300 Lines 1230 and 1300 form the outer FOR/NEXT loop. The outer loop must be executed 1 less time than the number of entries to be sorted (see the N3 − 1).

1230 FOR N1 = 0 TO N3 − 1

1240–1290 Lines 1240 and 1290 form the inner FOR/NEXT loop. The inner loop must be executed a varying number of times depending on whether this is the first, second, third, fourth, etc. pass through the sorting process. But no matter which pass is being made, the starting point of the inner loop is 1 greater than the starting point of the outer loop (see the N1 + 1).

1240 FOR N2 = N1 + 1 TO N3

1250–1280 Lines 1250 through 1280 make up the actual comparison and flipping process. For the four numbers, the comparison process takes the following steps.

The value in NUMBER (0) is compared with the value in NUMBER (1), see line 1250. For the sample data, 00123 is less than 09876, so the numbers are not flipped.

```
              Value
NUMBER (0) = 00123   Unchanged
NUMBER (1) = 09876   Unchanged
NUMBER (2) = 00001
NUMBER (3) = 00022
```

The value in NUMBER (0) is then compared with the value in NUMBER (2). If the value in NUMBER (0) is greater than the value in NUMBER (2), the two values are flipped. Since 00123 is greater than 00001, the two numbers are flipped (see lines 1260-1280). The flipping process is accomplished by saving NUMBER (0) in the hold area called **NUMBER**. The value in NUMBER (2) is then placed into the NUMBER (0). After the value in NUMBER (2) has been moved, the value which was saved in **NUMBER** is placed into NUMBER (2).

```
                  Value
NUMBER (0) = 00001   Flipped
NUMBER (1) = 09876   Unchanged
NUMBER (2) = 00123   Flipped
NUMBER (3) = 00022
```

The process is repeated until the value in NUMBER (0) has been compared with all the values in the table. After completion of the first iteration of the inner loop, the lowest value is in the first entry of the table: NUMBER (0).

After the first entry has been compared to all the other entries in the table, the outer FOR/NEXT instruction sets N1 up by 1, and the process of comparing the second entry with all the other table entries is carried out. If you follow the inner loop, you will see that during the second execution, two flip operations take place. First, 09876 and 00123 are flipped:

```
                  Value
NUMBER (0) = 00001   No longer used in comparison
NUMBER (1) = 00123   Flipped
NUMBER (2) = 09876   Flipped
NUMBER (3) = 00022
```

After NUMBER (1) and NUMBER (2) have been flipped, the new value in NUMBER (1) is compared with NUMBER (3), resulting in another flip.

```
                  Value
NUMBER (0) = 00001   No longer used in comparison
NUMBER (1) = 00022   Flipped
NUMBER (2) = 09876
NUMBER (3) = 00123   Flipped
```

Once NUMBER (1) has been compared with all the other entries in the table, the outer loop sets N1 up by 1, and the process of comparing the NUMBER (2) to all the other table entries is carried out. If you follow the inner loop one more time, you will see that during the third execution, one flip occurs. The value 09876 in NUMBER (2) is compared with 00123 in NUMBER (3), causing the values to be exchanged.

	Value	
NUMBER (0) =	00001	No longer used in comparison
NUMBER (1) =	00022	No longer used in comparison
NUMBER (2) =	00123	Flipped
NUMBER (3) =	09876	Flipped

Since there are only four entries in the table, N1 is now equal to 1 less than the number of entries, and the sort is completed.

Look through the code again and see how the sorting takes place. The outer loop of the REPLACEMENT sort takes one less pass (execution) than the number of entries in the table (4 − 1 = 3). The number of times the inner loop is executed may be computed by the following formula:

$$T(T - 1) / 2$$

where T = number of table entries.

For the example, the inner loop is executed six times:

$$4 (4 - 1) / 2 = 6$$

If the table contains all 100 entries, the inner loop is executed 4950 times:

$$100 (100 - 1) / 2 = 4950.$$

You can see why it takes several minutes for the computer to sort the table when it is completely full.

After the numbers are sorted, lines 1310 through 1430 display the values in groups of 20.

To see how the sorting program works, execute the following steps. First run the program by entering

RUN DIM SAMPLE1

The screen will clear and the following messages will be displayed:

ENTER FROM 2 TO 100 NUMBERS

ENTER Q TO QUIT
= ?

In response to the question mark, enter some numbers. The program must have at least two numbers in order to work. For this example enter the following numbers:

```
= 3
= 33
= 4
= 2
= 88
= Q        To terminate data entry process
```

After you enter a Q, the input routine will terminate and the sorting process will begin. During the sort, the following message is displayed:

SORTING NUMBERS

THE LENGTH OF TIME DEPENDS ON THE

NUMBER OF VALUES ENTERED.

After the sort is done, the five numbers are printed out in ascending order as follows:

```
2
3
4
33
88
THAT'S ALL FOLKS!
```

25. The READ/DATA/ RESTORE Instructions

The READ and DATA instructions must be used together. The RESTORE instruction is an optional instruction used to reset the pointer indicating the next variable to be read.

Instruction READ variable1,variable2,variable3,variable4,...
DATA value1,value2,value3,value4,...

....

RESTORE

Example READ INTEGER%,REAL,STRING$
DATA 25,10.5,'JOHN JONES'

Purpose The READ and DATA instructions provide a method of initializing variables to a starting value. The two instructions are especially helpful in loading arrays (DIMension entries).

Some programmers use the READ and DATA instructions in place of the INPUT instruction for entering data. With very few exceptions, this is not a good technique and should be avoided. When data are constant and only coded in one program, use the READ and DATA instructions. When data are subject to change or used by more than one program, create a disk file and use the INPUT instruction to read the data from disk. If the data change with each program, every time the program is run, code a routine in the program to allow the operator to INPUT the data.

The RESTORE instruction allows the programmer to reset the data pointers so the next time the READ instruction is executed, the first DATA entry is reread.

Rules for Use

1. If the READ instruction is used, there must be at least one DATA instruction in the program.
2. Each value within the DATA instruction MUST be separated by a comma.
3. The value in the DATA instruction must match the type of name used in the READ instruction, string values for string names and numeric names for numeric values.
4. Variable types may occur in any sequence within the READ and DATA instructions as long as the usage between the two instructions matches.

```
1000 READ STRING$,INTEGER%,REAL
1010 DATA JOHN JONES,25,5.25
```

5. A program can contain any number of READ instructions and DATA instructions. The number of READ instruction and the number of DATA instructions do not have to match. Each time a READ instruction is encountered, the next sequential data element is read.

```
1000 READ STRING$
1010 READ INTEGER%
1020 READ REAL
........
2000 DATA JOHN JONES
2010 DATA 25,5.25
```

6. If more variable names are used in the READ instruction(s) than there are values in the DATA instruction(s), an

OUT OF DATA ERROR IN ####

occurs and the program is canceled.

If more values are specified in the DATA instruction than are read by the READ instruction, the excess values are ignored.

7. For the very first value of the DATA instruction, a leading comma specifies a zero or null value (null means no value).

```
1000 READ N1,N2
1010 DATA ,25
1020 REM N1 WILL BE SET TO ZERO
1030 REM N2 WILL BE SET TO 25
```

For the very last value of the DATA instruction, a trailing comma specifies a zero or null value.

```
1000 READ NAME$,AGE,ADDRESS$
1010 DATA JOHN JONES,25,
1020 REM NAME$ = JOHN JONES
1030 REM AGE = 25
1040 REM ADDRESS$ = null value
```

Notice that the comma at the end of the DATA instruction is necessary to indicate the absence of the last value.

For other than the first or the last value, a zero or null string may be specified by using two consecutive commas.

```
1000 READ NAME$,AGE,ADDRESS$
1010 DATA JOHN JONES,,4953 WAGON WHEEL DR
1020 REM NAME$ = JOHN JONES
1030 REM AGE = 0
1040 REM ADDRESS$ = 4953 WAGON WHEEL DR
```

8. String values MUST be within quotation marks if leading or trailing blanks are to be included as part of the string value.

Illustration of the Rules

The first program consists of a date conversion subroutine which you may want to use in some of your programs. The program starts off by loading the name of each month into an array, and the maximum number of days for each month into a second array. The program is not set up to catch all types of data entry errors.

```
1000 REM READ DATA SAMPLE1
1010 HOME
1020 GOSUB 1210: REM EXECUTE ONLY ONCE
1030 PRINT "ENTER THE DATE IN MMDDYY FORMAT"
1040 INPUT " = ";DTE$
1050 GOSUB 1100: REM EDIT AND CONVERSION ROUTINE
1060 VTAB 10: PRINT DTE$
1070 END
1080 REM --------------------------
1090 REM EDIT AND CONVERT DATE
1100 MM = VAL ( LEFT$ (DTE$,2))
1110 IF MM < 1 OR MM > 12 THEN 1180
1120 DD = VAL ( MID$ (DTE$,3,2))
1130 IF DD < 1 OR DD > DD(MM) THEN 1180
1140 YY = VAL ( RIGHT$ (DTE$,2))
1150 IF YY < 0 OR YY > 99 THEN 1180
1160 DTE$ = MM$(MM) + " " + STR$ (DD) + ", 19" + RIGHT$ (DTE$,2)
1170 RETURN
1180 DTE$ = "ERROR"
1190 RETURN
1200 REM --------------------------
1210 REM BEGINNING ROUTINE
1220 DIM MM$(12),DD(12)
1230 REM --------------------------
1240 REM READ ALPHA MONTH NAME
1250 FOR N1 = 1 TO 12: READ MM$(N1): NEXT
1260 DATA " JANUARY"," FEBRUARY","    MARCH","    APRIL",
     "      MAY","     JUNE","     JULY","   AUGUST",
     "SEPTEMBER","  OCTOBER"," NOVEMBER"," DECEMBER"
1270 REM --------------------------
1280 REM READ NUMERIC DAY VALUE
1290 FOR N1 = 1 TO 12: READ DD(N1): NEXT
1300 DATA 31,29,31,30,31,30,31,31,30,31,30,31
1310 REM --------------------------
1320 RETURN
```

1000–1020   Before a date is accepted and converted into an alphanumeric format, the instructions related to loading the name of each month and the number of days in each month must be executed. These instructions must be executed only once at the start of the program. If you copy the subroutine, make sure you locate the code related to loading the array so it will only be executed once.

1030–1070   After the name of the month and the number of days are loaded, lines 1030 through 1070 accept a date from the operator and convert the numeric date into alphabetic format.

    Notice that the date is accepted from the operator as a string and not as a number. As a general rule, use strings for entering all data. Convert string format values to numeric format by using the VAL function.

1080–1190   Lines 1080 through 1150 edit the date entered to make sure it conforms to the MMDDYY format requested and each section of the date is within the specified limits. If the data entered fails any one of the tests, logic flow branches to line 1180, where a value of ERROR is returned in response to the conversion process. If the data entered passes all the tests, logic flow falls through to line 1160, where the various parts making up the date are connected to form the alphabetic date.

    Line 1130 uses the numbers read into the second array to check the value entered for the day. The number entered for the day is compared against the maximum value for the specific month. The value in MM is used within parentheses to point to the array entry.

1130 IF DD < 1 OR DD > DD(MM) THEN 1180

    Notice that the value of MM is edited prior to its use. If the value to be used as a pointer is entered by the operator, it should always be edited before being used. If the value to be used is generated by program code, there is no need to check the number.

1200–1220   Line 1220 defines the two arrays to be used in the program. The first array is used to store the string names of each month, while the second array is used to store the maximum number of days for each month. Applesoft does not allow the programmer to give starting values to the variables defined by the DIMension instruction. Any starting value other than a null value for string variables or a zero value for numeric variables must be loaded into each array entry.

1230–1320   Lines 1230 through 1320 make up the portion of the program which is related to the use of the READ and DATA instructions. The first loop reads the names of each month into the MM$ array. The second loop reads the number of days for each month into the DD array.

    The two loops could be combined into one single operation. The single loop version of the code is as follows:

```
1240 REM READ ALPHA MONTH NAME AND NUMERIC DAY VALUE
1250 FOR N1 = 1 TO 12: READ MM$(N1),DD(N1): NEXT
1260 DATA " JANUARY",31," FEBRUARY",29,"     MARCH",31,
     "     APRIL",30,"       MAY",31,"      JUNE",30,
     "      JULY",31,"    AUGUST",31,"SEPTEMBER",30,
     " OCTOBER",31," NOVEMBER",30," DECEMBER",31
```

Notice that since a string variable and a numeric variable are both read by the same statement, the DATA instruction must format the values in the same sequence as they are read.

Exercise 1: Entering a Valid Date

To check out the program and see how the program works, run the program using the following steps:

1. Enter

   RUN READ DATA SAMPLE1 <RETURN>

2. In response to the ENTER THE DATE message, key in your birthday.

   ENTER THE DATE IN MMDDYY FORMAT
   = 112244

3. As soon as you press the RETURN key, the computer will display the converted date in alphanumeric format:

   NOVEMBER 22, 1944

Exercise 2: Enter an Invalid Date

To see what happens when an invalid date is entered, use the following steps:

1. Since the program is still in memory just enter RUN and press RETURN.
2. In response to the ENTER THE DATE message, key in any of the following invalid dates:

   130182, 093182, 0101-1, or 000000

3. As soon as you press the RETURN key, the computer will display the word ERROR. If you are using the program as a subroutine within a larger program, the returned value should be tested for an error condition in order to tell if the user enters a valid date.

```
2000 GOSUB convert date
2010 IF DTE$ = "ERROR" THEN ...invalid date
2020 ...valid date
```

The second example shows how to use the RESTORE instruction to cause the values in the DATA instruction to be reread. Whenever you want to reuse the values included in the DATA instruction, the RESTORE instruction should be used.

The program asks you to enter the cost of merchandise and then multiplies the cost by 10 different markup percentages. The program can be reexecuted any number of times using the same values in the DATA instruction.

Key in the program, or load and list the program by entering

```
LOAD RESTORE SAMPLE1
LIST
```

```
1000 REM RESTORE SAMPLE1
1010 HOME
1020 INPUT "ENTER COST OF MERCHANDISE = ";CST
1030 HOME
1040 PRINT "COST OF MERCHANDISE = ";CST
1050 PRINT
1060 PRINT "% MARKUP     SALES PRICE"
1070 FOR N1 = 1 TO 10
1080 READ MARKUP
1090 DATA   .05,.15,.20,.25,.35,.45,.50,.60,.75,.90
1100 PRICE = (MARKUP + 1) * CST
1110 PRINT TAB( 3);MARKUP + 1 TAB( 15)PRICE
1120 NEXT
1130 PRINT : PRINT
1140 PRINT "PRESS  C  TO CONTINUE"
1150 PRINT "PRESS  Q  TO QUIT"
1160 GET X1$
1170 IF X1$ = "C" THEN  RESTORE : GOTO 1000
1180 IF X1$ = "Q" THEN  HOME : END
1190 GOTO 1160
```

1080–1090 The READ instruction retrieves a new markup percentage each time it is executed. The first time through, the cost is multiplied by 1.05. The tenth time through the loop, the cost is multiplied by 1.90.

1170 If the operator enters a C to continue the program, the RESTORE instruction on line 1170 resets the pointer. Once the DATA pointer is reset and the READ instruction is encountered, the first DATA value is reread.

Run the program and enter several values to see the RESTORE instruction in action.

26. The TRACE/NOTRACE Instructions

Instructions   Immediate Execution Mode:

TRACE
NOTRACE

Program Execution Mode:

1000 TRACE
1010 NOTRACE

Purpose   The TRACE and NOTRACE instructions are debugging instructions which can help you follow the logic flow through your program. Depending on how you use TRACE and NOTRACE, the instructions can be very helpful in providing you with the statement number of each line executed or can be overwhelming by listing too many statement numbers and flooding you with too much information.

Rules for Use

1. Use the keyword TRACE in either immediate or program execution mode to start the trace process. Use the keyword NOTRACE in either immediate or program execution mode to terminate the trace process.
2. Each statement number executed is displayed along with other data on the screen and therefore messes up any screen design format. If you are using the HOME, VTAB, or HTAB instructions to clear the screen or reposition the cursor, the statement numbers displayed by the TRACE function will be difficult to follow. Either slow the computer down with the SPEED command or use PR#1 to print all data displayed (if you have a printer).
3. The TRACE function can only be turned off by using the NOTRACE instruction or by resetting the machine. The LOAD and RUN instructions do not reset the TRACE operation.
4. The TRACE function cannot be used in a program which uses DOS instructions unless it is turned off prior to a DOS instruction and back on after a DOS instruction.

```
2000 NOTRACE        Turns trace off before DOS operation
2010 PRINT D$;"READ SEQUENTIAL FILE"
2020 INPUT A1RECORD$
2030 TRACE          Turns trace on after DOS operation
```

Illustration of the Rules

The first program is very short and is intended to show you how the TRACE/NOTRACE instructions work in immediate-execution mode. The program results in an endless loop and must be terminated by pressing CONTROL-C.

```
HOME
NEW
1000 REM TRACE SAMPLE1
1010 REM MAIN ROUTINE
1020 IF EOF$ = "YES" THEN END
1030 GOTO 1010
TRACE
```

Exercise 1: TRACE and NOTRACE in Immediate Execution Mode

Key in the short program. After the program has been entered, key in the TRACE instruction. Now RUN the program and watch how fast the screen fills up with statement numbers.

The new lines on the screen will appear as follows, starting with statement number 1000.

```
RUN
#1000 #1010 #1020 #1030 #1010 #1020 #103
0 #1010 #1020 #1030 #1010 #1020 #1030 #1
010 #1020 #1030 #1010 #1020 #1030 #1010
.............................................
BREAK IN ####
```

Notice that the cycle repeats in an endless loop. To cancel the program, press CONTROL-C.

After canceling the program, enter NOTRACE in order to terminate the TRACE process.

The second example shows how to use the TRACE instruction in the program execution mode and how to turn the trace process off and on within the program to cut down on the number of line numbers displayed. The program also uses the PRINT instruction as a debugging tool to help the programmer know which part of the program is being executed.

```
1000 REM TRACE SAMPLE2
1010 HOME
1020 REM MAIN ROUTINE
1030 PRINT "START OF OUTER LOOP"
1040 FOR N1 = 1 TO 5
1050 PRINT "START OF INNER LOOP"
1060 FOR N2 = 1 TO 5
1070 TRACE
1080 REM INNER FOR/NEXT INSTRUCTION
1090 NOTRACE
1100 NEXT
```

```
1110 PRINT "END OF INNER LOOP"
1120 NEXT
1130 PRINT "END OF OUTER LOOP"
1140 END
```

Exercise 2: TRACE and NOTRACE in Program Execution Mode

Study the code and run the program by entering

RUN TRACE SAMPLE2

The following screen image will be displayed:

```
START OF OUTER LOOP
START OF INNER LOOP
#1080 #1090 #1080 #1090 #1080 #1090 #108
0 #1090 #1080 #1090 END OF INNER LOOP
START OF INNER LOOP
#1080 #1090 #1080 #1090 #1080 #1090 #108
0 #1090 #1080 #1090 END OF INNER LOOP
START OF INNER LOOP
#1080 #1090 #1080 #1090 #1080 #1090 #108
0 #1090 #1080 #1090 END OF INNER LOOP
START OF INNER LOOP
#1080 #1090 #1080 #1090 #1080 #1090 #108
0 #1090 #1080 #1090 END OF INNER LOOP
START OF INNER LOOP
#1080 #1090 #1080 #1090 #1080 #1090 #108
0 #1090 #1080 #1090 END OF INNER LOOP
END OF OUTER LOOP
```

1070–1090 The TRACE and NOTRACE instructions are used in the innermost loop in order to limit the number of statement numbers displayed. Whenever you have a problem following what is happening in a block of code, use the TRACE and NOTRACE instructions to display the statements which are executed. Use the PRINT instruction to display routine names or values within specific variables.

27.   The PEEK Instruction

Instruction   variable = PEEK (address)

Example   PRINT "ERROR CODE = ";PEEK (219) * 256 + PEEK (218)

Prints the error number related to an **ONERR** condition.

FOR N1 = 0 TO 50: N2 = PEEK (− 16336): NEXT

Causes a short noise from the APPLE's speaker.

Purpose   The PEEK instruction is used to retrieve the contents of a byte of memory. The instruction returns a decimal number equal to the value stored at the specified address or flips a memory address switch.

Rules for Use   1.   The variable or expression following the keyword **PEEK** must be in parentheses and must be an address within the limits of the computer being used.
2.   Many of the addresses used in the **PEEK** and **POKE** instructions act as program switches. If the memory address is designated as a switch, either **PEEK**ing or **POKE**ing the address has the same effect of flipping the switch. Normally the shorter **POKE** instruction is used.

Illustration of the Rules

```
1000 REM NOISE ERROR ROUTINE
1010 HOME
1020 PRINT "ENTER A NUMBER BETWEEN 100 AND 1000"
1030 INPUT " = ";NUMBER
1040 IF NUMBER < 100 OR NUMBER > 1000 THEN 1000
1050 GOSUB 1090: REM MAKE NOISE
1060 END
1070 REM ----------------------
1080 REM NOISE SUBROUTINE
1090 FOR N1 = 0 TO NUMBER: N2 = PEEK ( − 16336): NEXT : RETURN
1100 REM ----------------------
```

Note: For another method see the **CALL** − 1052 instruction.

1070–1100   Line 1090 makes up the entire NOISE SUBROUTINE. The length of the noise is dependent on the value of NUMBER. If you use this instruction, you can substitute a numeric constant for NUMBER and simplify the operation.

```
1090 FOR N1 = 0 TO 100: X = PEEK ( −16336): NEXT
```

To get some idea of the noise and how long a FOR/NEXT loop you like, run the program and enter a variety of numbers from 100 to 1000. Enter:

```
RUN NOISE ERROR ROUTINE
100
RUN
500
RUN
1000
```

Some Useful PEEK Addresses

Some of the useful PEEK addresses are given below. For a more detailed listing of addresses to PEEK see the APPLE programming reference manual.

PEEK (36)   The memory address is used to store the current horizontal position of the cursor. The value ranges from 0 for the leftmost column to 39 for the rightmost column.

PEEK (37)   The memory address is used to store the current vertical position of the cursor. The value ranges from 0 for the first line to 23 for the bottom line.

PEEK (219) * 256   The memory locations 219 and 218 are used to store the line number of the statement
+ PEEK (218)   which caused an error condition to occur.

PEEK (222)   The memory address which contains the decimal number representing the type of error that occurred. A list of these numbers and the matching error message is included under the description of the ONERR GOTO instruction (see ONERR, p. 225).

PEEK (−16336)   This causes the speaker to produce a short click. For the click to be noticeable, the PEEK must be used in a FOR/NEXT loop and repeated several times (see CALL −1052, p. 242).

28. The POKE Instruction

Instruction   POKE address,number

Example   1000 REM RESET SCREEN SIZE
1010 HOME
1020 POKE 33,20: REM SETS THE WIDTH OF LINE TO 20 CHARACTERS
1030 POKE 32,10: REM SETS LEFT MARGIN TO START IN COLUMN 10
1040 POKE 34,4: REM SETS THE TOP MARGIN TO LINE 5
1050 POKE 35,20: REM SETS THE BOTTOM MARGIN TO LINE 20

The five instructions clear the screen and reset the size of the screen to a 20 character by 20 row format centered in the middle of the display unit. The instructions must be executed in program mode or else the outside margins are not clear.

Purpose   The POKE instruction is used to place a numeric value in a byte of memory or to flip a switch at a specific memory address.

Rules for Use   1. The variable or expression following the keyword POKE must consist of a machine address within the range of the computer and must be followed by a variable name or constant. The value of the variable name or numeric constant must be between 0 and 255.
2. Many of the addresses used in the PEEK and POKE instructions act as program switches. If the memory address is designated as a switch, either PEEKing or POKEing the address has the same effect of flipping the switch. Normally the shorter POKE instruction is used.

Illustration of the Rules   **Exercise 1: Changing the Text Window**

The first exercise modifies the text window, showing you how the POKE instruction works. The second exercise resets the window back to the normal mode.
Enter the following instructions and then run the program:

```
NEW
1000 HOME
1010 POKE 33,20    Sets the width of the line to 20 characters
1020 POKE 32,10    Sets the left margin to start in column 10
1030 POKE 34,4     Sets the top margin to line 5
1040 POKE 35,20    Sets the bottom margin to line 20
RUN
```

After the program has been run, enter the following single line program in the immediate execution mode:

FOR N1 = 1 TO 200: PRINT N1;: NEXT

The middle of the screen will fill with the numbers from 1 to 200. As the twentieth line is filled, the text window will scroll up for each new line displayed.

Exercise 2: Resetting the Text Window

The easy way to reset the text window is to press CONTROL-RESET or enter the TEXT command. The long way to reset the text is to rePOKE each memory address with the correct value as follows:

Long way:

```
HOME              Optional
POKE 32,0         Sets the left margin to start in column 0
POKE 33,40        Sets the width of the line to 40 characters
POKE 34,0         Sets the top margin to line 0
POKE 35,23        Sets the bottom margin to line 23
HOME
```

Short way:

```
TEXT
```

After resetting the window, enter the same command as used earlier and test the new setting of the text window.

FOR N1 = 1 TO 200: PRINT N1;: NEXT

Some Useful **POKE** Addresses

There are a large number of addresses which can be used with the POKE instruction when working with high resolution graphics or machine language.

For a more detailed listing of addresses used with the POKE instruction, see the APPLE programming reference manual.

POKE 32,number Memory location 32 contains a number from 0 to 39 indicating the starting column (leftmost column) to be used when displaying information on the screen. The left margin of the screen can be changed by POKEing a new value into memory location 32. Before the screen format is changed, the HOME command should be used to clear the screen or garbage may be left in the margins.

The left margin does not change until the cursor is repositioned to a new line. Also, the instruction does not change the width of the screen, which is controlled by memory location 33. When changing the size of the screen, either run a small program or use a single line of code in immediate execution mode as follows:

HOME : POKE 32,number : POKE 33,number : POKE 34,number : POKE 35,number : HOME

The instructions: clear the screen, reset the screen size, and reposition the cursor to the new location. The instructions must be executed as one line of code. If you execute each instruction individually, garbage will be left on the screen.

POKE 33,number Memory location 33 contains a number from 1 to 40 indicating the length of the lines to be displayed on the screen. A value of 0 cancels Applesoft.

For printing Applesoft programs, POKE 33,33 causes the third tab field to be ignored and can be used when making hard copies of Applesoft programs to print a full 80 columns.

To print a full 80 columns, enter

```
HOME          Optional
POKE 33,33    After the listing is done enter
PR#1
LIST
........
POKE 40,33
```

For editing Applesoft statements, POKE 33,33 causes the automatic formatting feature to eliminate extra spaces which are normally generated. Whenever you are using the edit keys to make changes to either remarks or lines containing string constants, the POKE instruction helps simplify the editing process.

```
POKE 33,33
LIST statement to be changed
... Make changes
POKE 33,40
```

POKE 34,number   Memory location 34 contains a value from 0 to 23 indicating the starting line on the screen to be used as the top margin. Needless to say, the top margin should not be set below the bottom margin.

POKE 35,number   Memory location 35 contains a value from 0 to 23 indicating the ending line on the screen to be used as the bottom margin. The bottom margin should not be set higher than the top margin.

29. The ONERR GOTO Instruction

Instruction   ONERR GOTO statement number

Example   1000 REM BEGINNING ROUTINE
1010 ONERR GOTO 3000

....

3000 REM ERROR ROUTINE

Purpose   The ONERR instruction allows the programmer to intercept an error situation and handle the recovery process within the program. By coding a special error routine, the programmer may terminate the program in an orderly fashion, give the operator special instructions, or restart the program.

Rules for Use   1.   If an error occurs prior to execution of an ONERR GOTO instruction, the program displays the statement number in error and the related error message. Once an ONERR GOTO instruction has been executed and an error occurs, the computer branches to the instruction indicated by the statement number following the keyword GOTO.

2.   Any number of ONERR GOTO instructions may be used in a program, but only the statement number associated with the last ONERR instruction is kept.

ONERR GOTO 2000
...   If an error occurs, logic flow branches to
...   statement 2000
ONERR GOTO 3000
...   Execution of a second ONERR statement changes
...   the code so that if an error occurs, logic flow
...   branches to statement 3000

3.   When an error occurs, the pointers associated with the FOR/NEXT instruction and the stacks associated with the GOSUB instruction are cleared (destroyed).

4.   Some of the related memory addresses are the following:
  222   Contains a decimal number between 0 and 255 indicating the type of error which occurred (see program listing).
  216   Bit 7 of memory address 216 acts as a switch, indicating whether or not

an ONERR instruction has been encountered. If you wish to turn off an ONERR instruction, execute the instruction POKE 216,0.

218 and 219 Memory addresses 218 and 219 contain the line number on which the error occurred.

The error subroutine shown in the following program provides a check for all the Applesoft errors. The program does not check for the DOS errors. See the DOS manual for DOS error values. There is really no advantage to using the subroutine unless you wish to change the wording of the error messages or wish to display some special instructions to the operator.

```
1000 REM ONERR SAMPLE1
1010 ONERR GOTO 1040
1020 HOME
1030 A = X$: REM CAUSES MISMATCH ERROR
1040 REM ---------------------
1050 ONERR SUBROUTINE
1060 VTAB 21: HTAB 1: CALL - 958
1070 E1 = PEEK (222)
1080 E2 = PEEK (219) * 256 + PEEK (218)
1090 PRINT "LINE="E2" ERROR="E1
1100 IF E1 = 0 THEN PRINT "NEXT WITHOUT FOR": GOTO 1290
1110 IF E1 = 16 THEN PRINT "SYNTAX ERROR": GOTO 1290
1120 IF E1 = 22 THEN PRINT "RETURN WITHOUT GOSUB": GOTO 1290
1130 IF E1 = 42 THEN PRINT "OUT OF DATA": GOTO 1290
1140 IF E1 = 53 THEN PRINT "ILLEGAL QUANTITY": GOTO 1290
1150 IF E1 = 69 THEN PRINT "OVERFLOW ERROR": GOTO 1290
1160 IF E1 = 77 THEN PRINT "OUT OF MEMORY": GOTO 1290
1170 IF E1 = 90 THEN PRINT "UNDEFINED STATEMENT": GOTO 1290
1180 IF E1 = 107 THEN PRINT "BAD SUBSCRIPT": GOTO 1290
1190 IF E1 = 120 THEN PRINT "REDIMENSIONED ARRAY": GOTO 1290
1200 IF E1 = 133 THEN PRINT "DIVISION BY ZERO": GOTO 1290
1210 IF E1 = 163 THEN PRINT "TYPE MISMATCH": GOTO 1290
1220 IF E1 = 176 THEN PRINT "STRING TOO LONG": GOTO 1290
1230 IF E1 = 191 THEN PRINT "FORMULA TOO COMPLEX": GOTO 1290
1240 IF E1 = 224 THEN PRINT "UNDEFINED FUNCTION": GOTO 1290
1250 IF E1 = 254 THEN PRINT "BAD RESPONSE TO AN INPUT
     STATEMENT": GOTO 1290
1260 IF E1 = 255 THEN PRINT "CONTROL-C INTERRUPT ATTEMPTED":
     GOTO 1290
1270 PRINT "UNDETERMINED ERROR"
1280 REM ---------------------
1290 REM INCLUDE SPECIAL INSTRUCTIONS TO OPERATOR?
1300 END
```

The only lines which may need explaining are those using the PEEK instruction.

```
1070 E1 = PEEK (222)
1080 E2 = PEEK (219) * 256 + PEEK (218)
1090 PRINT "LINE = "E2" ERROR = "E1
```

The first PEEK instruction sets E1 equal to the error number stored in memory location 222. The second PEEK instruction sets E2 equal to the line number which caused the error. Since the APPLE stores the numbers in reverse format and using the hexadecimal numbering system, the instruction may look a little complicated. Just use the instruction as shown, and it will give you the line number of the statement in error.

Note: After an error occurs, you can continue execution of the program at the start of the instruction which caused the error by using the RESUME instruction. In actual practice the RESUME instruction is not used since the GOSUB stacks and FOR/NEXT pointers are destroyed whenever an error occurs (see Rule 3).

```
2000 ONERR GOTO 3000
........
3000 REM HANDLE THE ERROR SITUATION
........
3100 RESUME
```

30. The STOP/CONTinue Instructions

Instruction　Program Execution Mode: 1000 STOP
Immediate Execution Mode: CONT

Purpose　By allowing the use of the CONTinue instruction with the END or STOP instructions, Applesoft provides the programmer with a way to pause while the operator reads messages on the screen.

> Note: For all the programs in this book the GET instruction is used in place of the CONT instruction to cause the programs to pause for a response from the operator. Since the STOP and CONT instructions result in messages being displayed they cannot be used with formal screen designs.

Rules for Use　1.　The CONTinue instruction can only be used in the immediate execution mode.

2.　The CONTinue instruction can be used when the program has been halted either by the STOP instruction, by the END instruction, or by the operator's pressing CONTROL-C. Note that the CONT instruction does not work if the operator presses CONTROL-C in response to an INPUT instruction.

3.　Once the program pauses in response to either the STOP, the END, or the CONTROL-C, the CONT command must be the next entry entered or the continuation process most likely will not work.

Illustration of the Rules　One program will be used to illustrate all the rules related to using the CONTinue instruction. Most of the program consists of print instructions to indicate what to do at each step. Look at how the STOP and END instructions are used on lines 1030 and 1060.

```
1000 REM CONT SAMPLE1
1010 HOME: SPEED= 150
1020 PRINT "1. TYPE IN 'CONT' TO CONTINUE"
1030 STOP: PRINT
1040 PRINT "VERY GOOD": PRINT: PRINT
1050 PRINT "2. TYPE IN 'CONT' TO CONTINUE"
1060 END: PRINT
1070 PRINT "VERY GOOD": PRINT: PRINT
1080 PRINT "3. PRESS CONTROL-C WHILE NUMBERS ARE"
1090 PRINT "   BEING DISPLAYED.  TYPE IN 'CONT'"
1100 PRINT "   TO TRY TO CONTINUE AFTER CONTROL-C."
```

```
1110 FOR N1 = 1 TO 100: PRINT N1;: NEXT: PRINT
1120 PRINT "VERY GOOD": PRINT: PRINT
1130 PRINT "4. TYPE IN 'CONT' TO TRY TO CONTINUE"
1140 PRINT "   AFTER ERROR MESSAGE IS DISPLAYED."
1150 SPEED = 255
1160 FOR N1 = 1 TO 999999: N1% = 2 * (N1% + 1): NEXT
1170 REM PROGRAM ENDS IN AN ERROR
```

Run the program by entering

RUN CONT SAMPLE1

After the program has displayed the first message and paused, go through Exercises 1 through 5 to see how the CONTinue instruction works in various situations.

Exercise 1: CONTinuing in Response to the STOP Instruction

Lines 1020 through 1040 relate to the first exercise.

```
1020 PRINT "1. TYPE IN 'CONT' TO CONTINUE"
1030 STOP: PRINT
1040 PRINT "VERY GOOD": PRINT: PRINT
```

After the message on line 1020 is displayed, type in CONT and press RETURN. The PRINT instruction on line 1030 causes a blank line to be displayed followed by the VERY GOOD message and two additional blank lines. The PRINT instruction on line 1030 is important for you to note. The instruction is the second statement on line 1030 and is executed after you key in the CONT instruction. This is an important point. The CONT instruction picks up with the next instruction immediately following the STOP.

The lines on the screen related to this exercise will appear as

```
1. TYPE IN 'CONT' TO CONTINUE
BREAK IN 1030
CONT

VERY GOOD
```

Exercise 2: CONTinuing in Response to the END Instruction

Lines 1050 through 1070 relate to the second exercise.

```
1050 PRINT "2 TYPE IN 'CONT' TO CONTINUE"
1060 END: PRINT
1070 PRINT "VERY GOOD": PRINT: PRINT
```

After the message on line 1050 is displayed, type in CONT and press RETURN. The END instruction does not cause a break message to be displayed. The program simply ends with a blinking cursor on the screen.

The lines on the screen related to this exercise will appear as

```
2. TYPE IN 'CONT' TO CONTINUE
CONT
VERY GOOD
```

The difference between the STOP and END instruction is that the STOP prints a message while the END does not.

Exercise 3: CONTinuing in Response to a CONTROL-C Termination

Lines 1080 through 1120 relate to the third exercise.

```
1080 PRINT "3. PRESS CONTROL-C WHILE NUMBERS ARE"
1090 PRINT " BEING DISPLAYED. TYPE IN 'CONT'"
1100 PRINT "TO TRY TO CONTINUE AFTER CONTROL-C"
1110 FOR N1 = 1 TO 100: PRINT N1;: NEXT: PRINT
1120 PRINT "VERY GOOD": PRINT: PRINT
```

In order to provide you with time to press the CONTROL-C, line 1110 displays the numbers from 1 to 100 at a SPEED of 150. While the numbers are being displayed, press CONTROL-C to cancel the program. Without entering anything else, enter CONT to continue the program. The program will start up right where it left off in the middle of the FOR/NEXT loop.

When you pressed CONTROL-C.

1. The current statement was canceled.
2. You entered CONTinue.
3. The program restarted right where you interrupted it.

The lines on the screen related to this exercise will appear as

```
3. PRESS CONTROL-C WHILE NUMBERS ARE
   BEING DISPLAYED. TYPE IN 'CONT'
   TO TRY TO CONTINUE AFTER CONTROL-C.
```

1234567891011121314 1516... Depends on where you interrupted program
BREAK IN 1110
CONT
252627282930313233 3435... Depends on where you interrupted program
VERY GOOD

Exercise 4: Trying to Continue in Response to an Error Message

Lines 1130 through 1170 relate to the fourth exercise.

```
1130 PRINT "4. TYPE IN 'CONT' TO TRY TO CONTINUE"
1140 LPRINT "AFTER ERROR MESSAGE IS DISPLAYED."
1150 SPEED = 255
1160 FOR N1 = 1 TO 999999: N1% = 2 * (N1% + 1): NEXT
1170 REM PROGRAM ENDS IN AN ERROR
```

Line 1160 results in an error message, since the equation results in a value too large to be stored in the integer field N1%. In response to the error message, type in CONT and press RETURN. After you enter CONTinue, a second error message will be displayed, indicating that the program cannot continue. The lines on the screen related to this exercise will appear as

```
4. TYPE IN 'CONT' TO TRY TO CONTINUE
   AFTER ERROR MESSAGE IS DISPLAYED.

?ILLEGAL QUANTITY ERROR IN 1160
CONT
?CAN'T CONTINUE ERROR
```

Exercise 5: Trying to Continue After Something Other Than CONT Has Been Entered Following a Program Pause

Run the program again, but this time in response to the first message, enter a new statement and then enter the word CONT as follows:

1000 REMNEW STATEMENT
CONT

When you entered the new statement, you voided the program's ability to continue. Any attempt to continue after program modification or cancellation of an INPUT instruction results in the CAN'T CONTINUE ERROR.

The lines on the screen related to this exercise will appear as

```
1. TYPE IN 'CONT' TO CONTINUE
1000 REMNEW STATEMENT
CONT

?CAN'T CONTINUE ERROR
```

31. The FRE (0) Instruction

Instruction variable = FRE (0)

Example N1 = FRE (0)

Purpose The FREe instruction is used to condense memory by eliminating unused areas of string memory. The instruction also returns the amount of free memory available after storage is condensed.

 If a program uses a large number of strings variables, Applesoft automatically reorganizes memory when there is no longer any free space available for assigning new values.

 The length of time the machine takes to condense string memory depends on the number of string variables used and whether or not large tables have been used (DIM instruction).

 By using the FRE instruction, the programmer can control the time and position within the program when memory is condensed.

Rules for Use

1. The FRE instruction must be specified in an equation format

 X = FRE (0)

 The variable to the left of the equal sign is set equal to the number of free bytes left after storage is condensed.

2. The value following the keyword FRE is required and must be in parentheses. Although the value of the parameter is ignored, it must be included and must be either an equation or a constant which can be interpreted by Applesoft. To save time and effort, code the instruction as FRE (0).

3. If your program uses high resolution graphics, you must use the FRE command to ensure that the high resolution pages are not destroyed.

 Three examples are used to help illustrate the FRE instruction and show how string memory is used. The first example shows how strings are stored in memory before and after execution of the FRE instruction. The second example uses a subroutine which determines when the FRE instruction should be executed. The third example illustrates the difference between freeing memory when no DIMension entries are used (DIM 0 entries), when a small table is used (DIM 100 entries), and when a large table is used (DIM 500 entries).

For more information on how the APPLE uses memory, see the APPLE programming reference manual.

Before getting started with the first example, let's review how the machine associates values with variable names.

Each variable name has an associated address which points to the area of memory where the related data is stored.

Type of Variable	Name	Address	
Real number	N1	2000	Address remains constant; value in memory location changes
Integer Number	N1%	2100	Address remains constant; value in memory location changes
String Variable	NAME$	10000	Value of address changes to reflect location of new string

For numeric variables, the area of memory remains constant, and the value within the memory area is changed as calculations are done.

For string variables, the address associated with the name changes each time the value of the string is changed.

Example 1: FREeing Memory

The first program fills up approximately 30 bytes of memory, displays how the 30 bytes look before using the FRE instruction, frees string memory, and then redisplays the 30 bytes.

The objective of the program is to show you how the machine allocates string memory and what happens after you use the FRE instruction.

```
1000 REM FRE SAMPLE1
1010 REM ---------------------------
1020 HOME
1030 FOR N1 = 1 TO 20:X1$ = STR$ (N1):NEXT
1040 LOW = PEEK (112) * 256 + PEEK (111)
1050 HIGH = PEEK (116) * 256 + PEEK (115) - 1
1060 PRINT "   LOW = "LOW"  HIGH = "HIGH
1070 FOR N1 = LOW TO HIGH: PRINT CHR$ ( PEEK (N1));: NEXT
1080 PRINT : PRINT : PRINT
1090 N1 = FRE (0)
1100 X1$ = "CONSTANT"
1110 PRINT "OLD LOW = "LOW"  HIGH = "HIGH
```

```
1120 FOR N1 = LOW TO HIGH: PRINT CHR$ ( PEEK (N1));: NEXT
1130 LOW = PEEK (112) * 256 + PEEK (111)
1140 PRINT : PRINT : PRINT "NEW LOW =."LOW
1150 END
```

Look over the code before running the program. After you run the program, the screen should appear as follows. The memory addresses vary depending on the memory size of the machine and the software being used.

```
   LOW = 34754 HIGH = 34784
2019181716151413121110987654321


OLD LOW = 34754 HIGH = 34784
2019181716151413121110987654420

NEW LOW = 34783
```

1030 Line 1030 generates 20 string values ranging from 1 to 20. As the numeric value of N1 changes so does the string value of X1$. But while N1 is stored in a fixed area of memory, the string X1$ continues to be reassigned new areas of memory each time it changes. At the end of the FOR/NEXT loop, X1$ is equal to 20. All the previous string values are garbage, taking up memory.

```
   LOW = 34754 HIGH = 34784
2019181716151413121110987654321
↑ ----- garbage strings ------
   └─── current value of X1$
```

Take time to study the way the machine stores each string. First a string value of 1 is stored in memory location 34784. Next a string value of 2 is stored in memory location 34783. Each new string value is stored in a lower and lower memory address. Remember, the machine uses string memory starting at the high addresses and working down. Finally a value of 20 is placed in memory addresses 34754 and 34755.

1040 Line 1040 finds the low address of string memory (address where last string value was stored). This value changes each time a string is placed into memory. Since the instruction is executed after the FOR/NEXT loop, the address points to the last string placed into memory (the '20').

To find the starting location of string memory, use the PEEK instruction along with memory locations 112 and 111.

Remember, the APPLE stores numbers in a format that appears backward to us. In order to convert the hexadecimal number to base 10, the high address (most significant digit) is multiplied by 256 and added to the value in the low address (least significant digit).

1050   The high end of string memory starts 1 byte below the HIMEM (HIgh MEMory) area of the machine. The high memory address varies with the size of the computer and the type of programs being run, but the value can be retrieved by PEEKing into memory locations 115 and 116.

In order to convert the hexadecimal number to base 10, the most significant digit is multiplied by 256 and added to the least significant digit. Then 1 is subtracted from the value in order to show the address of the last (highest) byte of string storage.

1060–1080   Lines 1060 through 1080 display the contents of each memory location starting at the lowest memory location and working upward to the highest memory location. The PEEK instruction is used to retrieve the binary value in each memory location, while the CHR$ function is used to convert the binary number to printable character format.

1090   Only the last two characters of the approximately 30 memory locations used reflect the current value of X1$. The FRE instruction condenses string memory by moving the active string values into high memory, changing the pointers associated with each string, and finally changing the address in location 112 and 111 to reflect the new start of string memory.

1100   Line 1100 is included in the program to point out how the APPLE works with constants and equal string values. If you study the program and screen closely, you will see that even though X1$ is set equal to the string CONSTANT, the value does not appear in the printout of string memory. To conserve memory space, the address associated with X1$ is set equal to the address of the constant within the Applesoft program.

```
1100 X1$ = "CONSTANT" : Y1$ = X1$ : Z1$ = X1$
              ↑
X1$ pointer   |
Y1$ pointer   |
Z1$ pointer   |
```

The last part of the line is included to illustrate what happens whenever a string variable is set equal to another variable. When a string is set equal to another variable, only the string's pointer is changed. The value is not duplicated in string memory. Assuming that CONSTANT starts in memory location 2000, all three variables will point to memory location 2000 after execution of line 1100.

Variable	Address in Pointer
X1$	2000
Y1$	2000
Z1$	2000

So, whenever you assign a string name to a constant or assign several string names to the same value, no additional memory is used.

1110–1140 Lines 1110 through 1140 show the content of memory after the FRE instruction has been used. At the time the FRE instruction was executed, X1$ was equal to 20. Since the 20 was the only active string value in memory, it was moved to the highest string address. After condensing memory, the machine reset the address in locations 112 and 111 to reflect the starting address of string memory.

```
OLD LOW = 34754 HIGH = 34784
201918171615141312111 0987654420
                                 ↑
NEW LOW = 34783——————————
```

The 4 preceding the 2 is not a typing mistake. If you play around with the FRE instruction, you will find that the character preceding the next available string address is always duplicated.

```
OLD LOW = 34754 HIGH = 34784
201918171615141312111 0987654420
                                ↑
Next available string
address should have
remained a 3————————————
but changed to character in preceding byte
(only the APPLE knows why)
```

Exercise 2:

The second example shows how to use the FREE MEMORY SUBROUTINE and emphasizes once more how string memory is allocated.

The program creates an endless loop consisting of two operations. The first part of the loop assigns a string value to a variable. The second part of the loop executes the FREE MEMORY SUBROUTINE to see if there is still room to continue the program. If there is plenty of memory available, the loop continues. If the start of string storage falls below 16384 (end of high resolution page 1), then the FRE MEMORY SUBROUTINE displays a message to the operator and executes the FRE instruction.

Make sure to let the program keep running until it pauses and displays a message. For the system I am using, the loop is executed 483 times. After the program frees memory and you respond by pressing the space bar, the program starts the endless loop again. To cancel the program, press CONTROL-C.

Key in and run the following program, or run the program by entering

RUN FRE SAMPLE2.

```
1000 REM FRE SAMPLE2
1010 REM ----------------------
1020 HOME
1030 FILLER$ = "...................."
1040 ADDRESS = PEEK (112) * 256 + (111)
1050 VTAB 10: HTAB 10
1060 PRINT "FROM "ADDRESS" TO "ADDRESS + 20"    "
1070 VTAB 11: HTAB 10
1080 PRINT "--------------------"
1090 VTAB 12: HTAB 10
1100 STRING$ = RIGHT$ (FILLER$ + STR$ (NUMBER),20)
1110 PRINT STRING$
1120 GOSUB 1160: REM CHECK AMOUNT OF MEMORY LEFT
1130 NUMBER = NUMBER + 1
1140 GOTO 1040
1150 REM ----------------------
1160 REM FREE MEMORY ROUTINE
1170 STARTING = PEEK (112) * 256 + PEEK (111): IF STARTING >
16384 THEN 1240
1180 VTAB 23: HTAB 1: INVERSE
1190 PRINT " FREEING MEMORY - PLEASE WAIT" TAB( 38)" "
1200 STARTING = FRE (0)
1210 PRINT " DONE - PRESS SPACE BAR TO CONTINUE   ";: NORMAL
1220 GET X1$: IF X1$ < > " " THEN 1220
1230 VTAB 23: HTAB 1: PRINT TAB( 39)" ": PRINT TAB( 39)" ";
1240 RETURN
1250 REM ----------------------
```

Each time the variable STRING$ is assigned a new value, the memory addresses used are displayed along with the string value. The program produces a screen like the following.

```
FROM 34785 TO 34805
--------------------
...................0
```

Press CONTROL-S to stop the program periodically so you can see the memory addresses being displayed. Start the program back up by pressing any key.

You should use the FREE MEMORY SUBROUTINE in any program which does a large amount of string processing. The subroutine has the following advantages:

1. It does not free memory until the space is needed.
2. While it is freeing memory, it lets the operator know what is going on.

To use the subroutine, simply include it in your program and use a GOSUB to branch to the first line.

Example 3:

The last FRE example shows how slow the machine is when freeing memory if large dimension entries are used.

Look over the following code and then run the program to get an idea of the time difference between freeing memory when no table entries are used (less than 1 second), when 100 table entries are used (around 3 seconds), and when 500 table entries are used (around 20 seconds).

```
1000 REM FRE SAMPLE3
1010 REM -----------------------
1020 DIM TABLE$(500)
1030 HOME
1040 N = 0: GOSUB 1090
1050 N = 100: GOSUB 1200: GOSUB 1090
1060 N = 500: GOSUB 1200: GOSUB 1090
1070 END
1080 REM -----------------------
1090 REM DISPLAY MESSAGE
1100 PRINT "FREE WITH "N" TABLE ENTRIES"
1110 PRINT
1120 PRINT "PRESS ANY KEY TO START FRE OPERATION";
1130 GET X1$
1140 N = FRE (0)
```

```
1150 PRINT : PRINT
1160 PRINT "FRE DONE - PRESS ANY KEY TO CONTINUE";
1170 GET X1$
1180 RETURN
1190 REM ----------------------
1200 REM LOAD ROUTINE
1210 HOME
1220 PRINT "LOADING "N" ENTRIES"
1230 PRINT
1240 FOR M = 1 TO N
1250 TABLE$(M) = STR$(N)
1260 NEXT
1270 RETURN
1280 REM ----------------------
```

For two dimensional entries TABLE$(100,100), the FRE operation can take several minutes. Some examples I have worked with take over 5 minutes to condense memory. That is why it is important to let the operator know what is going on and approximately how long it will take.

32.

Instructions Relating to Machine Language Routines

Four instructions are described in this section: CALL, USR(variable), LOMEM, and HIMEM. The instructions are normally used when working with either machine language subroutines or high-resolution shape tables. Since this book does not cover either of these two topics, only a brief description of the four instructions is given.

Check with the APPLE programming reference manual for further details about how to use the instructions and the memory allocation used by the computer.

The CALL Instruction

Instruction CALL address

The CALL instruction is used to execute a machine language subroutine. The address following the keyword CALL indicates the starting location of the machine subroutine.

There are a number of prewritten machine language subroutines which are available to the Applesoft user. If you intend to use your Applesoft programs on other than an APPLE II computer, do not get into the habit of using the machine language subroutines. The machine language subroutines make your program much more computer dependent than it already is.

Descriptions of the various machine language subroutines are provided in various locations of the APPLE II manuals. Some of the more useful routines are shown below with their calling addresses.

In the following descriptions, the term *text window* is used. The text window means the same as the full viewing screen unless you have changed the text window by poking new values into memory locations 32, 33, 34, or 35. If you have modified the screen settings, the following instructions relate to the smaller screen.

1000 CALL −868 The instruction clears from the current position of the cursor to the end of the line.

1000 CALL −912 The instruction causes data currently displayed in the text window to scroll up one line.

1000 CALL −922 The instruction issues a line feed, thereby causing the cursor to move one line down (cursor remains in the same column but one line down).

1000 CALL −926 The instruction causes a line feed and repositions the cursor to the leftmost position of the next line.

1000 CALL −936 The instruction clears the text window and repositions the cursor to the HOME position. The instruction is the same as the HOME instruction. Since the HOME instruction is easier to read than the CALL instruction, you should use the HOME instruction.

1000 CALL −958 The instruction clears the text window from the current cursor position to the bottom right character of the text window. The clearing operation clears to a dark background even if the computer is in INVERSE or FLASH mode.

1000 CALL −998 The instruction causes the cursor to move up one line without changing the horizontal position.

1000 CALL − 1008 This causes the cursor to back up one position. It is the same as the instruction PRINT CHR$(08)

1000 CALL -1052 The instruction beeps the speaker for 1/10 of a second. When it is used with a FOR/NEXT loop and a multiple of 10, you can set the number of seconds you want the speaker to beep.

The USR(variable) Instruction

Instruction USR(variable)

The USR (USeR subroutine) instruction is much like the CALL instruction but allows the Applesoft program to pass an argument (number) to the user written machine langauge subroutine. No further explanation will be given. If you are advanced enough to use this instruction, you don't need an explanation.

The **LOMEM** Instruction

Instruction   LOMEM: variable or expression

The low memory instruction is used to reset the lowest memory location in RAM (Random Access Memory) which will be available to the Applesoft program.

The computer uses various parts of memory for different purposes. The computer automatically protects the lower area of the storage by setting the value of low memory when the computer is started. The computer assumes memory between the low memory location and the high memory location is available for it to use as needed. If you are using shape tables for high-resolution graphics or if you are using a machine language subroutine, the operating system does not keep track of these items for you. You must locate them in either low memory or high memory and protect them from the operating system by resetting the value of low or high memory.

If you want to see the address for low memory for your computer, type in the following instructions:

```
NEW
PRINT "LOMEM = "; PEEK (106) * 256 + PEEK (105)
```

The instruction NEW destroys any program and resets low memory down to the original value designated by the system.

The address of low memory is in storage locations 105 and 106. Location 106 contains the most significant digits of the address, and location 105 contains the least significant digits. To convert the hexadecimal number to base 10, the computer multiplies the first digit by 256 and adds this to the second.

The **HIMEM** Instruction

Instruction   HIMEM: variable or expression

The high memory instruction is used to reset the highest memory location in RAM which will be available to the Applesoft program.

The upper area of the computer is used for storing the DOS control program and for I/O buffers. After DOS is loaded, it resets high memory in order to protect itself.

If you want to see the address of high memory for your computer, type in the following instructions:

```
NEW
PRINT "HIMEM = "; PEEK (116) * 256 + PEEK (115)
```

33. Other Applesoft Instructions

This section gives a brief description of some of the less used Applesoft instructions, high-resolution graphics instructions, and low-resolution graphic instructions. For a detailed description see the related APPLE manuals.

The DEF FN Instruction

Instruction   DEF FN function name (real variable) = arithmetic expression

Example   Definition:
1100 DEF FN MONTHLYINTEREST (AMT) = RATE * AMT / 12
Usage:
2000 MONTHLYINTEREST = FD MONTHLYINTEREST(AMT)

Purpose   The DEFine FuNction instruction allows the programmer to associate a symbolic name with an arithmetic formula. After the function is defined, the name can be used thoughout the program in place of the formula without having to recode the equation.

Rules for Use
1. The function instruction cannot be used to define string functions or integer functions.
2. The definition of the function may be only one statement long (one equation).
3. The DEF FN instruction must be executed prior to any use of the FN instruction.
4. As with all Applesoft names, only the first two characters of the function name are recognized and must be unique.
5. Functions may be redefined during execution of the program.

1100 DEF FN INTEREST (W) = INTERESTRATE * W

....

1200 YEARLYINTEREST = FN INTEREST (AMT)

....

2100 DEF FN INTEREST (W) = INTERESTRATE * W / 12

....

2200 MONTHLYINTEREST = FN INTEREST (AMT)

....

6. The function name may be used in any instruction where an arithmetic expression is acceptable. Thus

DEF FN AA (X) = X * 12 + (X − 3)
BB = FN AA(4)

results in the equation

BB = 4 * 12 + (4 − 3)
   = 49

and

CC = FN AA(2) * FN AA(3)

results in the equation

CC = (2 * 12 + (2 − 3)) * (3 * 12 + (3 − 3))
   = (23) * (36) = 828

The DEF FN instruction should be coded whenever a formula is repeatedly used thoughout a program. The instruction ensures that the formula is repeated correctly with each use and makes the program easier to code and modify.

The CLEAR Instruction

The CLEAR instruction is used to reset all variables, arrays, and strings to zero or null values. Pointers and stacks related to the FOR/NEXT and GOSUB instructions are also reset. The instruction may be used at the end of a program to reset all values prior to branching back to the first line to reexecute the program.

Example   1000 REMFIRST LINE OF PROGRAM

....

5000 CLEAR
5010 GOTO 1000
5020 REM CLEAR AND GOTO HAVE THE SAME EFFECT AS
5030 REM ENTERING THE RUN COMMAND.

The TEXT Instruction

The TEXT instruction is used to reset the screen from either low-resolution graphics mode or high-resolution graphics mode. The instruction sets the text window to the full-screen format and positions the cursor on the bottom line (line 24). The TEXT instruction can be used to reset the text window after any of the addresses 32, 33, 34, or 35 have been POKEd with new values.

The POS(0) Instruction

H1 = POS(0)

The POSition instruction returns a number from 0 to 39 indicating the current horizontal position of the cursor. The value within parentheses is required and must be interpretable by Applesoft even though it does not change the value returned.

The FP Instruction

FP is used in immediate execution mode to place the APPLE into Applesoft language mode after the machine has been executing either an Integer BASIC or machine language program. The use of the instruction varies depending on the options purchased with the APPLE computer. The APPLE II has Integer BASIC residing in

ROM (Read Only Memory). The APPLE II + and the APPLE IIe has Applesoft BASIC residing in ROM. Although all three machines can run either language the version of BASIC which does not reside in ROM must be loaded from a diskette into program memory (RAM) before use. For specific usage see the user manual for your APPLE.

The PR# Instruction

The PR# instruction is followed by a number from 0 to 7. The PR# instruction specifies that all further PRINT instruction output is to be directed to the slot number indicated. The statement PR#0 means the output will be directed to the standard data screen. Other than using PR#0, you must know what peripheral cards are in each slot prior to using the instruction. If you use the instruction with a slot number which does not contain a device, the computer locks up.

PR#0   Standard data screen connected to APPLE video jack
PR#1   Standard slot for printer interface card
PR#2-5 User optional interface cards
PR#6   Standard slot for disk drive control card
PR#7   User optional interface card

The IN# Instruction

The IN# instruction is followed by a number from 0 to 7. The IN# instruction specifies that all further INPUT instruction will read data from the specified slot. IN#0 indicates all further data are to be read from the keyboard. IN#6 indicates that all further data are to be read from the device located in slot 6.

Low-Resolution Graphics Instructions

GR   This instruction sets the computer to low-resolution GRaphics mode. Low-resolution graphics redefines the first 20 lines of the screen into a matrix of 40 by 40 dots. The last four lines of the screen remain in text mode and act as the text window. Reset the computer to normal mode by using the TEXT command.

Poking address -16302 converts the screen to full low-resolution graphics consisting of a 40 by 48 dot matrix.

POKE $-16302,0$

COLOR = number   Where number ranges from 0 to 15. This sets the color to be used in displaying low-resolution points. Sixteen colors are available in low-resolution graphics:

0 = Black	5 = Gray	10 = Gray (see 5)
1 = Magenta	6 = Medium blue	11 = Pink
2 = Dark blue	7 = Light blue	12 = Green
3 = Purple	8 = Brown	13 = Yellow
4 = Dark green	9 = Orange	14 = Aqua
		15 = White

PLOT x,y   The PLOT instruction is used to place a dot at a specific coordinate of position x,y. The value of x may vary from 0 to 39, while the value of y may vary from 0 to 47.

HLIN x,y,z   The HLIN (Horizontal LINe) instruction is used to draw a line starting with the point x,z and ending with the point y,z. The third parameter (z) indicates the horizontal line of the matrix, while the values of x and y indicate the starting and ending column positions. The value of x and y may range from 0 to 39.

VLIN x,y,z   The VLINe (Vertical LINe) instruction is used to draw a line starting with the point x,z and ending with the point y,z. The third parameter (z) indicates the vertical column of the matrix, while the values of x and y indicate the starting and ending line positions. The value of x and y may range from 0 to 47.

SCRN (x,y)   The SCReeN command is used to find out the color of a specific spot on the screen. The values of x and y indicate the coordinates of the position on the screen which is to be tested. The value returned ranges from 0 to 15, matching the color assignments.

High-Resolution Graphics Instructions

HGR This instruction sets the computer to high-resolution GRaphics mode. High-resolution graphics redefines the first 20 lines of the screen into a matrix of 280 by 160 dots. The last four lines of the screen remain in text mode and act as the text window. Reset the computer to normal mode by using the TEXT command.

Poking address −16302 converts the screen to full high-resolution graphics consisting of a 280 by 192 dot matrix.

POKE −16302,0

HGR2 High-resolution graphics uses two pages in memory. Using HGR2 causes the contents of the second page located in memory locations 16K to 24K to be displayed.

HCOLOR This instruction sets the color to be used in displaying high-resolution points. Eight colors are available in high-resolution graphics.

0 = Black1	3 = White1	6 = Depends on TV
1 = Green	4 = Black2	7 = White2
2 = Blue	5 = Depends on TV	

The colors of black1, black2, white1, and white2 depend on how the colors of the two corresponding dots within the matrix are set.

HPLOT HPLOT x,y
HPLOT TO x,y
HPLOT a,b TO x,y

The HPLOT instruction has three formats. The first format plots a single dot at the coordinates of x and y. The second option draws a line starting at the last position plotted and continuing to the coordinates of x and y. The third option plots a line starting at coordinates (a,b) and continuing to coordinates (x,y).

Shape Tables Shape tables are drawings made up of binary patterns. The shapes are used in high-resolution graphics and can be manipulated by five commands. For a detailed explanation of how to build and use shape tables, see the APPLE manuals.

The five instructions used with shape tables are DRAW, XDRAW, ROT (rotate),

SCALE, and SHLOAD. DRAW is used to place a shape on the high-resolution screen. XDRAW is normally used to erase the shape. ROTate is used to cause movement of the shape. SCALE is used to enlarge or reduce the size of the drawing. SHLOAD is used to load a shape table from cassette tape.

Game Controls

PDL Function The PaDdLe function returns a numeric value ranging from 0 to 255 indicating the setting of one of the game paddles.

X = PDL (0) Returns the value for paddle 0.
Y = PDL (1) Returns the value for paddle 1.

Magnetic Tape

RECALL This instruction is used to recall an array from cassette tape.

STORE This instruction is used to store an array on cassette tape.

Section II Creating and Using Disk Files

1. Information Storage on Disks

Disk Terms and Data Organization

1. Tracks (35 per disk)
2. Sectors (16 per track with 256 bytes per sector)
3. Directory and VTOC (Volume Table Of Contents)
4. Diskette Directory
5. Files

Track A track is one complete circle consisting of 16 sectors.

Sector A sector is a single recording strip consisting of 256 characters.

Catalog (Diskette Directory) The catalog consists of information about the disk and about each file stored on the disk. The directory contains an entry for all 560 sectors indicating whether the sector is being used (indicated by a 1 bit) or not used (indicated by a 0 bit). The directory contains four entries for each file on the disk:

1. The name of the file
2. The type of file (Text, Applesoft BASIC, Integer BASIC, Binary)
3. The number of sectors the file occupies
4. The address of the file's track/sector list. The track/sector list consists of information on each track and sector used by the file.

VTOC The VTOC is a small part of the directory and, among other things, provides DOS with information on which sectors of the disk are currently in use.

For each file on the disk, the directory contains the address of the related track/sector list. The track/sector list in turn gives the address of each sector which contains data related to the file.

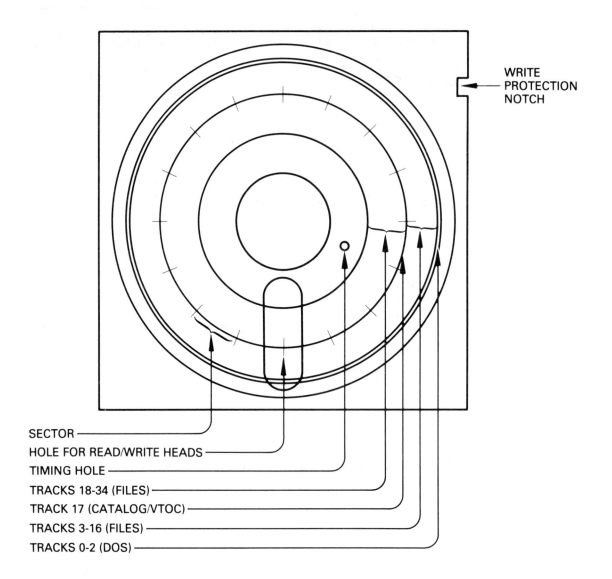

WRITE PROTECTION NOTCH

SECTOR
HOLE FOR READ/WRITE HEADS
TIMING HOLE
TRACKS 18-34 (FILES)
TRACK 17 (CATALOG/VTOC)
TRACKS 3-16 (FILES)
TRACKS 0-2 (DOS)

The file name in the directory points to the track/sector list.
The track/sector list points to the sectors used by the file.
The sectors contain the data making up the file.

So each file you define actually consists of two parts: the track/sector list and the actual data. APPLE designed the file structure in this manner so that the files can be expanded and all sectors of the disk may be used.

To help you see how the disk operates, let's follow through what occurs when information is written to a sequential disk file. For each instruction, two explanations are given: what happens when an existing file is opened and written to, and what happens when a new file is opened and written to.

The sequence varies for reading records and working with random files, but the basic ideas are the same. The following is a general description of what occurs and is not intended to reflect all the steps or the exact sequence of steps which actually occur when writing to a sequential file.

```
1000 D$ = CHR$(4)
1010 PRINT D$;"OPEN FILE NAME"
1020 PRINT D$;"WRITE FILE NAME"
1030 PRINT RECNAME$
1040 PRINT D$;"CLOSE FILE NAME"
1050 END
```

1000–1010   When DOS encounters the OPEN instruction, it checks the disk directory (also called catalog) for a matching file name.

1. If the file name currently exists, DOS extracts the location of the track/sector list from the directory and reuses the area already assigned to the file.
2. If the file does not exist, DOS enters the file name into the directory (catalog) and searches the VTOC to find an available sector. When an available sector is found, it is used to start a track/sector list for the file.

1020   The first time the WRITE instruction is encountered, the file buffer is cleared to binary zeros, and the sector pointers are cleared. The buffer and pointers are cleared even if the file previously existed and had sectors assigned (the old copy is lost).

There is one exception to this process. If the file exists and is LOCKed, any attempt to write on the file causes an error message to be displayed and the program to be canceled.

1. If the file does not exist, DOS clears the buffer and locates an available sector on the disk.
2. For all executions of the WRITE instruction other than the first, DOS simply directs any additional PRINT operations to send the data to the output buffer related to the specified file name.
3. Any data on an existing UNLOCKed file is now lost.

   Note: When a file is recreated, DOS does not update the VTOC to free sectors. When recreating new files with the same file name, it is best to delete the old file in order to free the space and then create a new file with a new track/sector list.

1030   When the PRINT instruction is executed, the data is placed in the output buffer. If all the data fits into the buffer, program execution continues to the next instruction. If the buffer becomes full during the data transfer operation, that is, if 256 characters have been sent to the buffer, then the following steps take place:

1. The filled buffer is written to the allocated disk sector as specified in the file's track/sector list.
2. A new unused sector is located in the VTOC and flagged as being in use (sector bit set to 1).
3. The address of the new sector is placed in the file's track/sector list.
4. The buffer is cleared, and any remaining data which did not fit during the PRINT operation is placed at the start of the buffer.

1040 When the CLOSE instruction is encountered, DOS writes out any remaining data which exists in the output buffer and adds an EOF (End-Of-File) marker. The disk directory is then updated to indicate the number of sectors assigned to the file.

A Commonly Asked Question

If the outer tracks of the disk are larger than the inner tracks, why do they hold the same amount of data?

The answer is that since the disk rotates at a constant speed and the computer writes at a constant speed, the bits recorded in the inner tracks are closer together than the bits recorded on the outer tracks.

```
Outer track:   1    0    1    1    0    1    1    0
Middle track:  1  0  1  1  0  1  1  0
Inner track:     10110110
```

The outer tracks are not recorded to their maximum density because of the difficulty in developing the necessary control logic and timing hardware to fully utilize all the recording surface.

2.

Introduction to DOS Disk Instructions

If you purchased the program diskette along with the book, be sure to copy the sample disk programs to a new disk before attempting to run them. The program disk does not have sufficient free space for additional files.

Use the APPLE's FID (FIle Developer) program to copy the programs; or, if you do not have access to the FID program, you may transfer each program by using the LOAD and SAVE commands:

LOAD program name,Dnumber
SAVE program name,Dnumber

Remember to INITialize any new disk before trying to use it.
For this chapter, copy the following programs to another disk:

```
SAMPLE SEQUENTIAL OPEN PROG
SAMPLE RANDOM OPEN PROG
SAMPLE APPEND PROG
SAMPLE SEQUENTIAL WRITE PROG
SAMPLE RANDOM WRITE PROG
SAMPLE SEQUENTIAL READ PROG
SAMPLE RANDOM READ PROG
```

If you do not have the program disk and are planning to key in the example programs, you should start off with a new disk. The programs presented in the last half of the book use the majority of space on one diskette.

There are a few specialized instructions which are used when working with disk files. Some of these instructions are used in every program which work with disk files, while others are only used for special situations. The more commonly used instructions are OPEN, READ, WRITE, and CLOSE. The instructions MON and NOMON are used when debugging programs which work with disk files. The APPEND instruction is used to add information to the end of a sequential file.

Since the instructions are so closely related, it is difficult to write an example which does not use several of the instructions at the same time. Before reading the detailed explanation of each instruction, look over the general descriptions below to get an idea how each instruction is used.

MON

The MONitor instruction is used to turn ON a debugging option of DOS in which any I/O operations to the disk are displayed on the screen. The MONitor instruction causes the computer to display on the screen any data read from the disk, data written to the disk, or any disk instruction being executed.

NOMON

The NOMONitor instruction is used to turn OFF the debugging feature of DOS in which information is displayed on the screen during disk I/O operations.

OPEN

The OPEN instruction must be executed once prior to any READ or WRITE operations using the disk.

APPEND

This is a method of opening an existing sequential file that allows records to be added to the end of the file. When a sequential file is opened with the APPEND instruction, DOS is set up so that any new records are written starting at the end of the existing file.

The APPEND instruction is ONLY used in conjunction with the WRITE instruction to add records to the end of an existing SEQUENTIAL file.

WRITE

This is a preparatory DOS instruction used prior to PRINTing information on the disk. The instruction is used in conjunction with the Applesoft PRINT instruction.

READ

This is a preparatory DOS instruction used prior to INPUTing information from the disk. It is used in conjunction with the Applesoft INPUT instruction.

CLOSE

The CLOSE instruction must be executed once after all processing for a file has been completed.

ONERR

This is an Applesoft instruction used to override the normal default option of the APPLE. When an error is encountered by the computer, the normal process is to cancel the program and display an error message. When the ONERR instruction is used, the program intercepts the error process and handles the error without canceling the program. The ONERR instruction is used by some programmers when working with sequential files to test for an EOF (End-Of-File) condition.

The following two instructions are infrequently used, but you should be familiar with them.

VERIFY

This is an instruction used to check to see if data have been written correctly on the disk or to see if a file is damaged.

MAXFILES

This is an instruction used to allocate additional buffer space when more than three files are going to be open at the same time in one program.

Other DOS commands related to disk operations which you should already know how to use in either immediate execution mode or program execution mode include the LOCK, UNLOCK, DELETE, and RENAME commands.

These commands were covered in detail in the first part of the book and are not covered in this part.

LOCK

This locks the file so it cannot be deleted or written over.

UNLOCK

This unlocks the file so it may be deleted or renamed, or records may be written to the file.

DELETE

This removes the file name (label) from the catalog.

RENAME

This is used to change the name of an existing file.

The **MON/NOMON** Disk Instructions

Instruction   MON I,C,O
NOMON I,C,O

Where

I   indicates to display all data being read from the disk. Any data read from the disk is displayed on the screen exactly as read.

C   indicates to display all DOS instructions which are executed. Although any DOS instruction used by the program is displayed, we are only concerned with the following instructions: READ, WRITE, OPEN, CLOSE, APPEND, MON, NOMON, LOCK, UNLOCK, and DELETE.

O   indicates to display all output disk operations. Any data written to the disk is displayed on the screen exactly as written.

Example   Immediate Execution Mode:

MON I,C,O	Turns on all the DOS monitor functions
NOMON I,C,O	Turns off all the DOS monitor functions
MON I,O	Turns on only the DOS input and output monitor functions

Program Execution Mode:

```
1000 PRINT D$;"MON I,C,O"
2000 PRINT D$;"NOMON I,C,O"
where D$ = CHR$(4)
```

Purpose   The purpose of the MON/NOMON instruction is to aid the programmer in debugging programs which use the disk. By using the instruction, the programmer can see all the operations and data which are directed toward the disk.

Rules for Use   1.   Once the MON (monitor) instruction is executed, it stays in effect until either the NOMON instruction is executed or the machine is reset by turning it off and back on, pressing CONTROL-RESET, or entering PR#6 and pressing RETURN.

2. The parameters I,C,O may occur in any sequence or combination.
3. At least one parameter must be used. If more than one is used, each parameter must be separated by a comma.

Illustration of the Rules

Immediate Execution Mode

MON I	Displays only disk input operations
MON C	Displays only disk instructions
MON O	Displays only disk print operations
MON I,C,O	Turns on all monitoring operations; this is the format you should normally use
NOMON I,C,O	Turns off all monitoring operations; this is the format you should normally use

Program Execution Mode: See any of the sample disk programs used to describe the OPEN, APPEND, WRITE, or READ instructions.

The OPEN Instruction

Instruction

Sequential Files
Fixed Format: PRINT D$;"OPEN file name,Dnumber"
or Variable Format: PRINT D$;"OPEN";variable$;",D";variable

Random Files
Fixed Format: PRINT D$;"OPEN file name,Lnumber,Dnumber"
or Variable Format: PRINT D$;"OPEN";variable$;",L";
                                    variable;",D";variable

Although slot number, drive number, and volume number may be used, only the drive number is illustrated in the formats.

Example

Sequential Files
Fixed Format: PRINT D$;"OPEN SEQ PAYROLL FILE,D1"
or Variable Format: PRINT D$;"OPEN";FILEID$;",D";FDRIVE

where FILEID$ = the label of the file to be opened.
      FDRIVE = a value of 1 or 2 indicating the drive on which the file is located.

Random Files
Fixed Format: PRINT D$;"OPEN RANDOM PAYROLL FILE,L10,D2"
or Variable Format: PRINT D$;"OPEN";FILEID$;",L";RECLEGTH;",D";
                       FDRIVE

where FILEID$ = the label of the file to be opened.
      RECLEGTH = the length of the records in the file.
      FDRIVE   = a value of 1 or 2 indicating the drive on which the file is
                  located.

Purpose   The OPEN instruction causes DOS to search the disk catalog to see if there is a matching file name. If a matching label is found, information about the file is extracted from the catalog. If no matching label is found, then a new entry is placed in the catalog.

Rules for Use
1. The OPEN instruction must be executed prior to any I/O operation which uses the file.
2. If the file name following the keyword OPEN does not currently exist on the disk, a label is added to the catalog and an area on the disk is assigned to the file.
3. For sequential files the OPEN instruction indicates to start with the first record of the file. For sequential files DOS keeps track of the location of the next record to be read or the location where the next record is to be written. If you open an *existing* sequential file and then use a WRITE instruction, *all existing* data on the file will be lost.
4. When you open a random file, the ,L parameter of the OPEN instruction must be included and must be followed by a whole number indicating the length of the record. For a random file all records must be the same length, or you must specify the length of the longest record. When computing the length of a record, remember to include the length of each variable making up the record, plus one additional character for the EOR (End-Of-Record) marker.

   For random files the maximum record length within the file must be included as part of the OPEN instruction. DOS must know the length of the records on the file in order to compute the location of an individual record. Exactly how DOS calculates the relative address of each record will not be shown here, but for random files the machine must know both the length of the records on the file and the record number which is to be read. The record number MUST be provided by the READ or WRITE instruction prior to the actual I/O operation.

   A common error made by beginning programmers is to incorrectly specify the record length in the OPEN instruction. This error becomes obvious when you attempt to read the random file. The computer beeps and prints a backward slash (\). No attempt will be made here to explain the error in detail. Just be aware that if the computer beeps and prints a backward slash, the records written on the file are longer than the length specified in the OPEN instruction.
5. As with all file processing, it is strongly suggested that you have a backup copy

of the file and/or that the current copy of the file is LOCKed to protect it from being accidentally written over.

6. The drive number is optional unless the file to be opened is located on a drive other than the last drive referenced. If the file is not located on the last drive referenced, then the drive number must be used.

PRINT D$;"OPEN file name,D1"

or

PRINT D$;"OPEN file name,D2"

7. When commas are shown in the example formats, the commas must be within quotes (",L" and ",D").

Illustration of the Rules (Sequential Files)
The following program creates a sequential file label on a specific disk drive. All the program does is OPEN a file and CLOSE the file. When you open and close the file, a label is placed in the disk catalog.

```
1000 REM SAMPLE SEQUENTIAL OPEN PROG
1010 TEXT : NORMAL : HOME : SPEED= 255
1020 D$ = CHR$ (4)
1030 FILEID$ = "SEQUENTIAL FILE NAME"
1040 D1DRIVE = 1
1050 PRINT D$;"MON I,O,C"
1060 PRINT D$;"OPEN ";FILEID$;",D";D1DRIVE
1070 REM insert instructions to process data
1080 PRINT D$;"CLOSE ";FILEID$
1090 PRINT D$;"NOMON I,O,C"
```

1010 At the start of each program you should include the instructions to ensure that the computer is operating in the mode you want. This instruction specifies to set the computer in NORMAL TEXT mode, clear the screen, and set the speed to the maximum.

1020 D$ = CHR$(4)

All DOS instruction must be preceded by a CONTROL-D symbol.

D$ is the standardized name used to represent a CONTROL-D symbol. Any program which uses disk files should initialize the variable D$ equal to the character value 4 (same as pressing CONTROL-D).

The D$ variable is used in the PRINT instruction to precede every DOS command. Whenever the computer encounters the CONTROL-D value, it knows that the information following the character is a disk instruction. The CONTROL-D value is also used to indicate termination of a disk operation.

1030   FILEID$ = "SEQUENTIAL FILE NAME"

Although some of the sample programs in this book do not use the variable format of the DOS instructions, you should make it a standard practice to always use variable file names. You will find programming easier if you set a variable name equal to the file label at the start of your program and then use that variable name in all the DOS instructions. By using the variable format you

1.   Make sure that the file label is spelled the same in all the DOS instructions.
2.   Save having to type a long label in each instruction.
3.   Make your program easier to modify. All occurances of the file label can be changed by simply changing the instruction which defines the name (FILEID$ = "*new label*").

1040   A variable may also be used for the drive number. For the example programs, D1DRIVE is be set equal to 1 for drive 1 and D2DRIVE is set equal to 2 for drive 2.

1050   PRINT D$;"MON I,O,C"

This turns on the debugging tool for monitoring disk input, output, and command operations.
        If you run the program, the screen will clear, and the following lines will be printed:

```
OPEN SEQUENTIAL FILE NAME,D1
CLOSE SEQUENTIAL FILE NAME
NOMON I,O,C
```

1060   PRINT D$;"OPEN ";FILEID$;",D";D1DRIVE

Creates a label called SEQUENTIAL FILE NAME on disk drive 1 unless the label already exists.This instruction could have been written in a fixed format by using the values in each variable:

1060 PRINT D$;"OPEN SEQUENTIAL FILE NAME,D1"

1080   PRINT D$;"CLOSE ";FILEID$

For output files or in this case newly created files, the CLOSE instruction causes any data which is in the write buffer to be written onto the disk and an EOF marker to be written following the last record. In this case no records were written, so only an EOF marker is written on the file. This instruction could have been written in a fixed format by using the values in each variable:

1080 PRINT D$;"CLOSE SEQUENTIAL FILENAME,D1"

1090   PRINT D$;"NOMON I,O,C"

The monitor functions are turned off by the **NOMON** instruction. You should always make it a practice to see that any function you set on in a program is turned off prior to ending the program.

For the example the monitor instructions on lines 1050 and 1090 are not necessary. These lines are only included to let you see the disk instructions in action.

Illustration of the Rules (Random Files) The following program serves only to show how the **OPEN** instruction is used with a random file.

Although this example creates a random file label, it is suggested that you do not use this format. In the chapter on random file processing, a more complete example will show how to create both the file label and dummy records. Creating dummy records (whatever dummy records are) makes working with random files easier.

```
1000 REM SAMPLE RANDOM OPEN PROG
1010 TEXT : NORMAL : HOME : SPEED= 255
1020 D$ = CHR$ (4)
1030 PRINT D$;"MON I,O,C"
1040 PRINT D$;"OPEN RANDOM FILE NAME,D1,L10"
1050 REM insert processing instructions
1060 PRINT D$;"CLOSE RANDOM FILE NAME"
1070 PRINT D$;"NOMON I,O,C"
```

1030   Line 1030 turns on the debugging tool for monitoring disk input, output, and command operations.

If you run the program the screen will clear, and the following lines will be displayed:

```
OPEN RANDOM FILE NAME,D1,L10
CLOSE RANDOM FILE NAME
NOMON I,O,C
```

1040   PRINT D$;"OPEN RANDOM FILE NAME,D1,L10"

The computer checks the disk in drive 1 to see if the file label **RANDOM FILE NAME** exists. If a matching label is not found, then the file label is created and an area assigned for the file. If a matching label is found, then the file is located and prepared for use.

In addition to providing the file label, the OPEN instruction also indicates to DOS that the records will be 9 bytes (characters) long.

Notice that the length specified in the OPEN *instruction is 1 greater than the number of characters to be written.*

Remember, DOS adds an EOR (End-Of-Record) indicator to each record written.

1060 For output files, or in this case newly created files, the CLOSE instruction causes any data which is in the write buffer to be written to the disk.

The APPEND Instruction

Instruction PRINT D$;"APPEND file name,Dnumber"
or PRINT D$;"APPEND";variable$;",D";variable

Example PRINT D$;"APPEND SEQ ADDRESS FILE,D1"
or PRINT D$;"APPEND";FILEID$;",D";D1DRIVE

Purpose The APPEND instruction is used to open a file and indicate to DOS that any new records written to this file are to be placed following the existing records.

Rules for Use
1. The APPEND instruction is used ONLY with sequential files.
2. The file label MUST EXIST prior to use of the APPEND instruction. The APPEND instruction cannot be used to create the file label.
3. Once the APPEND instruction is executed, records may only be written to the file. Any attempt to read from the file results in an error condition.
4. As with all file processing, it is strongly suggested that you have a backup copy of the file.

Illustration of the Rules The following program first creates a label for the file and then closes the file. The opening and closing of the file is not done in a normal APPEND program. It is done in this example in order to ensure that the file label exists prior to trying to use the APPEND instruction. If the APPEND instruction is used and the file label does not exist, an I/O error occurs. In the program the label is created by lines 1050 and 1060.

After the file label has been created, the program reopens the file using the APPEND instruction. The program then writes 10 records containing two variables each. The first variable consists of the numbers from 1 to 10, and the second variable is a running sum of the numbers from 1 to 10. These records serve no purpose other than to provide a simple file structure for the example. After execution of the program, the file contains the following records:

```
Record   1 = 1,1
         2 = 2,3
         3 = 3,6
         4 = 4,10
         5 = 5,15
         6 = 6,21
         7 = 7,28
         8 = 8,35
         9 = 9,44
        10 = 10,54
```

```
1000 REM SAMPLE APPEND PROG
1010 TEXT : NORMAL : HOME : SPEED= 255
1020 D$ = CHR$(4)
1030 REM -----
1040 PRINT D$;"NOMON C,I,O"
1050 PRINT D$;"OPEN SEQUENTIAL FILE NAME"
1060 PRINT D$;"CLOSE SEQUENTIAL FILE NAME"
1070 REM -----
1080 PRINT D$;"MON C,I,O"
1090 PRINT D$;"APPEND SEQUENTIAL FILE NAME"
1100 FOR N1 = 1 TO 10
1110 PRINT D$;"WRITE SEQUENTIAL FILE NAME"
1120 SUM = SUM + N1
1130 PRINT N1","SUM
1140 PRINT D$: REM TERMINATES DISK OPERATIONS
1150 PRINT N1,SUM
1160 NEXT
1170 PRINT D$;"CLOSE SEQUENTIAL FILE NAME"
1180 PRINT D$;"DELETE SEQUENTIAL FILE NAME"
1190 PRINT D$;"NOMON I,O,C"
1200 END
```

There are three points you should understand from the program.

1. The APPEND instruction is used in place of the OPEN instruction to gain access to a sequential file.
2. Since the data being written to disk is also going to be displayed on the screen, the operations to write to the disk must be started and stopped for each record. That is, a CONTROL-D must precede and follow the data written on the disk.
    If data is to be written both to the disk and to the screen, then the WRITE instruction must be executed prior to every PRINT instruction which is directed

to the disk. Following the PRINT instruction which writes to the disk, a CON-TROL-D character must be printed to terminate the disk operation. If the disk operation is not terminated correctly, then the data which is intended to be printed on the screen is directed to the disk instead.

```
1100 FOR N1 = 1 TO 10
... Start disk output ...
1110 PRINT D$;"WRITE SEQUENTIAL FILE NAME"
1120 SUM = SUM + N1
1130 PRINT N1","SUM


... Terminate disk output ...
1140 PRINT D$: REM TERMINATES DISK OPERATIONS

... Start screen output ...
1150 PRINT N1,SUM
1160 NEXT
```

If your program is only going to write data to the disk, then the WRITE instruction needs to be executed only once, and all PRINT instructions will go to the disk until another D$ character is encountered. The logic for writing continuously to the disk is shown below. Notice that the WRITE instruction is outside the FOR/NEXT loop. The WRITE instruction is executed once, while the PRINT instruction is executed 10 times with all printing directed toward the disk file.

```
1100 PRINT D$;"WRITE SEQUENTIAL FILE NAME"
1110 FOR N1 = 1 TO 10
1120 SUM = SUM + N1
1130 PRINT N1","SUM
1140 NEXT
1150 PRINT D$:REM TERMINATES DISK OPERATIONS
```

3. When you write data to the disk, the comma between variables, if used, must be in quotes. The reason for using the comma and why it must be enclosed within quotes will be explained in greater detail as part of the random disk system. For now just remember the following:

When writing to disk the comma is between quotes.

```
1130 PRINT N1","SUM
```

When writing to screen the comma is NOT between quotes.

```
1150 PRINT N1,SUM
```

1010 The first line to be executed in all the example programs follows the format of line 1010. The computer is set to TEXT mode in case you were using a program which ended while in high resolution graphics. The screen display format is set to NORMAL, and the screen is cleared by using the HOME instruction. The SPEED instruction resets the computer in case the last program ended with the speed set at a slower value.

After all program testing is done, a line should be added to turn off the monitor function in case it was left on by a previous program. The instruction should not be included during the testing phase, since you may want to monitor disk operations.

```
1015 PRINT CHR$(4);"NOMON I,O,C"
```

Remember, MON and NOMON are DOS instructions and must be preceded with a CONTROL-D value.

Since we want to monitor this program, the instruction has been left out.

1030–1060 Lines 1030 through 1060 open and close the file to ensure that the file label exists. If the file label does not exist, you *cannot* use the APPEND instruction.

1070–1090 Line 1080 turns on all the options of the MONitor instruction so you can see all the instructions being executed and the data being written to the disk. Line 1090 opens the file using the APPEND instruction.

1100–1140 Lines 1100 through 1140 represent the first half of a FOR/NEXT loop in which data is written to the disk. In the last half of the FOR/NEXT loop, the same data is displayed on the screen. The WRITE instruction on line 1110 is executed each time through the loop to tell DOS that any PRINT operation which follows should be directed toward the disk. The PRINT instruction on line 1130 causes the values of N1 and SUM to be written on the disk separated by a comma. The comma must be in quotes as shown. When the data is read, the comma serves as a variable separator to tell DOS where variables start and end.

Look over the code again. Lines 1110, 1130, and 1140 all work together to write data on the disk.

```
1100 FOR N1 = 1 TO 10
1110 PRINT D$;"WRITE SEQUENTIAL FILE NAME"
1120 SUM = SUM + N1
1130 PRINT N1","SUM
1140 PRINT D$: REM TERMINATES DISK OPERATIONS
```

Line 1140 prints what I call a *dummy* CONTROL-D. In order to terminate the disk operation, a single CONTROL-D symbol must be printed. If this instruction is not included, the PRINT instruction on line 1150 ends up writing on the disk.

1150–1160   Lines 1150 and 1160 make up the last half of the FOR/NEXT loop. Line 1150 displays on the screen the same data which was written on the disk. The NEXT instruction causes the variable N1 to be incremented by 1 and then tested to see if it is greater than 10. If N1 is 10 or less the loop is repeated.

1170–1200   Lines 1170 through 1200 wrap up the program by closing the file, deleting the file, and turning off the monitor functions. You should look at line 1180, where the DELETE instruction is used in program execution mode to remove the file label from the disk catalog. This is the first time this instruction has been used in this way.

1180 PRINT D$;"DELETE SEQUENTIAL FILE NAME"

This program creates the file label, appends data to the end of the file, and turns around and deletes the file so you do not have to delete it yourself.

If you run the program, the first few lines of the screen will appear as follows:

```
APPEND SEQUENTIAL FILE NAME
WRITE SEQUENTIAL FILE NAME
1,1                     Note: prints on disk

1                  1 Note: prints on screen
WRITE SEQUENTIAL FILE NAME
2,3                     Note: prints on disk

2                  3 Note: prints on screen
WRITE SEQUENTIAL FILE NAME
3,6                     Note: prints on disk

3                  6 Note: prints on screen
```

The MONitor function causes each of the DOS instructions to be displayed (see APPEND and WRITE messages). The MONitor instruction also causes the data which is written to the disk to be displayed exactly as it is written (see notes on screen). Notice that the PRINT instruction used to write to the disk includes the comma.

Once more, when the data is written to the disk, the value of each variable is separated by the comma within quotation marks. When the data is displayed to the screen, the comma is not placed within quotation marks. If the comma is not placed within quotes, it is interpreted by the computer as an automatic tab function, and the computer skips to column 17 before writing the second variable.

If you do not place the comma in quotes when writing to the disk, two errors occur. First, the computer interprets the comma as an automatic tab function and tabs over, generating extra blanks on the disk.

```
Disk                    1           2
Column          12345678901234567890
Record 1        1    <blanks>     1
```

Second, since the comma is not written to the disk, you have problems in trying to read the data. The computer treats the data as one variable since there is no separator (comma). To the computer this is one variable containing a leading 1, followed by 15 blanks, followed by a trailing 1.

Once more, use the APPEND and WRITE instructions to add data to the end of an existing file.

The WRITE Instruction

Instruction Sequential Files
Fixed Format: PRINT D$;"WRITE file name"
or Variable Format: PRINT D$;"WRITE";variable$

Random Files
Fixed Format: PRINT D$;"WRITE file name,Rnumber"
or Variable Format: PRINT D$;"WRITE";variable$;",R";variable

Example Sequential Files
Fixed Format: PRINT D$;"WRITE SEQ PAYROLL FILE"
Variable Format: PRINT D$;"WRITE ";FILEID$
where FILEID$ = the name of the file on which the record is to be written.

Random Files
Fixed Format: PRINT D$;"WRITE RANDOM PAYROLL FILE,R5"
where the fifth record of the file is going to be written.

Very seldom, if ever, do you use a random write instruction with a constant record number. As written, the instruction always writes record 5, and there is no way to vary the record number to write other records.

Variable Format: PRINT D$;"WRITE";FILEID$;",R";RECNUMBER
where FILEID$ = the name of the file on which the record is to be written.
RECNUMBER = the number of the record to be written.

Each record on a random file is accessed using the relative record number. For more information, see the chapter on how to work with random files.

Purpose The WRITE instruction serves as a preparatory command to tell the DOS system that a PRINT instruction follows and the information is to be written on the disk.

Rules for Use
1. For sequential files any number of records may be written after the WRITE instruction is executed.
2. For random files the WRITE instruction must be executed prior to each PRINT instruction and must indicate which record is to be written.
3. For the WRITE instruction the slot, volume, and drive parameters are not used. This information is only specified on the OPEN or APPEND instructions.

Illustration of the Rules (Sequential Files)

The following program writes 10 records containing two variables each. The first variable consists of the numbers from 1 to 10, and the second variable is a running sum of the numeric values from 1 to 10.

This program is not intended to be productive but only to serve as an example.

```
1000 REM SAMPLE SEQUENTIAL WRITE PROG
1010 TEXT : NORMAL : HOME : SPEED= 255
1020 D$ = CHR$ (4)
1030 PRINT D$;"MON C,I,O"
1040 PRINT D$;"OPEN SEQUENTIAL FILE NAME"
1050 FOR N1 = 1 TO 10
1060 PRINT D$;"WRITE SEQUENTIAL FILE NAME"
1070 SUM = SUM + N1
1080 PRINT N1",""SUM
1090 PRINT D$: REM TERMINATES DISK OPERATIONS
1100 PRINT N1,SUM
1110 NEXT
1120 PRINT D$;"CLOSE SEQUENTIAL FILE NAME"
1130 PRINT D$;"NOMON C,I,O"
1140 END
```

1040 The OPEN instruction checks the disk for a matching label. If a matching label is found, the existing file is opened. An OPEN followed by a WRITE command destroys an existing sequential file.

If a matching label is found and the file is LOCKed, any attempt to write on the locked file results in an error message and the termination of the program.

If no matching label exists on the disk, the file label is created.

1060 The WRITE instruction serves as a preparatory command telling DOS that until another DOS command is executed, all further PRINT operations are to be directed to the disk.

1080 Notice that when PRINTing variables on the disk, a comma is used to separate each variable name.

When you write on the disk, the variable separator (comma) must be enclosed within quotation marks.

1090–1100 Normally you want to display the data which is written on the disk either prior to writing the data or after it is written. To break the disk I/O instructions, you must print a dummy D$ (CONTROL-D). The sample program shows the normal sequence of instructions for writing on the disk:

Line 1060 indicates to DOS that a record is to be written on the disk.
Line 1080 prints a record on the disk.
Line 1090 terminates DOS operations.

1120–1140 Before the program is terminated, the file is closed and the monitor functions are turned off.

If you run the program, the first few lines of the screen will appear as follows:

```
OPEN SEQUENTIAL FILE NAME
WRITE SEQUENTIAL FILE NAME
1,1                        Note: prints on disk

1                  1 Note: prints on screen
WRITE SEQUENTIAL FILE NAME
2,3                        Note: prints on disk

2                  3 Note: prints on screen
WRITE SEQUENTIAL FILE NAME
3,6                        Note: prints on disk

3                  6 Note: prints on screen
```

Illustration of the Rules (Random Files) The following program writes 10 records containing two variables each. The first variable consists of the numbers from 1 to 10, and the second variable is a running sum of the numeric values from 1 to 10 (sounds very familiar).

This program is not intended to be productive but is only to serve as an example.

```
1000 REM SAMPLE RANDOM WRITE PROG
1010 TEXT : NORMAL : HOME : SPEED= 255
1020 D$ = CHR$ (4)
1030 PRINT D$;"MON C,I,O"
1040 PRINT D$;"OPEN RANDOM FILE NAME,L6"
1050 FOR N1 = 1 TO 10
1060 PRINT D$;"WRITE RANDOM FILE NAME,R";N1
1070 SUM = SUM + N1
1080 PRINT N1",";"SUM
1090 PRINT D$: REM TERMINATES DISK OPERATIONS
1100 PRINT N1,SUM
1110 NEXT
1120 PRINT D$;"CLOSE RANDOM FILE NAME"
1130 PRINT D$;"NOMON C,I,O"
1140 END
```

1040 PRINT D$;"OPEN RANDOM FILE NAME,L6"

The OPEN instruction checks the disk for a matching label. If a matching label is found, the existing file is opened. If no matching label is found, the label is placed in the disk catalog. DOS keeps track of the length of each record as indicated by the ",L" parameter in the OPEN statement. Each time a record is written, DOS uses the record length and record number to determine where on the file the record is to be placed. For this example the maximum length of each record is 6 bytes.

Maximum size of NUMBER	= 2
Maximum size of SUM	= 2
Number of commas	= 1
End-of-record indicator	= 1
Total	= 6

Once more, in order to open a random file properly, you must indicate the maximum length of the records making up the file. The maximum length is computed by the following formula:

Maximum record length = Maximum size of all variables
+ 1 for each comma used to separate variables
+ 1 for an EOR marker which is automatically written by DOS at the end of each record but which you must count as part of the record length

Total = Length used in the OPEN statement

Once the file has been created, the size of the records cannot be changed.

1060–1100 PRINT D$;"WRITE RANDOM FILE NAME,R";N1

The WRITE instruction serves as a preparatory command telling DOS that a record is to be written on the disk and indicates which record is to be written.

For random files the WRITE instruction *must* be specified prior to each PRINT in order to indicate which record is to be written.

Notice that lines 1060 through 1090 consist of the same basic sequence for writing on the disk.

Line 1060 indicates to DOS that a record is to be written.
Line 1080 PRINTs the record.
Line 1090 terminates DOS operations.

If you run the program, the first few lines of the screen will appear as follows:

```
OPEN RANDOM FILE NAME,L6
WRITE RANDOM FILE NAME,R1
1,1                    Note: prints on disk

1                   1 Note: prints on screen
WRITE RANDOM FILE NAME,R2
2,3

2                   3
WRITE RANDOM FILE NAME,R3
3,6

3                   6
WRITE RANDOM FILE NAME,R4
4,10

4                   10
```

Did you notice that for random files the WRITE instruction indicates which record number is to be written? (See lines 2, 6, 10, and 14.)

The READ Instruction

Instruction Sequential Files
Fixed Format: PRINT D$;"READ file name"
or Variable Format: PRINT D$;"READ";variable$

Random Files
Fixed Format: PRINT D$;"READ file name,Rnumber"
or Variable Format: PRINT D$;"READ";variable$;",R";variable

Example Sequential Files
Fixed Format: PRINT D$;"READ SEQ ADDRESS FILE"
or Variable Format: PRINT D$;"READ";ADDRFILE$
where ADDRFILE$ = the name of the file to be opened.

Random Files
Fixed Format: PRINT D$;"READ RAN ADDRESS FILE,R5"
or Variable Format: PRINT D$;"READ";ADDRFILE$;",R";RECNUMBER
where ADDRFILE$ = the name of the file to be opened.
      RECNUMBER = the number of the record to be read.

Purpose   The READ instruction serves as a preparatory command telling DOS an INPUT or GET instruction follows and the data is to be transferred from the disk to the computer's memory.

Rules For Use
1. For sequential files any number of records may be read after the READ instruction is executed.
2. For random files the READ instruction must be executed prior to each INPUT instruction and must indicate which record is to be read.
3. Once OPENed, a sequential file must be either continuously read or continuously written. Do not attempt to mix the READ and WRITE instructions for one OPEN operation of a sequential file.
4. For the READ instruction the slot, volume, and drive parameters are not used. This information is only specified on the OPEN instructions.

Illustration of the Rules (Sequential Files)   In order for the following program to work, you must have previously created records for it to read. The records are created by running the SAMPLE SEQUENTIAL WRITE PROG. If the records are not created before you run this program, an error occurs and the message END OF DATA is displayed.

The program reads and displays the 10 records written by the SAMPLE SEQUENTIAL WRITE PROG.

```
1000 REM SAMPLE SEQUENTIAL READ PROG
1010 TEXT : NORMAL : HOME : SPEED= 175
1020 D$ = CHR$ (4)
1030 PRINT D$;"MON C,I,O"
1040 PRINT D$;"OPEN SEQUENTIAL FILE NAME"
1050 FOR N1 = 1 TO 10
1060 PRINT D$;"READ SEQUENTIAL FILE NAME"
1070 INPUT NUMBER,SUM
1080 PRINT D$: REM TERMINATES DISK OPERATIONS
1090 PRINT NUMBER,SUM
1100 NEXT
1110 PRINT D$;"CLOSE SEQUENTIAL FILE NAME"
1120 PRINT D$;"NOMON I,C,O"
1130 SPEED= 255
1140 END
```

1040   The OPEN instruction checks the disk for a matching label. If no matching label exists, DOS creates one, but when the program attempts to read the file, the computer cancels the program and displays an END OF DATA message.

1060–1090   The READ instruction serves as a preparatory command telling DOS that until another DOS instruction is executed, all further INPUT is to come from the disk.

When you INPUT variables from a disk a comma is used to separate each variable name. Unlike the PRINT instruction, which WRITEs data to the disk, the INPUT instruction does *not* enclose the comma within quotes.

Also, when reading variables from a disk, be sure to read the same number of variables which were written. If the number of variables read does not match the number of variables written, an error message is displayed and the program canceled.

Right: PRINT variable1","variable2","variable3

        ....

    INPUT variable1,variable2,variable3   Exact match

Wrong: PRINT variable1","variable2","variable3

        ....

    INPUT variable1,variable2   Not enough

or   INPUT variable1,variable2,variable3,variable4   Too many

Normally you want to display the data which is read from the disk prior to reading another disk record. To break the disk I/O instruction, you must PRINT a dummy D$ (CONTROL-D). The program shows the normal sequence of instructions for reading data from disk and displaying it on the screen.

Line 1060 indicates to DOS that a disk file is to be read.
Line 1070 inputs a record.
Line 1080 terminates DOS operations.
Line 1090 displays the data read.

1110–1130   Prior to terminating any program which uses disk files, make sure you close the files and reset any options you have set on, such as MONitor or SPEED.

If you run the program, the first few lines of the screen will appear as follows:

```
OPEN SEQUENTIAL FILE NAME
READ SEQUENTIAL FILE NAME
?1,1              Note: reads from disk

1             1 Note: prints on screen
READ SEQUENTIAL FILE NAME
?2,3              Note: reads from disk

2             3 Note: prints on screen
READ SEQUENTIAL FILE NAME
?3,6              Note: reads from disk
```

Did you notice the question mark in front of each disk read? This is generated by the INPUT instruction.

**Illustration
of the Rules
(Random Files)**
In order for the following program to work, you must have previously created records for it to read. The records are created by running the SAMPLE RANDOM WRITE PROG. If the records are not created before this program is run, an error occurs and the message END OF DATA is displayed.

The program reads and displays the 10 records created by the SAMPLE RANDOM WRITE PROG in reverse order. Since this is a random file, the records may be read in any sequence. Rather than jumping around in the file in a random sequence, the computer reads the records starting with record 10 and reading backward to record 1.

```
1000 REM SAMPLE RANDOM READ PROG
1010 TEXT : NORMAL : HOME : SPEED= 175
1020 D$ = CHR$ (4)
1030 PRINT D$;"MON C,I,O"
1040 PRINT D$;"OPEN RANDOM FILE NAME,L6"
1050 FOR N1 = 10 TO 1 STEP -1
1060 PRINT D$;"READ RANDOM FILE NAME,R"N1
1070 INPUT NUMBER,SUM
1080 PRINT D$: REM TERMINATES DISK OPERATIONS
1090 PRINT NUMBER,SUM
1100 NEXT
1110 PRINT D$;"CLOSE RANDOM FILE NAME"
1120 PRINT D$;"NOMON C,I,O"
1130 SPEED= 255
1140 END
```

1040   PRINT D$;"OPEN RANDOM FILE NAME,L6"

One last time, the OPEN instruction checks the disk for a matching label. If a matching label is found, the existing file is opened. DOS keeps track of the record length as indicated by the L parameter in the OPEN instruction. For this example the maximum length of each record is 6 bytes.

Maximum size of NUMBER	= 2
Maximum size of SUM	= 2
Number of commas	= 1
End-of-record indicator	= 1
Total	= 6

If no matching label exists, any attempt to read the file results in an END OF DATA message and program termination.

1050   Line 1050 shows how to use the STEP parameter to count backward. Normally the STEP option is not used because the instruction automatically counts in increments of 1, and for most applications this is what we want.

In this example we want to start with a value of 10 and decrease N1 each time until it reaches a value of 1. The STEP −1 causes the value of N1 to be decreased each time through the FOR/NEXT loop.

1060 PRINT D$;"READ RANDOM FILE NAME,R"N1

↑ record number

For random files the READ instruction must be specified prior to each INPUT instruction in order to indicate which record is to be read.

1070 When you INPUT variables from a disk, a comma is used to separate each variable name. Unlike the PRINT instruction, which WRITEs data to the disk, the INPUT instruction does NOT enclose the comma within quotes.

Also, when reading variables from a disk, be sure to read the same number of variables which were written. If the number of variables read does not match the number of variables written, an error message results.

1080–1090 The disk operations are terminated by line 1080, and then the data read is displayed by line 1090.

1110–1130 Before the program is terminated, the file is closed, the monitor functions are turned off, and the speed is reset.

If you run the program, the first few lines of the screen will appear as follows:

```
OPEN RANDOM FILE NAME,L6
READ RANDOM FILE NAME,R10
?10,55              Note: reads from disk

10          55   Note: prints on screen
READ RANDOM FILE NAME,R9
?9,45               Note: reads from disk

9           45   Note: prints on screen
READ RANDOM FILE NAME,R8
?8,36

8           36
```

Once more, did you notice that before each record is read, the READ instruction tells the computer which random record is to be read? In this case the records were read sequentially starting with record 10 and working backward. For random files the records may be read in any order.

The CLOSE Instruction

Instruction Fixed Format: PRINT D$;"CLOSE file name"
or Variable Format: PRINT D$;"CLOSE";variable$

Example PRINT D$;"CLOSE SEQ ADDRESS FILE"
or PRINT D$;"CLOSE";FILEID$

Purpose
1. When used with an input file, the CLOSE instruction removes program access to the input buffer.
2. When used with an output file, the CLOSE instruction causes the current contents of the output buffer to be written on the file. For sequential files, the CLOSE instruction also records an EOF marker.

Rules for Use
1. The CLOSE instruction *must be executed* if the WRITE instruction has been used in conjunction with the file. Unless the CLOSE instruction is executed before the program is terminated, the last few records in the output buffer may not get written out to the file, and the file may not be properly closed.
2. The CLOSE instruction is optional if information has only been read from an existing file. Even though it is optional for input files, you should get into the habit of closing all files.
3. For the CLOSE instruction the slot, volume, and drive parameters are not used. This information is only specified on the OPEN or APPEND instructions.

For use of the CLOSE instruction, see any of the programs presented earlier in this chapter.

The ONERR GOTO Instruction (With Sequential Files)

The ONERR GOTO instruction is used with sequential disk files to indicate when the end of the file has been reached.

There are basically two ways to tell when you come to the end of a sequential disk file. One way is to use a trailer record consisting of a special set of characters.

By testing each record to see if it is the trailer record, the program may find the end of the file.

The second method is to use the ONERR GOTO instruction and let the machine automatically branch to a specific instruction when the computer encounters the END OF DATA error.

Using a Trailer Record to Indicate End of File

An easy and therefore common way to check for the EOF condition is to use a record consisting of all 9s, as shown below.

Sequential Disk File with Trailer Record

| 12345JOHN DOE | 4955 WEST STREET | MEXICO MO | 55543 |
| 22222MARY SMITH | 32 HIGH ST APT 5 | KANSAS CITY MO | 55432 |

....

| 88989BOB ZINK | 123 HARRY ST | OAK RIDGE ARK | 43322 |

999999999999999999999999999999999999999999999999999999999

Program Logic Flow for Using Trailer Record

```
PRINT D$;"READ DISK FILE"
INPUT REC$
IF LEFT$(REC$,5) = "99999" THEN goto end-of-file routine
...continue processing
```

Using ONERR GOTO to Indicate the EOF

If the ONERR GOTO instruction is going to be used to indicate the end of the file, the instruction must be executed as part of the beginning logic to specify where logic flow is to branch when the computer encounters an error condition.

```
1000 REM BEGINNING ROUTINE
1010 ONERR GOTO 9000
........
2000 PRINT D$;"READ DISK FILE"
2010 ...
........
9000 REM ENDING ROUTINE
9010 ...
```

When the computer encounters the EOF or *any other error*, it automatically branches to statement 9000.

For a working example, see the SEQUENTIAL DISK UPDATE PROGram.

Although the sequential example in the book uses the ONERR instruction, I prefer to use the trailer record technique. Using the ONERR GOTO instruction causes problems when trying to debug your program and if done correctly is more difficult to code.

If you do use the ONERR GOTO instruction, you should PEEK memory address 222 and test it for a value of 5 (END OF DATA error). If the error is an END OF DATA, the program may continue. If the error is not an END OF DATA, your program should display the error code, an error message indicating the type of error, and the line number on which the error occurred (see the sequential file UPDATE program).

The VERIFY Instruction

Instruction   VERIFY "filename,Dnumber"

Example   Fixed Format: VERIFY "MONTHLY EXPENSE FILE"
Variable Format: VERIFY FILEID$

Purpose   The instruction is used to check to see if data are written correctly on the disk or if the file has been damaged.

Rules for Use   1.   The VERIFY instruction may be executed in either immediate or program execution mode.
2.   After execution of the instruction, two things may happen. If processing continues with no error messages, the file has been verified and is correct. If an I/O error occurs, some portion of the file is incorrectly recorded or is damaged.

The computer reads each sector of the file and accumulates a check figure for each sector indicating the number of bits recorded. The check figure is matched against the check figure which was originally recorded on the sector when the data was written to disk. If the figures match, then the sector passes the edit test. If the figures differ, an I/O error has occurred.

The VERIFY instruction only needs to be used when you have a question about the quality of the diskette or the disk drive being used.

The **MAXFILES** Instruction

Instruction   Immediate execution mode: MAXFILES number
Program execution mode: PRINT D$;"MAXFILES "number
where number may range from 1 to 16

Example   MAXFILES 4
PRINT D$;"MAXFILES "4

Purpose   The MAXFILES instruction is used to allocate memory area for disk file buffers.

Rules for Use   1. Although the number may range from 1 to 16, in actual practice the upper limit is 15 since DOS requires one buffer in order to execute the DOS commands.

2. When more than two files are going to be open at the same time in a program, the MAXFILES instruction must be used.

3. The MAXFILES instruction can be executed in either immediate or program execution mode. If MAXFILES is used in program execution mode, it must be the very first instruction in the program since it resets high memory. The resetting of the high memory destroys any string variables which have been defined.

DOS automatically allocates enough memory to handle three files. DOS uses one and leaves the other two for you to use.

Each file takes 595 bytes of memory: a 256 byte area for I/O operations, a 256 byte area for the track/sector list, and additional area for handling the I/O operations.

If you execute an I/O instruction without an adequate number of buffers, the NO BUFFERS AVAILABLE message is displayed; or if the ONERR GOTO instruction is used within the program, a branch to the error routine occurs.

3. The GET Subroutine

Purpose   The GET subroutine provides a method of entering data which eliminates problems which occur when using the INPUT instruction. The subroutine is used in all the sample programs which require large amounts of input from the operator.

It is written specifically to make efficient use of string memory, to provide a controlled method of reading data from the screen, and to prevent the operator from entering either the comma or the colon.

At the first of the book the terms variable and field were defined as synonyms. Although they are synonyms, a slight distinction will be made for the rest of the book. Variable will be used when referring to names within the program. Field will be used when referring to information entered by the operator, or areas on the screen where the operator enters the information.

Why Use the GET Subroutine?

The INPUT instruction has several problems which make it unsuitable for the average computer user. The following is a list of problems with the INPUT instruction. If you do not understand the list, go back to the first half of the book and review the INPUT instruction.

1.   Commas or colons may be entered incorrectly within the data.
2.   Too many fields may be entered. (Remember, the term field is being used to distinquish information entered by the operator.)
3.   Too few fields may be entered.
4.   When the RETURN key is pressed, the INPUT instruction causes the remainder of the line to be cleared.
5.   The INPUT instruction does not provide a way to control the number of characters entered by the operator.
6.   The operator must press the RETURN key after entering each field.
7.   When working with the disk, commas or colons cause problems if included in the data. The INPUT instruction allows the operator to enter colons, whereas the GET subroutine does not allow commas or colons to be entered.

Like the INPUT instruction, the GET subroutine also has some disadvantages. Since it uses a fixed portion of high memory to store the data being entered, there is one line of code which *must be* executed at the very start of the program. If the line is not used at the very beginning of the program to define a portion of high memory, the subroutine *does not work*. Also, just as with any instruction, you must understand how to use it and must follow the rules related to its use.

But the advantages of the GET subroutine outweigh the disadvantages. The subroutine has the following advantages:

1. It allows you to control the number of characters entered by the operator.
2. The operator does not have to press the RETURN key if the maximum number of characters is entered.
3. The subroutine returns a numeric value equal to the number of characters entered. The main use of this value is to tell if the operator entered data or just pressed the RETURN key.
4. The subroutine may easily be modified to accept only numeric information (see p. 294).
5. Since the subroutine uses a machine language routine to read the keyboard, it can accept any characters except CONTROL-RESET.
6. The subroutine does not allow any control characters to be entered which might cause problems when printing. All values from 31 on down are rejected (CONTROL key values).

Don't let the size or complexity of the routine scare you off. You will see it is very simple to use and can make your efforts much more professional.

Instructions for Using the GET Subroutine

The remainder of this discussion is divided into two sections. The first section indicates how to use the subroutine. No knowledge of the instructions within the subroutine is necessary in order to use it. For those of you who want to know how the routine works, the second section gives a line by line explanation and indicates why each line is necessary.

There is one line of code which *must be the first executable* instruction in your program in order for the GET subroutine to work. This is the one part of the subroutine I do not like, but it is necessary in order to use string memory efficiently. The instruction defines a variable called GA\$ in high memory. The variable serves as a work area for all input operations. The numbers between the quotes are not important; they only serve to allocate memory. The format and sequence of the instruction are important. Code it exactly as shown.

```
1000 REM NAME OF PROGRAM
1010 REM --------------------
1020 CLEAR :G1 = PEEK (116) * 256 + PEEK (115) - 40
     :GA$ = "12345678901234567890" + "12345678901234567890"
1030 REM --------------------
1040 ... start program here ...
```

You MUST NEVER use the variable name GA$, other than as shown on line 1020. Line 1020 above defines the variable, and it will be used once again in the subroutine, but you MUST NEVER use it within your code or the subroutine WILL NOT WORK!

Now for the easy part. As you go through the programs, you will see a basic pattern for using the GET subroutine. The pattern consists of three or four instructions depending on the type of processing being done.

Before the subroutine is used, two instructions must be executed.

1. First the cursor must be positioned to the correct line and column at which the data is to be entered. The best way to position the cursor is to use the VTAB and HTAB instructions. For example,

```
1000 VTAB 10: HTAB 15
```

2. Second, the variable GALEGTH must be set equal to the number of characters to be read. For example,

```
1010 GALEGTH = 25
```

The subroutine does not test the value in GALEGTH to see if it is within the acceptable limits (1 to 40). To keep the subroutine as small as possible, all error checks were left out. It is up to you to follow the rules and set the variable equal to a value from 1 to 40 before executing the subroutine.

3. Once the cursor is positioned and the length specified, then execute the subroutine by way of the GOSUB instruction. For example,

```
1020 GOSUB 2000: REM EXECUTE GET SUBROUTINE
........
2000 REM GET SUBROUTINE
...    RETURN
```

After returning from the GET subroutine, three variables contain values which may be used in evaluating the data entered.

1. GBANSWER$ contains the data entered or is set equal to spaces if only the RETURN key is pressed.

Normally you want to set a variable name equal to the value returned. Remember, GBANSWER$ is in string format and must be converted for numeric operations. For example,

1030 NAME$ = GBANSWER$ String variables
or 1030 NUMBER = VAL(GBANSWER$)   Numeric variables

2. GCCHAR contains the number of characters keyed in by the operator. If the operator only presses the RETURN key, GCCHAR contains a value of zero.

GCCHAR is tested when updating data to see if the operator wants to change the value in a field or accept the old value.

When data is updated, you should display the old value and allow the operator a chance to accept it as is or change it. If the operator enters one or more characters, the variable is set equal to the new value entered by the operator. If the operator does not enter any characters (only presses RETURN), the instruction for resetting the variable is skipped.

Example:

```
1000 VTAB 10: HTAB 1: PRINT "NAME = (";NAME$;")"
1010 VTAB 10: HTAB 9: GALEGTH = 25: GOSUB 2000
1030 IF GCCHAR = 0 THEN 1050: REM SKIP CHANGING FIELD
1040 NAME$ = GBANSWER$: REM CHANGE DATA TO NEW VALUE
1050 REM NO CHANGE IN DATA
........
2000 REM GET SUBROUTINE
........
```

3. GB contains the numeric value of the last character entered (ASCII value). The value is of little use, but you may find a need to know which character was entered last.

I encourage you to use the GET subroutine in your programs, but *if you key in the subroutine, be extremely careful!* Every semicolon and line number in the subroutine is important. The subroutine has been condensed to the smallest number of lines possible without changing the method by which it operates.

If you have the sample disk, use the copy of the subroutine which is on the disk. If you do not have the sample disk, carefully enter the subroutine and save it. Once you have a good copy of the subroutine, you can load it into memory and use the RENUMBER program to merge it into your programs. Remember, the RENUMBER program is on the DOS diskette which comes with the APPLE and is one of the first utility programs which you should learn how to use. Do not try to rekey the subroutine for each program.

Let's do a little review before going on to the detailed description of instructions within the subroutine.

1. The following line MUST be the first executable instruction in your program:

```
1020 CLEAR :G1 = PEEK (116) * 256 + PEEK (115) − 40
     :GA$ = "12345678901234567890" + "12345678901234567890"
```

2. You MUST NEVER use the variable name GA$ in your own code.
3. Each time you use the routine you should
   a. Position the cursor
   b. Set GALEGTH equal to the number of characters to be read
   c. Set a variable name equal to the value returned in GBANSWER$

If you study the sample disk programs and follow through their logic, you will see how easy the subroutine is to use.

Really, you will.

The GET Subroutine Listing

To keep the statement numbers within the subroutine consistent with the code used in the sample disk programs, the line numbers start at 1100.

```
1020 CLEAR :G1 = PEEK (116) * 256 + PEEK (115) − 40: GA$ =
     "12345678901234567890" + "12345678901234567890"
. . . . . . . . . . . . . . . . . . . . . . . . . . . . . . . . . . . . . . . . . . . . . . . . . . . . . . .
1100 REM ------------------------
1110 REM GET SUBROUTINE
1120 IF G3 = 0 THEN GOSUB 1270
1130 G3 = G1 + GA − 1: FOR G2 = G1 TO G3: POKE G2,32: NEXT :
     G2 = G1
1140 CALL 768:GB = PEEK (775) − 128: IF GB = 08 THEN 1210
1150 IF GB = 13 THEN 1230
1160 IF GB = 21 THEN PRINT CHR$ ( PEEK (G2));: GOTO 1190
1170 IF GB = 44 OR GB = 58 OR GB < 32 THEN 1140
1180 PRINT CHR$ (GB);: POKE G2,GB
1190 G2 = G2 + 1: IF G2 > G3 THEN 1260
1200 GOTO 1140
```

```
1210 G2 = G2 - 1: IF G2 < G1 THEN G2 = G1: GOTO 1140
1220 PRINT CHR$ (8);: GOTO 1140
1230 IF G1 = G2 THEN 1250
1240 FOR GC = G2 TO G3: PRINT " ";: NEXT
1250 FOR GC = G2 TO G3: POKE GC,32: NEXT
1260 GB$ = LEFT$ (GA$,GA):GC = G2 - G1: RETURN
1270 POKE 768,32: POKE 769,12: POKE 770,253: POKE 771,141: P
OKE 772,07: POKE 773,03: POKE 774,96: RETURN
1280 REM
1290 REM ----------------------
```

Cross Reference Listing

G1 1130, 1210, 1230, 1260
G2 1130, 1160, 1180, 1190, 1210, 1230, 1240, 1250, 1260
G3 1120, 1130, 1190, 1240, 1250
GA 1130, 1260
GA$ 1260
GB 1140, 1150, 1160, 1170, 1180
GB$ 1260
GC 1240, 1250, 1260

Since each instruction making up the lines of code is important to the operation of the subroutine, in the following discussion each line is repeated and then broken down into the individual instructions as needed.

1020 CLEAR :G1 = PEEK (116) * 256 + PEEK (115) − 40: GA$ = "12345678901234567890" + "12345678901234567890"

CLEAR

The CLEAR instruction is used at the beginning of the line just in case you did not follow the rules and have defined a string variable before coding this line. The CLEAR instruction wipes out all previous string and numeric values.

There is one exception in which the CLEAR instruction should be removed. If you are going to use the MAXFILES instruction within your program, it must be coded before this line, and the CLEAR instruction must be removed from the line.

G1 = PEEK (116) * 256 + PEEK (115) − 40:

The variable G1 is used to store the starting address of GA$. Since GA$ is the first string defined in high memory, its starting address is equal to the address of high memory minus the length of GA$. If you want to change the subroutine to accept bigger fields, change the −40 to −nn, where nn is equal to the maximum size you want the subroutine to handle.

```
+-----------------------+
|                       |
|         DOS           |
|                       |
+-----------------------+
|                       |
|  .........GA$.........|
|  High memory          |         <   Address of high
|  Used for strings     |         memory and location of GA$
|                       |
+-----------------------+
|                       |
|  Low memory           |
|  Used for numeric     |
|  Variables and your   |
|  program              |
|                       |
|                       |
|                       |
|                       |
|                       |
+-----------------------+
```

Machine addresses 115 and 116 contain the address of high memory. The address is stored in hexadecimal, with the most significant digit in memory location 116. To convert the number to decimal, the value in 116 is multiplied by 256 and added to the value in memory location 115.

GA$ = "12345678901234567890" + "12345678901234567890"

The variable GA$ is set equal to 40 characters, and the value is placed in the first 40 bytes of high memory. In order for the instruction to work, the 40 characters must be broken into two strings. If only one string value were used, Applesoft would not place the value in high memory but would simply set the pointer for GA$ equal to the location of the constant within the Applesoft program. When the constant is divided into two parts and then the parts combined into one value, the instruction is forcing Applesoft to store the complete value in high memory and to set the pointer for GA$ to the high memory address.

If you want to change the subroutine to be able to handle more than 40 characters, then set GA$ equal to the maximum number of characters you want to use. Make sure to divide the constant into two parts as shown.

```
1100 REM ---------------------
1110 REM GET SUBROUTINE
1120 IF G3 = 0 THEN GOSUB 1270
........
1270 POKE 768,32: POKE 769,12: POKE 770,253: POKE 771,141:
     POKE 772,07: POKE 773,03: POKE 774,96: RETURN
1280 REM
1290 REM ---------------------
```

1120   IF G3 = 0 THEN GOSUB 1270

The very first line of the subroutine checks to see if this is the first time the subroutine has been executed. If G3 is equal to zero, then the subroutine has not been executed, and logic flow branches to line 1270, where a machine language routine is Poked into memory locations 768 through 774.

No attempt will be made to try to explain the machine language program other than to say that this is the actual routine which reads the keyboard and stores the symbol pressed in memory location 775. Later, a PEEK instruction is used to retrieve the value entered.

During execution of the subroutine, G3 is set equal to a memory address and is never equal to zero again (unless you reset it).

1130   G3 = G1 + GA − 1: FOR G2 = G1 TO G3: POKE G2,32: NEXT : G2 = G1

Line 1130 is executed once for each execution of the subroutine. The line is responsible for setting G3 equal to the ending address of the field to be entered, blanking out the area of memory in which the field will be placed, and setting G2 equal to the starting address of the field.

Remember, the first instruction in the program reserves 40 bytes of high memory. Before executing the subroutine, you set GALEGTH equal to a value from 1 to 40 indicating the size of the area within the 40 bytes of high memory which is to be used:

1040 GALEGTH = 25

Therefore,

GA\$ = "12345678901234567890123456789012345678901234567890"
G1 =   └Starting address
G3 =   Ending address ────────────┘

Using the starting and ending address of the field, the FOR/NEXT instruction blanks out the area of memory to be used for the input operation. Notice that only an area of memory equal to the size of the data to be entered is blanked out.

GA\$ = "   678901234567890"
G1 =   └Starting address
G3 =   Ending address ────────────┘

After the area is blanked out, G2 is set equal to the starting address of the field (G1).

1140   CALL 768:GB = PEEK (775) − 128: IF GB = 08 THEN 1210

CALL 768

The CALL instruction executes the machine language program at memory location 768 (see line 1270). The machine language routine puts the value of the key pressed in memory location 775.

GB = PEEK (775) − 128

The PEEK instruction is used to retrieve the value from memory. That's the easy part of the explanation. Now, why subtract 128?

When a key is pressed, the value of the key is placed into a specific memory address by the APPLE, and the first bit of that address is set on. The first bit acts as a switch, indicating that a key has been entered (bit on) or has not been entered (bit off). By testing this bit, the machine language routine knows when a key has been pressed and when to return a value. Once the value is returned, we must subtract 128 to turn off the high order bit.

```
  1100 0001 = ?   With bit on gives incorrect pattern
− 1000 0000 = 128   To take off first bit
= 0100 0001 = A   Correct bit pattern for letter A
```

IF GB = 08 THEN 1210

The value returned is tested to see if a left arrow key was pressed (08 = left arrow key; see Appendix A). If the left arrow key was pressed, logic flow branches to line 1210, where the instructions related to moving the cursor to the left are located.

1150 IF GB = 13 THEN 1230

The value is tested to see if the RETURN key was pressed (13 = RETURN key). If the RETURN key is pressed before reaching the end of the field, logic flow branches to line 1230, where a group of instructions blanks out the remainder of the field.

1160 IF GB = 21 THEN PRINT CHR$ (PEEK (G2));: GOTO 1190

The value is tested to see if a right arrow key was pressed (21 = right arrow key). If the right arrow key was pressed, the character at the current location of the cursor is printed. The printing of the character has the effect of moving the cursor over one position to the right. After the cursor is moved, logic flow branches to line 1190 to increment the position of the cursor and check to see if the end of the field has been reached.

1170 IF GB = 44 OR GB = 58 OR GB < 32 THEN 1140

If a comma (44), colon (58), or a control character (0 to 31), has been entered, the values are rejected, and logic flow branches back to accept a valid character.

If the RETURN key was pressed in any position other than the first, both FOR/NEXT instructions are executed. The first FOR/NEXT instruction blanks out the remainder of the field on the screen, while the second FOR/NEXT blanks out the remainder of the field in memory.

1260   GB$ = LEFT$ (GA$,GA):GC = G2 – G1: RETURN

After the value has been entered and placed in high memory, this instruction extracts the correct number of characters and places the value in GBANSWER$. Also, before the subroutine returns to the calling GOSUB, the value of GCCHAR is set equal to the number of characters entered (not necessarily the same as the size of the field).

All the variable names in the subroutine start with G:

G1, G2, G3, GA, GA, GB, GB$, GC,

If you use the subroutine, you should not use any of the variable names above except in conjunction with the GET subroutine.

The following variables are used as parameters to and from the routine:

GALEGTH   This must be set equal to the length of the variable to be read prior to executing the subroutine.

GBANSWER$ After returning from the subroutine, this variable contains the value read in.

GCCHAR   After completion of the subroutine, this variable contains the number of characters keyed in by the operator.

All the other variables used in the GET subroutine are necessary to its internal operation. The following list gives the full program name and a short description of each variable used by the subroutine.

G1   This variable contains the starting address of the GA$.

G2   This variable contains the address where the character being entered is to be placed.

G3   This variable contains the ending address of the GA$.

GALEGTH   This variable contains the number of characters to be read by the subroutine. The subroutine is set up to read from 1 to 40 characters.

GBCHAR   During execution of the subroutine this variable is used to store the ASCII value of the character keyed in. This allows for more readable code in testing for various keystrokes. After returning from the subroutine, the variable contains the numeric value of the last key pressed. If the RETURN key was pressed, the variable has a value of 13.

GBANSWER$ At the end of the subroutine, GBANSWER$ is set equal to the value keyed in.

GCCHAR   After execution of the subroutine, the variable GCCHAR contains a value equal to the number of characters keyed in. If no characters were entered, that is, if only the RETURN key was pressed, GCCHAR contains a value of zero.

This ends the explanation of the GET subroutine. Hopefully you understand how to use it and how it does what it does. Study the example disk programs for more complete examples of how to interact with the routine.

Feel free to use the subroutine in your programs in place of the INPUT instruction.

Note 1: To modify the GET subroutine so that it only accepts numeric characters, insert the following line.

1171 IF GB < 43 OR GB > 57 OR GB = 47 THEN 1140

Note 2: To modify the GET subroutine so that the operator must always press RETURN to enter a value, add the following two lines of code:

1141 IF GB = 13 AND G2 > G3 THEN 1260
1151 IF G2 > G3 THEN 1140

and change line 1190 to read

1190 G2 = G2 + 1

4. Serial and Sequential Disk Files

Before any of the programs which work with disk files are run, they must be copied to a new disk. The program disk does not have sufficient free space for additional files.

Use the APPLE's FID (FIle Developer) program to copy the programs; if you do not have access to the FID program, you can transfer each program by using the LOAD and SAVE commands.

LOAD program name,Dnumber
SAVE program name,Dnumber

Remember to INITialize any new disk before trying to use it.
For this chapter copy the following programs to another disk:

SEQ ADDR CREATE PROG
SEQ ADDR HELLO PROG
SEQ ADDR APPEND PROG
SEQ ADDR UPDATE PROG
SEQ ADDR LIST PROG
SEQ ADDR SEARCH PROG

If you want to make your disk operate like a turnkey system, use the following steps:

1. Use a new disk or one which no longer contains any files you wish to keep.
2. Load the SEQ ADDR HELLO PROG from the program disk. Enter

   LOAD SEQ ADDR HELLO PROG

3. REMOVE THE PROGRAM DISK and put in the disk you want to INITialize. After putting in the new disk, initialize the disk using the SEQ ADDR HELLO PROG currently in memory. Enter

   INIT SEQ ADDR HELLO PROG,Dnumber,Vnumber

   Fill in the drive and volume number as desired.
4. After the disk has been initialized, transfer the remaining programs from the program disk to the newly initialized disk.
5. In order to use the programs on the new disk, all you need to do is insert the disk into drive 1 and turn on the computer or key in PR#6 if the computer is

already turned on. The SEQ ADDR HELLO PROG will be executed automatically.

Note: The SEQ ADDR FILE CREATE PROG must be run before any of the other programs. The programs should be executed in the sequence presented.

A General Introduction to Serial and Sequential Files

Definition and Illustrations

Serial File: A file organization method in which the records are only accessible by reading the file sequentially and the records making up the file are not in any specific order.

Sequential File: A file organization method in which the records are only accessible by reading the file sequentially and the records are organized into either ascending or descending sequence by one or more variables within the record.

Both types of files are normally referred to as sequential files. But there is a fine line of difference between serial files and sequential files.

Serial file processing refers to the access method in which records must be read, processed, and written in a sequential manner. In order to access the last record, all previous records must be read. The first record is read and processed, then the second record is read and processed, etc.

The processing logic *is not dependent* on the records being in any specific sequence.

Example The following data is in serial order, that is, one record following another. The data is not in sequence by any of the variables making up the record. Therefore, it is technically NOT considered a sequential file. Even though it should be referred to as a serial file, most people would refer to the file as sequential.

Student Number	Student Name	Test Score
12345	JIM JOHNSON	080
54321	MARY SMITH	095
22222	TIMMY WILLIAMS	070
33333	JAMES MC DONALD	098
etc.		

Sequential file processing refers to the access method in which records must be read, processed, and written in a sequential manner. In order to access the last record, all previous records must be read. The first record is read and processed, then the second record is read and processed, etc.

The processing logic *is dependent on* the data within the file being in a specific sequence.

Example   The following table of data is in sequential order, that is, one record following another organized into either an ascending or a descending sequence by a key variable. The key variable is normally referred to as the record key. The record key is located in the same position on all records and serves to identify the record. Typical examples of record keys are Social Security number, student number, employee number, and driver's license number.

For this example the records are in ascending sequence by the student number.

Student Number	Student Name	Test Score
12345	JIM JOHNSON	080
22222	MARY SMITH	095
33333	TIMMY WILLIAMS	070
54321	JAMES MC DONALD	098
etc.		

In both serial and sequential files, the records are accessed sequentially. Thus the fine line of difference between a serial file and a sequential file is

1.   Serial files are not organized into any specific sequence.
2.   Sequential files are organized into either ascending or descending sequence by one or more variables within the record.

Systems Chart and Description of Sequential Processing

The following systems chart may be used to represent both the program which creates the file label and the program which adds records to the end of the file.

Step 1: Creating the File Label
Step 2: Adding Records to the End of a Sequential File

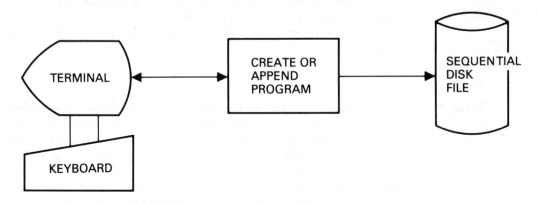

Before a sequential file can be accessed, the file label must be created. For the examples used in this book, the file labels are created by a separate program. After the label is created, records may be added (APPENDed) to the end of the file.

Step 3: Sequential File Update

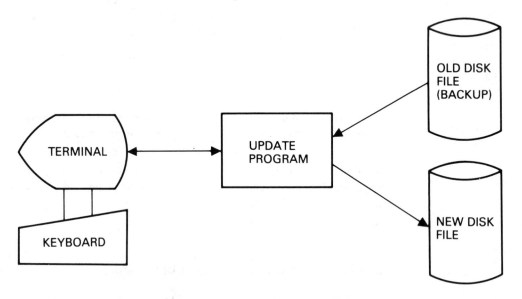

The update program provides the user with a method to keep data on the MASTER FILE current. Variables within existing records may be updated or changed. Records which are no longer needed may be deleted or purged from the file.

Step 4: Sequential Report Generation or Inquiry

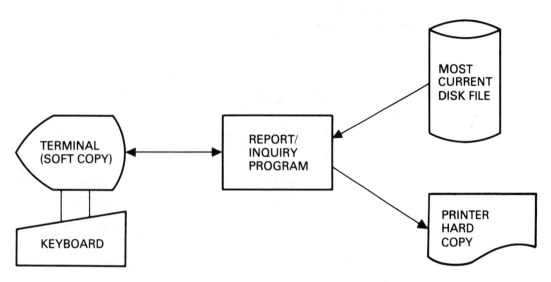

Once a file is created, the data on that file can be used to produce reports. Inquiries or reports related to the file may be displayed on the screen (soft copy) or sent to a printer to produce a hard copy. The term *inquiry* is normally used instead of *report* when a request is made to view a single record or a group of records. Inquiry also implies that the information will be displayed on a CRT.

The Advantages of Sequential and Serial Processing

Note: Even though there are some advantages to sequential files, they are normally not used on microcomputers or minicomputers because of the way the operator and the programs interact on smaller systems. Almost all systems developed for the APPLE use some form of random processing.

If *all* the records within a file *are normally* going to be accessed, sequential processing is faster than random processing.

Since the records are accessed sequentially, the machine does not have to compute the location of each record as it does when working with random files. This simplifies the I/O process and makes sequential file organization the preferred method when the majority of the records within a file are to be accessed.

A second advantage of sequential processing is that as part of the update operation, a second copy of the master file is created, thereby making an automatic backup of the file. As the OLD MASTER FILE is updated, a NEW MASTER FILE is created. The new master file is basically a copy of the old master file except for additions, changes, and deletions which are made during the update process. If for any reason you discover that errors have occurred during the update process, the old master is still available in its original state.

Disadvantages of Sequential and Serial Processing

For small computers which operate in an interactive mode (operator interacts with computer), the disadvantages of sequential files normally outweigh the advantages.

Sequential processing is normally limited to those systems in which information (transactions) may be grouped together in a batch and processed as a unit against the master file.

For example, in a sequential payroll application, time cards are batched at the end of the week and entered into the computer as a group. The time cards are *sorted* into the same sequence as the payroll master and then processed sequentially against the master file to produce a new updated master along with the checks, reports, etc.

Did you notice the word *sorted?*

For serial files the data does not have to be sorted, but for sequential files the data must be sorted prior to the updating of the master file.

The primary disadvantage of sequential processing is that the transactions (additions, changes, and deletions) must be in the same sequence as the master file in order to be processed.

The computer cannot insert new records into an existing sequential file. It can only add new records to the end of an existing sequential file. In order to insert new records, the entire file must be copied and the new records inserted in the proper sequence. Records which are to be changed or deleted must be processed in the sequence in which they occur on the master file.

A second disadvantage is that once a record is read from the old master file and written to the new master file, the computer cannot back up and reprocess it.

A third disadvantage is that even if only a few records are to be added, changed, or deleted, the entire sequential file must be read and rewritten.

If only a small portion of the records within a file are to be accessed during any given run or operation, then sequential processing should not be used. The time required to sequence the transactions, read the old sequential file, and write a new sequential file exceeds the time required to work with a few individual records in a random file.

A Summary of Sequential Files for Microcomputers

Sequential processing is fine for larger computers which can sort and process transactions in a batch mode, but for most applications on small computers, some form of random processing should be used.

Because the computer must process sequential files starting with the first record and continuing sequentially through the file, one record at a time, it is normally not the best technique for on-line, interactive programs.

Problem Specifications

A General Description of the Problem

Note: The data in this system is not in any specific order, and therefore the term *serial file* should be used. But the access method is sequential, so all references to the file and system are termed *sequential*.

The same problem is used to illustrate the three types of disk access methods with just a small variation on the screen design. The screen design for the sequential version of the client directory consists of the name, address, city, state, ZIP code, and telephone number as follows:

```
NAME      = (                        )
ADDRESS   = (                        )
CITY      = (                        )
STATE     = (   )
ZIP CODE  = (        )
PHONE     = (    -    -      )
```

The reason for using the same problem to illustrate all the disk programs is so you may concentrate on the structure of each type of program and the instructions related to file handling. Running the same data through each system also gives you a better chance to make a fair comparison of the advantages and disadvantages of each file processing technique.

Once you understand the logic of the various programs, you can easily copy the program structure to modify it for more involved applications. The overall logic for handling sequential files, random files, or index files is basically the same no matter what data is being manipulated.

So the problem is to design, write, and create a sequential system to keep track of client name, street address, city, state, ZIP code, and phone number. No client number or code is to be used as a record key, since this is a serial file and is not kept in any specific sequence.

Six programs are used to illustrate sequential processing:

1. A program for creating the file label in order to get the system started
2. A HELLO or MENU selection program which allows the operator a method of choosing which program is to be executed
3. A program for adding new records to the file
4. A program for updating existing records
5. A program for listing all the records on the file
6. A program for searching the file by last name for a specific client

The SEQ ADDR CREATE PROGram is needed to create a label on the disk. Once a label is created, the SEQ ADDR APPEND PROGram is used to add records to the end of the existing file.

The SEQ ADDR HELLO PROGram is used to display a menu to the person entering data. The operator enters a number matching the program which is to be executed (see below). With the exception of the SEQ ADDR CREATE PROGram and the SEQ ADDR HELLO PROGram, all programs within the system are executed by way of the menu.

```
SELECT ONE OF THE FOLLOWING:

    1. ADD NEW RECORDS.

    2. CHANGE EXISTING RECORDS.

    3. LIST RECORDS ON SCREEN.

    4. SEARCH FILE BY LAST NAME.

    5. QUIT PROCESSING.

SELECTION DESIRED = ( )



....... First error message line ......
....... Second error message line .....
```

The SEQ ADDR APPEND PROGram is used to add records to the end of an existing file. Since records are added to the end of the file in any sequence, the system uses SERIAL file processing logic. The system could be programmed to insert records into a specific sequence such as last name, but the logic is much more involved. Also, if records are inserted in sequence, there is no need to use the APPEND instruction. Since one of the objectives of this system is to illustrate how to use the APPEND instruction, all new records will be added to the end of the existing file.

The SEQ ADDR UPDATE PROGram is used to change one or more values in an existing record or to delete a complete record from the file. Again, if this were a sequential system instead of a serial system, then the program would be set up to allow records to be inserted (added) into the correct location.

The SEQ ADDR LIST PROGram is used to display all the names and addresses in the file.

The SEQ ADDR SEARCH PROGram is used to search the file and display all the records with a specific last name or part of a last name. This example is basically the same as the list program but shows how to search sequentially for a specific value within a record.

A Data Name Dictionary for the Sequential Address System

The following list describes the variables used in the sequential system.

Not all the names are used in each program. The dictionary is included here to give you a single source for the description of the variables used within the system. If you have a question about the use of one of the variables while looking at a program listing, return to this section for an explanation and a better understanding of the variable.

The names are listed in alphabetic order. Each name consists of a two character prefix followed by a descriptive name. The two character prefix or Applesoft name is given at the left with the full name and description at the right.

All the variable names starting with an A are part of the address record.

A1$ = A1REC$

This is the name used when reading the record from disk. It consists of all the variables making up the records.

AA$ = AANAME$

This contains the name of the client and has a fixed length of 25 characters. Data within the variable is left justified. The system is designed for the name to be entered using the format of FIRSTNAME LASTNAME. In order for the search program to work correctly, there must be a blank between the first and the last name. There can be no embedded blanks within the last name. For example, JOE MC DONALD has to be entered as JOE MCDONALD.

AB$ = ABADDR$

This contains the street address of the client and has a fixed length of 25 characters. The data within the variable should be left justified.

AC$ = ACCITY$

This contains the name of the city and has a fixed length of 15 characters. The data within the variable should be left justified.

FD = FDRIVE = Value of 1

The name stands for File DRIVE and is used in conjunction with PDRIVE (Program DRIVE) to indicate which disk drive is to be accessed.

FI$ = FILEID$

This contains the name of the file to be read. The variable is initialized in the BEGINNING ROUTINE of each program and used in all DOS instructions.

All the variable names starting with G are part of the GET subroutine. The following variables are used as parameters to and from the routine:

GA = GALEGTH

This must be set equal to the length of the variable to be read before the subroutine is executed. The subroutine is set up to read from 1 to 40 characters.

GB$ = GBANSWER$

After logic flow returns from the subroutine, this variable contains the value keyed in.

GC = GCCHAR

After completion of the subroutine, this variable contains the number of characters keyed in by the operator. GCCHAR is important only if you are testing whether the operator entered data or just pressed the RETURN key. If no characters are entered, that is, if only the RETURN key is pressed, the value in GCCHAR is zero.

You need to understand how the variables GALEGTH, GBANSWER$, and GCCHAR are used in order to follow the logic in the programs. You do not need to understand how the other variables in the GET subroutine are used in order to follow the program logic. For a detailed explanation of the variables GBCHAR, G1, G2 and G3 see the narrative presented earlier on the GET subroutine.

L1 through L9

The variables L1, L2, L3, L4, L5, L6, L7, L8, and L9 are used for vertical positioning of the cursor. The number in the second position of the name is not necessarily the number of the related line. VTAB L1 does not necessarily position the cursor on line 1. The variables are used for program flexibility and could have just as easily been called LA, LB, LC, LD, etc. (In fact, I wish I had: it would cause less confusion.)

MT = MTCHES

This variable is only used in the SEQ ADDR SEARCH PROGram. The variable is used to count the number of MaTCHES made when searching the file.

N1, N2, N3

N1, N2, and N3 (Numeric variable 1, 2, and 3) are used as general counters in FOR/NEXT instructions or for general numeric operations.

PD = PDRIVE = Value of 1

The name stands for Program DRIVE and is used in conjunction with FDRIVE (File DRIVE) to indicate which disk drive is to be accessed.

X1$, X2$

X1$ and X2$ are general string variables used in the GET instruction when requesting a response from the operator.

Disk Record Format Specifications

All the disk examples in this book work with fixed length records. That is, each variable in the record has a fixed length and each record has a fixed length.

For this example the record length is 83 characters. The table below shows the fixed size of each variable in the record.

Variable Name	= Length	− Record Position
AANAME$	25	1 to 25
ABADDR$	25	26 to 50
ACCITY$	15	51 to 65
ADSTE$	2	66 to 67
AEZIP$	5	68 to 72
AFPHNE$	10	73 to 82
EOR mark	1	83

The EOR or End-Of-Record indicator is written and controlled by the computer. It is included in the record description in case you are going to figure how much disk storage space is used.

When all these variables are combined and written onto the disk, the record has the following format:

```
                1         2         3         4         5
Column   12345678901234567890123456789012345678901234567890
         NNNNNNNNNNNNNNNNNNNNNNNNNAAAAAAAAAAAAAAAAAAAAAAAAA
```

```
              6          7          8
Column #   12345678901234567890123456789 0123
           CCCCCCCCCCCCCCCCSSZZZZZPPPPPPPPPP?
```

where N = name; A = street address; C = city; S = state; Z = ZIP code; P = phone number; ? = end-of-record marker

The Sequential File **CREATE** Program

Program Name   SEQ ADDR CREATE PROG

Program Objective   To create a label and EOF marker so that the APPEND program can add new records to the empty file.

Instructions for Running the Program

Note 1: Prior to running any of the programs in the sequential file system, you *must* copy the program from the program disk to a new disk. There is not enough room on the program disk to store any text files.

Note 2: Since all the programs are set up for a single drive system, the disk being used *must* be in drive 1 or the values for FDRIVE and PDRIVE must be changed in each program.

To keep this program as simple as possible, most of the responsibility for a successful run has been shifted from the program to the computer operator.

There are several situations which result in the program's failing to create the new empty file and file label.

1. If the file label already exists, the program simply OPENs and CLOSEs the existing file. The contents of the existing file remain unchanged.
2. If the disk is full, write protected, or not initialized, the program is canceled by DOS with an I/O ERROR message. The responsibility for handling these errors is left up to the operator.

Before running the program, you should make sure the file label (SEQ ADDR FILE) does not exist on the disk. Use the CATALOG command and check to see if the label exists. If the label exists and you are sure you want to destroy the data that is currently on the file, use the DELETE command to remove the file.

After you have made sure the file does not exist enter

RUN SEQ ADDR CREATE PROG <RETURN>

Program Listing

```
1000 REM SEQ ADDR CREATE PROG
1010 REM ----------------------
1020 TEXT : NORMAL : HOME : SPEED= 255
1030 D$ = CHR$ (4)
1040 FDRIVE = 1
1050 FILEID$ = "SEQ ADDR FILE"
1060 PRINT D$;"MON I,O,C"
1070 PRINT D$;"OPEN ";FILEID$;",D";FDRIVE
1080 PRINT D$;"CLOSE ";FILEID$
1090 PRINT D$;"NOMON I,O,C"
1100 PRINT D$
1110 PRINT
1120 PRINT "NORMAL END OF PROGRAM"
1130 REM ----------------------
1140 END
```

Explanation by Line Number

1020   As a coding standard, each of the programs in the systems start out with four instructions. The TEXT instruction makes sure the computer is in TEXT, mode. The NORMAL instruction makes sure the computer is set to light letters on a dark background.

Some instructions should be executed only while in the NORMAL mode. If you try to open a file while the system is in FLASH mode, the characters generated in the file name will not be the same as when the system is in NORMAL mode, and you will have problems retrieving the file in any mode other than FLASH. Also, the MONitor instruction, if used, must be executed while the system is in NORMAL mode.

The HOME instruction ensures that any information from a previous program is cleared from the screen as the program is starting. The SPEED instruction makes sure that any data displayed on the screen is displayed at the computer's normal speed of 255.

As a general guideline, start all your programs with this set of instructions. By always resetting these features, you are assured that the computer is set up correctly for your program. You need not be concerned if the last program used graphics, ended with the INVERSE or FLASH display options, left data on the screen, or slowed down the computer.

1030   The binary pattern for the CONTROL-D key must precede all DOS commands.

As a coding convention, most programmers use the variable name D$ to represent the CONTROL-D key. At the very beginning of the program, the string D$ is set equal to CHR$(4). CHaRacter$(4) represents the numeric value generated by the computer when both the CONTROL key and D key are pressed simultaneously.

The use of D$ in conjunction with the CHR$ function is the best way to code the CONTROL-D, but you may see programs which use other techniques.

DO NOT USE THE FOLLOWING CODING TECHNIQUE!

Bad Example: D$ = ": REM CONTROL-D IS BETWEEN QUOTES
or PRINT";"OPEN FILE NAME"

In this example the CONTROL-D key is hidden between the quotation marks. Since the CONTROL-D key is not a printable character, it does not show up on the screen or on printed listings of the program. You have no easy way of knowing what is between the two quotation marks.

Also, some printers use various control keys to indicate printer control operations such as skipping to the top of a page, changing the size or style of print, changing between graphics and text mode, etc.

If you attempt to list a program which has hidden control keys, you may become very frustrated.

Example: PRINT CHR$(4);"OPEN file name"
PRINT CHR$(4);"CLOSE file name"

If you have a limited number of places in your program which use the CONTROL-D value, you may code the CHR$ function in each location. This takes a little more coding, but some programmers prefer to see the actual control value rather than a variable.

1040 As a coding standard, the disk programs use the variable FDRIVE to represent the number of the disk drive on which the general data files are to be located.

The variable PDRIVE is used in other programs to represent the number of the disk drive on which the programs are located.

If you have one disk drive both fields will equal 1. If you have two disk drives normally the programs are located on drive 1 and the data files are located on drive 2.

1050 For the disk programs, a variable is used to specify the file name. The main advantage of using a variable for the file name rather than a constant is that there is no chance that the file labels will not match (at least within the program). When you key the name once, all the DOS instructions use the same value even if a keying error was made.

1060 The MONitor instruction is executed in order to provide you with some feedback on what the program is doing. As the files are opened and closed, you are able to see the instructions being executed. For operators who do not understand programming, you should display messages in more human oriented terms such as FILES OPENED, FILES CLOSED, and NORMAL END OF PROGRAM.

1070   The OPEN instruction allocates an area in the computer to prepare for handling either input from this file or output directed to the file.

The OPEN instruction also causes the file label to be entered into the disk catalog if the label does not currently exist.

1080   The CLOSE instruction causes any data which is in the output buffer and an EOF marker to be written.

The creation of a label on the disk and the writing of an EOF marker are the two objectives of this program. These objectives are not accomplished until the file is properly closed.

1090   The MONitor function is turned off since it is of no further use.

After the program completes execution, the screen will appear as follows:

```
OPEN SEQ ADDR FILE,D1
CLOSE SEQ ADDR FILE
NOMON I,O,C

NORMAL END OF PROGRAM
```

The Sequential File HELLO Program

Program Name   SEQ ADDR HELLO PROG

Program Objective   To provide a method of transition between the programs making up the ADDRESS SYSTEM so that the person using the system needs no technical knowledge of how to run a computer.

Every effort should be made to make an application package as simple for the user as possible. One technique to accomplish this is to program the system (application package) in such a way that the person using the computer needs only to know how to turn the computer on and follow directions.

The APPLE computer provides an ideal way of letting the programmer set up a turnkey system in which the user only needs to know how to insert a disk into drive 1 and turn the computer on.

When the computer is turned on, DOS automatically looks for the HELLO program which was stored on the disk during the disk INITialization process (see p. 295).

The HELLO program displays a menu and requests a response from the operator.

```
                                    ┌  1.   SEQ ADDR APPEND PROG
                                    │
                                    │  2.   SEQ ADDR UPDATE PROG
                                    │
     SEQ ADDR HELLO PROG    ┤  3.   SEQ ADDR LIST PROG
                                    │
                                    │  4.   SEQ ADDR SEARCH PROG
                                    │
                                    └  5.   QUIT PROCESSING
```

The SEQ ADDR HELLO PROG is executed automatically when the disk is placed in drive 1 and the computer is turned on (or PR#6 is entered). The operator selects a number from 1 to 5 indicating which operation is desired. The HELLO program then executes the matching program. Each program is set up to automatically return to the SEQ ADDR HELLO PROG when completed. Each time the HELLO program is executed, the operator has a choice between entering another number to run a program or entering 5 to quit processing.

The user never has to enter a RUN command for any of the processing programs.

The HELLO program and menu concept assume that only one system or set of programs is going to be located on the disk. For example, if cost is not a problem, you could put all the programs related to sequential file processing on one disk, all the programs related to random file processing on another disk, and all the programs related to indexed file processing on a third disk. Each system would have its own HELLO program, which would be executed when the system was turned on. Normally you do not want to store programs and files for more than one system on a single disk.

Use a separate disk for each system you develop. If possible, use one disk to store the programs and a separate disk to store the files.

Instructions for Running the Program

Make sure you have run the SEQ ADDR CREATE PROG before running any of the menu driven programs. The file label must exist before you run any of the programs which access the file.

Use the CATALOG command to check to see if the label exists and how many sectors are used. Scroll through the names looking for SEQ ADDR FILE. If you find the name, it should appear as

T 001 SEQ ADDR FILE

The T indicates that the file is a text file, and the 001 indicates that the file takes up 1 sector on the disk. Since a file cannot take less than a sector, you may assume the file is empty (contains no data). If the number of sectors used is greater than 1, the file most likely contains data.

After you are sure the file exists and does not contain any data, run the SEQ ADDR HELLO PROG by keying in

RUN SEQ ADDR HELLO PROG <RETURN>

The screen will clear and the menu screen will be displayed.

```
SELECT ONE OF THE FOLLOWING:

    1. ADD NEW RECORDS.

    2. CHANGE EXISTING RECORDS.

    3. LIST RECORDS ON SCREEN.

    4. SEARCH FILE BY LAST NAME.

    5. QUIT PROCESSING.

SELECTION DESIRED = ( )




....... First error message line ......
....... Second error message line .....
```

Normally you enter a number from 1 to 4 depending on which program you want to execute. But since you are just starting and there are no records currently on the SEQ ADDR FILE, you MUST RUN the APPEND program first in order to add records to the empty file.

Before you make a correct selection, press some of the following keys to see how the error messages are displayed.

1. Press the RETURN key

    No symbol is printed between the parentheses following the SELECTION message, but an error message is displayed at the bottom of the screen. Press the space bar to continue.

2. Press any key other than 1, 2, 3, 4, 5 or CONTROL-RESET.

The symbol is printed between the parentheses following the SELECTION message, and an error message is displayed at the bottom of the screen. Press the space bar to continue.

Before continuing you should look over the program listing and line explanation. After finishing with the SEQ ADDR HELLO PROGram, you will want to read all the information about the SEQ ADDR APPEND PROGram before actually adding any data.

Program Listing

```
1000 REM SEQ ADDR HELLO PROG
1010 REM --------------------
1020 TEXT : NORMAL : HOME : SPEED= 255
1030 D$ = CHR$ (4)
1040 PDRIVE = 1
1050 VTAB 5
1060 PRINT "SELECT ONE OF THE FOLLOWING:"
1070 PRINT
1080 PRINT "    1. ADD NEW RECORDS."
1090 PRINT
1100 PRINT "    2. CHANGE EXISTING RECORDS."
1110 PRINT
1120 PRINT "    3. LIST RECORDS ON SCREEN."
1130 PRINT
1140 PRINT "    4. SEARCH FILE BY LAST NAME."
1150 PRINT
1160 PRINT "    5. QUIT PROCESSING."
1170 PRINT
1180 PRINT "SELECTION DESIRED=( )"
1190 VTAB 15: HTAB 20
1200 PRINT " "; CHR$ (8); : REM CHR$(8) = BACKSPACE
1210 GET X1$: X1 = VAL (X1$): IF ASC(X1$) > 31 THEN PRINT  X1$;
1220 IF X1 < 1 OR X1 > 5 THEN 1270
1230 IF X1 = 5 THEN 1490
1240 VTAB 23: HTAB 1: INVERSE
1250 PRINT " LOADING PROGRAM - PLEASE WAIT        ": NORMAL
1260 ON X1 GOTO 1370,1400,1430,1460
1270 VTAB 23: HTAB 1: INVERSE
1280 PRINT "   INVALID ENTRY" TAB( 39)" "
1290 PRINT "   PRESS SPACE BAR AND TRY AGAIN" TAB( 38)" ";
1300 NORMAL : GET X1$
1310 IF X1$ < > " " THEN 1300
1320 VTAB 23: HTAB 1
1330 PRINT TAB( 39)" "
1340 PRINT TAB( 39)" ";
1350 GOTO 1190
1360 REM --------------------
1370 PRINT D$
1380 PRINT D$;"RUN SEQ ADDR APPEND PROG,D"PDRIVE
1390 REM --------------------
1400 PRINT D$
1410 PRINT D$;"RUN SEQ ADDR UPDATE PROG,D"PDRIVE
```

```
1420 REM -----------------------
1430 PRINT D$
1440 PRINT D$;"RUN SEQ ADDR LIST PROG,D"PDRIVE
1450 REM -----------------------
1460 PRINT D$
1470 PRINT D$;"RUN SEQ ADDR SEARCH PROG,D"PDRIVE
1480 REM -----------------------
1490 HOME
1500 PRINT "THAT'S ALL FOLKS!"
1510 END
```

Explanation by Line Number

Detailed explanations by line number follow.

1040

When designing a system, it is best to put all the programs on one disk and the data files on a second disk. This works fine for systems with two or more disk drives but does not work for single disk systems.

As a coding standard, all the programs which access information on the disk use two variables to indicate which disk drive is to be accessed. The name PDRIVE stands for Program DRIVE and contains the number 1, indicating the drive on which the programs are located. The name FDRIVE stands for File DRIVE and should contain either a 1 or 2 depending on how many drives you have on your system.

Rather than hard coding the OPEN and RUN instructions to use a specific disk, use variables to make the programs easier to change. If you code constants such as

PRINT D$;"RUN program name,D1"

or

PRINT D$;"OPEN file name,D2"

throughout your programs, the instructions will be difficult to change. If you code variables such as

PRINT D$;"RUN program name,D"PDRIVE

or

PRINT D$;"OPEN file name,D"FDRIVE

throughout your programs, then all the instructions may easily be changed by setting the drive variable equal to either a 1 or 2 at the beginning of each program.

By using a variable name to indicate which disk is to be accessed, you make your software much more flexible. In this book all the programs are set up to run with one disk drive. But you may change the value of FDRIVE to 2 and have the files located on drive 2.

1050–1190 Lines 1050 through 1170 display the menu indicating the possible choices to the operator. You should look at the last two lines to see how they are coded. Line 1180 provides a place for the operator to respond, and line 1190 is responsible for positioning the cursor within the parentheses.

1200 PRINT " "; CHR$ (8); : REM CHR$(8) = BACKSPACE

This PRINT instruction is beneficial only if the operator makes a mistake and enters a character other than 1, 2, 3, 4, or 5. For example, if you run the program and press the letter A, the A is displayed between the parentheses, and an error message is printed, indicating the mistake. After the error message is displayed, the operator is given another chance to enter a correct value. Before the operator is given another chance, line 1200 erases the A and backs up the cursor so it is located between the parentheses. The " " erases the position, while the CHR$(8) backs the cursor up one position.

1210 Line 1210 accepts a character, converts the symbol to a numeric value, and then checks and prints the character. The VAL function converts the single character string variable to a value from 0 to 9 so it can be used in the ON GOTO instruction. The ASC function converts the symbol to the binary value related to the character (see Appendix A). If the binary value of the character entered is greater than 31, it is not a control character and is displayed.

If you are using the GET instruction and want to display the character entered, you can follow the GET with a PRINT instruction; but be careful of control characters and the RETURN key. If you print the RETURN character on lines 1 through 23 and follow it with a semicolon, the screen will not scroll. But if you are using line 24 and the operator makes a mistake and presses the RETURN key instead of some acceptable character, there is a problem. When the RETURN symbol is printed on line 24, the screen scrolls up one line, even if the PRINT instruction ends with a semicolon.

If you are entering data on line 24, check the character entered for an ASC value of 13 (RETURN key), and do not print a RETURN symbol. Use the following sequence of instructions:

```
1000 GET X1$
1010 IF ASC (X1$) = 13 THEN PRINT " ";: GOTO 1030
1020 PRINT X1$;
1030 ... next instruction
```

1220 Line 1220 tests to make sure the value entered is within acceptable limits of the ON GOTO instruction. This test is not really necessary for this program since only a single digit may be entered. But it is a good practice to always precede an ON GOTO or an ON GOSUB with a test to make sure the value is not less than 0 or greater than 255.

If an invalid value is entered, logic flow skips to line 1270.

1230 If the operator enters a 5, the program is terminated.

1240–1250 Since there is a significant amount of time (several seconds) between the operator's entering a number and the execution of the next program, lines 1240 and 1250 display a message to indicate what is going on.

1260 ON X1 GOTO 1370,1400,1430,1460

Depending on the value keyed in, the ON number GOTO instruction causes program flow to branch to one of the four statement numbers following the GOTO or to fall through to the next instruction. If a 1 is entered, logic flow branches to statement 1370: a 2 causes a branch to 1400, a 3 to 1430, and a 4 to 1460.

1270 VTAB 23: HTAB 1: INVERSE

1280 PRINT "INVALID ENTRY" TAB(39)" "

1290 PRINT "PRESS SPACE BAR AND TRY AGAIN" TAB(38)" ";

1300 NORMAL : GET X1$

1310 IF X1$ < > " " THEN 1300

1320 VTAB 23: HTAB 1

1330 PRINT TAB(39)" "

1340 PRINT TAB(39)" ";

1350 GOTO 1190

The set of instructions from lines 1270 through 1350 represents a standard sequence for displaying an error message and waiting for a response from the operator.

As a design standard, all programs in this book use lines 23 and 24 of the screen for displaying error messages.

Lines 1270, 1280, and 1290 print the error message in the INVERSE mode. The lines look very simple, but there are several points you should make sure you understand.

Notice that the TAB function is used to cause inverse blanks to be printed all the way over to column 39. If the inverse blanks are not printed to column 39, the error message does not form a nice looking box. Also, notice that column 40 is not used on lines 23 and 24. When something is printed in column 40 of line 24, the screen automatically scrolls up one line even if the information is followed by a semicolon. The scrolling messes up the screen design, so none of the programs use column 40 of line 24.

Since a semicolon is used at the end of the PRINT instruction on line 1290, the cursor stays on line 24 in column 39 waiting for the operator to respond to the error message. If the semicolon is not used, the computer automatically scrolls up one line since the line just printed is the last line on the screen.

After the operator presses the space bar, lines 1320 through 1350 clear the error message and branch back to give the operator another chance at entering a correct value.

1370   PRINT D$

1380   PRINT D$;"RUN SEQ ADDR APPEND PROG,D"PDRIVE
....

1470   PRINT D$;"RUN SEQ ADDR SEARCH PROG,D"PDRIVE

If 1, 2, 3, or 4 is entered, logic branches to the matching RUN statement and causes the program to be run. Because of the way the GET and the DOS instructions work, there is a problem with trying to execute a DOS instruction after using the GET instruction. I will not try to explain why the problem exists but suggest that whenever you use the GET instruction and any DOS instructions in the same program, you should always print a dummy CONTROL-D prior to printing the actual DOS instruction.

The programs in this book always print a dummy D$ prior to executing a DOS instruction.

The Sequential File APPEND Program

Program Name   SEQ ADDR APPEND PROG

Program Objective   To provide the user with a method of adding new records to the SEQ ADDR FILE.

There are basically two methods for adding records to a file. The easiest method for both the operator and the programmer is to add new records to the end of an existing file. The harder method is to copy the old file and insert the new records in correct sequence as the new file is written out.

Since the objective of this program is to show how to use the APPEND instruction, the new records will be added to the end of the existing file (this also happens to be the easiest method to program).

Instructions for Running the Program

Make sure you have run the SEQ ADDR CREATE PROG. After the file has been created, run the SEQ ADDR HELLO PROG. In response to the menu, enter a 1, and the HELLO program will execute the APPEND program for you.

Those of you who want to bypass the HELLO program may run the program directly by entering

RUN SEQ ADDR APPEND PROG <RETURN>

After the program starts, the following screen will be displayed.

```
                    SEQ ADDR APPEND PROG


        NAME      = (                              )
        ADDRESS   = (                              )
        CITY      = (                    )
        STATE     = (   )
        ZIP CODE  = (      )
        PHONE     = (    -    -      )




        ( ) PRESS  A  TO ACCEPT THE ENTRY.
            PRESS  R  TO REJECT THE ENTRY.

        ( ) PRESS  Q  TO QUIT.
            PRESS THE SPACE BAR TO CONTINUE.




        ....... First error message line ......
        ....... Second error message line .....
```

When the screen is displayed, the cursor is positioned at the start of the quit or continue message. The program waits until you press Q to quit processing or the space bar to continue. When the space bar is pressed, the cursor is repositioned to the first data line. The] symbol indicates the position of the cursor on the screen.

(]) PRESS Q TO QUIT.
PRESS THE SPACE BAR TO CONTINUE.

In response to the first question, press the space bar. The cursor should now be in the first column of the name field.

```
NAME     = (]                        )
ADDRESS  = (                         )
```

Enter the name JOHN JONES and press RETURN. The cursor will move to the first column of the address field. Continue the data entry operation by keying in the address and the city as shown below. Since the data you are entering is shorter than the size of the field on the screen you must press RETURN after entering the last character of each field.

```
NAME     = (JOHN JONES               )
ADDRESS  = (1234 EASY STREET         )
CITY     = (NEW YORK       )
```

When you enter the state code, ZIP code, and phone number, the number of characters entered matches the maximum size of the field, and you do not need to press RETURN. As you press the last key of the character, the cursor automatically skips to the next field. Enter the state code, ZIP code, and phone number as follows:

```
STATE    = (NY)
ZIP CODE = (11111)
PHONE    = (222-333-4444)
```

After you enter the last digit of the phone number, the cursor is repositioned to the accept or reject message line, where it waits for you to check what you have entered.

(]) PRESS A TO ACCEPT THE ENTRY.
   PRESS R TO REJECT THE ENTRY.

If you did not make any mistakes on entering the data, then press A, and the record will be accepted. If you made a mistake and want to reject the data, enter an R.

The programs are designed to allow you to back up and change characters within the fields (by using the back arrow key) but are not designed to allow you to back up between fields. Once the cursor moves to the next field, you cannot return to the prior field. If you make a mistake and do not catch it until the cursor is positioned to a new field, then press the RETURN key until all the remaining fields have been skipped. Then reject the record and you will have another chance to reenter all the data correctly. This is not the best programming technique, but it is easy to code.

If you enter an A, the information is accepted, the screen is cleared, and the cursor is repositioned to the quit or continue message line to start the process over. Depending on how many records have been entered, the disk drive may or may not be activated (whirl and start up). Do not be concerned if the disk does not start up after accepting a record. Records are not written out to the disk until the output buffer is full. The buffer can hold a maximum of 256 characters, so data is written to the disk every three or four records (83 * 3 = 249; 83 * 4 = 332).

If you enter an R the screen is cleared, the data entered is rejected, and the cursor is repositioned to the quit or continue message line to start the process over.

If you press any key other than A or R, then the following error message is displayed at the bottom of the screen.

INVALID RESPONSE - PRESS SPACE BAR
TO CONTINUE

Continue entering a few records. Try to enter at least five records so you may see what happens when the buffer is filled. Hint: The red light on the disk turns on and buffer is written out.

After you are through entering data, press a Q in response to quit or continue message. The disk will whirl, any data currently in the output buffer will be written, and the file will be closed. After the file is closed, the SEQ ADDR HELLO PROGram is run, and the original menu is displayed.

The program must terminate normally in order for the last few records to be written out and the EOF marker to be correctly written.

If you want to see the data you entered, press a 3 in response to the menu to run the SEQ ADDR LIST PROGram.

Program Listing

```
1000 REM SEQ ADDR APPEND PROG
1010 REM ----------------------
1020 CLEAR :G1 = PEEK (116) * 256 + PEEK (115) - 40 :GA$  = "
     12345678901234567890" + "12345678901234567890"
1030 REM
1040 REM ----------------------
1050 REM DRIVE ROUTINE
1060 GOSUB 1870: REM BEGINNING
1070 GOSUB 1300: REM MAIN MOD
1080 GOTO 2280: REM END MODULE
1090 REM
1100 REM ----------------------
1110 REM GET SUBROUTINE
1120 IF G3 = 0 THEN GOSUB 1270
1130 G3 = G1 + GA - 1: FOR G2 = G1 TO G3: POKE G2,32: NEXT :
     G2 = G1
```

```
1140 CALL 768:GB = PEEK (775) - 128: IF GB = 08 THEN 1210
1150 IF GB = 13 THEN 1230
1160 IF GB = 21 THEN PRINT CHR$ ( PEEK (G2));: GOTO 1190
1170 IF GB = 44 OR GB = 58 OR GB < 32 THEN 1140
1180 PRINT CHR$ (GB);: POKE G2,GB
1190 G2 = G2 + 1: IF G2 > G3 THEN 1260
1200 GOTO 1140
1210 G2 = G2 - 1: IF G2 < G1 THEN G2 = G1: GOTO 1140
1220 PRINT CHR$ (8);: GOTO 1140
1230 IF G1 = G2 THEN 1250
1240 FOR GC = G2 TO G3: PRINT " ";: NEXT
1250 FOR GC = G2 TO G3: POKE GC,32: NEXT
1260 GB$ = LEFT$ (GA$,GA):GC = G2 - G1: RETURN
1270 POKE 768,32: POKE 769,12: POKE 770,253: POKE 771,141:
     POKE 772,07: POKE 773,03: POKE 774,96: RETURN
1280 REM
1290 REM ----------------------
1300 REM MAIN ROUTINE
1310 VTAB L8: HTAB 2: GET X1$
1320 IF X1$ = "Q" THEN 1840
1330 IF X1$ < > " " THEN 1310
1340 GOSUB 2180: REM CHECK ;MEMORY SPACE
1350 GALEGTH = 25: VTAB L1: HTAB 12: GOSUB 1110
1360 IF LEFT$ (GBANSWER$,1) = " " THEN 1350
1370 AANAME$ = GBANSWER$
1380 VTAB L2: HTAB 12: GOSUB 1110
1390 ABADDR$ = GBANSWER$
1400 GALEGTH = 15: VTAB L3: HTAB 12: GOSUB 1110
1410 ACCITY$ = GBANSWER$
1420 GALEGTH = 2: VTAB L4: HTAB 12: GOSUB 1110
1430 ADSTE$ = GBANSWER$
1440 GALEGTH = 5: VTAB L5: HTAB 12: GOSUB 1110
1450 AEZIP$ = GBANSWER$
1460 GALEGTH = 3: VTAB L6: HTAB 12: GOSUB 1110
1470 AFPHNE$ = GBANSWER$
1480 HTAB 16: GOSUB 1110
1490 AFPHNE$ = AFPHNE$ + GBANSWER$
1500 GALEGTH = 4: HTAB 20: GOSUB 1110
1510 AFPHNE$ = AFPHNE$ + GBANSWER$
1520 VTAB L7: HTAB 2: PRINT " "; CHR$(8);: REM CHR$(8) = BACKSPACE
1530 GET X1$: PRINT X1$;
1540 IF X1$ = "A" THEN 1680
1550 IF X1$ = "R" THEN 1750
1560 REM ----------------------
1570 REM ERROR MESSAGE
1580 VTAB L9: HTAB 1: INVERSE
1590 PRINT "INVALID RESPONSE - PRESS SPACE BAR" TAB( 39)" "
1600 PRINT "                    TO CONTINUE" TAB (38) " ";: NORMAL
1610 GET X1$: IF X1$ < > " " THEN 1610
1620 VTAB L9: HTAB 1
1630 PRINT TAB( 39)" "
1640 PRINT TAB( 39)" ";
1650 GOTO 1520
1660 REM
```

```
1670 REM ----------------------
1680 REM WRITE ON DISK
1690 PRINT D$
1700 PRINT D$;"WRITE ";FILEID$
1710 PRINT AANAME$;ABADDR$;ACCITY$;ADSTE$;AEZIP$;AFPHNE$
1720 PRINT D$
1730 REM
1740 REM ----------------------
1750 REM CLEAR SCREEN
1760 VTAB L1: HTAB 12: PRINT TAB( 36)" ": REM SPC CLEARED LINE
1770 VTAB L2: HTAB 12: PRINT TAB( 36)" "
1780 VTAB L3: HTAB 12: PRINT SPC( 15)
1790 VTAB L4: HTAB 12: PRINT "   "
1800 VTAB L5: HTAB 12: PRINT "        "
1810 VTAB L6: HTAB 12: PRINT "   -   -    "
1820 VTAB L7: HTAB 2: PRINT " "
1830 GOTO 1310
1840 RETURN
1850 REM
1860 REM ----------------------
1870 REM BEGINNING ROUTINE
1880 TEXT : NORMAL : HOME : SPEED= 255
1890 D$ = CHR$ (4)
1900 FDRIVE = 1:PDRIVE = 1
1910 FILEID$ = "SEQ ADDR FILE"
1920 L1 = 5:L2 = 6:L3 = 7:L4 = 8:L5 = 9:L6 = 10:L7 = 14:L8 =
     17: L9 = 23
1930 PRINT D$
1940 PRINT D$;"APPEND ";FILEID$;",D";FDRIVE
1950 PRINT D$
1960 REM
1970 REM ----------------------
1980 REM PRINT SCREEN IMAGE
1990 HOME
2000 PRINT
2010 PRINT "        SEQ ADDR APPEND PROG"
2020 VTAB L1: PRINT "NAME     =(" SPC( 25)")"
2030 VTAB L2: PRINT "ADDRESS  =(" SPC( 25)")"
2040 VTAB L3: PRINT "CITY     =(" SPC( 15)")"
2050 VTAB L4: PRINT "STATE    =(  )"
2060 VTAB L5: PRINT "ZIP CODE =(     )"
2070 VTAB L6: PRINT "PHONE    =(   -   -    )"
2080 VTAB L7
2090 PRINT "( ) PRESS  A  TO ACCEPT THE ENTRY."
2100 PRINT "    PRESS  R  TO REJECT THE ENTRY."
2110 VTAB L8
2120 PRINT "( ) PRESS  Q  TO QUIT."
2130 PRINT "    PRESS THE SPACE BAR TO CONTINUE."
2140 RETURN
2150 REM
2160 REM ----------------------
2170 REM FREE MEMORY ROUTINE
2180 STARTING = PEEK (112) * 256 + PEEK (111): IF STARTING >
     17000 THEN 2250
```

```
2190 VTAB L9: HTAB 1: INVERSE
2200 PRINT " FREEING MEMORY - PLEASE WAIT" TAB( 38)" "
2210 STARTING = FRE (0)
2220 PRINT " DONE - PRESS SPACE BAR TO CONTINUE   ";: NORMAL
2230 GET X1$: IF X1$ < > " " THEN 2230
2240 VTAB L9: HTAB 1: PRINT TAB( 39)" ": PRINT TAB( 39)" ";
2250 RETURN
2260 REM
2270 REM ----------------------
2280 REM ENDING ROUTINE
2290 PRINT D$
2300 PRINT D$;"CLOSE ";FILEID$
2310 HOME
2320 PRINT D$;"RUN SEQ ADDR HELLO PROG,D"PDRIVE
2330 REM
2340 REM ----------------------
```

Cross Reference Listing

Variable names used with the address record:

AA$ 1370, 1710
AB$ 1390, 1710
AC$ 1410, 1710
AD$ 1430, 1710
AE$ 1450, 1710
AF$ 1470, 1490, 1510, 1710

Variable names used with the disk commands:

D$ 1690, 1700, 1720, 1890, 1930, 1940, 1950, 2290, 2300, 2320
FD 1900, 1940
FI$ 1700, 1910, 1940, 2300
PD 1900, 2320

Variable names used with the GET subroutine:

G1 1020, 1130, 1210, 1230, 1260
G2 1130, 1160, 1180, 1190, 1210, 1230, 1240, 1250, 1260
G3 1120, 1130, 1190, 1240, 1250
GA 1130, 1260, 1350, 1400, 1420, 1440, 1460, 1500
GA$ 1020, 1260
GB 1140, 1150, 1160, 1170, 1180
GB$ 1260, 1360, 1370, 1390, 1410, 1430, 1450, 1470, 1490, 1510
GC 1240, 1250, 1260

Variable names used with displaying data on the screen:

L1 1350, 1760, 1920, 2020
L2 1380, 1770, 1920, 2030
L3 1400, 1780, 1920, 2040
L4 1420, 1790, 1920, 2050
L5 1440, 1800, 1920, 2060
L6 1460, 1810, 1920, 2070
L7 1520, 1820, 1920, 2080
L8 1310, 1920, 2110
L9 1580, 1620, 1920, 2190, 2240

Variable name used for general GET instruction in response to the screen messages:

X1$ 1310, 1320, 1330, 1530, 1540, 1550, 1610, 2230

Explanation By Line Number   Detailed explanations by line number follow.

1000   REM SEQ ADDR APPEND PROG

1010   REM ---------------------

1020   CLEAR :G1 = PEEK (116) * 256 + PEEK (115) − 40 :GA$ = "12345678901234567890" + "12345678901234567890"

1030   REM

1040   REM ---------------------

1050   REM DRIVE ROUTINE

1060   GOSUB 1790: REM BEGINNING

1070   GOSUB 1280: REM MAIN MOD

1080   GOTO 2070: REM END MODULE

With the exception of a few short programs in the system, each program starts off with the same basic set of instructions.

Line 1020 is used by the GET subroutine. The instruction must be coded exactly as shown and must be the first instruction in the program.

The first line of each program contains the name of the program as stored on the disk. If you follow the practice of always listing the first line of the program and then SAVEing the program under the name on line 1000, you are less likely to destroy a program by saving one under the wrong name.

Almost all programs may be broken down into three parts:

1. Those instructions which are to be executed once at the beginning of the program to start the program correctly (BEGINNING process)
2. Those instructions which are to be executed repeatedly to process each record (MAIN process)
3. Those instructions which are to be executed once at the end of the program to correctly terminate the program (ENDING process)

GOSUB instructions are used to execute the BEGINNING ROUTINE and the MAIN ROUTINE since they return to the DRIVE ROUTINE when done. A GOTO instruction is used to execute the ENDING ROUTINE since it starts execution of another program and does not return to the DRIVE ROUTINE.

Logically, the code is executed in the sequence of beginning instructions, main instructions, and ending instructions. Physically, the various parts of the program are located in a different sequence. The primary reason for having the code in a different sequence from that in which it is executed is that Applesoft and most BASIC languages execute faster if the most frequently used code is located toward the beginning of the program.

Therefore, one reason to place the most frequently used code toward the beginning of the program is to improve execution speed.

In working with programs, I have found it better to have the more difficult code toward the beginning of the program and the easier code toward the end; the most often referenced or changed code toward the beginning and the least often referenced code toward the end.

You may arrange your code in the same sequence as instruction execution if you like, but no matter what sequence you arrange the modules in, always code your programs in independent segments as shown in the example programs.

1100–1280 The GET subroutine was explained in detail earlier. If you want to review the GET subroutine, see p. 284.

1300 REM MAIN ROUTINE

1310 VTAB L8: HTAB 2: GET X1$

1320 IF X1$ = "Q" THEN 1840
....

1840 RETURN

The first line of the MAIN ROUTINE positions the cursor at the bottom of the screen to allow the operator to respond by pressing Q to quit or to press the space bar to continue.

(]) PRESS   Q   TO QUIT.
   PRESS THE SPACE BAR TO CONTINUE.

If the operator enters a Q, then the IF instruction causes a branch to line 1840, which in turn causes logic flow to RETURN to the DRIVE ROUTINE. Once back at the drive module, the GOTO instruction on line 1080 branches to the ENDING ROUTINE.

The RETURN and IF instruction could be combined and written as

1320 IF X1$ = "Q" THEN RETURN

The two instructions are separated because as a general rule it is best to have only one entry point to a module and one exit point from a module. The entry point is normally the first line of code, while the RETURN is normally the last line of code. This may require a little extra coding, but in the long run it is simpler to follow and debug.

Also, unless you are going to exclude all remarks from your program, I suggest you always branch to the REM instruction which names the module. This allows you to insert instructions at the very start of the module without having to worry about changing line numbers. Unfortunately, the example programs do not always follow this coding standard even though they should. This is one of those 'Do as I say and not as I do' situations.

```
                          1290 REM --------------------
GOSUB or GOTO to this line > 1300 REM MAIN ROUTINE
                          1310 VTAB L8: HTAB 2: GET X1$
```

1340 Because of the way in which the APPLE uses string memory, you should periodically check how much memory is available. If string memory becomes full, the APPLE automatically pauses and condenses memory, but does not let the operator know what it is doing. The operator can be in the middle of keying in a field when the cursor disappears for several minutes. By checking the amount of memory yourself, you can control when the memory is cleared and can display a message to the operator indicating what is going on (see FRE instruction p. 233).

1350   GALEGTH = 25: VTAB L1: HTAB 12: GOSUB 1110

1360   IF LEFT$ (GBANSWER$,1) = " " THEN 1350

1370   AANAME$ = GBANSWER$
....

1510   AFPHNE$ = AFPHNE$ + GBANSWER$

Most of the MAIN ROUTINE includes instructions for retrieving data from the screen and forms a repetitive pattern.

If you look closely at the code you will see a sequence of five instructions for each value entered.

1. Set GALEGTH to the length of the field to be read.
2. Position the cursor on the correct line.
3. Position the cursor at the correct column.
4. Execute the GET subroutine.
5. Set a variable equal to the value entered.

Lines 1460 through 1510 break the basic sequence by containing code which is dependent on prior lines to set up the correct field length and cursor position.

```
1460 GALEGTH = 3: VTAB L6: HTAB 12: GOSUB 1110
1470 AFPHNE$ = GBANSWER$
1480 HTAB 16: GOSUB 1110
1490 AFPHNE$ = AFPHNE$ + GBANSWER$
```

Line 1480 relies on line 1460 for setting GALEGTH to the correct length and for positioning the cursor on the correct line.

Since the phone number is all on the same line, no VTAB instruction is needed for the last two parts of the phone number. Also, since the first and second part of the phone number are the same length, the variable GALEGTH only has to be set equal to 3 one time. When code relies on prior lines to set up specific values, it is referred to as *dependent code*. This coding technique is more efficient in execution time but may make it harder to modify the program.

Any modification to the lines between 1460 and 1510 may result in an error unless the programmer is aware of the dependent code.

From a program maintenance standpoint it would be better to repeat the VTAB instruction and to set the length for each field to be read even though the code is redundant.

Some programmers like to make the program execute as fast as possible and take as few instructions as possible. They spend hours trying to eliminate redundant code. The resulting program executes slightly faster but is harder to change.

The problem with trying to eliminate redundant code is that the cost it takes in man hours to make a program operate more efficiently may not be recovered during the life of the program.

Most production shops are concerned with the number of correctly written and easily modifiable programs which may be turned out by a programmer rather than how efficiently the programs can be made to run.

1520–1530   VTAB L7: HTAB 2: PRINT " "; CHR$(8);: REM CHR$(8) = BACKSPACE GET X1$: PRINT X1$;

Once all the fields have been entered, lines 1520 and 1530 position the cursor and accept a response from the operator.

( ) PRESS A TO ACCEPT THE ENTRY.
   PRESS R TO REJECT THE ENTRY.

If the operator enters A, the program branches to the WRITE ROUTINE, where the record is written on the disk and the screen cleared. After the screen is cleared, logic flow branches back to the beginning of the MAIN ROUTINE to start the whole process over.

If the operator enters R, the program skips over the WRITE ROUTINE and branches to instructions for clearing the screen. After the screen is cleared, logic flow starts over from the beginning of the MAIN ROUTINE to allow the operator a choice of quitting or entering another record.

The only two allowable responses are A and R. Any other key causes program logic to fall through the two IF instructions and continue on to display an error message.

The last half of line 1520 is beneficial only if the operator made a mistake and entered a character other than A or R. The instruction PRINT " "; CHR$(8); blanks out any character which was printed between the two parentheses.

```
1560   REM ----------------------

1570   REM ERROR MESSAGE

1580   VTAB L9: HTAB 1: INVERSE

1590   PRINT "INVALID RESPONSE - PRESS SPACE BAR" TAB( 39)" "

1600   PRINT "                    TO CONTINUE" TAB (38)" ";: NORMAL

1610   GET X1$: IF X1$ < > " " THEN 1610

1620   VTAB L9: HTAB 1

1630   PRINT TAB( 39)" "

1640   PRINT TAB( 39)" ";

1650   GOTO 1520
```

The following narrative is a repeat, so if you understand the routine, skip to the next group of instructions.

The set of instructions from line 1560 through 1640 represents the standard sequence for displaying an error message and waiting for a response from the operator.

As a design standard, all the programs in this book use lines 23 and 24 of the screen for displaying error messages.

Lines 1580, 1590, and 1600 print the error message in the INVERSE mode. The lines look very simple, but there are several points you should understand.

Notice that the TAB function is used to cause INVERSE blanks to be printed all the way over to column 39. If the inverse blanks are not printed to column 39, the error message does not form a good looking box. Notice that column 40 is not used on lines 23 and 24. When something is printed in column 40 of line 24 a scrolling problem results. The scrolling messes up the screen design, so none of the programs use column 40 of line 24.

On the second line of the error message, the TAB function stops at column 38. Since the semicolon is used at the end of the PRINT instruction, the cursor stays on line 24 in column 39 waiting for the operator to respond to the error message.

```
1670    REM --------------------

1680    REM WRITE ON DISK

1690    PRINT D$

1700    PRINT D$;"WRITE";FILEID$

1710    PRINT AANAME$;ABADDR$;ACCITY$;ADSTE$;AEZIP$;AFPHNE$

1720    PRINT D$
```

There are several ways records may be written. One way is to write one fixed length record as shown above, and the other is to write each variable individually, separated by a comma within quotation marks.

```
1710 PRINT AANAME$","ABADDR$","ACCITY$","ADSTE$","AEZIP$"," AFPHNE$
```

There are advantages and disadvantages to each method.

1. Writing one fixed record (semicolon separation)
    a. Advantage: It takes less room on the disk when you are working with all string variables.

    b. Disadvantage: It requires a set of instructions when you are reading the record to break down the information into the individual variables. How to break down the record is shown in the update program.

    c. Disadvantage: Numeric variables must be converted to string format with a fixed size (not shown in examples).

2. Writing each individual variable (comma separation)

    a. Advantage: It is easier to code.

    b. Advantage: Numeric variables may be written directly to the disk without being converted to string format. Since numeric variables are stored in binary notation, they take less space on the disk than when converted to string format and stored.

    c. Disadvantage: It requires more room on the disk (unless you are working with numeric variables).

    d. Disadvantage: If any of the string variables written to the disk are blank or have leading spaces, the spaces will be suppressed when the values are read. This disadvantage is explained in the random disk system.

When individual variables are written to the disk, each comma separating the variables is also written on the disk. For this example, each record would take up an additional five characters on the disk (count the commas between the six variables).

The programs presented earlier to illustrate the READ and WRITE instruction explained how to use the commas when reading and writing disk files. All the sequential address programs use the technique of writing the variables separated by semicolons. When the semicolon is used, each variable is written immediately following the previous variable, and no separator (comma) is written within the record. The machine sees the record as one big string variable.

This technique should be used only when working with all string data. If you have records which contain numeric data, you should use commas between the numeric variables.

```
1740    REM --------------------

1750    REM CLEAR SCREEN

1760    VTAB L1: HTAB 12: PRINT TAB( 36)" "


........


1820    VTAB L7: HTAB 2: PRINT " "

1830    GOTO 1310

1840    RETURN
```

After the record is written or the data rejected, the screen is cleared. Notice only that the variable portion of the screen is cleared. The fixed titles remain on the screen.

The process for clearing a specific part of the screen is to first position the cursor at the area to be cleared (see line 1760). Once the cursor is at the correct location, then the PRINT instruction is used to print the correct number of blanks or to TAB to the last position and print a single blank (see lines 1760 and 1820). The TAB function clears to spaces all positions it passes over.

Two approaches are used for microcomputers when a screen format is displayed. Each has its own advantages and disadvantages.

1. Displaying a new screen for each entry
    a. Advantage: It is easier for the programmer to code.
    b. Disadvantages: The screen scrolls as lines are displayed, and this is harder on the operator's eyes. Also, since everything is redisplayed, this takes longer between data entry steps and slows down the operator.
2. Displaying the format once and clearing out the variable information after each entry
    a. Advantage: This gives faster execution and is easier on the operator's eyes.
    b. Disadvantage: It is harder for the programmer to code. Some computers do not have instructions corresponding to the VTAB and HTAB operations, leaving scrolling as the only method available.

After the screen is cleared, line 1830 causes program flow to branch back to the start of the MAIN ROUTINE. The RETURN instruction on line 1840 is executed only when the operator enters a Q to quit.

```
1860    REM --------------------

1870    REM BEGINNING ROUTINE

...............

1920    L1 = 5:L2 = 6:L3 = 7:L4 = 8:L5 = 9:L6 = 10:L7 = 14:L8 = 17: L9 = 23

1930    PRINT D$

1940    PRINT D$;"APPEND ";FILEID$:",D";FDRIVE

1950    PRINT D$
```

Line 1920 initializes the variable names for use in the **VTAB** instruction. When you use variables throughout the program code, it is much easier to redesign the screen by simply changing the values of the variable. If constants are used and you want to redesign the screen, you must locate and change each **VTAB** instruction in the program.

One word of warning. Only nine variable names are used on line 1920 (L1 to L9). If you need more than nine values, be sure to name them LA, LB, LC, etc. Remember, Applesoft only keeps track of the first two characters. To the computer, L10 is the same variable as L1.

Lines 1930 through 1950 instruct the computer to open the file and position the record pointer at the end of the file. Line 1930 prints a dummy disk control character. Since this set of code is executed at the very start of the program and no **GET** instruction has been executed, line 1930 may be eliminated. It is included here to be consistent with the sequence of

1. Printing a dummy control character because of the problems which occur when a DOS **PRINT** instruction follows a **GET** instruction
2. Printing a disk control character followed by the actual disk instruction
3. Printing a disk control character to terminate a disk instruction

```
1970   REM ---------------------

1980   REM PRINT SCREEN IMAGE

 ...............

2140   RETURN
```

As indicated earlier, the fixed portion of the screen is displayed only once. Two points you might want to study are represented on line 2020.

```
2020 VTAB L1: PRINT "NAME =(" SPC( 25)")"
```

When lines are displayed on the screen, the variables L1 though L9 are used in order to make the program easier to change. If for some reason you want to change the positions at which various lines are printed, only the line which defines the variables needs to be changed, and all **VTAB** operations using the variable automatically position the cursor to the correct location.

Another reason for using variables instead of constants is that Applesoft executes faster if variables are used.

When a large number of spaces are needed on the same line, the **SPC** function may be used. Using the **SPC** function is sometimes easier than counting out and keying the exact number of spaces.

```
2160   REM ---------------------
```

2170 REM FREE MEMORY ROUTINE

2180 STARTING = PEEK (112) * 256 + PEEK (111): IF STARTING > 17000 THEN 2250

....

2210 STARTING = FRE (0)

....

2250 RETURN

The FREE MEMORY ROUTINE tests to see when memory is becoming full. The advantages of the routine are the following:

1. It does not free memory until the space is needed.
2. While it is freeing memory, it lets the operator know what is going on.

To help explain why it is important to use the FRE instruction in programs which work extensively with string variables, let's review how string memory is used.

When Applesoft assigns a new value to a string variable, it does not put the value into a specific area of memory allocated for that variable. Instead Applesoft puts each new value into a new area of memory and then changes the pointer associated with the variable to indicate the address of the new data.

For the following two lines of code, assume the next available string memory location is 2000.

1000 STRING$ = STR$(123)

When line 1000 is executed, the characters 123 are placed into memory locations 1998, 1999, and 2000. Remember, strings are stored working from high memory addresses down. After moving the values into string memory, Applesoft changes the address pointer associated with STRING$ to point to the start of the variable (address 1998).

1010 STRING$ = STRING$ + STR$(456)

When STRING$ is set equal to a new value, the new value is not moved into locations 1998, 1999, and 2000. Instead, the value 123456 is moved into the next available memory locations (1992 to 1997) and the pointer for STRING$ is set equal to the start of the new value (1992). The old value of 123 is still in memory locations 1998 through 2000 but is no longer associated with the variable called STRING$. The value has become garbage and is just taking up memory.

As the program continues to use different values, the garbage (unused areas) continues to build. If your program is short and you have a lot of memory, you may never have any problems. But if the program does an extensive amount of string processing, you should periodically clear memory. Remember, the FREe instruction is only needed for condensing unused string values. Numeric variables are stored using fixed memory locations and do not cause problems by generating wasted storage.

Now back to why you should use the FREE MEMORY ROUTINE. If the program does not periodically free memory, the computer automatically frees memory when string storage starts to run into the numeric values stored in lower memory.

There are several problems in letting the computer do its own housecleaning whenever it wants to. The primary problem is that the computer does not let the operator know what is going on. When the computer frees memory, the cursor disappears and can take several minutes before returning.

Put yourself in the operator's position. If you were an operator and the cursor disappeared for several minutes, you might think the program had a bug and turn off the computer. This frees memory but also results in the loss of some processing and causes frustration for the operator.

Copy this routine and use it in any program which does an extensive amount of string processing. If possible, execute the routine during each main cycle (MAIN ROUTINE loop).

If you are writing extremely large programs or using page 2 of high resolution graphics, you should raise the address on line 2180 from 17000 to a higher value.

Note: If you use large tables DIM TABLE$(1000), the clearing process is very slow (minutes). If you do not use large DIM entries, the clearing process is very fast (fractions of a second). See the FRE instruction for more detail (p. 233).

```
2270   REM --------------------

2280   REM ENDING ROUTINE

2290   PRINT D$

2300   PRINT D$;"CLOSE ";FILEID$

2310   HOME

2320   PRINT D$;"RUN SEQ ADDR HELLO PROG,D"PDRIVE
```

The ENDING ROUTINE is the last module to be executed. There are two important instructions to consider within this set of code.

On line 2300 the SEQ ADDR FILE is closed. You MUST close all files which are used for output operations.

If you WRITE to a file and do not close the file, the last few records in the output buffer will not be written, and your file will not be properly closed. To be safe always close all files.

On line 2320 the SEQ ADDR HELLO PROG is executed, ending the operations associated with the APPEND program and giving the operator a chance to select a new process from the HELLO menu. The RUN command is executed just like any other DOS command. Notice that the program drive number is used as part of the RUN command. As indicated earlier, this allows a person with two disk drives to have the programs on one drive and the files on a second drive.

The Sequential File UPDATE Program

Program Name   SEQ ADDR UPDATE PROG

Program Objective   To provide the user with a method of changing and deleting records.

This is the hardest program in the book. If you can make it through this program, you can easily make it through any of the other programs.

In order for a file to be of any use, there must be a way to insert new information, change existing data on the file, and delete unwanted data from the file. The process of adding, changing, and deleting information is normally referred to as *updating the file*. In the sequential address system, the update process is broken down into two programs. The SEQ ADDR APPEND PROGram is used to add new records to the file, while the SEQ ADDR UPDATE PROGram is used to change and delete information.

Records cannot be changed and rewritten back to a sequential file, nor can records be deleted from an existing sequential file. In order for you to change or delete records, the update program must read the old sequential file and create a new sequential file.

Even if only one record is to be changed or deleted, the entire old sequential file must be read and rewritten to a new updated sequential file.

After the update process is complete, the new disk file becomes the *current copy* and the old disk file becomes the *backup copy*. If for some reason the new disk file contains a mistake or is lost, the backup copy can be renamed and used as input to the update program. The automatic creation of a backup copy each time the file is updated is one of the advantages of sequential file processing. (See diagram on top of page 335.)

Instructions for Running the Program   Make sure you have run the SEQ ADDR CREATE PROG and have added some records to the file by using the SEQ ADDR APPEND PROG. If you have not created the label and added records to the file, the update program will not have any records to change or delete and will not run correctly.

Run the program by entering

RUN SEQ ADDR HELLO PROG <RETURN>

System Flowchart of Sequential File Update Program

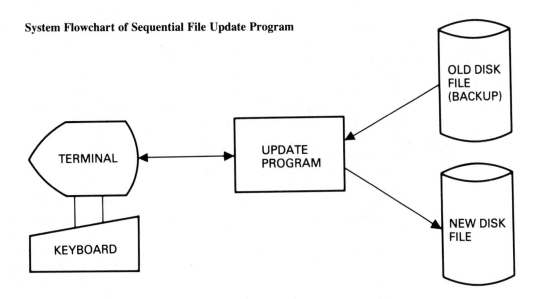

After the menu is displayed, enter a 2, and the HELLO program will start execution of the update program. After the update program has started, the following screen will be displayed:

```
       SEQ ADDR FILE UPDATE PROGRAM

   NAME     = (                        )
   ADDRESS  = (                        )
   CITY     = (               )
   STATE    = (   )
   ZIP CODE = (       )
   PHONE    = (    -    -      )




   ( ) PRESS  A  TO ACCEPT THE ENTRY.
       PRESS  R  TO REJECT THE ENTRY.

   ( ) ENTER CHARACTER CORRESPONDING TO
           PROCESS DESIRED.

   A TO ACCEPT THE RECORD.
   C TO CHANGE THE RECORD.
   D TO DELETE THE RECORD.
   Q TO QUIT PROCESSING.

   ....... First error message line ......
   ....... Second error message line .....
```

Once the screen layout has been displayed, the disk will whirl and the first record will be displayed in the variable portion of the screen. After displaying the record the computer will wait for you to enter either A, C, D, or Q.

If you want to accept the record as displayed, enter an A. The accepted record will be written to the new disk file, the next record in sequence will be displayed, and then you will be given another chance to select a processing code. In response to the first record, enter an A to accept the record.

D is entered to delete a record. If D is entered, instead of rewriting the record to the new disk file, the program ignores the old record and displays the next sequential record. The deleted record is still on the old (backup) file but does not exist on the new (current) file.

In response to the second record displayed, enter D and see what happens. Normally you do NOT see or hear any difference between the accepting process and the deleting process. Remember, the buffer for the new file is not written to the disk until either it is full or the CLOSE instruction is executed. By just looking at the screen, you are not able to tell if the record was actually accepted or deleted correctly. Later when you run the listing program, you can check to see how well the update process works.

If you want to change the record being displayed, you enter C. After a change is requested, the cursor is positioned at the first character of the name line.

If you want to change a field, you simply key in the new data over the old data and press RETURN. *You must reenter the entire field* even if only part of the field is incorrect. For example, if only the first name is incorrectly spelled, you must still reenter the entire field.

Old field contains   = JONH JONES
Key in all the characters = JOHN JONES <RETURN>

If you do not want to change a field, press the RETURN key without pressing any other keys.

Respond to the third record by entering C in order to change some of the fields. After you enter the C, the cursor will be positioned in the name field over the top of the first character of the first name.

NAME   = (]IRSTNAME LASTNAME   )

Press the RETURN key without hitting any other keys. The name will remain the same and the cursor will move to the first position of the address line. Type in a new address which is shorter than the original address, and then press RETURN. The unused portion of the address line will be blanked out and the cursor positioned to the first character of the city.

Follow the same procedure for the city, state, and ZIP code, pressing RETURN or making changes as you wish.

The phone number is broken down into three parts and is actually three separate fields. You may change any one of the three parts individually. That is, if you want to change the last four digits, you do not need to rekey the first six digits: simply press RETURN to skip over each subfield.

After you have been given a chance to change each of the fields, the cursor will be positioned on line 12, and the program will wait for you to check the fields.

(]) PRESS   A   TO ACCEPT THE ENTRY.
    PRESS   R   TO REJECT THE ENTRY.

If the changes are correct enter an A to indicate that the changes are to be accepted. When a record is accepted, it is written on the new file and the next record displayed.

If you want to reject the changes and start over, enter R. The changes will be rejected and the record redisplayed in its original form; no record will be written or read.

After either an A or R is entered the cursor will be repositioned to allow you to select another processing mode.

(]) ENTER CHARACTER CORRESPONDING TO
    PROCESS DESIRED.

There are two ways the program can end. You may enter Q to quit, or the program may reach the end of the old address file.

If you enter Q, then the program cannot just stop processing. All the remaining records on the old file must be read and rewritten to the new file. During this process the following screen is displayed.

```
READING AND WRITING REMAINING RECORDS
PLEASE BE PATIENT.
```

If the program reaches the end of the file, the update process is complete, and the program terminates without displaying any additional screens.

Program Listing

```
1000 REM SEQ ADDR UPDATE PROG
1010 REM --------------------
1020 CLEAR :G1 = PEEK (116) * 256 + PEEK (115) - 40 :GA$ = "
     12345678901234567890" + "12345678901234567890"
1030 REM
1040 REM --------------------
1050 REM DRIVE ROUTINE
```

```
1060 GOSUB 2380: REM BEGINNING
1070 GOTO 1310: REM MAIN MOD
1080 GOTO 2860: REM END MODULE
1090 REM
1100 REM ----------------------
1110 REM GET SUBROUTINE
1120 IF G3 = 0 THEN GOSUB 1270
1130 G3 = G1 + GA - 1: FOR G2 = G1 TO G3: POKE G2,32: NEXT :
     G2 = G1
1140 CALL 768:GB = PEEK (775) - 128: IF GB = 08 THEN 1210
1150 IF GB = 13 THEN 1230
1160 IF GB = 21 THEN PRINT CHR$ ( PEEK (G2));: GOTO 1190
1170 IF GB = 44 OR GB = 58 OR GB < 32 THEN 1140
1180 PRINT CHR$ (GB);: POKE G2,GB
1190 G2 = G2 + 1: IF G2 > G3 THEN 1260
1200 GOTO 1140
1210 G2 = G2 - 1: IF G2 < G1 THEN G2 = G1: GOTO 1140
1220 PRINT CHR$ (8);: GOTO 1140
1230 IF G1 = G2 THEN 1250
1240 FOR GC = G2 TO G3: PRINT " ";: NEXT
1250 FOR GC = G2 TO G3: POKE GC,32: NEXT
1260 GB$ = LEFT$ (GA$,GA):GC = G2 - G1: RETURN
1270 POKE 768,32: POKE 769,12: POKE 770,253: POKE 771,141:
     POKE 772,07: POKE 773,03: POKE 774,96: RETURN
1280 REM
1290 REM ----------------------
1300 REM MAIN ROUTINE
1310 GOSUB 2040: REM READ DISK
1320 GOSUB 2180: REM WRITE SCREEN
1330 GOSUB 2750: REM CHECK MEMORY
1340 VTAB L9: HTAB 2: GET X2$
1350 IF X2$ = "A" THEN 1820
1360 IF X2$ = "C" THEN 1430
1370 IF X2$ = "D" THEN 1900
1380 IF X2$ = "Q" THEN 2280
1390 GOTO 1340
1400 REM
1410 REM ----------------------
1420 REM CHANGE ROUTINE
1430 GALEGTH = 25: VTAB L1: HTAB 12: GOSUB 1120
1440 IF GCCHAR = 0 THEN 1470
1450 IF LEFT$ (GBANSWER$,1) = " " THEN 1430
1460 AANAME$ = GBANSWER$
1470 VTAB L2: HTAB 12: GOSUB 1120
1480 IF GCCHAR = 0 THEN 1500
1490 ABADDR$ = GBANSWER$
1500 GALEGTH = 15: VTAB L3: HTAB 12: GOSUB 1120
1510 IF GCCHAR = 0 THEN 1530
1520 ACCITY$ = GBANSWER$
1530 GALEGTH = 2: VTAB L4: HTAB 12: GOSUB 1120
1540 IF GCCHAR = 0 THEN 1560
1550 ADSTE$ = GBANSWER$
```

```
1560 GALEGTH = 5: VTAB L5: HTAB 12: GOSUB 1120
1570 IF GCCHAR = 0 THEN 1590
1580 AEZIP$ = GBANSWER$
1590 GALEGTH = 3: VTAB L6: HTAB 12: GOSUB 1120
1600 IF GCCHAR = 0 THEN 1620
1610 AFPHNE$ = GBANSWER$ + RIGHT$ (AFPHNE$,7)
1620 HTAB 16: GOSUB 1120
1630 IF GCCHAR = 0 THEN 1650
1640 AFPHNE$ = LEFT$ (AFPHNE$,3) + GBANSWER$ + RIGHT$ (AFPHN
     E$,4)
1650 GALEGTH = 4: HTAB 20: GOSUB 1120
1660 IF GCCHAR = 0 THEN 1680
1670 AFPHNE$ = LEFT$ (AFPHNE$,6) + GBANSWER$
1680 VTAB L7: HTAB 2: GET X1$
1690 IF X1$ = "A" THEN 1820
1700 IF X1$ = "R" THEN GOSUB 2080: GOTO 1320
1710 INVERSE: VTAB L9: HTAB 1
1720 PRINT "INVALID RESPONSE - PRESS SPACE BAR" TAB( 39)" "
1730 PRINT "                    TO CONTINUE" TAB (38)" ";: NO
     RMAL
1740 GET X1$: IF X1$ < > " " THEN 1740
1750 VTAB L9: HTAB 1
1760 PRINT TAB( 39)" "
1770 PRINT TAB( 39)" ";
1780 GOTO 1680
1790 REM
1800 REM ------------------------
1810 REM WRITE ON DISK
1820 PRINT D$
1830 PRINT D$;"WRITE ";FILEID$;" NEW"
1840 PRINT AANAME$;ABADDR$;ACCITY$;ADSTE$;AEZIP$;AFPHNE$
1850 PRINT D$
1860 IF X2$ = "Q" THEN RETURN
1870 REM
1880 REM ------------------------
1890 REM CLEAR SCREEN
1900 VTAB L1: HTAB 12: PRINT TAB( 36)" "
1910 VTAB L2: HTAB 12: PRINT TAB( 36)" "
1920 VTAB L3: HTAB 12: PRINT TAB( 26)" "
1930 VTAB L4: HTAB 12: PRINT "  "
1940 VTAB L5: HTAB 12: PRINT "      "
1950 VTAB L6: HTAB 12: PRINT "   -   -     "
1960 GOTO 1310
1970 REM
1980 REM ------------------------
1990 REM ONERR STATEMENT WILL BREAK
2000 THE LOOP.
2010 REM
2020 REM ------------------------
2030 REM READ DISK
2040 PRINT D$
2050 PRINT D$;"READ ";FILEID$
```

```
2060 INPUT A1ADDR$
2070 PRINT D$
2080 AANAME$ = LEFT$ (A1ADDR$,25)
2090 ABADDR$ = MID$ (A1ADDR$,26,25)
2100 ACCITY$ = MID$ (A1ADDR$,51,15)
2110 ADSTE$ = MID$ (A1ADDR$,66,2)
2120 AEZIP$ = MID$ (A1ADDR$,68,5)
2130 AFPHNE$ = RIGHT$ (A1ADDR$,10)
2140 RETURN
2150 REM
2160 REM --------------------
2170 REM WRITE ON SCREEN
2180 VTAB L1: HTAB 12: PRINT AANAME$
2190 VTAB L2: HTAB 12: PRINT ABADDR$
2200 VTAB L3: HTAB 12: PRINT ACCITY$
2210 VTAB L4: HTAB 12: PRINT ADSTE$
2220 VTAB L5: HTAB 12: PRINT AEZIP$
2230 VTAB L6: HTAB 12: PRINT LEFT$ (AFPHNE$,3)'-' MID$ (AFPHNE$,4,3)
     '-' RIGHT$ (AFPHNE$,4)
2240 RETURN
2250 REM
2260 REM --------------------
2270 REM READ/WRITE REST FILE
2280 HOME : VTAB 10
2290 PRINT 'READING AND WRITING REMAINING RECORDS.'
2300 PRINT
2310 PRINT 'PLEASE BE PATIENT.'
2320 GOSUB 1820: REM WRITE
2330 GOSUB 2040: REM READ
2340 GOTO 2320
2350 REM NO RETURN NEEDED - ONERR WILL TERMINATE LOOP
2360 REM
2370 REM --------------------
2380 REM BEGINNING ROUTINE
2390 TEXT : NORMAL : HOME : SPEED= 255
2400 ONERR GOTO 1080
2410 D$ = CHR$ (4)
2420 FDRIVE = 1 : PDRIVE = 1
2430 FILEID$ = 'SEQ ADDR FILE'
2440 L1 = 3:L2 = 4:L3 = 5:L4 = 6:L5 = 7:L6 = 8:L7 = 12:L8 = 15:
     L9 = 23
2450 PRINT D$
2460 PRINT D$;'OPEN ';FILEID$;',D';FDRIVE
2470 PRINT D$;'OPEN ';FILEID$;' NEW,D';FDRIVE
2480 PRINT D$
2490 REM
2500 REM --------------------
2510 REM PRINT SCREEN IMAGE
2520 HOME
2530 PRINT '    SEQ ADDR FILE UPDATE PROGRAM'
2540 VTAB L1: PRINT 'NAME     =(' SPC( 25)')'
2550 VTAB L2: PRINT 'ADDRESS  =(' SPC( 25)')'
2560 VTAB L3: PRINT 'CITY     =(' SPC( 15)')'
2570 VTAB L4: PRINT 'STATE    =(  )'
```

```
2580 VTAB L5: PRINT 'ZIP CODE =(        )'
2590 VTAB L6: PRINT 'PHONE     =(    -    -    )'
2600 VTAB L7
2610 PRINT '( ) PRESS  A  TO ACCEPT THE ENTRY.'
2620 PRINT '    PRESS  R  TO REJECT THE ENTRY.'
2630 VTAB L8
2640 PRINT '( ) ENTER CHARACTER CORRESPONDING TO '
2650 PRINT '          PROCESS DESIRED.'
2660 PRINT
2670 PRINT ' A  TO ACCEPT THE RECORD.'
2680 PRINT ' C  TO CHANGE THE RECORD.'
2690 PRINT ' D  TO DELETE THE RECORD.'
2700 PRINT ' Q  TO QUIT PROCESSING.'
2710 RETURN
2720 REM
2730 REM ----------------------
2740 REM FREE MEMORY ROUTINE
2750 STARTING = PEEK (112) * 256 + PEEK (111): IF STARTING >
     16000 THEN 2820
2760 VTAB L9: HTAB 1: INVERSE
2770 PRINT " FREEING MEMORY - PLEASE WAIT" TAB( 38)" "
2780 STARTING = FRE (0)
2790 PRINT " DONE - PRESS SPACE BAR TO CONTINUE   ";: NORMAL
2800 GET X1$: IF X1$ < > " " THEN 2800
2810 VTAB L9: HTAB 1: PRINT TAB( 39)" ": PRINT TAB( 39)" ";
2820 RETURN
2830 REM
2840 REM ----------------------
2850 REM ENDING ROUTINE
2860 ER = PEEK (222)
2870 IF ER < > 5 THEN 3050
2880 REM
2890 REM ----------------------
2900 NORMAL END OF FILE
2910 VTAB L9: HTAB 1: INVERSE
2920 PRINT " NORMAL END OF FILE - PLEASE WAIT      ": NORMAL
2930 PRINT D$
2940 PRINT D$;"CLOSE ";FILEID$
2950 PRINT D$;"CLOSE ";FILEID$;" NEW"
2960 ONERR GOTO 2980
2970 PRINT D$;"DELETE ";FILEID$;" BACKUP"
2980 PRINT D$;"RENAME ";FILEID$;",";FILEID$;" BACKUP"
2990 PRINT D$;"RENAME ";FILEID$;" NEW,";FILEID$
3000 HOME
3010 PRINT D$;"RUN SEQ ADDR HELLO PROG,D";PDRIVE
3020 REM
3030 REM ----------------------
3040 REM ABNORMAL TERMINATION ROUTINE
3050 HOME
3060 PRINT "*** NOTIFY PROGRAM SUPPORT ***"
3070 PRINT
3080 PRINT "ABNORMAL TERMINATION!!!!!"
3090 PRINT "ALL CHANGES WERE LOST!!!!"
3100 PRINT
```

```
3110 PRINT "ERROR CODE = "ER
3120 PRINT
3130 IF ER = 6 THEN PRINT "FILE NOT FOUND — CHECK DISKETTE":
     PRINT "AND TRY AGAIN"
3140 IF ER = 9 THEN PRINT "DISK FULL — FREE SPACE & START OVER"
3150 IF ER = 11 THEN PRINT "SYNTAX ERROR"
3160 PRINT
3170 PRINT "*** PROCESSING TERMINATED ***"
3180 END
3190 REM ----------------------
```

Cross Reference Listing

Variable names used with the address record:

A1$ 2060, 2080, 2090, 2100, 2110, 2120, 2130
AA$ 1460, 1840, 2080, 2180
AB$ 1490, 1840, 2090, 2190
AC$ 1520, 1840, 2100, 2200
AD$ 1550, 1840, 2110, 2210
AE$ 1580, 1840, 2120, 2220
AF$ 1610, 1640, 1670, 1840, 2130, 2230

Variable names used with the disk commands:

D$ 1820, 1830, 1850, 2040, 2050, 2070, 2410, 2450, 2460, 2470, 2480, 2910,
    2940, 2970, 2980, 2990, 3010
ER 2860, 2870, 3110, 3130, 3140, 3150
FD 2420, 2460, 2470
PD 2420, 3010

Variable names used with the GET subroutine:

G1 1020, 1130, 1210, 1230, 1260
G2 1130, 1160, 1180, 1190, 1210, 1230, 1240, 1250, 1260
G3 1120, 1130, 1190, 1240, 1250
GA 1130, 1260, 1430, 1500, 1530, 1560, 1590, 1650
GA$ 1020, 1260
GB 1140, 1150, 1160, 1170, 1180
GB$ 1260, 1450, 1460, 1490, 1520, 1550, 1580, 1610, 1640, 1670
GC 1240, 1250, 1260, 1440, 1480, 1510, 1540, 1570, 1600, 1630, 1660

Variable names used with displaying data on the screen:

L1 1430, 1900, 2180, 2440, 2540
L2 1470, 1910, 2190, 2440, 2550

L3 1500, 1920, 2200, 2440, 2560
L4 1530, 1930, 2210, 2440, 2570
L5 1560, 1940, 2220, 2440, 2580
L6 1590, 1620, 1650, 1950, 2230, 2440, 2590
L7 1680, 2440, 2600
L8 1340, 2440, 2630
L9 1710, 1750, 2440, 2760, 2810, 2920

Variable names used for general GET instruction in response to the screen messages:

X1$ 1680, 1690, 1700, 1740, 2800
X2$ 1340, 1350, 1360, 1370, 1380, 1860

Explanation by Line Number

Detailed explanations by line number follow.

1000   REM SEQ ADDR UPDATE PROG

1010   REM --------------------

1020   CLEAR :G1 = PEEK (116) * 256 + PEEK (115) − 40 :GA$ =
" 12345678901234567890" + "12345678901234567890"

1030   REM

1040   REM --------------------

1050   REM DRIVE ROUTINE

1060   GOSUB 2380: REM BEGINNING

1070   GOTO 1310: REM MAIN MOD

1080   GOTO 2860: REM END MODULE

1090   REM

With the exception of a few short programs in the system, each program starts off
with the same basic set of instructions.

This group of instructions was described at the first explanation for the SEQ ADDR APPEND PROG. For a detailed explanation of the instruction group, you may want to go back and review the first part of the SEQ APPEND PROG. The only statement which is different from that of the earlier program is line 1070. A GOTO instruction is used to execute the MAIN ROUTINE since an ONERR condition terminates the routine and forces logic to return to line 1080 to execute the ENDING ROUTINE (see ONERR line 2400).

```
1100    REM -------------------
```

```
1110    REM GET SUBROUTINE
```

The GET subroutine is explained in detail in Chapter 3 of Section II.

Lines 1290 through 1390 of the MAIN ROUTINE are responsible for reading a record, displaying a record, checking memory space, accepting a response from the operator, and executing the code related to the action requested by the operator.

```
1290    REM ---------------------
```

```
1300    REM MAIN ROUTINE
```

```
1310    GOSUB 2040: REM READ DISK
```

```
1320    GOSUB 2180: REM WRITE SCREEN
```

```
1330    GOSUB 2750: REM CHECK MEMORY
```

```
1340    VTAB L9: HTAB 2: GET X2$
```

```
1350    IF X2$ = "A" THEN 1820
```

```
1360    IF X2$ = "C" THEN 1430
```

```
1370    IF X2$ = "D" THEN 1900
```

```
1380    IF X2$ = "Q" THEN 2280
```

```
1390    GOTO 1340
```

To start the process of updating the file, a record is first read and displayed on the screen. After the record has been displayed, the operator is given a chance to respond by entering either A, C, D, or Q. A different sequence of instructions is executed depending on which character is entered.

If the operator enters A to accept the entry program logic branches to the sequence of code which writes the old record on the new file, clears the screen, and returns to line 1310 to read and display the next record.

If the operator enters C in order to change one or more fields on the existing record, program logic branches to the sequence of code which allows the operator to change any field. After changing one or more fields, the operator is given a chance to either accept or reject the changes which were made. If the operator accepts the record as changed, program logic writes the record on the new file, clears the screen, and returns to line 1310 to read and display the next record. If the operator rejects the changes that were·made, program logic returns to line 1320, which redisplays the existing record, giving the operator another chance to select the type of processing desired for this record.

If the operator enters D to delete the record, program logic branches to the sequence of code which clears the screen, and returns to line 1310 which reads and displays the next record. Since the record is not written to the new file, the effect is that of deleting the record.

If the operator enters Q, program logic must wrap up any loose ends before terminating. This is done by reading the old file and writing each record to the new file.

The responses A, C, D and Q are tested in alphabetic order, but this just happens to be a quirk of the letters selected. In actual practice you should ask the questions about the response in the sequence of most likely response first to least likely response last. For this program the assumption is that more records will be accepted as they exist than changed and more records will be changed than deleted. Since the operator will only enter Q once, it is the last value tested.

Notice that if the operator presses any key other than one of the four acceptable characters, no error message is displayed. The program simply branches back to the GET instruction and waits for the operator to enter a correct character (see line 1390). This is not necessarily the best technique but it is easy to code.

```
1410    REM --------------------

1420    REM CHANGE ROUTINE

1430    GALEGTH = 25: VTAB L1: HTAB 12: GOSUB 1120

1440    IF GCCHAR = 0 THEN 1470

1450    IF LEFT$ (GBANSWER$,1) = "  " THEN 1430
```

1460 AANAME$ = GBANSWER$

....

1670 AFPHNE$ = LEFT$ (AFPHNE$,6) + GBANSWER$

Lines 1410 through 1670 allow the operator to make changes to any of the fields within the record. If you look closely at the code, you will see a sequence of six instructions for each field.

1. Set GALEGTH to the length of the field to be read.
2 Position the cursor on the correct line.
3. Position the cursor at the correct column.
4. Execute the GET subroutine.
5. Check to see if the field was changed by testing to see if any data were entered.
6. If the field was changed place the new value in the related variable.

The IF instruction on line 1450 is included to make sure the operator does not enter leading blanks in the name field. Since the name is the first field in the record, any leading blanks cause problems when writing the record to the disk and trying to read it back. If the operator uses leading blanks, program logic branches back to line 1430 and makes the operator reenter the name.

The phone number is entered or changed using three executions of the GET subroutine. The first sequence of instructions accepts any change to the area code.

```
1590 GALEGTH = 3: VTAB L6: HTAB 12: GOSUB 1120
1600 IF GCCHAR = 0 THEN 1620
1610 AFPHNE$ = GBANSWER$ + RIGHT$ (AFPHNE$,7)
```

If the area code is changed, the new area code is added to the last seven digits of the old phone number, and the new number is placed back in AFPHNE$. The operator is given a chance to change the middle three digits. If the digits are changed, they replace the middle three digits of the current phone number, and the new phone number is put back in AFPHNE$ (see line 1640). The process is repeated for the last segment of the phone number.

1680–1780 Lines 1680 through 1700 give the operator a chance to look at the changes which were made and to enter A to accept the changes or to enter R to reject the changes and start over with the original display. Lines 1710 through 1780 consist of the standard sequence for displaying an error message; this has previously been described and will not be explained again.

If the operator enters an A, program logic writes out the record with the changes, clears the screen, and returns to the beginning of the MAIN ROUTINE to read and display the next record.

If the operator enters R, program logic rejects the changes by resetting all the variables back to their original values and redisplaying the screen. Look closely at how this is done.

First, the GOSUB branches into the middle of the READ ROUTINE, where the variables are set equal to specific columns within the record. As long as the variable A1$ is not used anywhere else in the program, it still contains the contents of the original record. All the variables are reset to their original contents prior to returning back to line 1700.

```
1700 IF X1$ = "R" THEN GOSUB 2080: GOTO 1320

........
2020 REM ---------------------
2030 REM READ DISK
2040 PRINT D$
2050 PRINT D$;"READ ";FILEID$
2060 INPUT A1ADDR$
2070 PRINT D$
———→2080 AANAME$ = LEFT$ (A1ADDR$,25)
2090 ABADDR$ = MID$ (A1ADDR$,26,25)
2100 ACCITY$ = MID$ (A1ADDR$,51,15)
2110 ADSTE$ = MID$ (A1ADDR$,66,2)
2120 AEZIP$ = MID$ (A1ADDR$,68,5)
2130 AFPHNE$ = RIGHT$ (A1ADDR$,10)
2140 RETURN
```

The GOSUB instruction may be used to branch into the middle of a routine, *but most programmers try to avoid this* because of problems in following the logic if and when changes are made to the program. As a general rule, each routine should have only one entry point and one exit point.

After the variables are reset, the GOTO instruction at the end of line 1700 branches to line 1320, skipping over the GOSUB which reads the next record, but executing the GOSUB which displays the record.

```
1700 IF X1$ = "R" THEN GOSUB 2080: GOTO 1320

........
1290 REM ---------------------
1300 REM MAIN ROUTINE
1310 GOSUB 2040: REM READ DISK
———→1320 GOSUB 2180: REM WRITE SCREEN
```

The old record is redisplayed and the process started over.

```
1800    REM ---------------------

1810    REM WRITE ON DISK

1820    PRINT D$
```

1830   PRINT D$;"WRITE ";FILEID$;" NEW"

1840   PRINT AANAME$;ABADDR$;ACCITY$;ADSTE$;AEZIP$;AFPHNE$

1850   PRINT D$

1860   IF X2$ = "Q" THEN RETURN

Lines 1800 through 1860 write the record to the new file. The logic is the same as in the APPEND program except for two things.

On line 1830 notice that the new file has the same name as the old file except for the last four characters (NEW).

Line 1860 tests to see if the operator has entered a Q in response to the terminate program message. If a Q was entered, the program returns to the calling module (see line 2270 in the READ/WRITE REST FILE ROUTINE).

```
2260 REM ---------------------
2270 REM READ/WRITE REST FILE
2280 HOME : VTAB 10
2290 PRINT "READING AND WRITING REMAINING RECORDS."
2300 PRINT
2310 PRINT "PLEASE BE PATIENT."
——→2320 GOSUB 1820: REM WRITE
2330 GOSUB 2040: REM READ
2340 GOTO 2320
2350 REM NO RETURN NEEDED - ONERR WILL TERMINATE LOOP
```

If the operator has not entered Q, logic flow continues to line 1870.

Line 1860 represents another break in the rule of one entry point and one exit point to a routine. In an effort to make the program shorter and not recode certain segments of the WRITE ROUTINE, the module is executed in two ways. During normal processing the WRITE ROUTINE is entered at line 1820 and falls through to the CLEAR SCREEN ROUTINE. But if the operator enters a Q to quit processing, line 1860 causes the routine to RETURN to the calling GOSUB instruction on line 2320 in the READ/WRITE REST FILE ROUTINE.

Normally it is better either to repeat a set of instructions or to make the instructions a separate module executed only by way of a GOSUB than to try to patch the code with a switch.

This is another case of "Do as I say and not as I do." The example programs are designed to show you a variety of coding techniques. When you are coding your own programs you should try to use good coding techniques, but when you are looking at another programmer's code, you must be able to follow any style of programming.

1880   REM --------------------

1890   REM CLEAR SCREEN

1900   VTAB L1: HTAB 12: PRINT TAB(36)"   "

....

1950   VTAB L6: HTAB 12: PRINT "   -   -   "

1960   GOTO 1310

Lines 1880 through 1960 clear the variable portion of the screen. The clearing process is really not necessary in this program as the next record is displayed immediately after the operator accepts or rejects the current record. The process of clearing the screen provides the operator with a visual feedback, since the screen is cleared prior to each new record. Study lines 1900 and 1950 to see the two ways the variable section of the lines are cleared. Line 1900 uses the TAB function to clear the area, while line 1950 uses spaces and dashes to erase the old data.

Line 1960 causes logic flow to return to the first line of the MAIN ROUTINE, where the entire process is started over. This looping process continues until one of the two following things occurs:

1. The end of the old SEQ ADDR FILE is reached and causes the ONERR instruction to be executed.
2. The operator enters a Q to quit.

If the end of the file is reached, the ONERR instruction branches to statement 1080.

```
2400 ONERR GOTO 1080
.......
1080 GOTO 2860: REM END MODULE
.......
```

2020   REM --------------------

2030   REM READ DISK

2040   PRINT D$

2050   PRINT D$;"READ ";FILEID$

```
2060   INPUT A1ADDR$

2070   PRINT D$

2080   AANAME$ = LEFT$ (A1ADDR$,25)

2090   ABADDR$ = MID$ (A1ADDR$,26,25)

2100   ACCITY$ = MID$ (A1ADDR$,51,15)

2110   ADSTE$ = MID$ (A1ADDR$,66,2)

2120   AEZIP$ = MID$ (A1ADDR$,68,5)

2130   AFPHNE$ = RIGHT$ (A1ADDR$,10)

2140   RETURN
```

Lines 2020 through 2140 cause a new record to be read and broken down into the individual variables making up the record.

As explained in the APPEND program, data may be written to the disk at the variable level:

```
2000 PRINT D$;"WRITE ";FILEID$
2010 PRINT AANAME$","ABADDR$","ACCITY$","ADSTE$","AEZIP$"," AFPHNE$
2020 PRINT D$
```

or as a single record.

```
2000 PRINT D$;"WRITE ";FILEID$
2010 PRINT AANAME$;ABADDR$;ACCITY$;ADSTE$;AEZIP$;AFPHNE$
2020 PRINT D$
```

When the record is read, it must be read USING EXACTLY THE SAME FORMAT AS THE ONE IN WHICH IT WAS WRITTEN. The names may vary, but the number of entries read must match the number of entries written whether or not single variables are read:

```
2100 PRINT D$;"READ ";FILEID$
2110 PRINT AANAME$,ABADDR$,ACCITY$,ADSTE$,AEZIP$,AFPHNE$
2120 PRINT D$
```

or as a single record:

```
2100 PRINT D$;"READ ";FILEID$
2110 PRINT A1ADDR$
2120 PRINT D$
```

Remember, if you write individual variables, the commas must be within quotation marks when writing and without quotation marks when reading.

If you are working mainly with string variables, use the format shown in the sequential programs. If you are working with numeric data, write each variable individually (separate with commas; see the random file UPDATE example).

```
2160    REM --------------------

2170    REM WRITE ON SCREEN

................

2180    VTAB L1: HTAB 12: PRINT AANAME$

2230    VTAB L6: HTAB 12: PRINT LEFT$ (AFPHNE$,3)"-" MID$ (AFPHNE$,4,3) "-" RIGHT$
        (AFPHNE$,4)

2240    RETURN
```

Lines 2160 through 2240 display the values read within the areas set aside for each variable.

Line 2230 is written a little differently from the rest of the statements because of the dashes which are inserted between the parts of the phone number (see line 2230). Each segment of the phone number is printed using the LEFT$, MID$, and RIGHT$ functions.

```
2260    REM --------------------

2270    REM READ/WRITE REST FILE

2280    HOME : VTAB 10

2290    PRINT "READING AND WRITING REMAINING RECORDS."

2300    PRINT
```

```
2310    PRINT "PLEASE BE PATIENT."

2320    GOSUB 1820: REM WRITE

2330    GOSUB 2040: REM READ

2340    GOTO 2320

2350    REM NO RETURN NEEDED - ONERR WILL TERMINATE LOOP
```

Lines 2260 through 2350 are executed when the operator presses Q prior to reaching the end of the SEQ ADDR FILE.

In order to copy all the records from the old file onto the new file, the READ ROUTINE and WRITE ROUTINE are executed repeatedly until the end of the old file is reached. Notice that the routines start off by writing the current record and then reading the next record.

If you check the program logic carefully, you will find that when the operator enters Q to quit, a record is being displayed. The record currently being displayed must be written before another record is read.

This group of instructions appears to cause an endless loop consisting of lines 2320, 2330, and 2340. The loop is broken when the EOF is reached and the computer breaks the sequence of execution in order to execute the ONERR instruction (see line 2400 in the BEGINNING ROUTINE). When the EOF is reached, logic flow branches to line 1080 of the DRIVE ROUTINE, where the ENDING ROUTINE is executed.

```
2370    REM --------------------

2380    REM BEGINNING ROUTINE

2390    TEXT : NORMAL : HOME : SPEED = 255

2400    ONERR GOTO 1080

        ...............

2460    PRINT D$;"OPEN ";FILEID$;",D";FDRIVE

2470    PRINT D$;"OPEN ";FILEID$;" NEW,D";FDRIVE

2480    PRINT D$

2490    REM
```

Lines 2370 through 2490 ensure that the computer is set up correctly for program execution, initializes some of the variables to the correct starting value, and opens the two files which are to be used within the program.

Line 2400 introduces the ONERR instruction and should be studied carefully.

There are several ways to handle coming to the end of a sequential file, but with the exception of the ONERR instruction, the alternatives are not compatible with the use of the APPEND instruction. Since the sequential system is designed with one of the programs using the APPEND instruction, the rest of the programs must rely on the ONERR instruction to indicate an EOF condition.

When the computer reaches the end of the file, it automatically interrupts the current sequence of code and branches to the line number indicated by the ONERR instruction.

Lines 2460 through 2470 open up the two files to be used within the program. When records are processed sequentially, the old file must be read and the new records written to another file. As a general rule you should use the same file names but follow the new file with a suffix to make the file name unique. In this example the suffix (NEW) is used to indicate the new file. At the end of the update process, the backup copy of the file is deleted, the old file is renamed as the backup copy, and the new file is renamed, making it the most current version.

```
2500   REM ---------------------

2510   REM PRINT SCREEN IMAGE

2520   HOME

      ...............

2710   RETURN

2720   REM
```

Lines 2500 through 2720 display the screen image and present no new concepts.

```
2730   REM ---------------------

2740   REM FREE MEMORY ROUTINE

2750   STARTING = PEEK (112) * 256 + PEEK (111): IF STARTING > 16000 THEN 2820

      ...............

2820   RETURN
```

The FREE MEMORY ROUTINE is important to any program which uses large numbers of string variables.

You do not need to completely understand the routine, but you should include it in every program which does a lot of string processing.

Lines 2840 through 3190 make up the ENDING ROUTINE. The ending set of instructions consists of three parts. The first few lines check to see how the program terminates. If the program terminates as expected, the instructions related to a normal ending are executed (lines 2890 throught 3020). If the program terminates in an unexpected manner, then the instructions related to an abnormal ending are executed (lines 3030 through 3190).

```
2840   REM --------------------

2850   REM ENDING ROUTINE

2860   ER = PEEK (222)

2870   IF ER < > 5 THEN 3050
```

Line 2860 finds out what the ending error code is by PEEKing into memory location 222. Line 2870 checks the error code. If the value is equal to 5 as expected, meaning EOF, then logic flow falls through to the next line. If the error code is any value other than 5, logic branches to line 3050, where the instructions related to an abnormal ending are executed, and the processing is terminated without returning to the HELLO program.

```
2890   REM --------------------

2900   NORMAL END OF FILE

2910   VTAB L9: HTAB 1: INVERSE

2920   PRINT " NORMAL END OF FILE - PLEASE WAIT      ": NORMAL

2930   PRINT D$

2940   PRINT D$;"CLOSE ";FILEID$

2950   PRINT D$;"CLOSE ";FILEID$;" NEW"
```

2960   ONERR GOTO 2980

2970   PRINT D$;"DELETE ";FILEID$;" BACKUP"

2980   PRINT D$;"RENAME ";FILEID$;",";FILEID$;" BACKUP"

2990   PRINT D$;"RENAME ";FILEID$;" NEW,";FILEID$

3000   HOME

3010   PRINT D$;"RUN SEQ ADDR HELLO PROG,D";PDRIVE

If the program ends normally, both files are closed. After the files are closed they are renamed so that each file reflects its status as a backup copy or a current copy.

Prior to closing:

SEQ ADDR FILE BACKUP	This is the prior master file (does not exist during first run).
SEQ ADDR FILE	This is the current master file.
SEQ ADDR FILE NEW	This is the new file being created.

After close:

SEQ ADDR FILE BACKUP	The oldest version of the file is deleted from the disk.
SEQ ADDR FILE	This becomes the backup copy after renaming it to SEQ ADDR FILE BACKUP
SEQ ADDR FILE NEW	This becomes the current master file after renaming it to SEQ ADDR FILE

The process of rotating the file names as shown provides you with the security of a backup copy of the file and makes sure the most recent copy of the file is always used as input by the processing programs.

Line 2970 deletes the backup copy prior to the renaming process. But there are a couple of situations in which there may not be a backup copy to delete.

1.   When you run the program the very first time, there is no backup copy.
2.   If for some reason you have problems with the current master file and have to rerun the UPDATE program using the backup copy, because of the rerun procedure (see below), there is no backup copy to delete.

Rerun Procedure   In order to rerun the UPDATE program using the backup copy, the operator must execute the following sequence of instructions in immediate execution mode:

```
DELETE SEQ ADDR FILE
RENAME SEQ ADDR FILE BACKUP,SEQ ADDR FILE
RUN program name
```

Since the backup copy has been renamed, the file name SEQ ADDR FILE BACKUP no longer exists, and any attempt to reference it results in an error.

2960   ONERR GOTO 2980

Line 2960 resets the statement number used in conjunction with the ONERR instruction. If the program attempts to delete a nonexistent file, the ONERR instruction is executed. Prior to this statement the ONERR was set to branch to line 1080 any time an error occurred.

```
2380 BEGINNING ROUTINE
........
2400 ONERR GOTO 1080
```

If the ONERR instruction is not reset as done by line 2960 and the backup copy does not exist, the computer will *incorrectly* end the program by executing the ABNORMAL TERMINATION ROUTINE.

The ONERR condition MUST be reset. The following rather lengthy narrative describes the logic flow which would occur if the ONERR instruction were not reset and the backup copy of the address file did not exist. The sequence of logic flow leading to the abnormal ending consists of the following:

1.   After the last record is read, an attempt is made to read another record, and the EOF marker is encountered. The resulting END OF DATA error causes the ONERR instruction to be executed.
2.   The ONERR instruction causes the program to branch to line 1080, which in turn branches to the ENDING ROUTINE.
3.   At the beginning of the ENDING ROUTINE, the error code is checked for a value of 5. Since the END OF DATA error code is equal to 5, logic flow continues to fall through and starts execution of the instructions related to a normal ending instructions.

Up to this point everything is going as it should.

4.   As part of the normal ending process, the two files are closed, and the DELETE instruction attempts to delete a nonexistent backup file. Since there is no file to delete, a code 6 error indicating FILE NOT FOUND occurs.

5. As soon as the FILE NOT FOUND error occurs the computer executes the ONERR instruction. Since the ONERR instruction was not reset, the program goes back to line 1080, which in turn sends the computer back to the beginning of the ENDING ROUTINE.

Are you still with me?

6. At the beginning of the ENDING ROUTINE, the ONERR code is checked. Since the code is not equal to 5, logic flow branches to the instructions to handle the abnormal ending.

Now hopefully you see why line 2960 resets the ONERR statement to branch to 2980 in case the backup file does not exist.

2970 PRINT D$;"DELETE ";FILEID$;" BACKUP"

Line 2970 deletes the backup copy of the address file if it exists. This must be done prior to the renaming process or there will be two files on the same disk with the same name.

2980 PRINT D$;"RENAME ";FILEID$;",";FILEID$;" BACKUP"

2990 PRINT D$;"RENAME ";FILEID$;" NEW,";FILEID$

Line 2980 and 2990 rename the two existing files to reflect their current status as backup copy and current copy.

After the files are properly renamed, the HELLO program is executed, returning once again to the original menu.

Lines 3030 through 3190 are executed only if an abnormal ending occurs. This should never happen, but if the disk becomes full, an I/O error occurs, or some other nonanticipated event occurs, the ABNORMAL TERMINATION ROUTINE displays a message and error code to the operator.

One important note. The backup copy of the file created by the sequential UPDATE program *Should not be your only backup copy.* There are two problems in relying on this backup copy.

1. The backup copy is on the same disk. If the disk is lost or damaged, both the original and the backup are lost.
2. The backup copy contains old data and does not reflect the most recent changes.

You should make it a standard practice to back up the latest version of your files on a separate disk, and to store the disk in a separate location.

The Sequential File LIST Program

Program Name SEQ ADDR LIST PROG

Program Objective To provide the user with a method of listing all the records in the address file.

Every system should have a way of listing the records either to the screen or to a printer. If the records are being printed, the program can read each record and print each record as fast as the printer operates. But if records are being displayed to the screen, the program must periodically pause to allow the records to be read by the computer operator.

The LISTing program displays three records per screen and then pauses. The program waits for a response from the operator and then continues. The program displays records in groups of three until either the end of the file is reached or the operator presses Q to terminate processing.

The three record screen format appears as follows:

```
NAME     = (                              )
ADDRESS  = (                              )
CITY     = (                   )
STATE    = (   )
ZIP CODE = (        )
PHONE    = (    -    -      )

NAME     = (                              )
ADDRESS  = (                              )
CITY     = (                   )
STATE    = (   )
ZIP CODE = (        )
PHONE    = (    -    -      )

NAME     = (                              )
ADDRESS  = (                              )
CITY     = (                   )
STATE    = (   )
ZIP CODE = (        )
PHONE    = (    -    -      )

PRESS   Q   TO  QUIT.
PRESS   C   TO  CONTINUE.
```

Instructions for Running the Program

Run the program by entering

RUN SEQ ADDR HELLO PROG <RETURN>

After the menu is displayed, enter a 3 to start execution of the listing program.

You may not like the idea of running the HELLO program to execute any of the other programs in the system. You do not always have to run the HELLO program. You may run any of the programs by entering RUN followed by the program name.

RUN SEQ ADDR LIST PROG <RETURN>

Remember in designing a computer system that the end user should only have to know how to put the program and file disk into the disk drives. After the operator places the disk in the disk drive and turns the computer on, the screen displays should guide the operator in using the system. The end user should not have to enter the RUN command and remember the various program names. But since you know more than the end user, you can execute the programs either way.

Once the program has started, the first three records are displayed on the screen. After the records are displayed, the computer waits until you enter either Q to quit or C to continue.

If you enter Q the program terminates and returns to the HELLO program. If you enter C the program reads and displays the next three records.

Program Listing

```
1000 REM SEQ ADDR LIST PROG
1010 REM --------------------
1020 REM DRIVE ROUTINE
1030 GOSUB 1410: REM BEGINNING
1040 GOSUB 1090: REM MAIN MOD
1050 GOTO 1500: REM END MODULE
1060 REM
1070 REM --------------------
1080 REM MAIN ROUTINE
1090 GOSUB 1280: REM READ DISK
1100 PRINT "NAME     =("AANAME$")"
1110 PRINT "ADDRESS  =("ABADDR$")"
1120 PRINT "CITY     =("ACCITY$")"
1130 PRINT "STATE    =("ADSTE$")"
1140 PRINT "ZIP CODE =("AEZIP$")"
1150 PRINT "PHONE    =("AFPHNE$")"
1160 N1 = N1 + 1
1170 IF N1 < 3 THEN PRINT: GOTO 1090
1180 PRINT
1190 PRINT "PRESS  Q  TO QUIT."
```

```
1200 PRINT "PRESS  C  TO CONTINUE.";
1210 GET X1$
1220 IF X1$ = "C" THEN HOME :N1 = 0: GOTO 1090
1230 IF X1$ = "Q" THEN RETURN
1240 GOTO 1210
1250 REM NO RETURN NEEDED
1260 REM ----------------------
1270 REM READ DISK
1280 PRINT D$
1290 PRINT D$;"READ SEQ ADDR FILE"
1300 INPUT A1ADDR$
1310 PRINT D$
1320 AANAME$ = LEFT$ (A1ADDR$,25)
1330 ABADDR$ = MID$ (A1ADDR$,26,25)
1340 ACCITY$ = MID$ (A1ADDR$,51,15)
1350 ADSTE$ = MID$ (A1ADDR$,66,2)
1360 AEZIP$ = MID$ (A1ADDR$,68,5)
1370 AFPHNE$ = MID$ (A1ADDR,73,3) + "-" + MID$ (A1ADDR$,76,3) +
     "-" + RIGHT$ (A1ADDR$,4)
1380 RETURN
1390 REM ----------------------
1400 REM BEGINNING ROUTINE
1410 TEXT : NORMAL : HOME : SPEED= 255
1420 ONERR GOTO 1050
1430 D$ = CHR$ (4)
1440 FDRIVE = 1 : PDRIVE = 1
1450 FILEID$ = "SEQ ADDR FILE"
1460 PRINT D$;"OPEN ";FILEID$;",D";FDRIVE
1470 RETURN
1480 REM ----------------------
1490 REM ENDING ROUTINE
1500 IF X1$ = "Q" THEN 1540
1510 IF N1 = 0 THEN 1540
1520 PRINT "PRESS  C  TO CONTINUE.";
1530 GET X1$: IF X1$ < > "C" THEN 1530
1540 PRINT D$
1550 PRINT D$;"CLOSE ";FILEID$
1560 PRINT D$;"RUN SEQ ADDR HELLO PROG,D"PDRIVE
1570 REM ----------------------
```

Cross Reference Listing

Variable names used with the address record:

```
A1$ 1300, 1320, 1330, 1340, 1350, 1360, 1370
AA$ 1100, 1320
AB$ 1110, 1330
AC$ 1120, 1340
AD$ 1130, 1350
AE$ 1140, 1360
AF$ 1150, 1370
```

Variable names used with the disk commands:

D$ 1280, 1290, 1310, 1430, 1460, 1540, 1550, 1560
FD 1440, 1460
FI$ 1290, 1450, 1460, 1550
PD 1440, 1560

General counters used to keep track of the number of records displayed on the screen:

N1 1160, 1170, 1220, 1510

Variable names used for general GET instruction in response to the screen messages:

X1$ 1210, 1220, 1230, 1500, 1530

Explanation by Line Number   Detailed explanations by line number follow.

1000   REM SEQ ADDR LIST PROG

1010   REM -------------------

1020   REM DRIVE ROUTINE

1030   GOSUB 1410: REM BEGINNING

1040   GOSUB 1090: REM MAIN MOD

1050   GOTO 1500: REM END MODULE

As with most of the programs in this book, the DRIVE ROUTINE contains the same three basic operations. A GOSUB instruction is used to execute those instructions necessary to get the program started. A GOSUB instruction is used to branch to the MAIN ROUTINE, which is executed repeatedly until all the records are displayed or the operator enters Q to quit processing. A GOTO instruction is used to branch to the ENDING ROUTINE to execute the instructions which terminate the program.

A GOSUB is used to execute the MAIN ROUTINE because it is possible for the operator to enter Q to quit processing. If Q is entered, logic RETURNs to the DRIVE ROUTINE. If the end of the file is reached, an ONERR instruction causes logic flow to go to line 1050, which in turn goes to the ENDING ROUTINE. This is the long way around, but it is an attempt to give the program a standardized logical structure.

The MAIN ROUTINE consists of two parts. The first half reads and displays the data, while the second half displays a message and waits for a response.

```
1070    REM -------------------

1080    REM MAIN ROUTINE

1090    GOSUB 1280: REM READ DISK

1100    PRINT "NAME      = ("AANAME$")"

................

1150    PRINT "PHONE     = ("AFPHNE$")"

1160    N1 = N1 + 1

1170    IF N1 < 3 THEN PRINT: GOTO 1090
```

Lines 1080 through 1170 are responsible for reading and displaying each record. Once three records have been displayed, the program pauses for the operator to view the information. Lines 1180 through 1240 consist of the standard logic for displaying and testing a response.

```
1260    REM --------------------

1270    REM READ DISK

................

1370    AFPHNE$ = MID$ (A1ADDR,73,3) + "-" + MID$ (A1ADDR$,76,3) + "-" + RIGHT$
        (A1ADDR$,4)

1380    RETURN
```

Lines 1260 through 1380 cause one record to be read; they consist basically of the same code as in all the sequential programs. The only difference is on line 1370, where hyphens are inserted into the phone number at the time the record is read.

```
1390   REM --------------------
```

```
1400   REM BEGINNING ROUTINE
```

```
1410   TEXT : NORMAL : HOME : SPEED = 255
```

```
1420   ONERR GOTO 1050
```

....

```
1470   RETURN
```

Lines 1410 through 1470 make sure the computer is set up correctly for program execution, initialize some of the variables to the correct starting value, and open the address file. Notice the **ONERR** statement on line 1420. If you are reading sequential files, you must allow for the error which occurs when the EOF is reached.

```
1480   REM --------------------
```

```
1490   REM ENDING ROUTINE
```

```
1500   IF X1$ = "Q" THEN 1540
```

```
1510   IF N1 = 0 THEN 1540
```

....

```
1560   PRINT D$;"RUN SEQ ADDR HELLO PROG,D"PDRIVE
```

Lines 1490 through 1560 are responsible for correctly terminating the program. The first few lines represent code which handles the various ways the program may terminate.

Some logic represented by the first few lines may not be immediately obvious but is necessary because there are three ways the program may terminate.

1. The program may terminate by the operator's entering Q at the end of one of the display screens. The operator may choose not to look at the entire file. If so, logic flow **RETURNs** to the DRIVE ROUTINE, which in turn executes the ENDING ROUTINE.

2. The program may terminate by encountering the EOF after displaying a full screen and prior to displaying any records on a new screen. That is, after three records are displayed, the operator responds by pressing C, but there are no more records to be read, so the ONERR instruction causes logic flow to execute the ENDING ROUTINE.

3. The program may terminate by encountering the EOF after displaying the first or second record of a new screen. The operator should have a chance to view and respond to the records which have just been displayed.

Each of these conditions requires a different sequence of instruction execution to correctly terminate the program.

1500 IF X1$ = "Q" THEN 1540

If the operator enters Q, there is no need to pause for any further response. If X1$ is equal to Q, logic flow skips over the messages and goes directly to the CLOSE instruction.

1510 IF N1 = 0 THEN 1540

If the program terminates by encountering the EOF prior to displaying any record on a new screen, there is no reason to pause and let the operator view the screen, so logic flow skips over the messages and goes directly to the CLOSE statement.

You may think all these checks are unnecessary, but can you imagine what the operator would think looking at a screen which was completely blank except for a message that said, PRESS C TO CONTINUE?

1520 PRINT "PRESS C TO CONTINUE.";

1530 GET X1$: IF X1$ <> "C" THEN 1530

If the program terminates with a partial screen (only one or two records displayed), the termination message is displayed, and the program waits for a response. The only response which is allowed is C. After C is entered, program logic falls through to the CLOSE instruction.

The Sequential File SEARCH Program

Program Name   SEQ ADDR SEARCH PROG

Program Objective   To provide the user with a method of scanning the file for a specific last name or scanning the file for all last names which start with a specific set of characters.

If the file is large, the user will not want to list all the records in sequence just to find one or two individuals. In order to make the system more usable, this program allows the operator to enter a last name or the first few characters of the last name, and the program searches the entire file for any records which match the characters entered.

The screen design is exactly the same as for the SEQ ADDR LISTING PROG except that there is a chance that no matching record will be found. If no record with a matching last name is found, an appropriate message is displayed, and the operator is given another chance to search the file.

Instructions for Running the Program   Run the program by entering

RUN SEQ ADDR HELLO PROG <RETURN>

After the menu is displayed, enter a 4 to start execution of the SEARCH program.

The first screen requests that you enter the last name or the first few characters of the last name to be used in searching the file.

```
ENTER THE LAST NAME OR FIRST FEW
LETTERS OF THE LAST NAME TO BE
USED WHEN SEARCHING THE FILE.

LAST NAME = (                    )
```

After receiving the value to be used during the search process, the program reads and displays any records which contain the same last name or partial last name. For example, if you enter JO as the characters to be used in searching the file, all the JOHNSONs, JOHNSTONs, JONESes, JORDANs, etc. are displayed.

```
NAME      = (JOHN JOHNSTON              )
ADDRESS   = (1234 EASY STREET           )
CITY      = (RICH TOWN       )
STATE     = (NY)
ZIP CODE  = (12345)
PHONE     = (222-333-4444)

NAME      = (MARY JONES                 )
ADDRESS   = (4321 FIRST STREET          )
CITY      = (MODEL TOWN       )
STATE     = (CA)
ZIP CODE  = (98765)
PHONE     = (444-333-2222)

NAME      = (JIM JORDAN                 )
ADDRESS   = (333 TRACK SIDE             )
CITY      = (BOX CAR         )
STATE     = (PA)
ZIP CODE  = (34343)
PHONE     = (252-252-2525)

PRESS   Q   TO QUIT.
PRESS   C   TO CONTINUE.
```

If three or more matches exist, the screen appears as just shown. If only one
or two matches are found before the EOF is reached, a partial screen is displayed,
and the operator is given a chance to enter C to continue. For a partial screen the
operator is not given a chance to enter Q, since the EOF has already been reached.

If no matches are found, a message is displayed as shown in the following
screen. Once the operator is through, C is entered to continue.

```
NO MATCHING RECORDS FOUND


PRESS   C   TO CONTINUE.
```

At the end of the program, the operator is given a chance to rerun the program
or to return to the menu program.

```
SELECT ONE OF THE FOLLOWING

    1. TO RUN THE PROGRAM AGAIN

    2. TO RETURN TO THE MENU


SELECTION DESIRED = (])
```

Program Listing

```
1000 REM SEQ ADDR SEARCH PROG
1010 REM ----------------------
1020 CLEAR :G1 = PEEK (116) * 256 + PEEK (115) - 40 :GA$ = "
     12345678901234567890" + "12345678901234567890"
1030 REM
1040 REM ----------------------
1050 REM DRIVE ROUTINE
1060 GOSUB 1690: REM BEGINNING
1070 GOSUB 1120: REM MAIN MOD
1080 GOTO 2150: REM END MODULE
1090 REM
1100 REM ----------------------
1110 REM MAIN ROUTINE
1120 GOSUB 1340: REM READ DISK
1130 GOSUB 1550: REM EXTRACT NAME
1140 IF FANAME$ < > FBNAME$ THEN 1120
1150 MTCHES = MTCHES + 1
1160 PRINT "NAME     =("AANAME$")"
1170 PRINT "ADDRESS  =("ABADDR$")"
1180 PRINT "CITY     =("ACCITY$")"
1190 PRINT "STATE    =("ADSTE$")"
1200 PRINT "ZIP CODE =("AEZIP$")"
1210 PRINT "PHONE    =("AFPHNE$")"
1220 N1 = N1 + 1
1230 IF N2 < 3 THEN PRINT: GOTO 1120
1240 VTAB 23: HTAB 1
1250 PRINT "PRESS  C  TO CONTINUE."
1260 PRINT "PRESS  Q  TO QUIT.";
1270 GET X1$
1280 IF X1$ = "C" THEN N2 = 0: GOSUB 1470: GOTO 1120
1290 IF X1$ = "Q" THEN N2 = 0: RETURN
1300 GOTO 1270
1310 REM
1320 REM ----------------------
1330 REM READ DISK
1340 PRINT D$
1350 PRINT D$;"READ ";FILEID$
1360 INPUT A1ADDR$
1370 PRINT D$
1380 AANAME$ = LEFT$ (A1ADDR$,25)
```

```
1390 ABADDR$ = MID$ (A1ADDR$,26,25)
1400 ACCITY$ = MID$ (A1ADDR$,51,15)
1410 ADSTE$ = MID$ (A1ADDR$,66,2)
1420 AEZIP$ = MID$ (A1ADDR$,68,5)
1430 AFPHNE$ = MID$ (A1ADDR,73,3) + "-" + MID$ (A1ADDR$,76,3) +
     "-" + RIGHT$ (A1ADDR$,4)
1440 RETURN
1450 REM
1460 REM ----------------------
1470 REM SEARCHING MESSAGE
1480 HOME : VTAB 24
1490 INVERSE : PRINT "   SEARCHING FILE - BE PATIENT" TAB( 38)
     " "; : NORMAL
1500 VTAB 1: HTAB1
1510 RETURN
1520 REM
1530 REM ----------------------
1540 REM EXTRACT NAME
1550 FOR N1 = 25 to 2 STEP - 1
1560 IF MID$ (AANAME$,N1,1) = " " THEN 1580
1570 GOTO 1590
1580 NEXT
1590 FOR N1 = N1 TO 1 STEP - 1
1600 IF MID$ (AANAME$,N1,1) = " " THEN 1620
1610 NEXT
1620 FBNAME$ = RIGHT$ (AANAME$,25 - N1)
1630 IF LEN (FBNAME$) > N3 THEN FBNAME$ = LEFT$ (FBNAME$,N3)
     : GOTO 1650
1640 IF LEN (FBNAME$) < N3 THEN FBNAME$ = FBNAME$ + " ": GOTO 1640
1650 RETURN
1660 REM
1670 REM ----------------------
1680 REM BEGINNING ROUTINE
1690 TEXT : NORMAL : HOME : SPEED= 255
1700 ONERR GOTO 1080
1710 D$ = CHR$ (4)
1720 FDRIVE = 1 : PDRIVE = 1
1730 FILEID$ = "SEQ ADDR FILE"
1740 PRINT D$
1750 PRINT D$;"OPEN ";FILEID$;",D"FDRIVE
1760 PRINT D$
1770 GOSUB 1820: REM INPUT NAME
1780 REM
1790 REM FALL THROUGH TO NEXT ROUTINE
1800 REM ----------------------
1810 REM INPUT NAME ROUTINE
1820 VTAB 5
1830 PRINT "ENTER THE LAST NAME OR FIRST FEW"
1840 PRINT "LETTERS OF THE LAST NAME TO BE"
1850 PRINT "USED WHEN SEARCHING THE FILE." : PRINT
1860 PRINT "LAST NAME = (" SPC( 20)")"
1870 VTAB 9: HTAB 14
1880 GALEGTH = 20: GOSUB 1960: IF LEFT$ (GBANSWER$,1) = " "   THEN 1870
```

```
1890 FANAME$ = LEFT$ (GBANSWER$,GCCHAR)
1900 N3 = GCCHAR
1910 GOSUB 1470
1920 RETURN
1930 REM
1940 REM --------------------
1950 REM GET SUBROUTINE
1960 IF G3 = 0 THEN GOSUB 2110
1970 G3 = G1 + GA - 1: FOR G2 = G1 TO G3: POKE G2,32: NEXT : G2 = G1
1980 CALL 768:GB = PEEK (775) - 128: IF GB = 08 THEN 2050
1990 IF GB = 13 THEN 2070
2000 IF GB = 21 THEN PRINT CHR$ ( PEEK (G2));: GOTO 2030
2010 IF GB = 44 OR GB = 58 OR GB < 32 THEN 1980
2020 PRINT CHR$ (GB);: POKE G2,GB
2030 G2 = G2 + 1: IF G2 > G3 THEN 2100
2040 GOTO 1980
2050 G2 = G2 - 1: IF G2 < G1 THEN G2 = G1: GOTO 1980
2060 PRINT CHR$ (8);: GOTO 1980
2070 IF G1 = G2 THEN 2090
2080 FOR GC = G2 TO G3: PRINT " ";: NEXT
2090 FOR GC = G2 TO G3: POKE GC,32: NEXT
2100 GB$ = LEFT$ (GA$,GA):GC = G2 - G1: RETURN
2110 POKE 768,32: POKE 769,12: POKE 770,253: POKE 771,141: P
     OKE 772,07: POKE 773,03: POKE 774,96: RETURN
2120 REM
2130 REM --------------------
2140 REM ENDING ROUTINE
2150 IF MTCHES = 0 THEN HOME: PRINT "NO MATCHES FOUND": PRINT
     : GOTO 2170
2160 IF N2 = 0 THEN 2190
2170 VTAB 24: PRINT "PRESS  C  TO CONTINUE." TAB( 39)" ";
2180 GET X1$: IF X1$ < > "C" THEN 2180
2190 PRINT D$
2200 PRINT D$;"CLOSE ";FILEID$
2210 PRINT D$
2220 HOME
2230 VTAB 5
2240 PRINT "SELECT ONE OF THE FOLLOWING"
2250 PRINT
2260 PRINT "    1. TO RUN THE PROGRAM AGAIN"
2270 PRINT
2280 PRINT "    2. TO RETURN TO THE MENU"
2290 PRINT
2300 PRINT
2310 PRINT "SELECTION DESIRED = ( )";
2320 VTAB 12: HTAB 22
2330 GET X1$: PRINT X1$
2340 IF X1$ = "1" THEN CLEAR : GOTO 1000
2350 IF X1$ = "2" THEN PRINT D$: PRINT D$;"RUN SEQ ADDR HELLO
     PROG,D"PDRIVE
2360 GOTO 2320
2370 REM
2380 REM --------------------
```

Cross Reference Listing

Variable names used with the address record:

A1$ 1360, 1380, 1390, 1400, 1410, 1420, 1430
AA$ 1160, 1380, 1560, 1600, 1620
AB$ 1170, 1390
AC$ 1180, 1400
AD$ 1190, 1410
AE$ 1200, 1420
AF$ 1210, 1430

Variables used for matching names:

FA$ 1140, 1890
FB$ 1140, 1620, 1630, 1640

Variable names used with the disk commands:

D$ 1340, 1350, 1370, 1710, 1740, 1750, 1760, 2190, 2200, 2210, 2350
FD 1720, 1750
PD 1720, 2350

Variable names used with the GET subroutine:

G1 1020, 1970, 2050, 2070, 2100
G2 1970, 2000, 2020, 2030, 2050, 2070, 2080, 2090, 2100
G3 1960, 1970, 2030, 2080, 2090
GA 1880, 1970, 2100
GB 1980, 1990, 2000, 2010, 2020
GB$ 1890, 2100
GC 1890, 1900, 2080, 2090, 2100

Variables used as general counters:

MT 1150, 2150
N1 1550, 1560, 1590, 1600, 1620
N2 1220, 1230, 1280, 1290, 2160
N3 1630, 1640, 1900

Variable names used for general GET instruction in response to the screen messages:

X1$ 1270, 1280, 1290, 2180, 2330, 2340, 2350

Explanation by Line Number

Detailed explanations by line number follow.

1000–1090 The DRIVE ROUTINE uses the same logic as previous programs. A GOSUB instruction is used to execute the BEGINNING ROUTINE. After returning from the BEGINNING ROUTINE, logic flow uses a GOSUB instruction to execute the MAIN ROUTINE.

The MAIN ROUTINE is executed until one of two conditions occurs. If the operator enters Q to quit, the MAIN ROUTINE is terminated by using a RETURN instruction. If the EOF is reached, the ONERR instruction breaks the GOSUB operation and branches to line 1080. In either case logic flow branches from line 1080 to the ENDING ROUTINE.

The logic of the MAIN ROUTINE consists of three smaller segments. Lines 1110 through 1140 read a record, extract the name, and test to see if there is a match. When a match does occur, lines 1150 through 1230 display the record and increment the counters related to the number of entries displayed. Lines 1240 through 1300 cause the computer to pause and give the operator a chance to respond if there are three matches.

```
1100    REM -------------------

1110    REM MAIN ROUTINE

1120    GOSUB 1340: REM READ DISK

1130    GOSUB 1550: REM EXTRACT NAME

1140    IF FANAME$ < > FBNAME$ THEN 1120
```

Line 1120 reads a record. After the record is read, a routine is executed which extracts the last name from AANAME$ and places it in the variable FBNAME$. If the name read is equal to the name entered by the operator, logic flow falls through the IF instruction, and the record is displayed. If the name is not equal, the record is rejected and a new record is read.

```
1150    MTCHES = MTCHES + 1

1160    PRINT "NAME      = ("AANAME$")"

    ...............

1210    PRINT "PHONE     = ("AFPHNE$")"

1220    N1 = N1 + 1

1230    IF N2 < 3 THEN PRINT: GOTO 1120
```

As each record is displayed, two counters are incremented. The first counter keeps track of the total number of matches. This counter is tested during the ENDING ROUTINE to determine if any records were displayed. If the value of MTCHES is equal to zero, that means that no matching records were found, and an appropriate message is displayed to the operator.

```
1150 MTCHES = MTCHES + 1
........
2140 REM ENDING ROUTINE
2150 IF MTCHES = 0 THEN HOME: PRINT "NO MATCHES FOUND": PRINT:
     GOTO 2170
```

The second counter keeps track of the number of records displayed on the screen. Once three records have been displayed, logic flow falls through the IF instruction and pauses while the operator is given a chance to view the data on the screen. After the operator has responded, the counter is reset and the process started over.

```
1220 N2 = N2 + 1
1230 IF N2 < 3 THEN PRINT: GOTO 1120
```

1240–1310 Lines 1240 through 1310 display the two options to the operator. If the operator enters Q, the MAIN ROUTINE is exited by way of the RETURN instruction. If the operator enters C, the screen is cleared and the search process continues.

If the operator fails to press Q or C, no message is displayed, but the GET instruction is reexecuted, giving the operator another chance to enter the right value.

1320–1450 Lines 1320 through 1450 consist of the READ ROUTINE, which was explained in the previous examples.

1460–1520 Since the process of searching the file is rather slow, a message is displayed on line 24 to let the operator know what is going on. The routine is different from other message routines in that the screen is cleared and then the message is displayed. After the message is displayed, the cursor is repositioned to line 1 column 1.

```
1530   REM --------------------
1540   REM EXTRACT NAME
1550   FOR N1 = 25 TO 2 STEP - 1
1560   IF MID$ (AANAME$,N1,1) = "   " THEN 1580
1570   GCTO 1590
```

1580 NEXT

1590 FOR N1 = N1 TO 1 STEP − 1

1600 IF MID$ (AANAME$,N1,1) = " " THEN 1620

1610 NEXT

1620 FBNAME$ = RIGHT$ (AANAME$,25 − N1)

1630 IF LEN (FBNAME$) > N3 THEN FBNAME$ = LEFT$ (FBNAME$,20): GOTO 1650

1640 IF LEN (FBNAME$) < N3 THEN FBNAME$ = FBNAME$ + " ": GOTO 1640

1650 RETURN

1660 REM

Lines 1530 through 1660 consist of the logic for extracting the last name from **AANAME$** and placing it in **FBNAME$**. The routine consists of three segments. The first segment of code locates the last character of the last name. The second segment of code locates the first character of the last name, and the third segment extracts all the characters making up the last name. In order for this routine to work, the name must be entered using the format of first name first, followed by a space, followed by the last name, followed by as many trailing spaces as necessary.

```
FIRSTNAME LASTNAME        (where ^'s point to blanks)
         ^        ^^^^^^^^
```

1530 REM --------------------

1540 REM EXTRACT NAME

1550 FOR N1 = 25 TO 2 STEP − 1

1560 IF MID$ (AANAME$,N1,1) = " " THEN 1580

1570 GOTO 1590

1580 NEXT

Line 1550 starts a **FOR/NEXT** loop in which each character of the string is examined starting from the rightmost character and working to the left.

```
        1         2
12345678901234567890012345
FIRSTNAME LASTNAME
```

The twenty-fifth character is checked first to see if it is equal to a blank. If it is equal to a blank, logic flow skips to line 1580, and N1 is decreased by 1 (see -1 on line 1550). After N1 is decreased, line 1560 is executed again to check to see if the twenty-fourth character is equal to a blank.

The FOR/NEXT loop continues to execute until a nonblank character is located or the counter reaches a value of 2. For the following example logic flow exits this segment of code when column 18 is checked for a blank. Notice that column 18 contains an E.

```
        1         2
12345678901234567890012345
FIRSTNAME LASTNAME
```

1590   FOR N1 = N1 TO 1 STEP − 1

1600   IF MID$ (AANAME$,N1,1) = "   " THEN 1620

1610   NEXT

After the last character of the name is found, the problem is to find the first character of the last name. Lines 1590 through 1610 accomplish this by starting a new search but this time for the blank between the first and the last name.

```
        1         2
12345678901234567890012345
FIRSTNAME LASTNAME
```

The FOR/NEXT loop is executed until N1 is equal to 10. When the blank in the tenth column is found, logic flow skips around the NEXT instruction and goes to line 1620.

1620   FBNAME$ = RIGHT$ (AANAME$,25 − N1)

1630   IF LEN (FBNAME$) > N3 THEN FBNAME$ = LEFT$ (FBNAME$,20): GOTO 1650

1640   IF LEN (FBNAME$) < N3 THEN FBNAME$ = FBNAME$ + "   ": GOTO 1640

1650   RETURN

1660   REM

After the blank preceding the last name is found, all that remains is to extract the correct number of characters from the start of the last name to the end of the string. This is done by using the RIGHT$ function.

    The variable FBNAME$ is set equal to the characters making up the right side of AANAME$. The portion of AANAME$ to be used is determined by subtracting N1 from 25 where

      25 = The length of the field
    − N1 = The position of the blank between the first and the last name
    = 15 = The number of characters to be extracted

```
          1         2
1234567890123456789012345
FIRSTNAME LASTNAME
          ---------------
```

After extracting the name, the remaining code ensures that the string contains the same number of characters as entered by the operator. This is done by either truncating the excess characters or padding the string with blanks on the right side.

    Lines 1810 through 1920 are executed after falling through the BEGINNING ROUTINE; they allow the operator to enter the name used in searching the address file. The rest of the BEGINNING ROUTINE consists of the same type of code as in all the previous examples.

1670   REM --------------------

1680   REM BEGINNING ROUTINE

....

1780   REM

1790   REM FALL THROUGH TO NEXT ROUTINE

1800   REM --------------------

1810   REM INPUT NAME ROUTINE

1820   VTAB 5

1830   PRINT "ENTER THE LAST NAME TO BE USED WHEN"

1840   PRINT "SEARCHING THE FILE."

1850   PRINT

1860   PRINT "LAST NAME = (" SPC(20)")"

1870   VTAB 8: HTAB 14

1880   GALEGTH = 20: GOSUB 1960: IF LEFT$ (GBANSWER$,1) = " " THEN 1870

1890   FANAME$ = LEFT$ (GBANSWER$,GCCHAR)

1900   N3 = GCCHAR

1910   GOSUB 1470

1920   RETURN

Lines 1800 through 1920 are responsible for retrieving the name from the operator. The IF instruction at the end of line 1880 makes sure the name starts with a nonblank character. Since the names extracted from the file will all start with a letter, the name entered by the operator must start with a letter. Line 1890 is important in that it determines how many characters were entered by the operator. One of the features of the GET subroutine is that it returns the number of characters entered in the variable GCCHAR. The program must know how many characters were entered in order to extract the matching number of characters from the name in each record.

   The name extracted from the record must be the same length as the name entered by the operator in order for the comparison to work correctly. You cannot correctly compare unequal size strings in Applesoft.

1950–2120   The GET subroutine is executed only once in this program and is placed toward the end of the program.

   The ENDING ROUTINE contains some interesting logic and a technique for restarting the program.

2130   REM --------------------

```
2140    REM ENDING ROUTINE

................

2340    IF X1$ = "1" THEN CLEAR : GOTO 1000

2350    IF X1$ = "2" THEN PRINT D$: PRINT D$;"RUN SEQ ADDR HELLO PROG,D" PDRIVE

2360    GOTO 2320

2370    REM

2380    REM --------------------
```

After the file is closed, the operator is given a chance to rerun the program or to return to the menu.

2130–2380 The operator must enter either a 1 or a 2. If a 1 is entered, all variables are CLEARed (set to 0) and the program is restarted. Since all variables are set to 0, the program *must* start over on the very first line so that variables can be initialized to the correct starting values and the files reopened.

5. Random Disk Files

Before any of the following programs are run, they must be copied to a new disk. The program disk does not have enough free space for additional files.

For this chapter copy the following programs to another disk:

RAN ADDR CREATE PROG
RAN ADDR HELLO PROG
RAN ADDR UPDATE PROG
RAN ADDR LIST PROG

If you want to make your disk operate like a turnkey system, use the following steps:

1. Use a new disk or one which no longer contains any files you wish to keep.
2. Load the **RAN ADDR HELLO PROG** from the program disk. Enter

   LOAD RAN ADDR HELLO PROG

3. *Remove the program disk* and put in the disk you want to initialize. After putting in the new disk, initialize the disk using the **RAN ADDR HELLO PROG** currently in memory. Enter

   INIT RAN ADDR HELLO PROG,Dnumber,Vnumber

   fill in the drive and volume number as desired.
4. After the disk has been initialized, transfer the remaining programs from the program disk to the newly initialized disk.
5. In order to use the programs on the new disk, all you need to do is to insert the disk into drive 1 and turn the computer on, or key in PR#6 if the computer is already on. The **RAN ADDR HELLO PROG** will be executed automatically.

A General Introduction to Random Files

Definition and Illustrations

The terms *random* or *direct access* are sometimes incorrectly used when referring to sequential files or indexed file structures. There is only one form of pure random processing, and the concepts used in accessing the record are basically the same for microcomputers as they are for large mainframe computers.

Random access refers to the access method whereby each record is assigned a *relative record number* and a specific location within the file. A record MAY ONLY BE ACCESSED (read or written) using the relative record number related to the record's location within the file.

Relative record number = a whole number starting at 0 and progressing upward in increments of 1 (0, 1, 2, 3, 4, etc.).

Each relative record number corresponds to an area reserved on the disk for a record. Since the computer starts counting at 0 and humans start counting at 1, the relative record number and the actual number of the record do not match (in human terms).

Relative record 0 = the first record in the file.
Relative record 1 = the second record in the file.
Relative record 2 = the third record in the file.

To overcome this discrepancy, some programmers ignore record 0 and do not use that area of the file.

Since the computer MUST HAVE THE RELATIVE RECORD NUMBER in order to locate a specific record, most programmers or systems analysts use the relative record number as the identifying variable for the record (record key).

```
0105JOHN JONES........
^^^^
```

The employee number serves as the relative record number. Mr. Jone's record is located on the disk in relative record location number 0105. The record is physically the 106th record.

Once more, the value for the relative record number starts at 0 and continues as a closed set of sequential numbers up to the maximum number of records to be stored on the file.

The term *closed set of sequential numbers* refers to the requirement that the relative record numbers start at 0 and progress in increments of 1 up to the maximum number of records to be stored on the file.

0, 1, 2, 3, 4, 5, 6, 7, ..., 495, 496, 497, 498, 499

On large computers each number has an area on the disk reserved for it even if the area is not used to store any data. For the APPLE the area in the text file is not reserved, but space in the track/sector list is reserved. The actual space in the text file is not used until the record is written.

Example 1: If record 1000 is written, DOS sets aside 1000 areas in the track/sector list to be used to store the pointers for the 1000 records (even though 1000 records do not currently exist on the file). Record 1000 is written in the first sector assigned to the file, and a pointer is placed in position 1000 of the track/sector list to indicate the location of the record. As other records are written to the file, the area within the track/sector list is updated to point to the location of the record. Records are physically stored in the sequence in which they are added to the file, but the track/sector list is maintained by relative record number.

Example 2: The following table of data shows the relationship between the relative record number and the related record. Each student is assigned a number. If the instructor is smart, the numbers are assigned starting with 01, 02, 03, etc., and the student number serves as the relative record number. For the following data the record key serves both to identify the student and to indicate the location of the record within the random file.

Since the student number equals the relative record number, it may be, but does not have to be, stored as part of the record. For example, when record 01 is retrieved, the student number (01) is already known, so why take up additional disk space by recording the student number on the file? For the data shown below, only the student name and test score are recorded on the disk.

Relative Record #	Student Name	Test Score
00	...Unused; space not allocated	
01	JIM JOHNSON	080
02	MARY SMITH	095
03	...Unused; space not allocated	
04	JAMES MC DONALD	070
. . .	. . . .	. . .
98	BOB NEXT-TO-LAST	065
99	JOHN LAST-RECORD	083

Each of the 100 records (00 to 99) is allocated space in the track/sector list whether or not all 100 records actually contain data.

Applesoft does not require that all the records be written out to the disk as shown in the example programs, but to code the programs so that they work with a partial random file creates more problems than the wasted disk space.

Because of the method used by the computer in locating the records on a random file, the space allocated for each record must be the same length. The maximum length of each record is specified when you OPEN the file prior to any I/O operations. When you READ or WRITE a record, the relative record number must be specified.

Once again, the computer needs two items of information in order to locate a record:

1. Length of the area reserved for each record (must be specified in the OPEN instruction).
2. Relative record number (must be specified by both the READ and WRITE instructions).

If you would like a more technical explanation, see the *APPLE DOS Manual*.

A Systems Chart and Description of Random Files

Step 1: Creating File Labels and Dummy Records

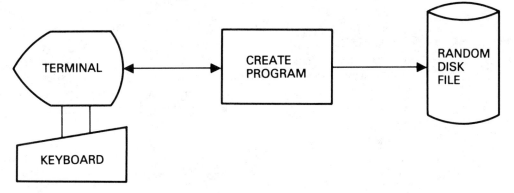

Before a random file is accessed, the file label should be created and dummy values written for each record making up the file. The dummy record values serve to allocate disk space and as a method of indentifying records which are not currently in use.

For example, to create the student file shown earlier, the program opens the random file and writes out 100 dummy records. In this case periods are used as filler or dummy data in creating the records making up the random file.

Relative Record #	Student Name	Test Score
00	. . . .	. . .
01	. . . .	. . .
02	. . . .	. . .
03	. . . .	. . .
04	. . . .	. . .
. .	. . . .	. . .
98	. . . .	. . .
99	. . . .	. . .

Step 2: Random File Update

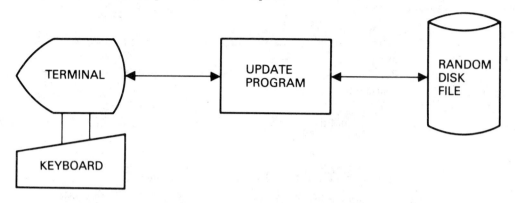

After the dummy file is created, records may be added to, changed, or deleted from the file. Records are added to the file by changing the dummy data (......) and writing the record back to disk. Changes to the file are made by reading the old record, changing the data within the record, and writing the record back to the disk in the same location that it was before. Deleting a record is done by writing dummy data (......) over the top of the old data, thereby destroying the old record.

Step 3: Random Report Generation or Inquiry

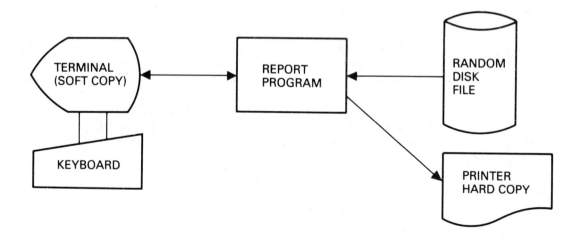

Once a file is created, the data on the file may be used to produce reports. Inquiries or reports related to the file may be displayed on the screen (soft copy) or sent to a printer to produce a hard copy.

The Advantages of Random Files

If the system you are developing requires an on-line direct inquiry, or if only a small portion of the records within a file are to be accessed by most programs, a form of random processing should be used.

Random files allow the operator to access any record within the file in any sequence. The operator may request information about the last record on the file and then turn around and inquire about the first record on the file without any problems.

Since the records may be processed in any order, the computer operator does not need to worry about the sequence of the transaction records. Only the records which are to be updated need to be read and rewritten. This greatly simplifies the job of the operator.

Unlike sequential file updating, in which the entire master file must be copied during the update cycle, random files need only rewrite the updated records. Since only the records which are changed need to be rewritten, the time required for I/O operations is reduced.

Disadvantages of Random Files

If the application you are developing cannot assign a closed set of sequential numbers to the records within the file, there will be problems in how the relative record number is associated with each record.

The computer must have the relative record number to be able to read and write information on the file. If the relative record number cannot serve as the record key, then for cross-reference purposes the record must contain both the record key and the relative record number, as shown in the following data.

```
SN#    R# Student Name              PTS

.....  00 ...Unused area ..........  ...
30303  01 JIM JOHNSON               080
10101  02 MARY SMITH                095
.....  03 ...Unused area..........  080
20202  04 JAMES MC DONALD           070
23134  98 BOB NEXT-TO-LAST          065
55328  99 JOHN LAST-RECORD          083
```

```
where SN# = student number (record key);
      R#  = relative record number;
      PTS = points
```

Having two ways to identify the record increases the disk space required and creates problems when working with the records.

When working with student number 10101 (Mary Smith), the computer user must know Mary's relative record number (02) or have a chart to help cross-reference the student number with the corresponding relative record number. The cross-referencing gets to be a major problem with large files.

A Summary of Random Files for Microcomputers

Random files are ideal for on-line interactive programs. The only drawback to using pure random files is designing the application so the relative record number also serves as the record key.

If the application you are developing can use a closed set of sequential numbers to identify each record, then random file processing should be your first choice.

The closed set of numbers does not have to start at 1. For example, say you are working with product numbers which start at 1000 and run continuously up to 1999. To arrive at a relative record number for accessing each record, simply subtract the starting number (1000) from each product number.

$1000 - 1000 =$ Relative record 000

....

$1010 - 1000 =$ Relative record 010

....

$1999 - 1000 =$ Relative record 999

The key to random file usage is a closed set of sequential numbers which identify each record.

Problem Specifications

A General Description of the Problem

The same problem is used to illustrate the three types of disk access methods with the sequential and random systems using the same screen design.

The basic fields making up the screen design for the random version of the client directory are as follows:

```
RECORD # = (   )
NAME     = (                              )
ADDRESS  = (                              )
CITY     = (                              )
STATE    = (   )
ZIP CODE = (         )
PHONE    = (    -    -    )
```

The problem is to design, write, and create a random system to keep track of the client's name, street address, city, state, ZIP code, and phone number. Each client is assigned a relative record number by which information is accessed.

Note: Since there is no logical way to tie the relative record number to a specific name and address, the client record system does not lend itself to using pure random file organization. In order to use the file you need to produce a cross-reference listing giving the relative record number and client name.

Four programs are used to illustrate random processing:

1. A program for creating the file label and dummy records
2. A HELLO program which allows the operator a method of choosing which program is to be executed
3. A program for updating existing records
4. A program for listing all the records on the file

The RAN ADDR CREATE PROGram is needed to create a label on the disk and to create the correct number of dummy records. Once the label and dummy records are created, other programs within the system may access the file.

The RAN ADDR HELLO PROGram is used to display a menu and execute the other programs in the system. With the exception of the RAN ADDR CREATE PROGram and the RAN ADDR HELLO PROGram, all programs within the system are executed by using the menu.

The RAN ADDR UPDATE PROGram is used to add, change, or delete records from the file. Records cannot actually be added since the space has already been allocated by the dummy records and space cannot be deleted from the file because of the way random files work. Additions to the file are made by writing over the dummy records with new data. Deletions to the file are made by writing over the old data with a dummy record containing all periods (......). Changes are made by reading the record, changing specific fields, and then rewriting the new record over the old record.

The RAN ADDR LIST PROGram is used to display all the names and addresses in ascending order by the client's last name.

A Data Name Dictionary for the Random Address System

The following list describes the variables used in the random system. Most of the names used are the same as those used for the sequential file system. You should scan the list and review the definition and use of each variable.

Not all the names are used in each program. The dictionary is included here to give a single source for the description of all the variables used within the system. If you have a question about the use of one of the variables while looking at a program listing, return to this section for an explanation and a better understanding of the variable.

The names are listed in alphabetic order. Each name consists of a two character prefix followed by a descriptive name. The two character prefix or Applesoft name is given at the left with the full name and description at the right.

All the variable names starting with an A are part of the address record.

AA\$ = AANAME\$

This contains the name of the client and has a fixed length of 25 characters. Data within the variable is left justified. The system is designed for the name to be entered using the format of FIRSTNAME LASTNAME.

AB\$ = ABADDR\$

This contains the street address of the client and has a fixed length of 25 characters. The data within the variable is left justified.

AC\$ = ACCITY\$

This contains the name of the city and has a fixed length of 15 characters. The data within the variable is left justified.

AD\$ = ADSTE\$

This contains a two digit code representing the state. The AT in stATe has to be omitted because of the way in which Applesoft recognizes keywords.

AE$ = AEZIP$

This contains the ZIP code. Although it should be numeric, no edit check is made.

AF$ = AFPHNE$

This contains the first three digits (area code) of the phone number.

AG$ = AGPHNE$

This contains the second set of three digits (prefix) of the phone number.

AH$ = AHPHNE$

This contains the last four digits of the phone number.

D$ = D$ = CONTROL-D character

At the beginning of the each program, the variable D$ is set equal to the character CHR$(4). The character is used when working with I/O operations on the disk.

FB = FBNUM

This variable is only used in the listing program. While records are read the variable serves as a counter, indicating how many valid client names have been read and loaded into a table. After the table has been loaded, the variable serves as a limit of how many times the SORT ROUTINE must be executed.

FB$ = FBNAME$

This variable is used only in the listing program during the process of extracting the last name. FBNAME$ is used to hold the last name of the client.

FB$(= FBNAME$(number)

The name represents the table used to store the last name and relative record number of each client. After the table is sorted by the last name, the corresponding record number is used to read and display each record.

FD = FDRIVE = Value of 1

The name stands for File DRIVE and is used in conjunction with PDRIVE (Program DRIVE) to indicate which disk drive is to be accessed.

FI = FILEID$

This contains the name of the file to be read. The variable is initialized in the BEGINNING ROUTINE of each program and used in all DOS instructions.

All the variable names starting with G are part of the GET subroutine. The following variables are used as parameters to pass data to and from the routine:

GALEGTH   = This variable must be set equal to the length of the field to be read before the subroutine is executed.

GBANSWER$ = After completion of the subroutine, the variable contains the value read in.

GCCHAR   = After completion of the subroutine, GCCHAR contains the number of characters keyed in by the operator. This variable is important only if you are testing whether the operator entered data or just pressed the RETURN key.

All the other variables starting with a G used in the GET subroutine are necessary to its internal operation and are not described in this chapter.

L1 through L9

The variables L1, L2, L3, L4, L5, L6, L7, L8, and L9 are used for vertical positioning of the cursor. The number in the name of the variable is not necessarily the number of the related line. VTAB L1 does not necessarily position the cursor on line 1.

L$ = L$ CONTROL-L Character

L$ is used only in the LIST program when the records are to be printed. L$ is set equal to a CONTROL-L. When this character is sent to a printer which recognizes the ASCII control codes, it causes the printer to skip to the top of the next sheet of paper.

LI = LINE

LINE is only used in the listing program when the records are printed. The variable actually counts the number of records printed, and the name is a little misleading. This is a case of choosing a bad descriptive name, but since the variable REC is used for other purposes, we'll just have to remember that LINE counts the number of records printed. Once a specific number of records have been printed and the page is full, logic causes the printer to skip to the top of the next page and start the listing process again.

N1, N2, N3

N1, N2, and N3 are general counters used with the FOR/NEXT instruction or for other general numeric operations.

PD = PDRIVE = Value of 1

The name stands for Program DRIVE and is used in conjunction with FDRIVE (File DRIVE) to indicate which disk drive is to be accessed.

RE = REC

The numeric variable RECord is used when reading or writing records to the random file. The variable contains a numeric whole number indicating the relative record number of the record to be accessed.

RE$ = REC$

This is the alphanumeric format of the relative record number. The variable is used whenever suppression of the leading 0 for the numbers 0 through 9 would cause a problem in how the data is stored or printed.

Warning: Whenever working with numbers in string format, you should make sure they are all the same length. Pad smaller numeric string variables with leading zeros to make all the strings the same size.

The following instruction makes sure the variable REC$ always contains three digits.

```
2000 IF LEN(REC$) < 3 THEN REC$ = "0" + REC$
```

Also, be careful of accidentally using the letter O instead of the numeric character 0.

SP$ = SPACE$

The variable is used for extending the size of variables read from the disk. When DOS reads in a string variable which contains leading blanks (spaces), the leading spaces are ignored and the data is shifted to the left until the first significant character is encountered. If the variable is completely blank, then the data is reduced to only one space. If the smaller variable is printed over a larger variable, it leaves garbage on the screen. To overcome this problem, each string variable is checked and extended to its maximum size before being displayed.

ST = STARTING

The variable is used in the FREE MEMORY ROUTINE as a general work area. If in your program you use a name which starts with ST, be careful of also using the FREE MEMORY ROUTINE.

X1$, X2$, X3$

X1$, X2$, and X3$ are general alphanumeric variables used with the GET instruction when requesting a response from the operator.

Disk Record Format Specifications

The technique used to write the records on the random file is different from the technique used in the sequential file example.

Instead of being written as one large record containing all the variables as was done in the sequential example, each variable is written as an individual unit separated by a comma. This takes more disk space and presents a problem with variables containing leading spaces but is normally easier for the programmer to code.

Note: This technique should be used when working mainly with numeric data. If you write numbers in string format on the disk, each character takes up 1 byte. If you write numeric variables to the disk, the condensed binary format takes far less space. For example the value 32000 takes 5 bytes in string format and 2 bytes in integer format.

All the variables written to the disk have a fixed length. Since commas are required between each variable, the total length of the record is 90 characters.

The following table shows the position of each variable and comma.

Variable Name	Length	Record Position	Required Comma
AANAME$	25	1 to 25	26
ABADDR$	25	27 to 51	52
ACCITY$	15	53 to 67	68
ADSTE$	2	69 to 70	71
AEZIP$	5	72 to 76	77
AFPHNE$	3	78 to 80	81
AGPHNE$	3	82 to 84	85
AHPHNE$	4	86 to 89	none
EOR Mark	1	90	

The (EOR) End of Record indicator is written and controlled by the computer. It is included in the record description to make sure you understand that it is part of the record length specified in the length parameter of the OPEN instruction.

When all the variables are combined and written onto the disk, the record has the following format:

```
            1         2         3         4         5
Column 123456789012345678901234567890123456789012345678901 2
       NNNNNNNNNNNNNNNNNNNNNNNNN,AAAAAAAAAAAAAAAAAAAAAAAAA,

            6         7         8         9
Column 345678901234567890123456789012345 67890
       CCCCCCCCCCCCCCC,SS,ZZZZZ,PPP,PPP,PPPP?
```

where N = name; A = street address; C = city; S = state; Z = ZIP code; P = phone number; ? = end-of-record marker.

Knowing the format of each record may not seem important to you, but it is very important that you are always aware of how many characters are being written to the disk, how big each variable is, and how the variables are being written out (string format or numeric format). If you write a record larger than the size specified when opening the file, you mess up the EOR marker and will have problems the next time you try to read the destroyed record.

If, while trying to read a random file, the computer beeps and prints a backward slash (\), then you have written larger records than specified by the OPEN instruction. The data on the file is bad and you have to recreate the file.

The Random File CREATE Program

Program Name RAN ADDR CREATE PROG

Program Objective To create a label and 100 dummy records so the UPDATE program may add, change, or delete records as necessary.

Instructions for Running The Program Note 1: Prior to running any of the programs in the random file system, you MUST copy the program from the program disk to a new disk. There is not enough room on the program disk to store any text files.

Note 2: Since all the programs are set up for a single drive system, the disk being used MUST be in drive 1 or the values for FDRIVE and PDRIVE must be changed in each program.

To keep the CREATE program as simple as possible, most of the responsibility for a successful run has been shifted from the program to the computer operator.

There are several situations which result in the program's failing to correctly create the new file.

1. The file label already exists and the file is locked. When the program is run it attempts to OPEN and WRITE on the file. DOS prevents an existing file from being written on if it is locked. The program is terminated with a FILE LOCKED error message.
2. The file label already exists and the file is unlocked. If this should happen, then the program writes dummy records over the existing data. If this is what you want, fine, but if not, the original data is lost.
3. The disk is full, write protected, not initialized, or some other situation not handled within the code of the program. If the program is run under any of these conditions, an I/O ERROR occurs. The responsibility for handling these errors is left up to the operator.

Before running the program, you should make sure the file label (RAN ADDR FILE) does not exist on the disk. Use the CATALOG command and check to see if the label exists. If the label exists and you are sure you want to destroy the data that is currently on the file, use the DELETE command to remove the file.

Even though record 0 is written out by the CREATE program, all other programs ignore the record. After the program starts, each WRITE command and related record will be displayed as follows:

```
WRITE RAN ADDR FILE,R1
. . . . . . . . . . . . . . . . . . . . . . . . . . . . . ,. . . . . . . . . . . . . . .
. . . . . . . . . . . . . . . . . . . . . . . . . . . ,. .,. . . . . . . ,. . .
,. . . .,. . . .
WRITE RAN ADDR FILE,R2
. . . . . . . . . . . . . . . . . . . . . . . . . . . . ,. . . . . . . . . .
. . . . . . . . . . . . . . . ,. . . . . . . . . . . ,. .,. . . . . . . ,. . .
,. . . .,. . . .
```

Program Listing

```
1000 REM RAN ADDR CREATE PROG
1010 REM ---------------------
1020 TEXT : NORMAL : HOME : SPEED= 255
1030 D$ = CHR$ (4)
1040 FDRIVE = 1
1050 FILEID$ = "RAN ADDR FILE"
1060 REM ------
1070 REM SET UP DUMMY RECORDS
1080 REM PROBLEM WITH SPACES
1090 REM ------
1100 AA$ = "........................."
1110 AB$ = "........................."
1120 AC$ = "..............."
1130 AD$ = ".."
1140 AE$ = "....."
1150 AF$ = "..."
1160 AG$ = "..."
1170 AH$ = "...."
1180 REM ------
1190 REM CREATE 100 DUMMY REC'S ON FILE.
1200 REM MUST OPEN AS ONE CHARACTER GREATER THAN SIZE OF RECORD.
1210 REM ------
1220 PRINT D$;"MON I,0,C"
1230 PRINT D$;"OPEN ";FILEID$;",L90,D";FDRIVE
1240 FOR REC = 0 TO 99
1250 PRINT D$;"WRITE ";FILEID$;",R";REC
1260 PRINT AA$",""AB$","AC$","AD$","AE$","AF$","AG$","AH$
1270 NEXT
1280 PRINT D$;"CLOSE ";FILEID$
1290 PRINT D$;"NOMON I,0,C"
1300 END
1310 REM ---------------------
```

Explanation by   Detailed explanations by line number follow.
Line Number

1000–1040   As a coding standard, each of the disk programs starts out with this set of instruc-
                tions. (See the SEQ ADDR CREATE PROG for greater detail.)

1050   FILEID$ = "RAN ADDR FILE"
           A variable is used to represent the file name. You should always use a variable to
           prevent problems with keying errors and to make the programs easier to change.

1100   AA$ = "......................"
....

1170   AH$ = "...."
           When writing string variables out to the disk and reading the variables back into
           memory, the APPLE has a problem in that it suppresses leading blanks. If you allow
           string variables to be blank or have leading spaces, you should extend the variables
           to their maximum length before they are displayed.
               For this book periods are used in place of spaces when writing out dummy
           records. Using periods or some dummy value helps overcome the problem of leading
           spaces and provides a visual reference to the operator. To create the correct number
           of periods, each variable is set to a string of periods equal to the length of the
           variable.

1220   The MONitor instruction is executed in order to provide you with feedback on what
           the program is doing. As the file is opened, records written, and the file closed, you
           are able to see the instructions in execution.

1230   PRINT D$;"OPEN ";FILEID$;",L90,D";FDRIVE
           The OPEN instruction allocates an area in the computer to prepare for handling of
           either input from the file or output directed to the file. If the file label does not
           currently exist on the disk, the label is created in the disk directory.
               For a random file the length parameter L is required. The length must be 1
           greater than the number of characters which are to be written on the disk. In this
           case there are 83 characters making up the data plus six commas used to separate
           the variables, for a total of 89 characters. The file is opened with a length of 90, 1
           greater than 89.

1240   FOR REC = 0 TO 99

1250   PRINT D$;"WRITE ";FILEID$;",R";REC

1260   PRINT AA$","AB$","AC$","AD$","AE$","AF$","AG$","AH$

1270   NEXT

Lines 1240 through 1270 are responsible for writing out the 100 dummy records. The important thing to notice is that the WRITE instruction is inside the FOR/NEXT loop. Each time through the loop, the value of REC is incremented by 1. The first time through the loop, relative record 0 is written; the second time, relative record 1, third time, relative record 2; etc.

The WRITE instruction MUST BE EXECUTED prior to the PRINT instruction which causes the information to be recorded on the disk.

After the 100th record is written (relative record 99), the FOR/NEXT loop is terminated and the file is closed.

You should look closely at line 1260, where each variable is printed individually separated by a comma. When writing to the disk, the comma separating each variable MUST BE WITHIN QUOTATION MARKS. The comma is written to the disk as part of the record. If you forget to put the quotes around the comma, the computer tabs and writes blanks on the disk.

1280   The CLOSE instruction causes any data which is in the output buffer and an EOF marker to be written on the file.

If for some reason you cancel a program while disk files are open, use the CLOSE instruction in immediate execution mode to clear the I/O buffers. After pressing CONTROL-RESET or CONTROL-C enter

CLOSE <RETURN>

Once the program has terminated, you may want to use the CATALOG command to list the disk directory and see how many sectors the RAN ADDR FILE takes up. The file should take up around 36 sectors.

```
      90   character per record
*    100   number of records on the file
=   9000   total number of characters stored
/    256   per sector
= 35.15    sectors (round to 36)
```

If you list the directory you will find that the file actually takes up 37 sectors. The one sector difference represents the single sector used for the track/sector list which DOS builds for all disk files.

The Random File **HELLO** Program

Program Name   RAN ADDR HELLO PROG

Program Objective   To provide a method of transition between the programs making up the random address system.

   The explanation of this program is brief. The material was covered in detail as part of the narrative on the SEQ ADDR HELLO PROG. If you did not read the chapter on sequential file handling, go back and read about the HELLO program.

Instructions for Running the Program   Make sure you have run the RAN ADDR CREATE PROG before running any of the menu driven programs. The file label and the dummy records must exist before you run any of the programs which access the file.

   Use the CATALOG command to check if the label exists and how many sectors are used. Scroll through the names looking for RAN ADDR FILE. If you find the name, it should appear as

T 037 RAN ADDR FILE

After you are sure the file exists enter

RUN RAN ADDR HELLO PROG <RETURN>

   Once the program starts the screen will be cleared and the menu displayed.

```
            SELECT ONE OF THE FOLLOWING:

               1. UPDATE ADDRESS FILE.

               2. LIST RECORDS.

               3. QUIT PROCESSING.

            SELECTION DESIRED = ( )
```

   Don't be overwhelmed by the large number of selections. The random address system is set up to allow you to either update the file or list the records, that's all. The APPEND and SEARCH options which were part of the sequential example are not repeated here. The APPEND instruction is used only with sequential files. If records need to be added to the end of a random file, all you need to do is to modify the **CREATE** program to write out more dummy records starting at relative record number 100: 100, 101, 102, 103, etc. The **SEARCH** program is not repeated since it would consist of almost exactly the same logic. Since random files can be accessed only by the relative record number, each record in the file would have to be read and compared with the search value in order to locate a specific name within the file.

When you are finished reviewing the code for the **HELLO** program, enter a 1 to start execution of the **UPDATE** program. Since this is the first time you have executed the random **UPDATE** program, the file will not contain any valid data. You must start off by adding three or four records to the file.

See the narrative on **RAN ADDR UPDATE PROG**ram for instructions on how to enter data.

Program Listing

```
1000 REM RAN ADDR HELLO PROG
1010 REM ----------------------
1020 TEXT : NORMAL : HOME : SPEED= 255
1030 D$ = CHR$ (4)
1040 PDRIVE = 1
1050 VTAB 5
1060 PRINT "SELECT ONE OF THE FOLLOWING:"
1070 PRINT
1080 PRINT "    1. UPDATE ADDRESS FILE."
1090 PRINT
1100 PRINT "    2. LIST RECORDS."
1110 PRINT
1120 PRINT "    3. QUIT PROCESSING."
1130 PRINT
1140 PRINT "SELECTION DESIRED=( )"
1150 VTAB 13: HTAB 21
1160 PRINT CHR$(8);: REM CHR$(8) = BACKSPACE
1170 GET X1$: PRINT X1$;:X1 = VAL (X1$)
1180 IF X1 < 1 OR X1 > 3 THEN 1150
1190 IF X1 = 3 THEN 1320
1200 VTAB 23: HTAB 1: INVERSE
1210 PRINT " LOADING PROGRAM - PLEASE WAIT        "
1220 NORMAL
1230 ON X1 GOTO 1260,1290
1240 GOTO 1150
1250 REM ----------------------
1260 PRINT D$
1270 PRINT D$;"RUN RAN ADDR UPDATE PROG,D"PDRIVE
1280 REM ----------------------
1290 PRINT D$
1300 PRINT D$;"RUN RAN ADDR LIST PROG,D"PDRIVE
1310 REM ----------------------
1320 HOME
1330 PRINT "THAT'S ALL FOLKS!"
1340 END
```

Explanation by Line Number   Detailed explanations by line number follow.

1000–1040   See prior programs.

1050–1160   Lines 1050 through 1130 display the menu indicating the possible choices to the operator. You should look at the last three lines to see how they are coded. Line 1140 provides a place for the operator to respond. Line 1150 positions the cursor one column beyond where we want the cursor to end up. Line 1160 backs up the cursor so it is blinking over the space between the parentheses.

The reason for the rather complex sequence of instructions is obvious only when the operator enters an invalid value. When an invalid character is entered, it is printed between the parentheses, and then the cursor is moved backward so it is blinking over the invalid character. The operator can see the invalid character and realize the mistake (or try to outwait the computer).

1170   `GET X1$ : PRINT X1$; : X1 = VAL (X1$)`
The GET instruction allows the operator to enter one character. The symbol is printed and the character converted to a numeric value so it can be tested prior to use in the ON GOTO instruction.

1180   When accepting a value from the screen, you should always edit it to make sure it is within the expected limits. If the value is not between 1 and 3, the operator must try again.

1190   The IF tests to see if the operator wants to end processing. If the operator wants to end processing, logic flow skips to the end of the program and displays an ending message.

1200–1220   The UPDATE program is rather long and takes awhile to load. To let the operator know what is going on, a message is displayed at the bottom of the screen. It is always nice to let the operator know what is going on. Think how you feel when the computer is busy and you don't know why.

1230–1300   Depending on the value keyed in, the ON number GOTO instruction causes program flow to branch to one of the two statement numbers following the GOTO. If 1 is entered, logic branches to statement 1260. If 2 is entered, statement 1290 is executed. Since the value of X1 was edited earlier, there is no need to code the GOTO following the ON GOTO instruction. The statement is coded to prevent future errors. If someone changes the code and does not correctly edit the value, the GOTO prevents logic flow from falling through to the DOS commands.

The Random File **UPDATE** Program

Program Name   RAN ADDR UPDATE PROG

Program Objective   To provide the user with a method of adding, changing, and deleting records.

In order for a file to be of any use, there must be a way to add new information, change existing data on the file, and delete unwanted data. The process of adding, changing, and deleting information is normally referred to as *updating the file*.

One of the major benefits of random file processing is that records may be read, changed, and rewritten back to the same file. Unlike sequential file processing, random file processing does not require rewriting the entire file just to change one record.

System Flowchart of Random File Update Program

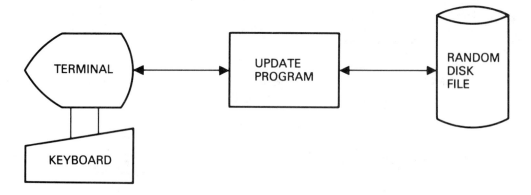

One of the disadvantages of random file processing is that no backup copy is created as part of the update process. You would be wise to periodically make a backup copy of any random file you create.

The biggest investment you make in working with the computer is not the cost of the equipment but the cost of your time in programming and entering data. Do not waste your time by failing to make a backup copy of all your work.

Instructions for Running the Program   Make sure the RAN ADDR CREATE PROG has been run. If you do not create the label and dummy records, the update program will terminate with an END OF DATA error message the first time you try to read a record.

Run the program by entering

RUN RAN ADDR HELLO PROG <RETURN>

After the menu is displayed, enter 1 to start execution of the UPDATE program. The UPDATE program uses the following screen for data entry:

```
                    RAN ADDR FILE UPDATE PROG

        RECORD #  = (   )

        NAME      = (                              )
        ADDRESS   = (                              )
        CITY      = (                    )
        STATE     = (   )
        ZIP CODE  = (       )
        PHONE     = (    -    -       )

                    ? SELECTION

        ADD    CHANGE    DELETE    LIST    QUIT

        ....... First error message line ......
        ....... Second error message line .....
```

The screen differs from the sequential example in three areas. First, the program options have been shortened to a single word with the first letter of each option displayed in INVERSE mode. Second, the operator enters the selection over the top of the question mark preceding the word SELECTION. Last and most important, the operator must enter a number from 1 to 99 corresponding to the record to be processed (see RECORD # = ( ) at top of screen).

Remember: RANDOM ACCESS FILES ARE BASED ON THE USER'S KNOW-
ING THE RELATIVE RECORD NUMBER OF EACH RECORD.

Once you enter a relative record number from 01 to 99, the record is read and displayed.

Exercise 1: Adding a Record

To add a record enter an A and a relative record number. One of two things will happen. If the relative record number you enter refers to an unused record (dummy record), the cursor will be positioned on the first line, allowing you to enter data. If the relative record number you enter contains an existing record (no periods in first five characters of name), an error message will be displayed on the last two lines of the screen.

To test these two situations, execute the following steps:
First, add a record to the file.

1. Enter A in response to the ? SELECTION message.
2. Enter 01 in response to the RECORD # = message.
3. All the fields displayed will contain periods unless you have already added information to record 1.
4. Enter a name, address, city, state, ZIP code, and phone number. After the last digit of the phone number is entered, the record will be rewritten to the disk, and the cursor will be repositioned for another selection.

Second, try to add a record to the file which already exists (one which you added earlier).

1. Enter A in response to the ? SELECTION message.
2. Enter 01 in response to the RECORD # = message.
3. The data entered previously will be displayed followed by an error message at the bottom of the screen indicating this record already contains data.
4. To erase the error message, press the space bar and start over.

Exercise 2: Changing a Record

To change a record enter C and a relative record number. To keep the program short, no check is made to see if the record you are changing contains good data or dummy periods.

To test the logic for changing a record, run through the following two exercises. First, change a record with existing data.

1. Enter C in response to the ? SELECTION message.
2. Enter 01 in response to the RECORD # = message.
3. The fields will be displayed as previously entered.
4. Change any or all of the fields, but remember that if you want to change a field you must reenter the entire field even if only part of the field is incorrect. After the last field is finished, the record will be rewritten to the disk, and the cursor will be repositioned for another selection.

Second, change a record with dummy data.

1. Enter C in response to the ? SELECTION message.
2. Enter 02 in response to the RECORD # = message.
3. The fields displayed will contain periods, indicating a dummy record.
4. Change any or all of the fields. After the last field is changed, the record will be rewritten to the disk, and the cursor repositioned for another selection. Technically the program should not allow you to change a record in which valid data does not exist.

Exercise 3: Deleting a Record

To delete a record enter a D and a relative record number.

To test the logic for deleting a record:

1. Enter D in response to the ? SELECTION message.
2. Enter 01 in response to the RECORD # = message.
3. The fields will be displayed with the current contents.
4. At the bottom of the screen a message will be displayed asking you if you are sure this is the record you want deleted. To delete the record, enter Y. To avoid deleting the record, press any other key.
5. Enter Y to delete the record. You will not see any change in the data displayed. To check your work list the record (see following exercise).

Exercise 4: Listing a Record

To list a record enter L and the relative record number.

1. Enter L in response to the ? SELECTION message.
2. Enter 01 in response to the RECORD # = message.
3. The fields will be displayed with periods, indicating that the record has been deleted.
4. After the data is displayed, the cursor will be repositioned to the selection line ready for the next inquiry.

Exercise 5: Quit Processing

Prior to quitting, make sure you add several records to the file. If you do not add records to the file, there will be no records for the listing program to display. To see how the listing program works, you should enter at least four records.

To terminate the program enter Q. The screen will be cleared and the HELLO program will be executed, allowing you to make another program selection.

Program Listing

```
1000 REM RAN ADDR UPDATE PROG
1010 REM --------------------
1020 CLEAR :G1 = PEEK (116) * 256 + PEEK (115) - 40 :GA$ = "
12345678901234567890" + "12345678901234567890"
1030 REM
1040 REM --------------------
1050 REM DRIVE ROUTINE
1060 GOSUB 2710: REM BEGINNING
1070 GOSUB 1300: REM MAIN MOD
1080 GOTO 3140: REM END MODULE
```

```
1090 REM
1100 REM ----------------------
1110 REM GET SUBROUTINE
1120 IF G3 = 0 THEN GOSUB 1270
1130 G3 = G1 + GA - 1: FOR G2 = G1 TO G3: POKE G2,32: NEXT : G2 = G1
1140 CALL 768:GB = PEEK (775) - 128: IF GB = 08 THEN 1210
1150 IF GB = 13 THEN 1230
1160 IF GB = 21 THEN PRINT CHR$ ( PEEK (G2));: GOTO 1190
1170 IF GB = 44 OR GB = 58 OR GB < 32 THEN 1140
1180 PRINT CHR$ (GB);: POKE G2,GB
1190 G2 = G2 + 1: IF G2 > G3 THEN 1260
1200 GOTO 1140
1210 G2 = G2 - 1: IF G2 < G1 THEN G2 = G1: GOTO 1140
1220 PRINT CHR$ (8);: GOTO 1140
1230 IF G1 = G2 THEN 1250
1240 FOR GC = G2 TO G3: PRINT " ";: NEXT
1250 FOR GC = G2 TO G3: POKE GC,32: NEXT
1260 GB$ = LEFT$ (GA$,GA):GC = G2 - G1: RETURN
1270 POKE 768,32: POKE 769,12: POKE 770,253: POKE 771,141:
     POKE 772,07: POKE 773,03: POKE 774,96: RETURN
1280 REM
1290 REM ----------------------
1300 REM MAIN ROUTINE
1310 VTAB L7: HTAB 1: INVERSE
1320 PRINT "          ? SELECTION" TAB( 39)" "
1330 NORMAL : VTAB L7: HTAB 12: GET X2$: PRINT X2$
1340 IF X2$ = "Q" THEN RETURN
1350 GOSUB 3040: REM CHECK MEMORY SPACE
1360 IF X2$ = "A" OR X2$ = "C" OR X2$ = .'D" OR X2$ = "L" THEN 1380
1370 GOTO 1330
1380 VTAB L0: HTAB 12: GALEGTH = 2: GOSUB 1120
1390 REC = VAL (GBANSWER$)
1400 IF REC < 1 OR REC > 99 THEN 1380
1410 GOSUB 2460: REM READ DISK
1420 GOSUB 2550: REM WRITE SCR
1430 IF X2$ = "A" THEN GOSUB 1540: GOTO 1300
1440 IF X2$ = "C" THEN GOSUB 1880: GOTO 1300
1450 IF X2$ = "D" THEN GOSUB 2200: GOTO 1300
1460 REM
1470 REM ----------------------
1480 REM LIST ROUTINE
1490 REM NO EDIT CHECK IS MADE
1500 REM TO SEE IF VALID RECORD.
1510 GOTO 1300
1520 REM
1530 REM ----------------------
1540 REM ADD ROUTINE
1550 IF LEFT$ (AANAME$,5) < > "....." THEN GOSUB 1770: GOTO 1740
1560 GALEGTH = 25: VTAB L1: HTAB 12: GOSUB 1120
1570 IF LEFT$ (GAANSWER,1) = " " THEN 1560
1580 AANAME$ = GBANSWER$
1590 VTAB L2: HTAB 12: GOSUB 1120
1600 ABADDR$ = GBANSWER$
1610 GALEGTH = 15: VTAB L3: HTAB 12: GOSUB 1120
```

```
1620 ACCITY$ = GBANSWER$
1630 GALEGTH = 2: VTAB L4: HTAB 12: GOSUB 1120
1640 ADSTE$ = GBANSWER$
1650 GALEGTH = 5: VTAB L5: HTAB 12: GOSUB 1120
1660 AEZIP$ = GBANSWER$
1670 GALEGTH = 3: VTAB L6: HTAB 12: GOSUB 1120
1680 AFPHNE$ = GBANSWER$
1690 VTAB L6: HTAB 16: GOSUB 1120
1700 AGPHNE$ = GBANSWER$
1710 GALEGTH = 4: VTAB L6: HTAB 20: GOSUB 1070
1720 AHPHNE$ = GBANSWER$
1730 GOSUB 2360: REM WRITE REC
1740 RETURN
1750 REM
1760 REM --------------------
1770 REM ADD ERROR ROUTINE
1780 VTAB L9: HTAB 1: INVERSE
1790 PRINT "   RECORD ALREADY EXIST - CANNOT ADD   "
1800 PRINT "   PRESS SPACE BAR AND TRY AGAIN       ";
1810 NORMAL : GET X1$: IF X1$ < > " " THEN 1810
1820 VTAB L9: HTAB 1
1830 PRINT TAB( 39)" "
1840 PRINT TAB( 39)" ";
1850 RETURN
1860 REM
1870 REM --------------------
1880 REM CHANGE ROUTINE
1890 REM NO EDIT CHECK IS MADE
1900 REM TO SEE IF VALID RECORD
1910 GALEGTH = 25: VTAB L1: HTAB 12: GOSUB 1120
1920 IF GCHAR = 0 THEN 1950
1930 IF LEFT$ (GBANSWER$,1) = " " THEN 1910
1940 AANAME$ = GBANSWER$
1950 VTAB L2: HTAB 12: GOSUB 1120
1960 IF GCCHAR = 0 THEN 1980
1970 ABADDR$ = GBANSWER$
1980 GALEGTH = 15: VTAB L3: HTAB 12: GOSUB 1120
1990 IF GCCHAR = 0 THEN 2010
2000 ACCITY$ = GBANSWER$
2010 GALEGTH = 2: VTAB L4: HTAB 12: GOSUB 1120
2020 IF GCCHAR = 0 THEN 2040
2030 ADSTE$ = GBANSWER$
2040 GALEGTH = 5: VTAB L5: HTAB 12: GOSUB 1120
2050 IF GCCHAR = 0 THEN 2070
2060 AEZIP$ = GBANSWER$
2070 GALEGTH = 3: VTAB L6: HTAB 12: GOSUB 1120
2080 IF GCCHAR = 0 THEN 2100
2090 AFPHNE$ = GBANSWER$
2100 VTAB L6: HTAB 16: GOSUB 1120
2110 IF GCCHAR = 0 THEN 2130
2120 AGPHNE$ = GBANSWER$
2130 GALEGTH = 4: VTAB L6: HTAB 20: GOSUB 1120
2140 IF GCCHAR = 0 THEN 2160
2150 AHPHNE$ = GBANSWER$
```

```
2160 GOSUB 2360: REM WRITE ON DISK
2170 RETURN
2180 REM
2190 REM ----------------------
2200 REM DELETE ROUTINE
2210 REM NO EDIT CHECK IS MADE
2220 REM TO SEE IF VALID RECORD
2230 VTAB L9: HTAB 1: INVERSE
2240 PRINT "ARE YOU SURE?    ENTER Y TO DELETE THE "
2250 PRINT "RECORD.  ANY OTHER KEY TO KEEP RECORD ";
2260 NORMAL : GET X1$
2270 VTAB L9: HTAB 1
2280 PRINT TAB( 39)" "
2290 PRINT TAB( 39)" ";
2300 IF X1$ < > "Y" THEN 2300
2310 AANAME$ = "......................":ABADDR$ = "......
     ........................":ACCITY$ = "..............":A
     DSTE$ = "..":AEZIP$ = ".....":AFPHNE$ = "...":AGPHNE$ =
     "...":AHPHNE$ = "...."
2320 GOSUB 2370: REM WRITE ON DISK
2330 RETURN
2340 REM
2350 REM ----------------------
2360 REM WRITE ON DISK
2370 VTAB 1: HTAB 39
2380 PRINT D$
2390 PRINT D$;"WRITE ";FILEID$;",R";REC
2400 PRINT AANAME$","ABADDR$","ACCITY$","ADSTE$","AEZIP$","A
     FPHNE$","AGPHNE$","AHPHNE$
2410 PRINT D$
2420 RETURN
2430 REM
2440 REM ----------------------
2450 REM READ DISK
2460 VTAB 1: HTAB 39
2470 PRINT D$
2480 PRINT D$;"READ ";FILEID$;",R";REC
2490 INPUT AANAME$,ABADDR$,ACCITY$,ADSTE$,AEZIP$,AFPHNE$,AGP
HNE$,AHPHNE$
2500 PRINT D$
2510 RETURN
2520 REM
2530 REM ----------------------
2540 REM WRITE ON SCREEN
2550 IF LEN (ABADDR$) < 25 THEN ABADDR$ = LEFT$ (ABADDR$ + SPACES$,25)
2560 IF LEN (ACCITY$) < 15 THEN ACCITY$ = LEFT$ (ACCITY$ + SPACES$,15)
2570 IF LEN (ADSTE$) < 2 THEN ADSTE$ = LEFT$ (ADSTE$ + SPACES$,2)
2580 IF LEN (AEZIP$) < 5 THEN AEZIP$ = LEFT$ (AEZIP$ + SPACES$,5)
2590 IF LEN (AFPHNE$) < 3 THEN AFPHNE$ = LEFT$ (AFPHNE$ + SPACES$,3)
2600 IF LEN (AGPHNE$) < 3 THEN AGPHNE$ = LEFT$ (AGPHNE$ + SPACES$,3)
2610 IF LEN (AHPHNE$) < 4 THEN AHPHNE$ = LEFT$ (AHPHNE$ + SPACES$,4)
2620 VTAB L1: HTAB 12: PRINT AANAME$
2630 VTAB L2: HTAB 12: PRINT ABADDR$
2640 VTAB L3: HTAB 12: PRINT ACCITY$
```

```
2650 VTAB L4: HTAB 12: PRINT ADSTE$
2660 VTAB L5: HTAB 12: PRINT AEZIP$
2670 VTAB L6: HTAB 12: PRINT AFPHNE$"-"AGPHNE$"-"AHPHNE$
2680 RETURN
2690 REM
2700 REM ----------------------
2710 REM BEGINNING ROUTINE
2720 TEXT : NORMAL : HOME : SPEED= 255
2730 D$ = CHR$ (4)
2740 FDRIVE = 1: PDRIVE = 1
2750 FILEID$ = "RAN ADDR FILE"
2760 L0 = 4:L1 = 6:L2 = 7:L3 = 8:L4 = 9:L5 = 10:L6 = 11:L7 =
     14:L8 = 16:L9 = 23
2770 SPACES$ = "                               "
2780 PRINT D$
2790 PRINT D$;"OPEN ";FILEID$;",L90,D"FDRIVE
2800 PRINT D$
2810 REM
2820 REM ---------------------
2830 REM PRINT SCREEN IMAGE
2840 HOME
2850 PRINT
2860 PRINT "    RAN ADDR FILE UPDATE PROG"
2870 VTAB L0: PRINT "RECORD # =(  )"
2880 VTAB L1: PRINT "NAME      =(" SPC( 25)")"
2890 VTAB L2: PRINT "ADDRESS   =(" SPC( 25)")"
2900 VTAB L3: PRINT "CITY      =(" SPC( 15)")"
2910 VTAB L4: PRINT "STATE     =(  )"
2920 VTAB L5: PRINT "ZIP CODE  =(      )"
2930 VTAB L6: PRINT "PHONE     =(    -   -     )"
2940 VTAB L8
2950 INVERSE : PRINT "A";: NORMAL : PRINT "DD      ";
2960 INVERSE : PRINT "C";: NORMAL : PRINT "HANGE     ";
2970 INVERSE : PRINT "D";: NORMAL : PRINT "ELETE      ";
2980 INVERSE : PRINT "L";: NORMAL : PRINT "IST     ";
2990 INVERSE : PRINT "Q";: NORMAL : PRINT "UIT"
3000 RETURN
3010 REM
3020 REM ---------------------
3030 REM FREE MEMORY ROUTINE
3040 STARTING = PEEK (112) * 256 + PEEK (111): IF STARTING >
17000 THEN 3110
3050 VTAB L9: HTAB 1: INVERSE
3060 PRINT " FREEING MEMORY - PLEASE WAIT" TAB( 38)" "
3070 STARTING = FRE (0)
3080 PRINT " DONE - PRESS SPACE BAR TO CONTINUE   ";: NORMAL
3090 GET X1$: IF X1$ < > " " THEN 3090
3100 VTAB L9: HTAB 1: PRINT TAB( 39)" ": PRINT TAB( 39)" ";
3110 RETURN
3120 REM
3130 REM ---------------------
3140 REM ENDING ROUTINE
3150 PRINT D$
3160 PRINT D$;"CLOSE"
```

```
3170 HOME
3180 PRINT D$;"RUN RAN ADDR HELLO PROG,D"PDRIVE
3190 REM
3200 REM ------------------------
```

Cross Reference Listing

Variable names used with the address record:

AA$ 1550, 1580, 1940, 2310, 2400, 2490, 2620
AB$ 1600, 1970, 2310, 2400, 2490, 2550, 2630
AC$ 1620, 2000, 2310, 2400, 2490, 2560, 2640
AD$ 1640, 2030, 2310, 2400, 2490, 2570, 2650
AE$ 1660, 2060, 2310, 2400, 2490, 2580, 2660
AF$ 1680, 2090, 2310, 2400, 2490, 2590, 2670
AG$ 1700, 2120, 2310, 2400, 2490, 2600, 2670
AH$ 1720, 2150, 2310, 2400, 2490, 2610, 2670

Variable names used with the disk instruction:

D$ 2380, 2390, 2410, 2470, 2480, 2500, 2730, 2780, 2790, 2800, 3150, 3160, 3180
FD 2740, 2790
FI$ 2390, 2480, 2750, 2790
PD 2740, 3180
RE 1390, 1400, 2390, 2480

Variable names used with the GET subroutine:

G1 1020, 1130, 1210, 1230, 1260
G2 1130, 1160, 1180, 1190, 1210, 1230, 1240, 1250, 1260
G3 1120, 1130, 1190, 1240, 1250
GA 1130, 1260, 1380, 1560, 1610, 1630, 1650, 1670, 1710, 1910, 1980, 2010, 2040, 2070, 2130
GA$ 1020, 1260
GB 1140, 1150, 1160, 1170, 1180
GB$ 1260, 1390, 1570, 1580, 1600, 1620, 1640, 1660, 1680, 1700, 1710, 1720, 1930, 1940, 1970, 2000, 2030, 2060, 2090, 2120, 2150
GC 1240, 1250, 1260, 1920, 1960, 1990, 2020, 2050, 2080, 2110, 2140

Variable names used when displaying data on the screen:

L0 1380, 2760, 2870
L1 1560, 1910, 2620, 2760, 2880
L2 1590, 1950, 2630, 2760, 2890

L3 1610, 1980, 2640, 2760, 2900
L4 1630, 2010, 2650, 2760, 2910
L5 1650, 2040, 2660, 2760, 2920
L6 1670, 1690, 1710, 2070, 2100, 2130, 2670, 2760, 2930
L7 1310, 1330, 2760
L8 2760, 2940
L9 1780, 1820, 2230, 2270, 2760, 3050, 3100
SP$ 2550, 2560, 2570, 2580, 2590, 2600, 2610, 2770

Variable names used for general GET instruction in response to screen messages:

X1$ 1810, 2260, 2300, 3090
X2$ 1330, 1340, 1360, 1430, 1440, 1450

Explanation by Line Number

Detailed explanations by line number follow.

1000 REM RAN ADDR UPDATE PROG

1010 REM ---------------------

1020 CLEAR :G1 = PEEK (116) * 256 + PEEK (115) − 40 :GA$ =
"12345678901234567890" + "12345678901234567890"

1030 REM

1040 REM ---------------------

1050 REM DRIVE ROUTINE

1060 GOSUB 2710: REM BEGINNING

1070 GOSUB 1300: REM MAIN MOD

1080 GOTO 3140: REM END MODULE
Lines 1000 through 1280 consist of the same code as used in earlier programs. For
a detailed explanation see the sequential file UPDATE program.

1100 REM ---------------------

1110 REM GET SUBROUTINE

The **GET** subroutine is explained in detail in Chapter 3 of Section II.

Lines 1290 through 1460 of the **MAIN ROUTINE** are responsible for the following:

1. Accepting a response from the operator indicating what type of processing is to be done
2. Checking to see if string memory is full
3. Accepting the record number of the entry to be processed
4. Reading the record
5. Displaying the record
6. Executing the routine requested by the operator

1290 REM --------------------

1300 REM MAIN ROUTINE

1310 VTAB L7: HTAB 1: INVERSE

1320 PRINT "   ? SELECTION" TAB(39)"   "

1330 NORMAL : VTAB L7: HTAB 12: GET X2$: PRINT X2$

1340 IF X2$ = "Q" THEN RETURN

Even though the operator enters Q only once, it must be tested first. If the operator wants to quit, the program must exit the **MAIN ROUTINE** prior to asking the operator to enter a record number.

1350 GOSUB 3040: REM CHECK MEMORY SPACE

During each cycle through the **MAIN ROUTINE**, the amount of string memory is checked. If string memory is full, a message is displayed and string memory is condensed (see **FREE MEMORY ROUTINE** p. 238).

1360 IF X2$ = "A" OR X2$ = "C" OR X2$ = "D" OR X2$ = "L" THE N 1380

1370 GOTO 1330

The character entered is tested before the operator is asked to enter a record number. There is no point in asking the operator to enter a record number if an invalid processing code has been entered. If an acceptable character is entered, then logic flow skips to line 1380. If the character fails the edit, the logic flow goes back to line 1330 and makes the operator reenter the data.

1380   VTAB L0: HTAB 12: GALEGTH = 2: GOSUB 1120

1390   REC = VAL (GBANSWER$)

1400   IF REC < 1 OR REC > 99 THEN 1380
The value entered is tested to make sure it is within the limits of the file. You may think this is not necessary since the operator can enter only two digits (01 to 99). But there is always a possibility that the operator might accidently enter negative or decimal values which would cancel the program (-1 through -9 or .1 through .9).

The check also eliminates record 0 as an acceptable choice. There are two reasons for not using record 0. First, ignoring record 0 keeps the program working in human terms. Second, while entering the record number it is very easy to make a mistake which results in a record number of 0. For example, if the operator enters a leading alpha character instead of a number, the VAL function returns a value of 0, and the wrong record is read.

1410   GOSUB 2460: REM READ DISK

1420   GOSUB 2550: REM WRITE SCR

1430   IF X2$ = "A" THEN GOSUB 1540: GOTO 1300

1440   IF X2$ = "C" THEN GOSUB 1880: GOTO 1300

1450   IF X2$ = "D" THEN GOSUB 2200: GOTO 1300

1460   REM

1470   REM --------------------

1480   REM LIST ROUTINE (Logic flow falls through IF instructions to the LIST ROUTINE.)
After the relative record number has been entered, the matching record is read and displayed. After displaying the record, logic flow continues to one of the four routines related to processing the record.

Notice that only the A, C and D codes are checked. Since the character has already been edited by line 1360, the last code is not checked. When the operator requests a listing operation, logic flow falls through all the IF instructions and executes the LIST ROUTINE.

1480–1520 Lines 1480 through 1520 consist of the code related to the LIST ROUTINE. Since the record has already been read and displayed, there is nothing for the LIST ROUTINE to do but to branch back to the start of the MAIN ROUTINE. To keep the program simpler, no check is made to see if the record being listed contains dummy information (all periods) or good data.

1530 REM --------------------

1540 REM ADD ROUTINE

1550 IF LEFT$ (AANAME$,5) < > "....." THEN GOSUB 1770: GOTO 1740

....

1740 RETURN
At the very start of the ADD ROUTINE, the record just displayed is checked to see if the name starts off with periods. If the name does contain periods, the entry is a dummy record and logic flow continues to the next line. If the name does not contain periods, then the program assumes that the information displayed represents a valid record and an error has been made in trying to add a new record over an existing one. If the record already contains data, an error message is displayed, and logic flow returns to the beginning of the MAIN ROUTINE.

1560 GALEGTH = 25: VTAB L1: HTAB 12: GOSUB 1120

1570 IF LEFT$ (GAANSWER$,1) = " " THEN 1560

1580 AANAME$ = GBANSWER$

1590 VTAB L2: HTAB 12: GOSUB 1120

1600 ABADDR$ = GBANSWER$

1610 GALEGTH = 15: VTAB L3: HTAB 12: GOSUB 1120

1620 ACCITY$ = GBANSWER$

....

1730 GOSUB 2360: REM WRITE REC

1740 RETURN

1750   REM

Lines 1560 through 1750 represent the code which allows the operator to enter data into each field. If a more realistic (longer) example was coded, each value entered would be edited in some manner to see if the value was left justified, numeric, within a specific range, or any other edit check which improves the validity of the file. The more you edit the data entered by the operator, the better the file and reports will be. Unlike the examples shown in this book, your programs should completely edit each value entered.

Lines 1560 and 1570 show how you can check the data entered to make sure the operator left justifies the field (enters the first letter of the name in the first column). If the first character entered by the operator is equal to a space, the program branches back and makes the operator reenter the data.

Line 1590 through 1750 consist of the basic pattern for adding data. This pattern is illustrated by lines 1610 and 1620.

```
1610 GALEGTH = 15: VTAB L3: HTAB 12: GOSUB 1120
1620 ACCITY$ = GBANSWER$
```

1. Set GALEGTH equal to the length of the field to be read.
2. Position the cursor on the correct line.
3. Position the cursor at the correct column.
4. Execute the GET subroutine.
5. Edit the value entered the ensure that it is as valid as possible (this is not shown in the example).
6. If the value passes the edit check, set the receiving variable equal to the value read (GBANSWER$).

1760–1860   Lines 1760 through 1860 consist of the standard error routine in which a message is displayed and the program waits for the operator to read the message and respond. The message is then cleared and processing resumes.

1870   REM --------------------

1880   REM CHANGE ROUTINE
....

1980   GALEGTH = 15: VTAB L3: HTAB 12: GOSUB 1120

1990   IF GCCHAR = 0 THEN 2010

2000   ACCITY$ = GBANSWER$
....

2160   GOSUB 2360: REM WRITE ON DISK

2170 RETURN

The CHANGE ROUTINE is exactly like the ADD ROUTINE except for one extra instruction in the logic pattern. The pattern is illustrated by lines 1980 through 2000.

Same as ADD	1. Set GALEGTH to the length of the field to be read.
Same as ADD	2. Position the cursor to the correct line and in the correct column.
Same as ADD	3. Execute the subroutine.
Only on CHANGE	4. Check to see if any data was entered (line 1990). If no data was entered, skip to the next field.
Same as ADD	5. If a value was entered, edit the value prior to accepting it. (This is not shown in the example.)
Same as ADD	6. If the field was changed, set the receiving variable equal to the value entered.

2190 REM ----------------------

2200 REM DELETE ROUTINE

2210 REM NO EDIT CHECK IS MADE

2220 REM TO SEE IF VALID RECORD

2230 VTAB L9: HTAB 1: INVERSE

2240 PRINT "ARE YOU SURE? ENTER Y TO DELETE THE "

2250 PRINT "RECORD. ANY OTHER KEY TO KEEP RECORD ";

2260 NORMAL : GET X1$

2270 VTAB L9: HTAB 1

2280 PRINT TAB(39)"   "

2290 PRINT TAB(39)"   ";

2300 IF X1$ < > "Y" THEN 2300

2310 AANAME$ = "........................":ABADDR$ = "............................":ACCITY$ = "...............":A DSTE$ = "..":AEZIP$ = "....":AFPHNE$ = "...":AGPHNE$ = "...":AHPHNE$ = "...."

2320 GOSUB 2370: REM WRITE ON DISK

2330 RETURN

2340 REM
The **DELETE ROUTINE** consists mainly of coding to ask the operator if the record displayed is really the one which is to be deleted. If the operator responds to the message by entering Y, each individual variable is set equal to the correct number of periods prior to being rewritten back to the disk.

If any value other than Y is entered, the record is not deleted, and logic flow returns to the **MAIN ROUTINE**. Always have the operator check twice when deleting a record.

2350 REM --------------------

2360 REM WRITE ON DISK

2370 VTAB 1: HTAB 39

2380 PRINT D$

2390 PRINT D$;"WRITE ";FILEID$;",R";REC

2400 PRINT AANAME$","ABADDR$","ACCITY$","ADSTE$","AEZIP$","A FPHNE$", "AGPHNE$","AHPHNE$

2410 PRINT D$

2420 RETURN
In programming circles, line 2370 is called a *patch*. For some reason, before line 2370 was inserted, whenever the **WRITE ROUTINE** was executed the position of the cursor on the screen was cleared. To overcome this problem (after hours of trying to solve it in other ways) a program patch was put in to "correct" the situation. The cursor is moved to the upper right corner where it can do no harm.

The programmer's motto is "If all else fails, PATCH IT."

```
2440    REM --------------------

2450    REM READ DISK

2460    VTAB 1: HTAB 39

2470    PRINT D$

2480    PRINT D$;"READ ";FILEID$;",R";REC

2490    INPUT   AANAME$,ABADDR$,ACCITY$,ADSTE$,AEZIP$,AFPHNE$,AGP  HNE$,
        AHPHNE$

2500    PRINT D$

2510    RETURN

2520    REM
```

Lines 2440 through 2510 make up the READ ROUTINE for the random file. You should pay special attention to two of the lines. First, line 2460 is another patch to keep the cursor from clearing data from the screen when reading a record. Again the cursor is sent to the upper right corner. Second, line 2480 tells the computer which record is to be read. Every time a record is read from a random file, the relative record number must be specified by the READ instruction.

```
2530    REM --------------------

2540    REM WRITE ON SCREEN

2550    IF LEN (ABADDR$) < 25 THEN ABADDR$ = LEFT$ (ABADDR$ + SPACES$,25)

2560    IF LEN (ACCITY$) < 15 THEN ACCITY$ = LEFT$ (ACCITY$ + SPACES$,15)
.................
2620    VTAB L1: HTAB 12: PRINT AANAME$

2630    VTAB L2: HTAB 12: PRINT ABADDR$
.................
2680    RETURN
```

Before any data is displayed, lines 2550 through 2610 ensure that all the variables are set to the maximum length. Any strings which do not contain the maximum number of characters are padded with spaces on the right.

If you display a shorter variable over the top of a longer variable, the display shows all of the short value and part of the long value. To prevent this from happening, always use fixed length strings.

Example   Old field: "INDIANAPOLIS"
New field: "SALEM"
Display: CITY   = (SALEMNAPOLIS   )
You may think padding the variable with extra spaces is not necessary since fixed length variables were written and read from the disk. Remember, there is a problem with leading spaces. The computer WRITEs out spaces correctly and READs in the spaces. But sometime during the READ process, leading spaces in a value are eliminated. So for a completely blank variable, you get only one blank character. For variables that contain leading blanks, the data is moved to the left and the variable shortened.

Example   When writing: ABADDR$ = "   25 spaces   "
After reading: ABADDR$ = " "   1 space

(What goes out as 25 spaces comes back as 1.)

Example   When writing: ABADDR$ = "   1234 MIDDLE STREET   "

(Notice the value is not left justified.)

After reading: ABADDR$ = "1234 MIDDLE STREET   "

(Notice the leading spaces are suppressed and the value is shortened by the number of leading spaces.)

You might question why we did not have this problem with the sequential address system. Remember, the sequential system reads and writes one complete string (record) which starts with a nonblank character.

2700-2810   The BEGINNING ROUTINE presents no new instructions or coding techniques.

2820   REM --------------------

2830   REM PRINT SCREEN IMAGE

2940   VTAB L8

2950 INVERSE : PRINT "A";: NORMAL : PRINT "DD ";

2960 INVERSE : PRINT "C";: NORMAL : PRINT "HANGE ";

2970 INVERSE : PRINT "D";: NORMAL : PRINT "ELETE ";

2980 INVERSE : PRINT "L";: NORMAL : PRINT "IST ";

2990 INVERSE : PRINT "Q";: NORMAL : PRINT "UIT"

3000 RETURN
Lines 2950 through 2990 combine to print one line on the screen. The leading character of each option is printed in INVERSE format to let the operator know which character to enter when making a selection. The remaining characters in the word are printed in NORMAL format with each PRINT intruction ending with a semicolon. This form of display is common among purchased software.

3020 REM --------------------

3030 REM FREE MEMORY ROUTINE

3040 STARTING = PEEK (112) * 256 + PEEK (111): IF STARTING > 17000 THEN 3110
....

3070 STARTING = FRE (0)
....

3110 RETURN
Each time a string variable is set equal to a new value, additional memory is used. The FREE MEMORY ROUTINE checks the amount of free space available. If there is still plenty of memory, the routine quickly returns to the calling GOSUB. If the start of string memory falls below 17000, the FRE instruction is executed and string memory is condensed.
The memory address 17000 was chosen because it is well past the end of any of the programs in this book. The larger programs use around 14000 bytes of memory.
For a detailed explanation of the routine, see the sequential UPDATE program.

3130 REM --------------------

3140 REM ENDING ROUTINE

3150   PRINT D$

3160   PRINT D$;"CLOSE"

3170   HOME

3180   PRINT D$;"RUN RAN ADDR HELLO PROG,D"PDRIVE

3190   REM

3200   REM --------------------
The ENDING ROUTINE consists of no new instructions but does show a different format for the CLOSE instruction. When the CLOSE instruction is used without a file name, DOS CLOSEs all the open files used in the program.

The Random File LIST Program

Program Name   RAN ADDR LIST PROG

Program Objective   To provide the user with a method of displaying all the records on the screen or printing a hard copy of the records.

The random address LIST program varies in several ways from the sequential LIST program shown earlier. The random address LIST program:

1. Allows the user either to display the records on the screen or to print each record.
2. Sorts the records into alphabetic sequence by the client's last name.
3. Does not use the DRIVE ROUTINE as in previous examples. The coding still uses modules and limits the use of the GOTO instruction, but because of the nature of the program, logic flow is allowed to simply fall through each module as it is executed.

The random address LIST program displays two records to the screen or prints three records per page. When displaying the records the program pauses at the end of each screen and waits for a response from the operator. When printing records the program does not pause.

The two-record screen format appears as follows:

```
          RECORD #  = (   )

          NAME      = (                        )
          ADDRESS   = (                        )
          CITY      = (              )
          STATE     = (   )
          ZIP CODE  = (       )
          PHONE     = (    -    -     )


          RECORD #  = (   )

          NAME      = (                        )
          ADDRESS   = (                        )
          CITY      = (              )
          STATE     = (   )
          ZIP CODE  = (       )
          PHONE     = (    -    -     )



          PRESS THE SPACE BAR TO CONTINUE
```

Instructions for Running the Program

Run the program by entering

RUN RAN ADDR HELLO PROG <RETURN>

After the menu is displayed, enter 2 to start execution of the listing program.

After the listing program has started the screen will be cleared, and the following message will be displayed.

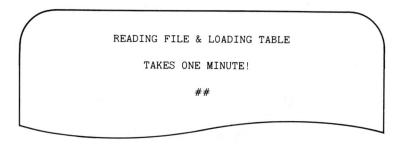

```
          READING FILE & LOADING TABLE

               TAKES ONE MINUTE!

                    ##
```

As each record is read, the record number is displayed to give the operator visual feedback about what the program is doing.

Each record in the file must be read and examined to see if it contains a valid name, the last name extracted, and the name placed into a table. With a random file it is possible for the operator to skip around and enter data for any record in the file.

To ensure that each name in the file is found, all 99 records making up the file are read and checked for a valid name. Be patient, as the program must read from record 01 to record 99.

After all the records have been read and the last name of each client is placed into a table, the table is sorted. The length of time it takes the program to sort the table depends on how many records are found. If only a few records contain information, you cannot even tell that the sorting is taking place (except for the message on the screen). But if every record on the file contains a name, the sorting takes around 1½ minutes to sequence the records.

The **SORT ROUTINE** uses the following screen format:

```
             SORTING TABLE ENTRIES

                PASS ## OF ##



     SORT DONE - PRESS SPACE BAR TO CONT.
```

During the sorting process, two numbers are displayed. The last number indicates the total number of passes needed to sort the table, while the first number indicates which pass the computer is currently working on. The length of time the first number is displayed depends on the number of entries in the table. Toward the end of the sorting the numbers change very rapidly.

After the sort is done, the operator must press the space bar to continue. The pause is put in so the operator has a chance to see the screen and know what is going on. If there are only a few entries in the table, the sorting is done in a matter of seconds. If there were no pause, the message would flash on the screen, the sort would be done, and a new message would be displayed before the operator knew what happened.

The current version of the program does not give the operator any method of terminating the program early. Once the program has started, it continues to execute until all the records have been displayed or printed. The display portion of the program should be modified to allow the operator a method of continuing or ending the program. The operator will most likely not want to look at every name in the file two at a time. This is another case of "Do as I say and not as I do." When displaying records on the screen you should always make the operator respond with a specific key in order to continue and always give the operator a way to end the program gracefully (gracefully means without canceling the program or pulling the plug on the computer).

As the program is written, the operator's only options are to wait until processing has been completed or to cancel the program.

After the sort is done and the operator has responded, the next screen is displayed. The screen allows the operator to enter either D to display the records on the screen or P to print the records.

```
          ENTER  D  TO  DISPLAY  THE  NAMES

          ENTER  P  TO  PRINT     THE  NAMES

                   RESPONSE  =   ↑
```

If the operator chooses to display the records, then the display process is started. If the operator wants to print the records, another screen is displayed, and the program pauses to give the operator time to make sure the printer is ready.

```
              PRESS  SPACE  BAR  WHEN:

              1.  PRINTER  IS  TURNED  ON.

              2.  FORMS  ARE  ALIGNED.
```

Program Listing

```
1000 REM RAN ADDR LIST PROG
1010 REM ------------------------
1020 REM BEGINNING ROUTINE
1030 DIM FBNAME$(99)
1040 TEXT : NORMAL : HOME : SPEED= 255
1050 D$ = CHR$ (4)
1060 FDRIVE = 1:PDRIVE = 1
1070 FILEID$ = "RAN ADDR FILE"
1080 SPACES$ = "                          "
1090 REM L$ = TO-TOP-OF-PAGE
1100 L$ = CHR$ (12)
1110 VTAB 10: HTAB 5
1120 PRINT "READING FILE & LOADING TABLE"
1130 VTAB 12: HTAB 10
1140 PRINT "TAKES ONE MINUTE!"
1150 PRINT D$
```

```
1160 PRINT D$;"OPEN ";FILEID$;",L90,D"FDRIVE
1170 PRINT D$
1180 REM
1190 REM --------------------
1200 REM MAIN ROUTINE
1210 FOR REC = 1 TO 99
1220 REM -----MUST READ ALL FIELDS OR EXTRA IGNORED MESSAGE
IS DISPLAYED
1230 GOSUB 2070: REM READ DISK
1240 VTAB 15: HTAB 19: PRINT REC
1250 REM
1260 REM --------------------
1270 IF LEFT$ (AANAME$,1) = "." THEN 1460
1280 REM
1290 R (AANAME$,N1,1) = " " THEN N2 = N1:N1 = 1
1370 NEXT
1380 IF N2 = 25 THEN FBNAME$ = LEFT$ (AANAME$,20): GOTO 1420
1390 FBNAME$ = RIGHT$ (AANAME$,25 - N2)
1400 IF LEN (FBNAME$) > 20 THEN FBNAME$ = LEFT$ (FBNAME$,20)
: GOTO 1420
1410 IF LEN (FBNAME$) < 20 THEN FBNAME$ = LEFT$ (FBNAME$ + SPACES$,20)
1420 REC$ = STR$ (REC)
1430 IF LEN (REC$) < 2 THEN REC$ "0" + REC$
1440 FBNAME$(FBNUM) = FBNAME$ + REC$
1450 FBNUM = FBNUM + 1
1460 NEXT
1470 REM
1480 REM --------------------
1490 REM SORT ROUTINE
1500 HOME : VTAB 10: HTAB 5
1510 PRINT "SORTING TABLE ENTRIES"
1520 N3 = FBNUM - 1: IF N3 < 1 THEN 1670
1530 FOR N1 = 0 TO N3 - 1
1540 VTAB 12: HTAB 9: PRINT "PASS "N1 + 1" OF "N3
1550 :: FOR N2 = N1 + 1 TO N3
1560 :::: IF FBNAME$(N1) < FBNAME$(N2) THEN 1600
1570 :::: X1$ = FBNAME$(N1)
1580 :::: FBNAME$(N1) = FBNAME$(N2)
1590 :::: FBNAME$(N2) = X1$
1600 :: NEXT
1610 NEXT
1620 VTAB 24: HTAGB 1
1630 INVERSE : PRINT " SORT DONE - PRESS SPACE BAR TO CONT.  ";:NORMAL
1640 GET X1$: IF X1$ < > " " THEN 1640
1650 REM
1660 REM --------------------
1670 REM SELECT DEVICE
1680 HOME
1690 PRINT : PRINT
1700 PRINT "ENTER D TO DISPLAY THE NAMES"
1710 PRINT
1720 PRINT "ENTER P TO PRINT   THE NAMES"
1730 PRINT
1740 PRINT "      RESPONSE = ";: GET X2$: PRINT X2$;
```

```
1750 IF X2$ = "D" THEN HOME : GOTO 1910
1760 IF X2$ = "P" THEN 1780
1770 GOTO 1680
1780 HOME
1790 PRINT "PRESS SPACE BAR WHEN:"
1800 PRINT
1810 PRINT "  1. PRINTER IS TURNED ON."
1820 PRINT
1830 PRINT "  2. FORMS ARE ALIGNED.";
1840 GET X1$: IF X1$ < > " " THEN 1840
1850 HOME
1860 PRINT D$
1870 PRINT D$;"PR#1"
1880 REM
1890 REM --------------------
1900 REM PRINT TABLE ENTRIES
1910 FOR N1 = 0 TO N3
1920 REC$ = RIGHT$ (FBNAME$(N1),2)
1930 REC = VAL (REC)
1940 GOSUB 2080: REM READ DISK
1950 GOSUB 2160: REM WRITE PRT
1960 NEXT
1970 IF X2$ = "D" AND LINE > 0 THEN VTAB 22: HTAB 1: PRINT " PRESS
     THE SPACE BAR TO CONTINUE";: GET X1$: IF X1$ < > " " THEN 1970
1980 IF X2$ = "D" THEN 2010
1990 PRINT L$;L$
2000 PRINT D$: PRINT D$;"PR#0"
2010 PRINT D$: PRINT D$;"CLOSE"
2020 PRINT D$;"RUN RAN ADDR HELLO PROG,D"PDRIVE
2030 REM
2040 REM --------------------
2050 REM *** SUBROUTINES ***
2060 REM --------------------
2070 REM READ DISK
2080 PRINT D$
2090 PRINT D$;"READ ";FILEID$;",R"REC
2100 INPUT AANAME$,ABADDR$,ACCITY$,ADSTE$,AFPHNE$,AGPHNE$,AHPHNE$
2110 PRINT D$
2120 RETURN
2130 REM
2140 REM --------------------
2150 REM PRINT SCREEN IMAGE
2160 IF LEN (ABADDR$) < 25 THEN ABADDR$ = LEFT$ (ABADDR$ + SPACES$,25)
2170 IF LEN (ACCITY$) < 15 THEN ACCITY$ = LEFT$ (ACCITY$ + SPACES$,15)
2180 IF LEN (ADSTE$) < 2 THEN ADSTE$ = LEFT$ (ADSTE$ + SPACES$,2)
2190 IF LEN (AEZIP$) < 5 THEN AEZIP$ = LEFT$ (AEZIP$ + SPACES$,5)
2200 IF LEN (AFPHNE$) < 3 THEN AFPHNE$ = LEFT$ (AFPHNE$ + SPACES$,3)
2210 IF LEN (AGPHNE$) < 3 THEN AGPHNE$ = LEFT$ (AGPHNE$ + SPACES$,3)
2220 IF LEN (AHPHNE$) < 4 THEN AHPHNE$ = LEFT$(AHPHNE$ +
     SPACES$,4)
2230 PRINT
2240 PRINT "RECORD # =("REC$")"
2250 PRINT
2260 PRINT "NAME     =("AANAME$")"
```

```
2270 PRINT "ADDRESS  =("ABADDR$")"
2280 PRINT "CITY     =("ACCITY$")"
2290 PRINT "STATE    =("ADSTE$")"
2300 PRINT "ZIP CODE =("AEZIP$")"
2310 PRINT "PHONE    =("AFPHNE$"-"AFPHNE$"-"AFPHNE$")"
2320 PRINT : PRINT
2330 REM
2340 REM ----------------------
2350 IF X2$ = "D" THEN 2410
2360 LINE = LINE + 1
2370 IF LINE > 4 THEN PRINT L$: LINE = 0
2380 RETURN
2390 REM
2400 REM ----------------------
2410 LINE = LINE + 1
2420 IF LINE < 2 THEN 2460
2430 PRINT "PRESS THE SPACE BAR TO CONTINUE ";
2440 GET X1$: IF X1$ < > " " THEN 2440
2450 HOME: LINE = 0
2460 RETURN
2470 REM
2480 REM ----------------------
```

Cross Reference Listing

Variable names used with the address record:

AA$ 1270, 1320, 1360, 1380, 1390, 2100, 2260
AB$ 2100, 2160, 2270
AC$ 2100, 2170, 2280
AD$ 2100, 2180, 2290
AE$ 2100, 2190, 2300
AF$ 2100, 2200, 2310
AG$ 2100, 2210, 2310
AH$ 2100, 2220, 2310

Variable names used with the disk instructions:

D$ 1050, 1150, 1160, 1170, 1860, 1870, 2000, 2010, 2020, 2080, 2090, 2110
FD 1060, 1160
FI$ 1070, 1160, 2090
PD 1060, 2020

Variable names used when working with finding and storing the last name:

FB 1440, 1450, 1520
FB$ 1380, 1390, 1400, 1410, 1440
FB$(1030, 1440, 1560, 1570, 1580, 1590, 1920

Other general purpose variable names:

L$ 1100, 1990, 2370
LI   1970, 2360, 2370, 2410, 2420, 2450
N1   1310, 1320, 1330, 1350, 1360, 1530, 1540, 1550, 1560, 1570, 1580, 1910, 1920
N2   1330, 1350, 1360, 1380, 1390, 1550, 1560, 1580, 1590
N3   1520, 1530, 1540, 1550, 1910
RE   1210, 1240, 1420, 1930, 2090
RE$ 1420, 1430, 1440, 1920, 1930, 2240
X1$ 1570, 1590, 1640, 1840, 1970, 2440
X2$ 1740, 1750, 1760, 1970, 1980, 2350

Explanation by Line Number

Detailed explanations by line number follow.

1000   REM RAN ADDR LIST PROG
....

1030   DIM FBNAME$(99)
....

1090   REM L$ = TO-TOP-OF-PAGE

1100   L$ = CHR$ (12)
....

1160   PRINT D$;"OPEN ";FILEID$;",L90,D"FDRIVE

There are four instructions in the BEGINNING ROUTINE you should look at closely. The first instruction sets up the table used to store the client's last name. A table (also called list or array) provides the programmer with an easy way to reference many values by using a single variable name followed by a number.

FBNAME$ (0) = First table entry
FBNAME$ (1) = Second table entry
FBNAME$ (2) = Third table entry
....
FBNAME$ (99) = 100th table entry

Instead of a constant (0, 1, 99), a variable is used following the table name, allowing the programmer to access each table entry by varying the value within the parentheses. Looking ahead at lines 1440 and 1450 shows us how the table is loaded.

.... Find a name in the file and then put it in the table
1440 FBNAME$(FBNUM) = FBNAME$ + REC$
1450 FBNUM = FBNUM + 1

Each time a name is found in the file, the name and matching record number are placed in the table. The very first time line 1440 is executed, FBNUM is equal to 0, so FBNAME$ (0) is set equal to the value of FBNAME$ + REC$. After a value is put FBNAME$ (0), FBNUM is incremented to point to the next table entry. The next time line 1440 is executed, FBNAME$ (1) is set equal to the value of FBNAME$ + REC$ and FBNUM is incremented to point to FBNAME$ (2). The process is repeated for each name found in the file.

If you have trouble understanding how the table is being used, go back and review the DIM instruction in Chapter 24 of Section I.

The second line to review sets L$ equal to CONTROL-L.

1090 REM L$ = TO-TOP-OF-PAGE
1100 L$ = CHR$ (12)

The CONTROL-L is used to cause the printer to advance to the top of the next page. By printing the character (sending the character to the printer), the printer automatically advances the form to the top of the next page.

The third line you should examine is the OPEN instruction, which specifies the length of the records making up the random address file.

1160 PRINT D$;"OPEN ";FILEID$;",L90,D"FDRIVE

Although it has been stated several times before, remember that when using random files the maximum length of each record must be specified as part of the OPEN instruction. The length must include the number of characters per variable, any commas used to separate the variables, and one character for the EOR indicator.

The MAIN ROUTINE consists of one large FOR/NEXT loop, which is executed 99 times.

1190   REM --------------------

1200   REM MAIN ROUTINE

1210   FOR REC = 1 TO 99

1220   REM -----MUST READ ALL FIELDS OR EXTRA IGNORED MESSAGE IS DISPLAYED

1230   GOSUB 2070: REM READ DISK

1240   VTAB 15: HTAB 19: PRINT REC

1250 REM

1260 REM --------------------

1270 IF LEFT$ (AANAME$,1) = "." THEN 1460

....

1460 NEXT

Each time the **MAIN ROUTINE** is executed, a record is read and the name checked
to see if it starts with a period. If the name starts with a period, logic flow branches
to line 1460, where the **NEXT** instruction either causes the FOR/NEXT loop to be
repeated (REC = 01 to 99) or drops through to line 1470 (REC > 99).

Line 1220 has been inserted to remind you that even though you may be
interested in only one or two variables within the record, all the variables making
up a record must be read or else an error message is displayed indicating that the
extra data was ignored. The first time through the file, the only variable needed is
the last name. The name is required in order to sort the names prior to rereading
the file and displaying the records in last name sequence. But in order to retrieve
the name, all the variables making up the record must be read.

Lines 1300 through 1460 consist of the logic for extracting the last name. The
routine is basically the same as in the **SEQ ADDR SEARCH PROG**. You may want
to study it again in detail or skim over the material and go to the explanation of the
next module.

The routine consists of three segments. The first segment of code locates the
last character in the last name. The second segment of code locates the first character
of the last name, and the third segment extracts all the characters making up the last
name. In order for the routine to work, the name must have been entered using the
format of first name, followed by a space, followed by the last name, followed by
as many trailing spaces as necessary.

```
FIRSTNAME LASTNAME
         ^          ^^^^^^   Where ^ points to blank positions
```

1290 REM --------------------

1300 REM EXTRACT NAME

1310 FOR N1 = 25 TO 1 STEP − 1

1320 IF MID$ (AANAME$,N1,1) = "   " THEN 1340

1330 N2 = N1:N1 = 1

1340 NEXT

Line 1310 starts a FOR/NEXT loop in which each character of the variable is examined starting from the rightmost character and working to the left.

```
          1         2
1234567890123456789012345
FIRSTNAME LASTNAME
```

The twenty-fifth character is checked to see if it is equal to a blank. If it is equal to a blank, logic flow skips to line 1340 where N1 is decreased by 1 (see -1 on line 1310). After N1 is reduced, line 1320 is executed again to check to see if the twenty-fourth character is equal to a blank. The FOR/NEXT loop is continued until a nonblank character is located or the counter reaches a value of 2. For the example, logic flow exits the segment of code when column 18 is checked for a blank. Notice that column 18 contains an E.

```
          1         2
1234567890123456789012345
FIRSTNAME LASTNAME
```

After the last character of the name is found, the problem is finding the first character of the last name. Lines 1350 through 1370 accomplish this by starting a new search, but this time for the blank between the first and the last name.

1350 FOR N1 = N2 TO 1 STEP $-$ 1

1360 IF MID$ (AANAME$,N1,1) = " " THEN N2 = N1:N1 = 1

1370 NEXT

The FOR/NEXT loop is executed until a blank is found or N1 is less than 1. For the example the loop stops when N1 reaches 10. When the blank is found, N2 is set equal to the current value of N1 (which is 10), and N1 is set equal to 1 in order to terminate the FOR/NEXT loop. Since the FOR/NEXT loop is set up to terminate when N1 is less than 1, logic flow falls through statement 1370 to 1380 (remember the NEXT statement subtracts 1 from N1 and tests for a LESS THAN condition).

We now know that the last name is between the value in N2 (10) and the last column.

```
          1         2
1234567890123456789012345
FIRSTNAME LASTNAME
         ^ N2              ^ Last Byte of field
```

1380 IF N2 = 25 THEN FBNAME$ = LEFT$ (AANAME$,20): GOTO 1420

1390   FBNAME\$ = RIGHT\$ (AA NAME\$,25 − N2)

But there is a very slight chance that the client's last name takes up the entire 25 characters. If the name takes up the entire 25 characters, the formula used to extract the name results in an error.

If N2 = 25, then RIGHT\$ (AANAME\$,25 − N2)
                 = RIGHT\$ (AANAME\$,0)

The second parameter of the RIGHT\$ function cannot be 0.

To handle this unlikely situation, the value of N2 is checked to see if it is equal to 25. If it is equal to 25, only the leftmost 20 characters of the variable are used (see line 1380).

For a name less than 25 characters long, FBNAME\$ is set equal to the characters making up the right side of AANAME\$. The portion of AANAME\$ to be used is determined by subtracting N1 from 25 where

    25 = The length of the FBNAME\$
 − N1 = The position of the blank between the first and the last name
 = 15 = The number of characters to be extracted

```
        1         2
123456789012345678901 2345
FIRSTNAME LASTNAME
        ---------------
```

1400   IF LEN (FBNAME\$) > 20 THEN FBNAME\$ = LEFT\$ (FBNAME\$,20) : GOTO 1420

1410   IF LEN (FBNAME\$) < 20 THEN FBNAME\$ = LEFT\$ (FBNAME\$ + SPACES\$,20)

After the last name has been extracted, the remaining code guarantees that the variable contains exactly 20 characters. In order for the sort to work, all the variables must be exactly the same length. Strings being compared in Applesoft must be the same size or the shorter string will be considered less than the longer string.

1420   REC\$ = STR\$ (REC)

1430   IF LEN (REC\$) < 2 THEN REC\$ " " + REC\$

1440   FBNAME\$(FBNUM) = FBNAME\$ + REC\$

1450   FBNUM = FBNUM + 1

1460   NEXT   (Remember the FOR on line 1210)

1470 REM
Once the last name has been found, lines 1420 through 1450 attach the relative
record number to the name and place both entries into the table.

```
LASTNAME            00
^^^^^^^^^^^^^^^^^^^^ Name
                    ^^Relative record number
```

Both the name and the relative record number are needed. The last name is
needed in order to sort the records, and the relative record number is needed after
the names are sorted so the records can be read in the same sequence as they were
sorted.

For example, if the following three names were on the file

| | Record |
Name..............	Number
BOOTH	05
SMITH	15
ADAMS	20

after the sort they would appear as

| | Record |
Name..............	Number
ADAMS	20
BOOTH	05
SMITH	15

Record 20 is read first: record 5, second: and record 15, third.

Lines 1490 through 1640 make up the logic for sorting the table entries into
ascending order. The program uses a replacement sort, which is the easiest sorting
technique for the programmer to code. Unfortunately, the replacement sort is one
of the most inefficient methods of sorting if you are considering the amount of time
it takes for the computer to complete the sort.

Basically, the sort logic consists of two **FOR/NEXT** loops. The inner loop is
responsible for doing the comparisons and switching the values, while the outer
loop resets the counters and determines how many times the inner loop is executed.

Look over the complete routine and then follow through the line by line explanation. The **FOR/NEXT** loops have been indented by using leading colons to help
you follow the logic.

1480 REM --------------------

1490 REM SORT ROUTINE

```
1500    HOME : VTAB 10: HTAB 5

1510    PRINT "SORTING TABLE ENTRIES"

1520    N3 = FBNUM − 1: IF N3 < 1 THEN 1670

1530    FOR N1 = 0 TO N3 − 1

1540    VTAB 12: HTAB 9: PRINT 'PASS 'N1 + 1' OF 'N3

1550    :: FOR N2 = N1 + 1 TO N3

1560    :::: IF FBNAME$(N1) < FBNAME$(N2) THEN 1600

1570    :::: X1$ = FBNAME$(N1)

1580    :::: FBNAME$(N1) = FBNAME$(N2)

1590    :::: FBNAME$(N2) = X1$

1600    :: NEXT

1610    NEXT

1620    VTAB 24: HTAGB 1

1630    INVERSE : PRINT " SORT DONE - PRESS SPACE BAR TO CONT. ";:NORMAL

1640    GET X1$: IF X1$ < > " " THEN 1640

1520    N3 = FBNUM − 1: IF N3 < 1 THEN 1670
```

Line 1520 sets N3 equal to the number of names in the table. If you go back to line 1450, you will see that FBNUM points to the next empty location of the table. By subtracting 1 from the value of FBNUM, the program sets N3 equal to the exact number of entries in the table. After 1 is subtracted, an IF is used to make sure there are two or more entries. The sort is bypassed if the file contains only one record. No allowance is made for an empty file.

To help explain the logic, let's use the following table values:

	Name.........	Record Number
FBNAME$ (0) =	SMITH	03
FBNAME$ (1) =	ADAMS	04
FBNAME$ (2) =	JOHNSON	08
FBNAME$ (3) =	BOOTH	11

The name in FBNAME$ (0) is compared with the name in FBNAME$ (1) (see line 1560). If the name in FBNAME$ (0) is greater than the name in FBNAME$ (1), the two names (including record numbers) are exchanged (see lines 1570 to 1590). The exchange or flipping process is accomplished by setting X1$ equal to FBNAME$ (0) in order to prevent the value from being lost. The name in FBNAME$ (1) is then placed into FBNAME$ (0). After the name in FBNAME$ (1) has been moved, the first value, which was saved in X1$, is placed into FBNAME$ (1).

	Name.........	Record Number
FBNAME$ (0) =	ADAMS	04 Flipped
FBNAME$ (1) =	SMITH	03 Flipped
FBNAME$ (2) =	JOHNSON	08
FBNAME$ (3) =	BOOTH	11

The name in FBNAME$ (0) is then compared with the name in FBNAME$ (2). If the name in FBNAME$ (0) is greater than the name in FBNAME$ (2), the two names are flipped.

The process is repeated until the name in the first entry has been compared with all the names in the table. After the first iteration of the inner loop is completed, the lowest name is in the first entry of the table, FBNAME$ (0).

After the first entry has been compared to all the other entries in the table, the outer FOR/NEXT instruction sets N1 up by 1 and the inner FOR/NEXT instructions are executed again in order to compare the second entry with all the other table entries. If you follow the inner loop, you will see that during the second execution two flip operations take place. First, SMITH and JOHNSON are flipped.

	Name.........	Record Number
FBNAME$ (0) =	ADAMS	04 No longer used in comparison
FBNAME$ (1) =	JOHNSON	08 Flipped
FBNAME$ (2) =	SMITH	03 Flipped
FBNAME$ (3) =	BOOTH	11

Then, when JOHNSON is compared with BOOTH, those names are flipped.

	Name.........	Record Number
FBNAME$ (0) =	ADAMS	04 No longer used in comparison
FBNAME$ (1) =	BOOTH	11 Flipped
FBNAME$ (2) =	SMITH	03
FBNAME$ (3) =	JOHNSON	08 Flipped

Once the FBNAME$ (1) has been compared with all the other entries in the table, the outer loop sets N1 up by 1 and the process of comparing FBNAME (2) with all the other table entries is carried out. If you follow the inner loop one more time, you will see that during the third execution, one flip occurs. SMITH is compared with JOHNSON causing the names to be exchanged.

	Name.........	Record Number
FBNAME$ (0) =	ADAMS	04 No longer used in comparison
FBNAME$ (1) =	BOOTH	11 No longer used in comparison
FBNAME$ (2) =	JOHNSON	08 Flipped
FBNAME$ (3) =	SMITH	03 Flipped

Since there are only four entries in the table, N1 is now equal to 1 less than the number of entries, and the sort is done.

Look through the code again and see how the sorting takes place. The outer loop of the replacement sort takes one less pass (execution) than the number of entries in the table ($4 - 1 = 3$). The number of times the inner loop is executed may be computed by the following formula:

Number of table entries * (number of table entries $- 1) / 2$

For the example, the inner loop is executed six times.

$4 * (4 - 1) / 2 = 6$

If the table contained 100 entries, the inner loop would be executed 4950 times:

$100 * (100 - 1) / 2 = 4950.$

You can see why it takes several minutes for the computer to sort the table when it is completely full.

```
1660   REM --------------------


1670   REM SELECT DEVICE
       ................
```

1860   PRINT D$

1870   PRINT D$;"PR#1"
Lines 1660 through 1870 allow the operator to decide whether the records are to be displayed on the screen or printed. The only line which you should find new is 1870.

The PRINT instruction is telling DOS to channel all further output to slot 1, where the printer control board is located. If you have a printer, the interface board is located in slot 1, and the printer is turned on, the statement is executed correctly and data printed. If the printer is not turned on, the cursor disappears and waits for you to turn on the printer. If you do not have a printer interface board in slot 1 when the statement is executed, the cursor disappears and the computer LOCKS UP. You must reset the computer and start over.

1890   REM --------------------

1900   REM PRINT TABLE ENTRIES

1910   FOR N1 = 0 TO N3

1920   REC$ = RIGHT$ (FBNAME$(N1),2)

1930   REC = VAL (REC$)

1940   GOSUB 2080: REM READ DISK

1950   GOSUB 2160: REM WRITE PRT

1960   NEXT
Lines 1890 through 1960 display all the entries which were loaded into the table. The FOR/NEXT instruction is executed from 0 to N3 times, where N3 is equal to the total number of entries in the table.

Line 1920 extracts the relative record number but leaves it in a string format so it can be printed without suppression of the leading 0 (01 through 09). Line 1930 converts the relative record number from string format to numeric format so it can be used in the READ module to retrieve the record.

After the record number has been extracted, the record is read and the data displayed.

The FOR/NEXT loop continues to read and display the records until all the entries in the table have been displayed.

```
1970    IF X2$ = "D" AND LINE > 0 THEN VTAB 22: HTAB 1: PRINT " PRESS THE
        SPACE BAR TO CONTINUE";: GET X1$: IF X1$ < > "  " THEN 1970

1980    IF X2$ = "D" THEN 2010

1990    PRINT L$;L$

2000    PRINT D$: PRINT D$;"PR#0"

2010    PRINT D$: PRINT D$;"CLOSE"

2020    PRINT D$;"RUN RAN ADDR HELLO PROG,D"PDRIVE

2030    REM
```

After all the entries are printed or displayed logic flow falls through to line 1970. If records are being displayed and there is a record on the screen, logic flow gives the operator a chance to view the last record before continuing. If the records were being displayed but there are none on the screen, logic flow skips to line 2010.

If the records were being printed, lines 1990 and 2000 are executed. On line 1990 two CONTROL-Ls are printed. The first L$ causes the last page being printed to eject. The second L$ causes a blank page to be ejected so the operator can easily tear off the last page of the printout. This may waste one or two sheets of paper but makes the job of the operator much easier.

After positioning the paper, line 2000 tells DOS to direct all further displayed data to the screen. The PR#0 stands for the console screen (slot #0).

Whether the data was displayed or printed, the file is closed and the HELLO program run.

```
2060    REM --------------------

2070    REM READ DISK

2080    PRINT D$

2090    PRINT D$;"READ ";FILEID$;",R"REC

2100    INPUT AANAME$,ABADDR$,ACCITY$,ADSTE$,AFPHNE$,AGPHNE$,AHPHNE$

2110    PRINT D$
```

2120 RETURN

2130 REM
For the READ DISK ROUTINE you should make sure you understand lines 2090 and 2100. Before a record on a random file is read the READ instruction MUST be executed, indicating which record is to be read. The INPUT instruction which reads the random record MUST match the format and style of that in which the data were written.
The PRINT SCREEN ROUTINE consists of three segments. Lines 2160 through 2320 make sure the variables are the correct length, and display both headings and data at the same time. Lines 2360 through 2380 are used when the data are being directed to a printer. Lines 2410 through 2460 are used when the data are being directed to the screen.

2140 REM --------------------

2150 REM PRINT SCREEN IMAGE

2160 IF LEN (ABADDR$) < 25 THEN ABADDR$ = LEFT$ (ABADDR$ + SPACES$,25)
....

2230 PRINT

2240 PRINT "RECORD # = ("REC$")"

2250 PRINT

2260 PRINT "NAME   = ("AANAME$")"
To make all the records fit the same format, each variable is set to its maximum length prior to being displayed. One point you may want examine is how the data and headings are displayed at the same time (see lines 2240 through 2310).

2340 REM --------------------

2350 IF X2$ = "D" THEN 2410

2360 LINE = LINE + 1

2370 IF LINE > 4 THEN PRINT L$: LINE = 0

2380   RETURN

Line 2350 checks to see if the data is being displayed or printed. If the data is being displayed to the screen, logic flow skips to line 2410. If the data is being printed, LINE is incremented by 1 and tested to see if a full page has been printed. Once a page is full, the PRINT L\$ command causes the printer to skip up to the top of the next page. When a new page is started, Do not forget to reset the line counter. The last instruction on line 2370 resets LINE to 0. This is an important instruction. If you do not reset the line counter to 0 it continues to increase, and the printer skips to the top of a new page for every record printed after record 4. Forgetting to reset the line counter is a common error made by new programmers.

2400   REM --------------------

2410   LINE = LINE + 1

2420   IF LINE < 2 THEN 2460

2430   PRINT "PRESS THE SPACE BAR TO CONTINUE ";

2440   GET X1\$: IF X1\$ < > " " THEN 2440

2450   HOME: LINE = 0

2460   RETURN

Records being displayed to the screen must be handled differently from records being printed. In order to give the operator time to read the records, the program pauses after displaying two records. Once the operator has viewed the two records and pressed the space bar, the program continues to the next two records.

Do not forget to reset the line counter after a screen is full.

The program did not use the FREE MEMORY ROUTINE in order to keep the listing short. The FREE MEMORY ROUTINE should have been used prior to and during the sort. Anytime you sort string variables, large amounts of memory are used up.

6. Index Disk Files

Before any of the following programs are run, they must be copied to a new disk. The program disk does not have enough free space to create additional files.

For this chapter copy the following programs to another disk:

INDEX FILE CREATE PROG
IND ADDR FILE CREATE PROG
IND ADDR HELLO PROG
IND ADDR UPDATE PROG
IND ADDR LIST PROG
IND ADDR SEARCH PROG

If you want to make your disk operate as a turnkey system, use the following steps:

1. Use a new disk or one which no longer contains any files you wish to keep.
2. Load the IND ADDR HELLO PROG from the program disk. Enter

   LOAD IND ADDR HELLO PROG <RETURN>

3. REMOVE THE PROGRAM DISK and put in the disk you want to initialize. After putting in the new disk, initialize the disk using the IND ADDR HELLO PROG currently in memory. Enter

   INIT IND ADDR HELLO PROG,Dnumber,Vnumber <RETURN>

   Fill in the drive and volume number as desired.
4. After the disk has been initialized, transfer the remaining programs from the program disk to the newly initialized disk.
5. In order to use the programs on the new disk, all you need to do is to insert the disk into drive 1 and turn the computer on, or key in PR#6 if the computer is already on. The IND ADDR HELLO PROG will be executed automatically.

A General Introduction to Index Files

Definitions and Illustrations

Sequential and random file processing are the only two types of file handling supported by the APPLE and most microcomputers. Unfortunately, these two structures do not provide the flexibility most computer users need. In order to overcome the disadvantages of sequential files and pure random files, a third method is developed which we refer to as *indexed file processing*. This form of file processing allows the terminal user to access the records either sequentially or randomly according to a key field within the record.

Index files are constructed on the APPLE by combining two random files. The first random file consists of a table made up of the index used to identify each record. The second random file consists of the actual data. The first random file is called the index file, and the second random file is called the data file.

Index file structure = 1. Index file
2. Data file

The index is used just as you would use the index in a book. If you want to find a specific topic, you quickly scan through the abbreviated index until it is located. Once it is located, you turn to the page number indicated to read the information.

Unlike the user of random file processing, the user of an indexed file structure does not need to know the relative record number in order to access information. A short identifying key, normally part of the data, is associated with each record. The identifying key, or index, is used in the I/O operations associated with each record. For example, the most common index used for people is the Social Security number. Other common index keys include driver's license number and employee number. Normally the index is unique to the individual record. That is, no two records are identified by the same key.

Almost all systems developed for on-line operator interaction should be developed around some form of indexed file organization. Notice the words *some form*. There are many ways in which an index structure may be set up and associated with the data on a file. The method presented in this chapter is only one of the numerous methods, but the information gives you a good starting point for developing your own index files.

The following two tables show how the records appear within an index file and within the associated data file.

```
Records on the                    Records on the Data File
Index File
┌──────────────────────┐   ┌──────────────────────────────────────────┐
│                      │   │ Relative   Student              Test       │
│  Index   Record      │   │ Record     Name                 Score      │
│          Number      │   │ Number                                     │
│                      │   │                                            │
│  ADAMS   000         │   │ 000        JAMES ADAMS          087        │
│  BARNE   002         │   │ 001        JIM WILSON           080        │
│  BRENN   003         │   │ 002        MARY BARNES          095        │
│  MCDON   004         │   │ 003        TIMMY BRENNER        088        │
│  WILSO   001         │   │ 004        JAMES MCDONALD       070        │
│  .....   005         │   │ 005        . . . . . . . . . . . . . .  . . . │
│  .....   006         │   │ 006        . . . . . . . . . . . . . .  . . . │
│  etc.                │   │ etc.       . . . . . . . . . . . . . .  . . . │
└──────────────────────┘   └──────────────────────────────────────────┘
```

There are several things you should notice about the sample data.

1. There are actually two files. The first file consists of the indexes and associated relative record numbers. The second file consists of the actual data (student name and test score).

2. The indexes on the index file are in alphabetic sequence, but the relative record numbers are not in numeric sequence. When records are added to the file, they do not need to be entered in alphabetic sequence. Each time a student is added, the computer assigns the next available record location. Although the data is not in sequence by last name, the indexes can be sorted and kept in alphabetic sequence (for this example).

3. Within the index file unused record locations are given a dummy index key of "….." When a dummy value is assigned to each unused index within the file, the program can search through the index to find an unused area.

For this example the first five characters of the student's last name are used as the record index. When a record is added to the file, program logic locates an unused record (see "….." in index) and associates the matching relative record number with the index of the new record. The data for the student being added is written to the direct access file using the relative record number associated with the new index. Later, when accessing the data, the user of the system only needs to remember the first five characters of the student's last name. The program matches the five characters to the index in order to find out which relative record was used to store the data. After the relative record number is found, the student's record can be read.

A record can only be accessed randomly (read or written) using the relative record number associated with each record. The program must locate the index value within the index file and use the associated relative record number to actually read the data. This may appear to be a lot of coding, but remember that the objective of indexed file processing is to make it easier for the computer user, not the programmer.

Sequential processing of the file is controlled by program logic. In the previous example the index file is kept in alphabetic sequence. The program reads the index file sequentially and then reads the matching record on the data file. The computer operator does not need to know any of the record keys (index values).

For the index address example which follows, both the index file and the data file are created and filled with dummy values prior to letting the user enter any data. This is not the only approach but it is one of the simpler methods. Program logic is simplified by setting up the system to handle a maximum number of records and allocating all the disk space ahead of time.

A Systems Chart and Description of Index Files

Step 1: Creating File Labels and Dummy Records for the Index File

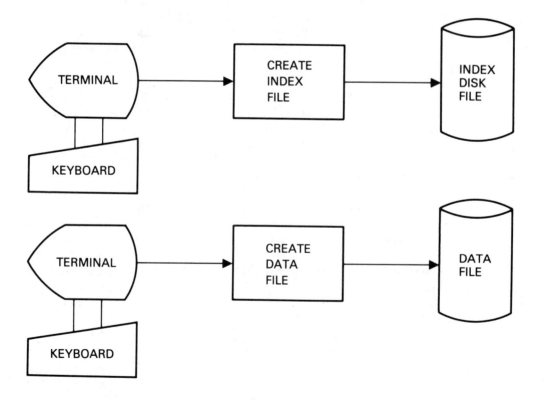

Before the index file structure can be used, two file labels must be created and dummy values written for each record making up the two files.

In order to create the files, we must determine the maximum number of records the file is to handle. This may sound like a problem, but we can always extend the file if more space is needed.

For the index file the dummy records consist of two variables. The first variable corresponds to the index value, while the second variable is the associated relative record number.

For the index file the dummy value of "....." indicates an unused index value.

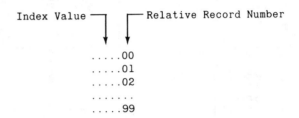

```
Index Value ─┐    ┌─Relative Record Number
             ↓    ↓
          .....00
          .....01
          .....02
          .......
          .....99
```

The second file represents the data, with dummy records written in order to initialize and allocate disk space.

For example, if the student file shown earlier is created, the program opens the data file and writes out dummy records. One record is written for each entry in the index file. If the index file is set up to handle 100 records, the data file must also contain 100 records.

Relative Record Number	Student Name	Test Score
00	....	...
01	....	...
02	....	...
03	....	...
04	....	...
..	....	...
98	....	...
99	....	...

Step 2: Index File Update

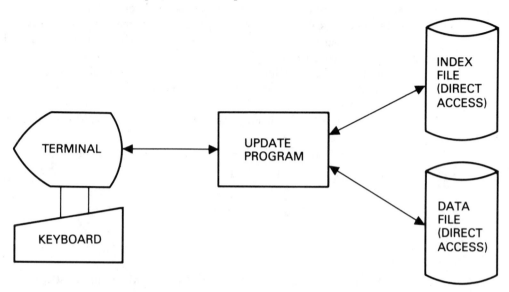

After the file is created, records may be added, changed, or deleted from the file.

Records are added to the data file by first finding an unused index entry in the index file.

Unused index ──┐   ┌── Relative record number
                   01

After an unused area is located, the related record is read from the data file and displayed. Once the operator has entered new information in place of the dummy values, the new data is written back to the data file.

New record
Name ────────┐   ┌── Test Score
         JOHN JONES 89

In addition to writing out the new record, the program must update the index file to reflect the new data.

New index value ────┐   ┌─Relative record number
              JONES01

Changes to the file are made by reading the old record, changing the data within the record, and writing the revised record back over the top of the old record. In order to change the record, the user must know the index key for the record. For the previous example the user must know the first five characters of the student's last name.

Deleting a record is done by writing dummy data (......) over the top of the old data, thereby destroying the old record. The index value within the index file is also reset to a dummy value of five periods ".....". In order to delete the record, the user must know the index key for the record.

Step 3: Index File Report Generation or Inquiry

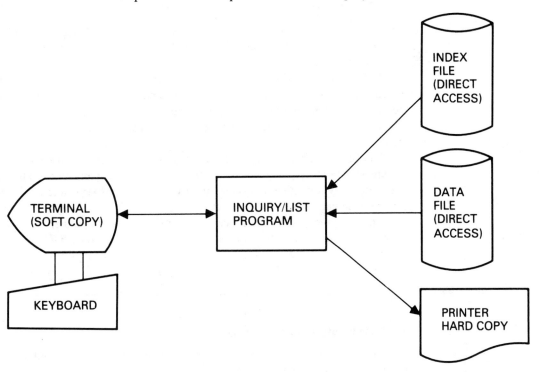

Once a file is created, the data on the file may be used to produce reports. Inquiries or reports related to the file may be displayed on the screen (soft copy) or sent to a printer to produce a hard copy.

The Advantages of Index Files

The advantages of index files are all directed toward the user of the system. There are no real advantages to the programmer in developing an index system except pride in accomplishment.

Although index systems are harder for the programmer to write, they are much easier for the user to work with, and therefore the majority of applications being developed for microcomputers use some form of index file handling.

You should develop an index system wherever

1. The system you are developing requires on-line inquiry, and/or
2. Only a small portion of the records within a file are to be accessed by most programs, and/or
3. The key for identifying the record cannot be a closed set of sequential numbers as used in random processing (001, 002, 003, 004, etc.)

Index file processing provides the user with the ability to access data either in a random mode or in an ascending or descending sequence by a specific field within the record (if programmed to do so).

Unlike the random file system, in which the user must remember the relative record number in order to retrieve the record randomly, the index system requires the user to remember only the value of the record key. Since the record key is normally part of the data, it is much easier for the user to remember than a relative record number.

Unlike the random file system, in which the record keys must be a closed set of sequential numbers, the index file system may use any combination of characters. Index files may use either alphanumeric or numeric record keys, and the keys may contain wide gaps (AAA, A01, 999, etc.).

Since the records may be processed in any order, the computer operator does not need to worry about the sequence of the transaction records. Only the records which are to be updated need to be read and written. This simplifies the job of the operator.

The Disadvantages of Index Files

The user must be able to remember all or part of the record key, depending on how flexibly the program has been written.

Although the index file structure is wonderful for the user, it is harder for the programmer to work with and requires more processing time than simpler random file structures.

A Summary of Index Files for Microcomputers

Almost all systems developed for the microcomputer should use an index file structure. The benefits for the end user include:

1. Being able to use meaningful record keys to retrieve a record
2. Faster access to record (faster than sequential files but slower than random files)

3. Faster searching options (faster than either sequential files or random files)
4. The ability to access a record by using multiple keys (if programmed with multiple indexes)

Problem Specifications

A General Description of the Problem

The same basic problem is used to illustrate the three types of disk access methods. The screen design for the index file contains two additional lines for comments about the client.

The basic screen design for the index version of the directory is as follows. The actual screen format varies with each program.

```
LAST NAME = (       )    Serves as index

NAME      = (                      )
ADDRESS   = (                      )
CITY      = (                      )
STATE     = (   )
ZIP CODE  = (       )

PHONE     = (    -    -      )

COMMENT#1 = (                )
COMMENT#2 = (                )
```

Six programs are used to illustrate index file processing:

1. A program for creating the index file label and dummy index records. Each index record consists of five periods and a relative record number ranging from 00 to 99.
2. A program for creating the data file label and dummy records consisting of 124 periods. The new record format includes two comment fields which make the record a total of 124 characters long.

3. A HELLO program which gives the operator a method of choosing which program is to be executed.
4. A program for updating existing records.
5. A program for listing all the records on the file in ascending sequence by the index value.
6. A program for searching the file for a specific record based on all or part of the index.

The INDEX FILE CREATE PROGram is needed to create a label on the disk and to create 100 dummy index records in the correct format. Both the index file and the random data file must be created before any of the other programs are run.

The IND ADDR FILE CREATE PROGram is needed to create a label on the disk and to create the correct number of dummy records. Once the label and dummy records are created, the UPDATE program can be run to add records to the file.

The IND ADDR HELLO PROGram is used to display a menu to the operator. The operator enters a number matching the program which is to be executed. With the exception of the INDEX FILE CREATE PROGram, the IND ADDR FILE CREATE PROGram, and the IND ADDR HELLO PROGram, all programs within the system are executed by using the menu.

The IND ADDR UPDATE PROGram is used to add, change, or delete records. Records cannot truly be added since the space has already been allocated by the dummy records, and space cannot be deleted from the file because of the way random files work. Additions to the file are made by writing over the dummy records with new data. Deletions to the file are made by writing over the old data with a dummy record containing all periods (.....). Changes are made by reading the record, changing specific fields, and then rewriting the new record over the old record.

Both the index file and the data file must be updated when adding, changing, or deleting records.

The IND ADDR LIST PROGram is used either to display or to print all the names and addresses in ascending order by the index (assumed to be the first five characters of the client's last name).

The IND ADDR SEARCH PROGram is used to search the file and display all the records with the same index value or partial index value. The program is set up to allow the operator to enter from one to five characters of the index. The program then searches through the index file and displays records with matching index values.

A Data Name Dictionary for the Index Address System

The following list describes the variables used in the index system. Most of the names are the same as those used for the sequential system and the random system. Some of the variable specifications have been changed. You should scan the list and review the definition and use of each variable.

Not all the names are used in each program. The dictionary is included here to give a single source for the description of all the variables used within the system. If you have a question about the use of one of the variables while looking at a program listing, return to this section for an explanation and a better understanding of the variable usage.

The names are listed in alphabetic order. Each name consists of a two character prefix followed by a descriptive name. The two character prefix or Applesoft name is given at the left with the full name and description at the right.

The variables X1$, X2$, X3$, N1, N2, N3, and a few others are used without complete descriptions and for multiple purposes. This is an example of bad (lazy) programming. It is true that Applesoft executes faster if fewer variables are used, but the program is very difficult to maintain when short multifunction variables are used.

Each variable should have a meaningful description and a single purpose within the program. If the variable is a general counter, indicate the use by the name. If the variable is a switch, use the term SWITCH within the name.

It is very easy to create new variable names. It takes a little more time to correctly define the variables. But the extra time it takes to do it right the first time is saved later when maintaining the program. This is one more case of "Do as I say and not as I do."

All the variable names starting with an A are part of the address record.

A1$ = A1ADDR$

This is the name used when reading the record. It consists of all the variables making up one record. The record must be broken down when read from the disk using the LEFT$, RIGHT$, and MID$ functions.

AA$ = AANAME$

This contains the name of the client and has a fixed length of 25 characters. The variable is left justified. The system is designed for the name to be entered using the format of FIRSTNAME LASTNAME.

AB$ = ABADDR$

This contains the street address of the client and has a fixed length of 25 characters. The variable should be left justified.

AC$ = ACCITY$

This contains the name of the city and has a fixed length of 15 characters. The variable should be left justified.

AD$ = ADSTE$

This contains a two digit code representing the state. The AT in stATe has to be omitted because of the way in which Applesoft recognizes keywords.

AE$ = AEZIP$

This contains the ZIP code. The variable is edited and must be either blank or contain all numeric characters.

AF$ = AFPHNE$

This contains the phone number, consisting of a three digit area code, a three digit prefix, and a four digit number. Each portion of the phone number is edited and must contain all spaces or all numbers. The O in phOne has to be omitted because of the way in which Applesoft recognizes keywords.

AG$ = AGCOM1$

This contains 21 characters of comments.

AH$ = AHCOM2$

This contains 21 characters of comments.

D$ = D$ = CONTROL-D character

At the beginning of each program, D$ is set equal to the character CHR$(4). The character is used when working with I/O operations on the disk.

F1 = F1FILEID$

This contains the name of the index file. The variable is initialized in the BEGINNING ROUTINE of each program and used in all DOS instructions directed toward the file.

F2 = F2FILEID$

This contains the name of the data file. The variable is initialized in the BEGINNING

ROUTINE of each program and used in all DOS instructions directed toward the file.

FD = FDRIVE = Value of 1

The name stands for File DRIVE and is used in conjunction with PDRIVE (Program DRIVE) to indicate which disk drive is to be accessed.

All the variable names starting with G are part of the GET subroutine. The following variables are used as parameters to pass data to and from the routine:

GALEGTH   Before execution of the subroutine GALEGTH must be set equal to the length of the field to be read.

GBANSWER$ After completion of the subroutine, GBANSWER$ contains the value read in.

GCCHAR   After completion of the subroutine, GCCHAR contains the number of characters keyed in by the operator.

All the other variables starting with G used in the GET subroutine are necessary to its internal operation and are not described in this chapter.

KE$ = KEY$

This variable is used when searching the index table. It contains the record key entered by the operator which is to be matched to the entry in the index table.

IN$(= INDEX$(99)

This is the name of the index table used to store the index file in memory. The table is loaded during the BEGINNING ROUTINE and continually updated as records are changed.

L1 through L9

The variables L1, L2, L3, L4, L5, L6, L7, L8, and L9 are used for vertical positioning of the cursor. The number in the name of the variable is not necessarily the number of the related line. VTAB L1 does not necessarily position the cursor on line 1.

L$ = L$ (CONTROL-L)

L$ is used only in the listing program when the records are to be printed. L$ is set equal to CHR$(12), which is a CONTROL-L symbol. When this character is sent to a printer which recognizes the ASCII control codes, it causes the printer to skip to the top of a new sheet of paper.

LI = LINE

The variable LINE is used only in the listing program when the records are to be printed. LINE is used to count how many records have been printed. Once a specific number of records have been printed and the page is full, logic causes the printer to skip to the top of the next page.

N1, N2, N3

N1, N2, and N3 are general counters used with the FOR/NEXT instruction or for other general numeric operations.

PD = PDRIVE = Value of 1

The name stands for Program DRIVE and is used in conjunction with FDRIVE (File Drive) to indicate which disk drive is to be accessed.

RE = REC

RECord is used when reading or writing records to the random file. The variable contains a numeric whole number indicating the relative record number of the record to be accessed.

RE$ = REC$

This is the alphanumeric format of the relative record number and is used whenever suppression of the leading 0 for the numbers 0 through 9 cause a problem in how the data is stored or how it is printed.

SI = SIZE

This variable is only used in the IND ADDR SEARCH PROG. It contains the size of the search key entered by the operator.

ST = STARTING

This variable is used by the FREE MEMORY ROUTINE as a general work area. If you use a name in your program which starts with ST, be careful of also using the FREE MEMORY ROUTINE.

X1$, X2$, X3$

X1$, X2$, and X3$ are general string variables used with the GET instruction when requesting a response from the operator.

X1$ may be used at any time, but X2$ and X3$ are used to pass information between subroutines and should be used with care. Changing the value of X2$ or X3$ without considering how their current value is being used could result in problems.

Disk Record Format Specifications

The technique used to write the records on the index file is the same as that used in the sequential file example.

One large record is written with no variable separators (commas). This technique requires slightly more coding by the programmer but saves disk space and eliminates the problem with leading spaces within individual variables.

All records written to the disk have a fixed variable and a fixed record length. Since comments have been added, the new record is 125 characters long. There are 124 characters in the record and one position for the end of record marker.

The record breakdown is as follows:

Variable Name =	Length	—	Record Position
AANAME$	25		1 to 25
ABADDR$	25		26 to 50
ACCITY$	15		51 to 65
ADSTE$	2		66 to 67
AEZIP$	5		68 to 72
AFPHNE$	10		73 to 82
AGCOM1$	21		83 to 103
AHCOM2$	21		104 to 124
EOR mark	1		125

The EOR or End-Of-Record indicator is written and controlled by the computer. It is included in the record description in case you are going to figure how much disk storage space is used.

When all these variables are combined and written to the disk, the record has the following format:

```
              1         2         3         4         5
Column  12345678901234567890123456789012345678901234567890
        NNNNNNNNNNNNNNNNNNNNNNNNNAAAAAAAAAAAAAAAAAAAAAAAAA


              6         7         8         9         10
Column  12345678901234567890123456789012345678901234567890
        CCCCCCCCCCCCCCCSSZZZZZPPPPPPPPPP11111111111111111111


            11                12
Column  1234567890123456789012345
        1112222222222222222222222?
```

where N = name; A = street address; C = city; S = state; Z = ZIP code; P = phone number; 1 comment 1; 2 = comment 2; ? end-of-record marker.

You should always know how many characters are being written to the disk and how the variables are being written out. If you write a record larger than the size specified when opening the file, you mess up the EOR marker and have problems the next time you try to read the file.

The Index File **CREATE** Index Program

Program Name INDEX FILE CREATE PROG

Program Objective Create a label and 100 dummy index records consisting of a five character index and a two digit relative record number.

Instructions for Running the Program Note 1: Prior to running any of the programs in the index file system, you MUST copy the program from the program disk to a new disk. There is not enough room on the example disk to store any text files.

Note 2: Since all the programs are set up for a single drive system, the disk being used MUST be in drive 1 or the values for FDRIVE and PDRIVE must be changed in each program.

To keep the two file **CREATE** programs as simple as possible, most of the responsibility for a successful run has been shifted from the program to the computer operator.

There are several situations which will cause the program to fail to create the new file correctly. These conditions were covered in the discussion of the **RAN ADDR CREATE PROG** and are not repeated here.

Before running the program, you should make sure the file label (INDEX FILE) does not exist on the disk. Use the CATALOG command and check to see if the label exists. If the label exists and you are sure you want to destroy any data that are currently in the file, use the DELETE command to remove the file.

After you have made sure the file does not exist enter

RUN INDEX FILE CREATE PROG <RETURN>

As the records are written to the file, both the WRITE command and the contents of the record will be displayed on the screen.

```
WRITE INDEX FILE,R0
.....00
WRITE INDEX FILE,R1
.....01
WRITE INDEX FILE,R2
.....02
etc.
```

Program Listing

```
1000 REM INDEX FILE CREATE PROG
1010 REM ------------------------
1020 TEXT : NORMAL : HOME : SPEED= 200
1030 D$ = CHR$ (4)
1040 FDRIVE = 1
1050 F1FILEID$ = "INDEX FILE"
1060 REM -----
1070 REM CREATE 100 DUMMY INDEX RECORDS
1080 INDEX$ = "....."
1090 REM -----
1100 PRINT D$;"MON I,O,C"
1110 PRINT D$;"OPEN ";F1FILEID$;",L8,D";FDRIVE
1120 FOR REC = 0 TO 99
1130 PRINT D$;"WRITE ";F1FILEID$;",R";REC
1140 REC$ = STR$ (REC)
1150 IF LEN (REC$) < 2 THEN REC$ = "0" + REC$
1160 PRINT INDEX$;REC$
1170 NEXT
1180 PRINT D$;"CLOSE"
1190 PRINT D$;"NOMON I,O,C"
1200 SPEED= 255
1210 REM ------------------------
```

Explanation by Line Number

Detailed explanations by line number follow.

1020 ...SPEED= 200

The SPEED instruction is used to slow down the rate at which the records are written on the disk. When you slow down the I/O speed, the operator can see the records as they are displayed on the screen. If the speed were not slowed down, the records would scroll by so fast on the screen that the operator could not read them.

1110 PRINT D$;"OPEN ";F1FILEID$;",L8,D";FDRIVE

The OPEN instruction allocates two areas in the computer to prepare for handling either input from the file or output directed to the file. If the file label does not currently exist on the disk, the label is written to the disk directory.

For a random file the L (length) parameter is required. The length must be 1 greater than the number of characters written on the disk. In this case seven characters make up the record: five characters for the index and two characters for the relative record number. The file is opened with a length of 8, 1 greater than the size of the data making up the record.

For a more detailed explanation, see the section on the random file CREATE program in Chapter 5.

1120 FOR REC = 0 TO 99

1130 PRINT D$;"WRITE ";F1FILEID$;",R";REC

1140 REC$ = STR$ (REC)

1150 IF LEN (REC$) < 2 THEN REC$ = "0" + REC$

1160 PRINT INDEX$;REC$

1170 NEXT

Lines 1120 through 1170 are responsible for writing out the 100 dummy index records. The important thing to notice is that the WRITE instruction is inside the FOR/NEXT loop. Each time through the loop, the value of REC is incremented by 1. The first time through the loop, relative record 0 is written: the second time, relative record 1: third time, relative record 2, etc.

The WRITE instruction must be executed prior to the PRINT instruction which causes the information to be recorded on the disk.

When the record numbers 0 through 9 are converted to a string format, they are only one character long. All the programs are set up to handle a two digit relative record number. The IF instruction on line 1150 places a leading 0 in front of the single digit numbers so all records are the same length. This instruction may seem relatively minor, but NONE of the other programs work correctly with records 0 through 9 unless it is included. Be sure to use it in any index structure you develop.

After the 100th record is written, the FOR/NEXT loop is terminated and the file is closed.

After the program has terminated, you may want to use the CATALOG command to list the disk directory and see how many sectors the INDEX FILE takes up. The file should take up around 4 sectors.

```
      8   character per record
  * 100   number of records on the file
  = 800   total number of characters stored
  / 256   per sector
  = 3.12  sectors (round to 4, always round up)
```

If you list the directory, you will find that the file actually takes up 5 sectors. Four sectors are used for the data and 1 sector for the track/sector index which DOS builds for all disk files.

The Index File CREATE Data Program

Program Name IND ADDR FILE CREATE PROG

Program Objective To create a label and 100 dummy records consisting of 124 periods. The dummy records serve to allocate space on the disk and to indicate an unused record.

Instructions for Running the Program To keep the two file CREATE programs as simple as possible, most of the responsibility for a successful run has been shifted from the program to the computer operator.

There are several situations which cause the program to fail to create the new file correctly. These conditions were covered in the discussion of the RAN ADDR CREATE PROG and are not repeated here.

Before running the program you should make sure the file label (IND ADDR FILE) does not exist on the disk. Use the CATALOG command and check to see if the label exists. If the label exists and you are sure you want to destroy any data that is currently in the file, use the DELETE command to remove the file.

After you have made sure the file does not exist enter

RUN IND ADDR FILE CREATE PROG <RETURN>

After the program starts, each WRITE command and related record will be displayed as follows:

```
WRITE IND ADDR FILE.R0
. . . . . . . . . . . . . . . . . . . . . . . . . . . . . . . . . . . . . . . . . . . . . . . .
. . . . . . . . . . . . . . . . . . . . . . . . . . . . . . . . . . . . . . . . . . . . . . . .
. . . . . . . . . . . . . . . . . . . . . . . . . . . . . . . . . . . . . . . . . . . . . . . .
. . . . ?
WRITE IND ADDR FILE.R1
. . . . . . . . . . . . . . . . . . . . . . . . . . . . . . . . . . . . . . . . . . . . . . . .
. . . . . . . . . . . . . . . . . . . . . . . . . . . . . . . . . . . . . . . . . . . . . . . .
. . . . . . . . . . . . . . . . . . . . . . . . . . . . . . . . . . . . . . . . . . . . . . . .
. . . . ?
etc.
```

Program Listing

```
1000 REM IND ADDR FILE CREATE PROG
1010 REM ----------------------
1020 TEXT : NORMAL : HOME : SPEED= 255
1030 D$ = CHR$ (4)
1040 FDRIVE = 1
1050 F2FILEID$ = "IND ADDR FILE"
1060 REM -----
1070 REM CREATE 100 DUMMY RECORDS
1080 FOR N1 = 1 TO 124
1090 A1ADDR$ = A1ADDR$ + "."
1100 NEXT
1110 REM -----
1120 PRINT D$;"MON I,O,C"
1130 PRINT D$;"OPEN ";F2FILEID$;",L125,D"FDRIVE
1140 FOR REC = 0 TO 99
1150 PRINT D$;"WRITE ";F2FILEID$;",R"REC
1160 PRINT A1ADDR$
1170 NEXT
1180 PRINT D$;"CLOSE"
1190 PRINT D$;"NOMON I,O,C"
1200 REM ----------------------
```

Explanation by Line Number

1080–1100   Rather than counting out 124 periods within a constant ("...124..."), lines 1080 through 1100 use a FOR/NEXT instruction to link 124 periods into one big variable.

1130   Once more, look at the OPEN instruction. For a random file the L (length) parameter is required. The length must be 1 greater than the number of characters which will be written to the disk. In this case 124 characters make up the record. The file is opened with a length of 125.

1140–1170   Lines 1140 through 1170 are responsible for writing out the 100 dummy records. The important thing to notice is that the WRITE instruction is inside the FOR/NEXT loop. Each time through the loop, the value of REC is incremented by 1. The first time through the loop, relative record 0 is written; the second time, relative record 1, third time, relative record 2, etc.

The WRITE instruction must be executed prior to the PRINT instruction which causes the information to be recorded on the disk.

After the 100th record is written (relative record 99), the FOR/NEXT loop is terminated and the file is closed.

After the program has terminated you may want to use the CATALOG command to list the disk directory and see how many sectors the INDEX FILE takes up. The file should take up around 49 sectors.

	125	character per record
*	100	number of records on the file
=	12,500	total number of characters stored
/	256	per sector
=	48.82	sectors (round to 49, always round up)

If you list the directory you will find that the file actually takes up 50 sectors. The 1 sector difference represents the single sector used for the track/sector list which DOS builds for all disk files.

The Index File HELLO Program

Program Name IND ADDR HELLO PROG

Program Objective To provide a method of transition between the programs making up the INDEX ADDRESS SYSTEM.

For a detailed explanation of the purpose of a HELLO program and how to set up the disk, see the SEQ ADDR HELLO PROG and the INITialize instruction.

Instructions for Running the Program Make sure you have run the INDEX FILE CREATE PROG and the IND ADDR FILE CREATE PROG before running any of the menu driven programs. Both files must exist prior to running any of the programs which access the two files.

After you are sure that both files exist, run the IND ADDDR HELLO PROG by keying in

RUN IND ADDR HELLO PROG <RETURN>

The HELLO program will display the following screen:

```
SELECT ONE OF THE FOLLOWING:

    1. UPDATE THE ADDRESS FILE.

    2. LIST OR DISPLAY RECORDS.

    3. SEARCH FILE BY INDEX.

    4. QUIT PROCESSING.

SELECTION DESIRED = (?)
```

When you are finished reviewing the code for the HELLO program, enter 1 to start execution of the UPDATE program. Since this is the first time you have executed the UPDATE program, the file will not contain any valid data. Use the UPDATE program to add records to the file.

See the narrative on IND ADDR UPDATE PROGram for instructions on how to enter data.

Program Listing

```
1000 REM IND ADDR HELLO PROG
1010 REM ----------------------
1020 TEXT : NORMAL : HOME : SPEED= 255
1030 D$ = CHR$ (4)
1040 PDRIVE = 1
1050 VTAB 5
1060 PRINT "SELECT ONE OF THE FOLLOWING:"
1070 PRINT
1080 PRINT "    1. UPDATE THE ADDRESS FILE."
1090 PRINT
1100 PRINT "    2. LIST OR DISPLAY RECORDS."
1110 PRINT
1120 PRINT "    3. SEARCH FILE BY INDEX."
1130 PRINT
1140 PRINT "    4. QUIT PROCESSING."
1150 PRINT
1160 PRINT "SELECTION DESIRE=(?)"
1170 VTAB 15: HTAB 21
1180 PRINT CHR$ (8) ;
1190 GET X1$: PRINT X;: X1 = VAL (X1$)
1200 IF X1 < 1 OR X1 > 4 THEN 1170
1210 IF X1 = 4 THEN 1340
1220 VTAB 23: HTAB 1: INVERSE
1230 PRINT " LOADING PROGRAM - PLEASE WAIT        "
1240 NORMAL
1250 ON X1 GOTO 1280,1300,1320
1260 GOTO 1170
1270 REM ----------------------
1280 PRINT D$;"RUN IND ADDR UPDATE PROG,D"PDRIVE
1290 REM ----------------------
1300 PRINT D$;"RUN IND ADDR LIST PROG,D"PDRIVE
1310 REM ----------------------
1320 PRINT D$;"RUN IND ADDR SEARCH PROG,D"PDRIVE
1330 REM ----------------------
1340 HOME
1350 PRINT "THAT'S ALL FOLKS!"
1360 END
```

Explanation by Line Number

The HELLO program is basically the same as the ones used in the sequential and the random system. The only difference you might notice is the absence of the dummy D$ prior to each DOS command.

If a PRINT instruction, which *Does not* end in a semicolon, is used after a GET instruction and before the DOS command, the dummy D$ (PRINT) is not necessary.

Since the message on line 1230 is printed before any of the DOS commands are executed, there should be no problem between using the GET instruction and executing the DOS commands.

The Index File UPDATE Program

Program Name   IND ADDR UPDATE PROG

Program Objective   To provide the user with a method of adding, changing, and deleting records.

Since the index file structure is actually a combination of two related random files, it has the advantages of random files. One of the major benefits of the index file structure is that records may be read, changed, and rewritten back to the same file. Unlike sequential file processing, index file processing does not require the user to rewrite the entire file just to change one record.

System Flowchart of Index File Update Program

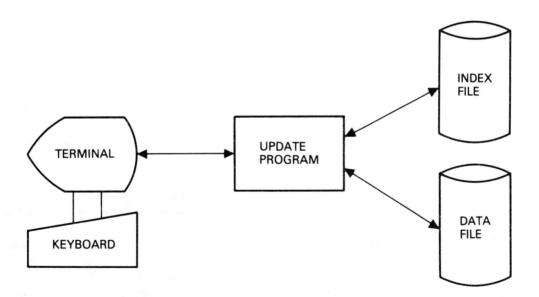

One of the disadvantages of index file processing is that no backup copy is created as part of the update process. You should periodically make a backup copy of both the index and the data file.

Instructions for Running the Program

Make sure you have run both the INDEX FILE CREATE PROG and the IND ADDR CREATE PROG. If you do not create the two index files correctly, the UPDATE program terminates with an END OF DATA error message the first time the program tries to read a record.

Run the program by entering

RUN IND ADDR HELLO PROG <RETURN>

After the menu is displayed, enter a 1 to start execution of the UPDATE program. the UPATE program uses the following screen:

```
    ADDRESS FILE UPDATE PROGRAM

LAST NAME = (      )
NAME      = (                          )
ADDRESS   = (                          )
CITY      = (                )
STATE     = (   )
ZIP CODE  = (        )
PHONE     = (    -    -      )

COMMENT#1 = (                      )
COMMENT#2 = (                      )

            ? SELECTION

ADD    CHANGE    DELETE    LIST    QUIT


.......  First error message line  .....
........  Second error message line  ....
```

After the entire screen has been displayed, the cursor is positioned over the question mark preceding the word SELECTION. The program then waits for you to enter A, C, D, L, or Q.

After you have entered any acceptable character other than Q, the cursor is repositioned to the top of the screen, where the program waits for you to enter the five character index used to identify the record being processed.

Once you enter the index value, the program either searches the index table for a matching value or searches the table for an unused area. If you are adding a record, the index table is searched for an empty location. If you are adding a record, the index table is searched for an empty location. If you are changing or deleting a record, the table is searched for a matching index value.

Exercise 1: Adding a Record

To add a record enter A and then an index value (LAST NAME=) from one to five characters long. The program searches through the index table looking for an unused record. Since this is the first record to be added to the file, the program finds periods in the first table position.

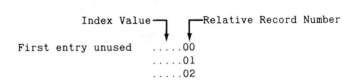

To test the ADD logic, execute the following steps:

1. Enter A in response to the SELECTION message.
2. Enter JOHNS in response to the LAST NAME = (message.
3. All the entries on the screen should be displayed as periods.
4. Enter

$$
\begin{aligned}
\text{Name} &= \text{MARY J JOHNSON} \\
\text{Address} &= \text{4444 HIGH STREET} \\
\text{City} &= \text{PORTLAND} \\
\text{State} &= \text{OR} \\
\text{ZIP code} &= \text{01234} \\
\text{Phone} &= \text{777-777-7777} \\
\text{Comment 1} &= \text{as desired} \\
\text{Comment 2} &= \text{as desired}
\end{aligned}
$$

After the last comment entry has been entered or skipped, the record will be written to the disk and the cursor repositioned for another selection.

Exercise 2: Changing a Record

To change a record you enter C and the index value to be used in searching for a matching record. Since more than one record can have the same five character index value, the program searches sequentially through the index table until it finds a match. Once a match is found, the program displays the record and asks you if it is the record you want to change. After looking at the record, if it is not the one you want to change, you respond with N for No, and the program continues to search for another matching index. If it is the correct record, you respond with Y for Yes, and the program allows you to make changes to the record just displayed.

To test the logic for changing a record, execute the following two sequences of instructions.

First, change a record with existing data.

1. Enter C in response to the SELECTION message.
2. Enter JOHNS in response to the LAST NAME = (message.
3. All the entries on the screen will be displayed as previously entered. On the last two lines of the screen a message will be displayed asking you if this is the record you want to change. In response to the question, key in Y for **Yes.**
4. Change any or all of the fields, but remember that if you want to change a field you must reenter the entire field even if only part of the field is incorrect.

If you change the last name, you should also change the five character index.
After the last field is entered, the record will be rewritten to the disk and the cursor repositioned for another selection.
Next, attempt to change a record that does not exist.

1. Enter C in response to the SELECTION message.
2. Enter JOHNS in response to the LAST NAME = (message.
3. All the entries on the screen will be displayed as previously entered. On the bottom two lines of the screen a message is displayed asking you if this is the record you want to change. In response to the question, key in N for **No.**
4. After you have rejected the current record, a second message will be displayed indicating that the record you are searching for does not exist. In response to the last message, press the space bar, and the program will continue.

Exercise 3: Deleting a Record

To delete a record you enter D and the index value to be used in searching for a matching record. Since more than one record can have the same five character index value, the program searches sequentially through the index table until it finds a match. Once a match is found, the program displays the record and asks you if it is the record you want to delete. If the record is not the one you want to delete, you respond with N (No), and the program continues to search for another matching index. Once the record you want to delete is found and you enter Y to indicate it is the correct record, a second message is displayed. The second message asks you if you are sure you want to delete the record. This gives you one last chance to change your mind and exit the DELETE ROUTINE.
To test the logic for deleting a record:

1. Enter D in response to the SELECTION message.
2. Enter JOHNS in response to the LAST NAME = (message.
3. All the entries on the screen will be displayed as previously entered. On the bottom two lines of the screen a message will be displayed asking you if this is the record you want to delete. In response to this question, key in Y for **Yes.**
4. On the bottom two lines of the screen a second message will be displayed asking you if you are sure this is the record you want deleted. To delete the record, enter Y. To avoid deleting the record, press any other key.

Since we will want to list this record later, press any key other than Y. The screen will be cleared and the cursor repositioned for the next transaction.

Exercise 4: Listing a Record

To list a record you enter L and the index value to be used in searching for a matching record. Since more than one record can have the same five character index value, the program searches sequentially through the index table until it finds a match. Once a match is found, the program displays the record and asks if it is the record you want. After looking at the record, if it is not the one you want, respond with N (No), and the program continues to search for another matching index value. Once the record you want listed is found, do not enter Y until you are finished with the record. Once you are done, enter Y, and the program sets up the screen for the next transaction.

To list a record enter L and the index value to be used in searching the index table.

1. Enter L in response to the SELECTION message.
2. Enter JOHNS in response to the LAST NAME = (message.
3. All the entries on the screen will be displayed as previously entered. On the bottom two lines of the screen a message will be displayed asking you if this is the record you want to list. Before entering Y, view the record, as it will be erased once the Y is entered.

Enter Y to terminate the listing operation. The screen will be cleared and the cursor repositioned for the next transaction.

Exercise 5: Quit Processing

Prior to running the LIST or SEARCH program, make sure you add several records to the file. If you do not add records to the file, there will be no records for the listing program to display.

To terminate the program, enter Q. The HELLO program will be executed, allowing you to make another program selection.

Program Listing

```
1000 REM IND ADDR UPDATE PROG
1010 REM ----------------------
1020 CLEAR :G1 = PEEK (116) * 256 + PEEK (115) - 40 :GA$ =
     "12345678901234567890" + "12345678901234567890"
1030 REM ----------------------
1040 REM DRIVE ROUTINE
1050 GOSUB 3590: REM BEGINNING
1060 GOSUB 1290: REM MAIN MOD
1070 GOTO 4030: REM END MODULE
```

```
1080 REM ----------------------
1090 REM GET SUBROUTINE
1100 IF G3 = 0 THEN GOSUB 1250
1110 G3 = G1 + GA - 1: FOR G2 = G1 TO G3: POKE G2,32: NEXT : G2 = G1
1120 CALL 768:GB = PEEK (775) - 128: IF GB = 08 THEN 1190
1130 IF GB = 13 THEN 1210
1140 IF GB = 21 THEN PRINT CHR$ ( PEEK (G2));: GOTO 1170
1150 IF GB = 44 OR GB = 58 OR GB < 32 THEN 1120
1160 PRINT CHR$ (GB);: POKE G2,GB
1170 G2 = G2 + 1: IF G2 > G3 THEN 1240
1180 GOTO 1120
1190 G2 = G2 - 1: IF G2 < G1 THEN G2 = G1: GOTO 1120
1200 PRINT CHR$ (8);: GOTO 1120
1210 IF G1 = G2 THEN 1230
1220 FOR GC = G2 TO G3: PRINT " ";: NEXT
1230 FOR GC = G2 TO G3: POKE GC,32: NEXT
1240 GB$ = LEFT$ (GA$,GA):GC = G2 - G1: RETURN
1250 POKE 768,32: POKE 769,12: POKE 770,253: POKE 771,141:
     POKE 772,07: POKE 773,03: POKE 774,96: RETURN
1260 REM
1270 REM ----------------------
1280 REM MAIN ROUTINE
1290 VTAB L8: HTAB 1: INVERSE : PRINT "          ? SELECTION"
     TAB( 38) " ";:NORMAL : HTAB 12: GET X2$: PRINT X2$
1300 IF X2$ = "Q" THEN 1380
1310 GOSUB 3490: REM CHECK MEMORY SPACE
1320 GOSUB 2680: REM CLEAR SCREEN
1330 IF X2$ = "A" THEN GOSUB 1460: GOTO 1290
1340 IF X2$ = "C" THEN GOSUB 1730: GOTO 1290
1350 IF X2$ = "D" THEN GOSUB 2170: GOTO 1290
1360 IF X2$ = "L" THEN GOSUB 2410: GOTO 1290
1370 GOTO 1290
1380 RETURN
1390 REM ----------------------
1400 REM SEARCH INDEX
1410 N2 = 100: FOR N1 = REC TO 99: IF LEFT$ (INDEX$(N1),5) =
     KEY$ THEN REC$ = RIGHT$ (INDEX$(N1),2):N2 = N1:N1 = 100
1420 NEXT
1430 RETURN
1440 REM ----------------------
1450 REM ADD ROUTINE
1460 REC = 0: KEY$ = ".....": GOSUB 1410
1470 IF N2 > 99 THEN GOSUB 3240: GOTO 1700
1480 REC = VAL (REC$)
1490 VTAB L0: HTAB 12: GALEGTH = 5: GOSUB 1090
1500 IF LEFT$(GBANSWER$,1) = " " THEN 1490
1510 KEY$ = GBANSWER$: INDEX$(N2) = KEY$ + REC$
1520 GOSUB 2800: REM READ DISK
1530 GOSUB 2960: REM WRITE SCR
1540 GALEGTH = 25: VTAB L1: HTAB 12: GOSUB 1090: IF LEFT$
     (GBANSWER$,1) = " " THEN 1540
1550 AANAME$ = GBANSWER$
1560 VTAB L2: HTAB 12: GOSUB 1090:ABADDR$ = GBANSWER$
1570 GALEGTH = 15: VTAB L3: HTAB 12: GOSUB 1090:ACCITY$ = GBANSWER$
```

```
1580 GALEGTH = 2: VTAB L4: HTAB 12: GOSUB 1090:ADSTE$ = GBANSWER$
1590 GALEGTH = 5: VTAB L5: HTAB 12: GOSUB 1090: GOSUB 3320:
     IF X1$ = "N" THEN 1590
1600 AEZIP$ = GBANSWER$
1610 GALEGTH = 3: VTAB L6: HTAB 12: GOSUB 1090: GOSUB 3320:
     IF X1$ = "N" THEN 1610
1620 AFPHNE$ = GBANSWER$
1630 HTAB 16: GOSUB 1090: GOSUB 3320: IF X1$ = "N" THEN 1630
1640 AFPHNE$ = AFPHNE$ + GBANSWER$
1650 GALEGTH = 4: HTAB 20: GOSUB 1090: GOSUB 3320: IF X1$ =
     'N" THEN 1650
1660 AFPHNE$ = AFPHNE$ + GBANSWER$
1670 GALEGTH = 21: VTAB L7: HTAB 12: GOSUB 1090:AGCOM1$ = GBANSWER$
1680 VTAB L7 + 1: HTAB 12: GOSUB 1090:AHCOM2$ = GBANSWER$
1690 GOSUB 2560: REM WRITE DISK
1700 RETURN
1710 REM ----------------------
1720 REM CHANGE ROUTINE
1730 VTAB L0: HTAB 12:GALEGTH = 5: GOSUB 1090
1740 IF LEFT$(GBANSWER$,1) = " " THEN 1730
1750 KEY$ = GBANSWER$
1760 REC = 0
1770 IF REC > 99 THEN GOSUB 3070: GOTO 2140
1780 GOSUB 1410: REM SEARCH INDEX
1790 IF N2 > 99 THEN GOSUB 3070: GOTO 2140
1800 REC = VAL (REC$)
1810 GOSUB 2800: REM READ DISK
1820 GOSUB 2960: REM WRITE SCR
1830 GOSUB 3150: REM MESSAGE
1840 IF X1$ = "N" THEN REC = REC + 1: GOTO 1770
1850 VTAB L0: HTAB 12: GALEGTH = 5: GOSUB 1090: IF GCCHAR =
     0 THEN 1880
1860 IF LEFT$(GBANSWER$,1) = " " THEN 1850
1870 INDEX$(N2) = GBANSWER$ + REC$
1880 GALEGTH = 25: VTAB L1: HTAB 12: GOSUB 1090: IF GCCHAR =
     0 THEN 1910
1890 IF LEFT$ (GBANSWER$,1) = " " THEN 1880
1900 AANAME$ = GBANSWER$
1910 VTAB L2: HTAB 12: GOSUB 1090: IF GCCHAR = 0 THEN 1930
1920 ABADDR$ = GBANSWER$
1930 GALEGTH = 15: VTAB L3: HTAB 12: GOSUB 1090: IF GCCHAR =
     0 THEN 1950
1940 ACCITY$ = GBANSWER$
1950 GALEGTH = 2: VTAB L4: HTAB 12: GOSUB 1090: IF GCCHAR =
     0 THEN 1970
1960 ADSTE$ = GBANSWER$
1970 GALEGTH = 5: VTAB L5: HTAB 12: GOSUB 1090: IF GCCHAR =
     0 THEN 2000
1980 GOSUB 3320: IF X1$ = "N" THEN 1970
1990 AEZIP$ = GBANSWER$
2000 GALEGTH = 3: VTAB L6: HTAB 12: GOSUB 1090: IF GCCHAR =
     0 THEN 2030
2010 GOSUB 3320: IF X1$ = "N" THEN 2000
2020 AFPHNE$ = GBANSWER$ + RIGHT$ (AFPHNE$,7)
```

```
2030 HTAB 16: GOSUB 1090: IF GCCHAR = 0 THEN 2060
2040 GOSUB 3320: IF X1$ = "N" THEN 2030
2050 AFPHNE$ = LEFT$ (AFPHNE$,3) + GBANSWER$ + RIGHT$(AFPHNE$,4)
2060 GALEGTH = 4: HTAB 20: GOSUB 1090: IF GCCHAR = 0 THEN 2090
2070 GOSUB 3320: IF X1$ = "N" THEN 2060
2080 AFPHNE$ = LEFT$ (AFPHNE$,6) + GBANSWER$
2090 GALEGTH = 21: VTAB L7: HTAB 12: GOSUB 1090: IF GCCHAR =
     0 THEN 2110
2100 AGCOM1$ = GBANSWER$
2110 VTAB L7 + 1: HTAB 12: GOSUB 1090: IF GCCHAR = 0 THEN 2130
2120 AHCOM2$ = GBANSWER$
2130 GOSUB 2560: REM WRITE DISK
2140 RETURN
2150 REM ----------------------
2160 REM DELETE ROUTINE
2170 GALEGTH = 5: VTAB L0: HTAB 12: GOSUB 1090
2180 IF LEFT$ (GBANSWER$,1) = " " THEN 2170
2190 KEY$ = GBANSWER$
2200 REC = 0
2210 IF REC > 99 THEN GOSUB 3070: GOTO 2380
2220 GOSUB 1410: REM SEARCH INDEX
2230 IF N2 > 99 THEN GOSUB 3070: GOTO 2380
2240 REC = VAL (REC$)
2250 GOSUB 2800: REM READ DISK
2260 GOSUB 2960: REM WRITE SCR
2270 GOSUB 3150: REM MESSAGE
2280 IF X1$ = "N" THEN REC = REC + 1: GOTO 2210
2290 VTAB L9: HTAB 1: INVERSE
2300 PRINT "ARE YOU SURE?  ENTER Y TO DELETE THE "
2310 PRINT "RECORD.  ANY OTHER KEY TO KEEP RECORD";
2320 GET X1$
2330 VTAB L9: HTAB 1: NORMAL
2340 PRINT TAB( 39)" "
2350 PRINT TAB( 39)" ";
2360 REM
2370 IF X1$ = "Y" THEN INDEX$(REC) = "....." + REC$: GOSUB 2560
2380 RETURN
2390 REM ----------------------
2400 REM LIST ROUTINE
2410 VTAB L0: HTAB 12: GALEGTH = 5: GOSUB 1090
2420 IF LEFT$ (GBANSWER$,1) = " " THEN 2410
2430 KEY$ = GBANSWER$
2440 REC = 0
2450 IF REC > 99 THEN GOSUB 3070: GOTO 2530
2460 GOSUB 1410: REM SEARCH INDEX
2470 IF N2 > 99 THEN GOSUB 3070: GOTO 2530
2480 REC = VAL (REC$)
2490 GOSUB 2800: REM READ DISK
2500 GOSUB 2960: REM WRITE SCR
2510 GOSUB 3150: REM MESSAGE
2520 IF X1$ = "N" THEN REC = REC + 1: GOTO 2450
2530 RETURN
2540 REM ----------------------
2550 REM WRITE ON DISK
```

```
2560 VTAB 1: HTAB 39
2570 PRINT D$
2580 PRINT D$;"WRITE ";F2FILEID$;",R";REC
2590 IF X2$ = "D" THEN PRINT R1RESET$: GOTO 2610
2600 PRINT AANAME$;ABADDR$;ACCITY$;ADSTE$;AEZIP$;AFPHNE$;AGCOM1$;
     AHCOM2$
2610 PRINT D$;"WRITE ";F1FILEID$;",R";REC
2620 PRINT INDEX$(REC)
2630 PRINT D$
2640 REM
2650 RETURN
2660 REM --------------------------
2670 REM CLEAR SCREEN
2680 VTAB L0: HTAB 12: PRINT "     "
2690 VTAB L1: HTAB 12: PRINT  TAB( 36)" "
2700 VTAB L2: HTAB 12: PRINT  TAB( 36)" "
2710 VTAB L3: HTAB 12: PRINT  TAB( 26)" "
2720 VTAB L4: HTAB 12: PRINT "  "
2730 VTAB L5: HTAB 12: PRINT "      "
2740 VTAB L6: HTAB 12: PRINT "    -  -    "
2750 VTAB L7: HTAB 12: PRINT  TAB( 32)" "
2760 VTAB L7 + 1: HTAB 12: PRINT  TAB( 32)" "
2770 RETURN
2780 REM --------------------------
2790 REM READ DISK
2800 VTAB 1: HTAB 39
2810 PRINT D$
2820 PRINT D$;"READ ";F2FILEID$;",R";REC
2830 INPUT A1ADDR$
2840 PRINT D$
2850 AANAME$ = LEFT$ (A1ADDR$,25)
2860 ABADDR$ = MID$ (A1ADDR$,26,25)
2870 ACCITY$ = MID$ (A1ADDR$,51,15)
2880 ADSTE$ = MID$ (A1ADDR$,66,2)
2890 AEZIP$ = MID$ (A1ADDR$,68,5)
2900 AFPHNE$ = MID$ (A1ADDR$,73,10)
2910 AGCOM1$ = MID$ (A1ADDR$,83,21)
2920 AHCOM2$ = RIGHT$ (A1ADDR$,21)
2930 RETURN
2940 REM --------------------------
2950 REM WRITE ON SCREEN
2960 VTAB L1: HTAB 12: PRINT AANAME$
2970 VTAB L2: HTAB 12: PRINT ABADDR$
2980 VTAB L3: HTAB 12: PRINT ACCITY$
2990 VTAB L4: HTAB 12: PRINT ADSTE$
3000 VTAB L5: HTAB 12: PRINT AEZIP$
3010 VTAB L6: HTAB 12: PRINT LEFT$ (AFPHNE$,3) "-" MID$ (AFPHNE$,
     4,3) "-" RIGHT$ (AFPHNE$,4)
3020 VTAB L7: HTAB 12: PRINT AGCOM1$
3030 VTAB L7 + 1: HTAB 12: PRINT AHCOM2$
3040 RETURN
3050 REM --------------------------
3060 REM REC NOT FOUND MESSAGE
3070 VTAB L9: HTAB 1: INVERSE
```

```
3080 PRINT "RECORD NOT ON FILE                    "
3090 PRINT "PRESS THE SPACE BAR TO TRY AGAIN      ";
3100 GET X1$: IF X1$ < > " " THEN 3100
3110 VTAB L9: HTAB 1: NORMAL : PRINT TAB( 39)" ": PRINT TAB( 39)" ";
3120 RETURN
3130 REM ----------------------
3140 REM IS THIS REC MESSAGE
3150 VTAB L9: HTAB 1: INVERSE
3160 PRINT "IS THIS THE RECORD YOU WANTED?        "
3170 PRINT "ENTER Y (YES) OR N (NO)              ";
3180 GET X1$: IF X1$ = "Y" OR X1$ = "N" THEN 3200
3190 GOTO 3180
3200 VTAB L9: HTAB 1: NORMAL : PRINT TAB( 39)" ": PRINT TAB( 39)" ";
3210 RETURN
3220 REM ----------------------
3230 REM FILE FULL MESSAGE
3240 VTAB L9: HTAB 1: INVERSE: SPEED= 100
3250 PRINT "THE ADDRESS FILE IS FULL-REC'S MUST BE"
3260 PRINT "DELETED BEFORE ANY MORE CAN BE ADDED. ";
3270 FOR N1 = 1 TO 10: CALL - 1052: NEXT
3280 VTAB L9: HTAB 1: NORMAL
3290 PRINT TAB( 39)" ": PRINT TAB ( 39)" ";: SPEED= 255
3300 RETURN
3310 REM ----------------------
3320 REM NUMERIC EDIT
3330 REM SPACES OR NUMBERS ONLY
3340 N2 = LEN (GBANSWER$)
3350 X1$ = "Y"
3360 FOR N1 = 1 TO N2
3370 IF MID$ (GBANSWER$,N1,1) < > " " THEN X1$ = "N": N1 = N2
3380 NEXT
3390 IF X1$ = "Y" THEN 3460
3400 X1$ = "Y"
3410 FOR N1 = 1 TO N2
3420 IF MID$ (GBANSWER$,N1,1) < "0" OR MID$ (GBANSWER$,N1,1)
     > "9" THEN X1$ = "N": N1 = N2
3430 NEXT
3440 IF X1$ = "Y" THEN 3460
3450 FOR N1 = 1 TO 30: N2 = PEEK ( - 16336): NEXT
3460 RETURN
3470 REM ----------------------
3480 REM FREE MEMORY ROUTINE
3490 STARTING = PEEK (112) * 256 + PEEK (111): IF STARTING >
     17000 THEN 3560
3500 VTAB L9: HTAB 1: INVERSE
3510 PRINT " FREEING MEMORY - PLEASE WAIT" TAB( 38)" "
3520 STARTING = FRE (0)
3530 PRINT " DONE - PRESS SPACE BAR TO CONTINUE   ";: NORMAL
3540 GET X1$: IF X1$ < > " " THEN 3540
3550 VTAB L9: HTAB 1: PRINT TAB( 39)" ": PRINT TAB( 39)" ";
3560 RETURN
3570 REM ----------------------
3580 REM BEGINNING ROUTINE
```

```
3590 TEXT : NORMAL : HOME : SPEED= 255
3600 D$ = CHR$ (4)
3610 FDRIVE = 1:PDRIVE = 1
3620 F1FILEID$ = "INDEX FILE"
3630 F2FILEID$ = "IND ADDR FILE"
3640 DIM INDEX$(99)
3650 L0 = 3:L1 = 5:L2 = 6:L3 = 7:L4 = 8:L5 = 9:L6 = 10:L7 =
     12:L8 = 17:L9 = 23
3660 FOR N1 = 1 TO 124:R1RESET$ = R1RESET$ + ".": NEXT
3670 HOME : PRINT "OPENING FILES AND LOADING INDEX TABLE."
3680 PRINT D$
3690 PRINT D$;"OPEN ";F1FILEID$;",L8,D";FDRIVE
3700 FOR REC = 0 TO 99
3710 VTAB 12: HTAB 15: PRINT "REC = ";REC
3720 PRINT D$;"READ ";F1FILEID$;",R";REC
3730 INPUT INDEX$(REC)
3740 PRINT D$
3750 NEXT
3760 PRINT D$;"OPEN ";F2FILEID$;",L125,D";FDRIVE
3770 PRINT D$
3780 REM ----------------------
3790 REM PRINT SCREEN IMAGE
3800 HOME
3810 PRINT "    ADDRESS FILE UPDATE PROGRAM"
3820 VTAB L0
3830 PRINT "LAST NAME=(      )"
3840 VTAB L1
3850 PRINT "NAME      =(" SPC( 25)")"
3860 PRINT "ADDRESS   =(" SPC( 25)")"
3870 PRINT "CITY      =(" SPC( 15)")"
3880 PRINT "STATE     =(  )"
3890 PRINT "ZIP CODE =(     )"
3900 PRINT "PHONE     =(   -   -     )"
3910 VTAB L7
3920 PRINT "COMMENT#1=(" SPC( 21)")"
3930 PRINT "COMMENT#2=(" SPC( 21)")"
3940 VTAB L8 + 2
3950 INVERSE : PRINT "A";: NORMAL : PRINT "DD    ";
3960 INVERSE : PRINT "C";: NORMAL : PRINT "HANGE    ";
3970 INVERSE : PRINT "D";: NORMAL : PRINT "ELETE    ";
3980 INVERSE : PRINT "L";: NORMAL : PRINT "IST    ";
3990 INVERSE : PRINT "Q";: NORMAL : PRINT "UIT"
4000 RETURN
4010 REM ----------------------
4020 REM ENDING ROUTINE
4030 PRINT D$
4040 PRINT D$;"CLOSE ";F1FILEID$
4050 PRINT D$;"CLOSE ";F2FILEID$
4060 HOME
4070 PRINT D$;"RUN IND ADDR HELLO PROG,D"PDRIVE
4080 REM
4090 REM ----------------------
```

Cross Reference Listing

Variable names used with the address record:

A1$ 2830, 2850, 2860, 2870, 2880, 2890, 2900, 2910, 2920
AA$ 1550, 1900, 2600, 2850, 2960
AB$ 1560, 1920, 2600, 2860, 2970
AC$ 1570, 1940, 2600, 2870, 2980
AD$ 1580, 1960, 2600, 2880, 2990
AE$ 1600, 1990, 2600, 2890, 3000
AF$ 1620, 1640, 1660, 2020, 2050, 2080, 2600, 2640, 2900, 3010
AG$ 1670, 2100, 2600, 2910, 3020
AH$ 1680, 2120, 2600, 2920, 3030

Variable names used with the disk commands:

D$ 2570, 2580, 2610, 2630, 2810, 2820, 2840, 3600, 3680, 3690, 3720, 3740,
     3760, 3770, 4030, 4040, 4050, 4070
F1$ 2610, 3620, 3690, 3720, 4040
F2$ 2580, 2820, 3630, 3760, 4050
FD   3610, 3690, 3760
PD   3610, 4070

Variable names used with the GET subroutine:

GA   1110, 1240, 1490, 1540, 1570, 1580, 1590, 1610, 1650, 1670, 1730, 1850,
     1880, 1930, 1950, 1970, 2000, 2060, 2090, 2170, 2410
GB$ 1240, 1500, 1510, 1540, 1550, 1560, 1570, 1580, 1600, 1620, 1640, 1660,
     1670, 1680, 1740, 1860, 1870, 1890, 1900, 1920, 1940, 1960, 1990, 2020,
     2050, 2080, 2100, 2120, 2180, 2190, 2420, 2430, 3340, 3370, 3420
GC   1220, 1230, 1240, 1850, 1880, 1910, 1930, 1950, 1970, 2000, 2030, 2050,
     2090, 2110

Variable names used with index table:

IN$(1410, 1510, 1870, 2370, 2620, 3640, 3730
KE$ 1410, 1460, 1510, 1750, 2190, 2430

Variable names used with displaying data on the screen:

L0 1490, 1730, 1850, 2170, 2410, 2680, 3650, 3820
L1 1540, 1880, 2690, 2960, 3650, 3840
L2 1560, 1910, 2700, 2970, 3650
L3 1570, 1930, 2710, 2980, 3650
L4 1580, 1950, 2720, 2990, 3650
L5 1590, 1970, 2730, 3000, 3650

L6   1610, 2000, 2740, 3010, 3650
L7   1670, 1680, 2090, 2110, 2750, 2760, 3020, 3030, 3650, 3910
L8   1290, 3650, 3940
L9   2290, 2330, 2360, 3070, 3110, 3150, 3200, 3240, 3280, 3500, 3550, 3650
R1$ 2590, 3660
RE   1410, 1460, 1480, 1760, 1770, 1800, 1840, 2200, 2210, 2240, 2280, 2370,
      2440, 2450, 2480, 2520, 2580, 2610, 2820, 3700, 3710, 3720, 3730
RE$ 1410, 1480, 1510, 1800, 1870, 2240, 2370, 2480

Variable names used for general GET instruction in response to screen messages and
for general counting in FOR/NEXT operations:

N1   1410, 3270, 3360, 3370, 3410, 3420, 3450, 3660
N2   1410, 1470, 1510, 1790, 1870, 2230, 2470, 3340, 3360, 3370 3410, 3420,
      3450
X1$ 1590, 1610, 1630, 1650, 1840, 1980, 2010, 2040, 2070, 2280, 2320, 2370,
      2520, 3100, 3180, 3350, 3370, 3390, 3400, 3420, 3440, 3540
X2$ 1290, 1300, 1330, 1340, 1350, 1360, 2590

Explanation by Line Number   Detailed explanations by line number follow.

1040–1070   The DRIVE ROUTINE consists of the same basic instruction group as in all the
example programs.

1080   REM --------------------

1090   REM GET SUBROUTINE
The GET subroutine is explained in detail in Chapter 3 of Section II.

1270   REM --------------------

1280   REM MAIN ROUTINE

1290   VTAB L8: HTAB 1: INVERSE : PRINT "   ? SELECTION"TAB(38)
" ";:NORMAL : HTAB 12: GET X2$: PRINT X2$

1300   IF X2$ = "Q" THEN 1380

1310   GOSUB 3490: REM CHECK MEMORY SPACE

```
1320    GOSUB 2680: REM CLEAR SCREEN

1330    IF X2$ = "A" THEN GOSUB 1460: GOTO 1290

1340    IF X2$ = "C" THEN GOSUB 1730: GOTO 1290

1350    IF X2$ = "D" THEN GOSUB 2170: GOTO 1290

1360    IF X2$ = "L" THEN GOSUB 2410: GOTO 1290

1370    GOTO 1290

1380    RETURN
```

Lines 1270 through 1380 of the **MAIN ROUTINE** are responsible for the following:

1. Displaying a message and accepting a response from the operator
2. Clearing memory between each record
3. Clearing the screen
4. Executing the routine corresponding to the processing code entered by the operator

One part you may want to review is the subroutine for clearing memory. The reason and the logic were explained in the **RAN ADDR UPDATE PROG** (see p. 398).

```
1390    REM --------------------

1400    REM SEARCH INDEX

1410    N2 = 100: FOR N1 = REC TO 99: IF LEFT$ (INDEX$(N1),5) = KEY$ THEN REC$
        = RIGHT$ (INDEX$(N1),2):N2 = N1:N1 = 100

1420    NEXT

1430    RETURN
```

As part of the **BEGINNING ROUTINE** logic, the index file is read and loaded into the table called **INDEX$(number)**. Once an index value is entered by the operator, this subroutine searches the table to find a matching value and the related record number.

Line 1410 contains a number of instructions. The first instruction sets N2 equal to 100. N2 serves as a switch after returning from the subroutine. If N2 still has a value of 100 after the SEARCH INDEX ROUTINE is done, this indicates that no matching index was found. If the value of N2 is changed during the search, this indicates that a match was found. The new value of N2 points to the matching entry within the index table.

The second instruction on line 1410 starts a FOR/NEXT loop. You may wonder why there are so many instructions on line 1410, while the NEXT instruction is on a line by itself. To make the SEARCH INDEX ROUTINE work faster, as many instructions as possible were put on one line. But since the FOR/NEXT loop includes an IF instruction, the entire loop cannot be put on one line. Whenever a FOR/NEXT instruction includes an IF, it must be written on two or more lines, and the keyword NEXT should not be part of the IF instruction.

The FOR/NEXT loop searches through the table until either a match is found or the entire table has been searched. If a match is found, REC$ is set equal to the relative record number located in the right two digits of the index record. After the relative record number is found, the variables N2 and N1 are reset. N2 is set equal to the location of the index within the table. N1 is set equal to 100 in order to terminate the FOR/NEXT loop.

```
FOR N1 = REC TO 99:
    IF LEFT$ (INDEX$(N1),5) = KEY$
        THEN REC$ = RIGHT$ (INDEX$(N1),2):
            N2 = N1:
            N1 = 100
NEXT
```

If no matching index value is found, N2 remains at 100, indicating that the index value does not exist within the program.

```
1440    REM --------------------

1450    REM ADD ROUTINE

1460    REC = 0: KEY$ = ".....": GOSUB 1410

1470    IF N2 > 99 THEN GOSUB 3240: GOTO 1700

1480    REC = VAL (REC$)

1490    VTAB L0: HTAB 12: GALEGTH = 5: GOSUB 1090
```

```
1500    IF LEFT$(GBANSWER$,1) = " " THEN 1490

1510    KEY$ = GBANSWER$: INDEX$(N2) = KEY$ + REC$

1520    GOSUB 2800: REM READ DISK

1530    GOSUB 2960: REM WRITE SCR

1540    GALEGTH = 25: VTAB L1: HTAB 12: GOSUB 1090: IF LEFT$ (G BANSWER$,1)
        = " " THEN 1540

1550    AANAME$ = GBANSWER$

1560    VTAB L2: HTAB 12: GOSUB 1090:ABADDR$ = GBANSWER$

1570    GALEGTH = 15: VTAB L3: HTAB 12: GOSUB 1090:ACCITY$ = GB ANSWER$
................
1610    GALEGTH = 3: VTAB L6: HTAB 12: GOSUB 1090: GOSUB 3320: IF X1$ = "N"
        THEN 1610

1620    AFPHNE$ = GBANSWER$
................
1690    GOSUB 2560: REM WRITE DISK

1700    RETURN

1460    REC = 0: KEY$ = ".....": GOSUB 1410
```

When a record is added to the file, an unused record location must be found. In order to find an unused area, the variable REC is given a starting value of zero. REC is used in the FOR/NEXT loop of the SEARCH INDEX ROUTINE to indicate the position within the table where the search is to begin.

```
1410 N2 = 100: FOR N1 = REC TO 99...
                          ^^^
```

For the ADD ROUTINE the table is always searched starting at the first entry. In the CHANGE ROUTINE, the DELETE ROUTINE, and the LIST ROUTINE, the point at which the table is searched varies depending on whether or not a previous match has already been found.

After REC is initialized, the variable KEY$ is set equal to the dummy value used on the index file (five periods). The five periods are compared with the indexes in the table until an unused record location is found.

1470   After logic flow returns from the SEARCH INDEX ROUTINE the value of N2 is checked to see if it is greater than 99. If N2 is greater than 99, it indicates that there were no unused record locations and the file is full. If the file is full, an appropriate message is displayed, and the GOTO skips the rest of the ADD ROUTINE.

1480   If the value of N2 is less than 100, the numeric variable REC is set equal to the relative record number which was located in the table. Remember, REC$ is used when printing on the screen or disk, and REC is used in the READ/WRITE commands.

1490   VTAB L0: HTAB 12: GALEGTH = 5: GOSUB 1090

1500   IF LEFT$(GBANSWER$,1) = " " THEN 1490

1510   KEY$ = GBANSWER$: INDEX$(N2) = KEY$ + REC$
Lines 1490 through 1510 allow the operator to enter a five character index. The first four instructions relate to the use of the GET subroutine. Line 1500 tests the value returned to make sure it does not start with a blank. Remember, any record written to the disk should not contain leading spaces.

Line 1510 sets KEY$ equal to the index value and places the new index value along with the related record number back into the table.

For example, when adding the first record, the SEARCH INDEX ROUTINE stops at the first entry in the table and returns a value of

.....00

where "....." is the dummy index and 00 the relative record number.

After the index value is correctly entered, line 1510 places the new index into the first table location.

KEY$ ⌐┐   ┌─ REC$
    JOHNS00

where JOHNS is the index value and 00 the relative record number.

1520–1530   After the index value has been entered, the matching record is read using the relative record number retrieved from the table. For the ADD ROUTINE the record read should contain all periods, indicating an unused record. Once the record is read, the periods are displayed on the screen.

1540   GALEGTH = 25: VTAB L1: HTAB 12: GOSUB 1090: IF LEFT$ (GBANSWER$,1) = " " THEN 1540

1550   AANAME$ = GBANSWER$

....

1610   GALEGTH = 3: VTAB L6: HTAB 12: GOSUB 1090: GOSUB 3320: IF X1$ = "N" THEN 1610

1620   AFPHNE$ = GBANSWER$

Lines 1490 through 1700 make up the body of the ADD ROUTINE and consist basically of the same sequence of instructions. The operator is given a chance to enter data for each field. The very first field in the record is checked to make sure there are no leading spaces. Numeric fields are edited to make sure the value is either all spaces or all numeric (see GOSUB 3320 and IF).

Once more, the name field is treated differently than the other fields because it is the first field in the record. Since the APPLE suppresses leading spaces when reading data back from the disk, the program makes sure the operator does not include any leading spaces in the name.

If the operator makes a mistake and starts the name off with a leading space, the IF instruction rejects the entry and has the operator start over.

Other than the instructions for the name the basic sequence of instructions is as follows:

1. Set GALEGTH equal to the length of the field to be read.
2. Position the cursor on the correct line.
3. Position the cursor at the correct column.
4. Execute the GET subroutine.
5. For numeric fields, edit the data entered and test the switch returned by the NUMERIC EDIT ROUTINE.
6. Once past the edit test set a variable equal to the value returned by the GET subroutine.

1690–1700   After all the fields have been entered, the new data is rewritten over the old dummy values. Once the record is added, logic flow returns to the main body of the program.

1710   REM ---------------------

1720   REM CHANGE ROUTINE

1730   VTAB L0: HTAB 12:GALEGTH = 5: GOSUB 1090

1740   IF LEFT$(GBANSWER$,1) = " " THEN 1730

1750   KEY$ = GBANSWER$

1760   REC = 0

Lines 1730 through 1750 allow the operator to enter the five character index. For all the processing codes except the A (Add), the first step is to have the operator enter the index value corresponding to the record to be read. After the index is entered, REC is set equal to zero so the searching process initially starts with the first entry in the table.

1770   Line 1770 has been inserted before the table is searched to handle a unique situation. The search process (lines 1770 through 1840) is executed repeatedly until either an acceptable match is found or the end of the index table is reached. A match on entry 99 can occur. If the ninety-ninth entry is not the desired one, the search routine is executed again starting at entry 100 (99 + 1 = 100).

1840 IF X1$ = "N" THEN REC = REC + 1: GOTO 1770

Whoops! There is no table entry 100. The number is beyond the end of the table and if used caused an error message to cancel the program. To prevent this from happening, line 1770 checks the value of REC before starting the search. If the value is greater than 99, then a message is displayed indicating that the record is not on the file, and logic flow exits the CHANGE ROUTINE.

1770   IF REC > 99 THEN GOSUB 3070: GOTO 2140 No match

1780   GOSUB 1410: REM SEARCH INDEX

1790   IF N2 > 99 THEN GOSUB 3070: GOTO 2140 No match

1800   REC = VAL (REC$) Yes match

1810   GOSUB 2800: REM READ DISK

1820   GOSUB 2960: REM WRITE SCR

1830   GOSUB 3150: REM MESSAGE

1840   IF X1$ = "N" THEN REC = REC + 1: GOTO 1770
Lines 1770 through 1840 make up the code which

1. Executes the SEARCH INDEX ROUTINE (GOSUB 1410)
2. Tests to see if a matching index value was NOT found (IF N2 > 99 THEN GOSUB 3070: GOTO 2140)
3. Reads and displays the matching record
4. Requests the operator to respond with a Y (Yes) or N (No) indicating whether or not the record displayed is the one to be changed

The GOSUB instruction (line 1780) executes the table SEARCH INDEX ROUTINE. After logic flow returns from the routine, the value of N2 is tested. If N2 is greater then 99, this indicates that no matching index was found. If no matching index was located, a message is displayed (GOSUB 3070), and logic flow exits the CHANGE ROUTINE (GOTO 2140).

If N2 is less than 100, a record is read and the information displayed. Since there could be more than one record with the same index, a standard message is displayed with each screen. The operator must respond, indicating whether or not the record displayed is the one to be processed.

If the operator enters Y, logic flow continues through the CHANGE ROUTINE. If the operator enters N, the value of REC is incremented by 1, and logic flow skips to line 1770, where the SEARCH INDEX ROUTINE is executed again. Take some time to study the use of the variable REC. Before the first execution of the SEARCH INDEX ROUTINE REC is set to 0, the routine starts looking through the table until a match is found. Once a match is found, REC contains the table position of the matching index. If the operator rejects the record, then the value of REC is incremented by 1 so it points to the table position following the last match. After the value of REC has been incremented, the SEARCH INDEX ROUTINE is executed again starting with the new value of REC.

```
1850    ........

1880    GALEGTH = 25: VTAB L1: HTAB 12: GOSUB 1090: IF GCCHAR = 0 THEN 1910

1890    IF LEFT$ (GBANSWER$,1) = " " THEN 1880

1900    AANAME$ = GBANSWER$
        ...............

2000    GALEGTH = 3: VTAB L6: HTAB 12: GOSUB 1090: IF GCCHAR = 0 THEN 2030

2010    GOSUB 3320: IF X1$ = "N" THEN 2000

2020    AFPHNE$ = GBANSWER$ + RIGHT$ (AFPHNE$,7)
```

Lines 1850 through 2140 consist of the instructions for allowing the operator to change the current value of any of the fields.

The points to remember are the following:

1. For the first variable in the record, make sure there are no leading spaces (lines 1880 and 1890).
2. When changes are made, you must test to see if any data were entered or if only the return key was pressed (IF GCCHAR = 0 THEN 1910).
3. If data are entered, then edit the value to make sure it was entered correctly (lines 1890 and 2010).
4. If the data entered pass the edit test, then set the variable name equal to the new value (lines 1900 and 2020).

Line 2000 through 2080 work with the phone number. Since the field is entered in three separate parts, care must be taken to combine the new information with the old. It is possible for the operator to change only part of the phone number.

2130–2140   Once all the changes have been made, the record is rewritten, and logic flow returns to the main portion of the program.

2150   REM ---------------------

2160   REM DELETE ROUTINE
The first part of the DELETE ROUTINE is the same as the first part of the CHANGE ROUTINE. The operator enters the index to be used in searching the file. If a matching value is found, the related record is read and displayed. After the record is displayed, the operator is given a chance to indicate whether or not this is the record to be deleted.

If the operator indicates that the current record is to be deleted, a second message is displayed. The operator is given a second chance to exit the routine and keep the record. If the operator presses any key other than Y, the record is not deleted.

If the operator enters Y in response to the second message, the index value in the table is set equal to periods, and then both the index and data records are rewritten (see related lines 2580, 2590, and 2620).

2390   REM ---------------------

2400   REM LIST ROUTINE
The LIST ROUTINE follows the same pattern as the ADD ROUTINE, the CHANGE ROUTINE, and the DELETE ROUTINE.

```
2540    REM --------------------

2550    REM WRITE ON DISK

2560    VTAB 1: HTAB 39

2570    PRINT D$

2580    PRINT D$;"WRITE ";F2FILEID$;",R";REC

2590    IF X2$ = "D" THEN PRINT R1RESET$: GOTO 2610

2600    PRINT AANAME$;ABADDR$;ACCITY$;ADSTE$;AEZIP$;AFPHNE$;AGC
        OM1$;AHCOM2$

2610    PRINT D$;"WRITE ";F1FILEID$;",R";REC

2620    PRINT INDEX$(REC)
```
Line 2560 is the program patch which keeps the cursor from erasing a position on the screen. Line 2590 or line 2600 writes the new information to the disk. If the record is being deleted, line 2590 writes 124 periods on the disk. If data is being added or changed, then line 2600 writes the information in one large 124 character record.

Either way, line 2620 writes the new index value back on the index file.

```
2680    REM --------------------

2690    REM CLEAR SCREEN
```
This routine does not present any new ideas. See the sequential file UPDATE program for a detailed explanation.

```
2780    REM --------------------

2790    REM READ DISK

2800    VTAB 1: HTAB 39

2810    PRINT D$
```

2820   PRINT D$;"READ ";F2FILEID$;",R";REC

2830   INPUT A1ADDR$

2840   PRINT D$

2850   AANAME$ = LEFT$ (A1ADDR$,25)

....

2930   RETURN
Lines 2780 through 2930 read the record and break it down into the individual variables.

2940   REM --------------------

2950   REM WRITE ON SCREEN
This routine does not present any new ideas. See the sequential file UPDATE program for a detailed explanation.

3050   REM --------------------

3060   REM REC NOT FOUND MESSAGE

3070   VTAB L9: HTAB 1: INVERSE

3080   PRINT "RECORD NOT ON FILE   "

3090   PRINT "PRESS THE SPACE BAR TO TRY AGAIN   ";

3100   GET X1$: IF X1$ < > " " THEN 3100

3110   VTAB L9: HTAB 1: NORMAL : PRINT TAB(39)" ": PRINT TAB(39)" ";

3120   RETURN
If the index value entered by the operator is not matched up to an index value in the table, the "RECORD NOT ON FILE" message is displayed. After the operator has read the message and pressed the space bar, the subroutine returns to the calling GOSUB.

3220   REM --------------------

3230   REM FILE FULL MESSAGE

3240   VTAB L9: HTAB 1: INVERSE: SPEED= 100

3250   PRINT "THE ADDRESS FILE IS FULL-REC'S MUST BE   "

3260   PRINT "DELETED BEFORE ANY MORE CAN BE ADDED. ";

3270   FOR N1 = 1 TO 10: CALL - 1052: NEXT

3280   VTAB L9: HTAB 1: NORMAL

3290   PRINT TAB(39)" ": PRINT TAB (39)" ";: SPEED= 255

3300   RETURN

This routine handles the error message differently than previous error routines. The INVERSE and SPEED commands are used on line 3240 to attract the operator's attention to the message being displayed and to slow the computer down so the operator has time to view the message.

Line 3270 sets up a FOR/NEXT loop which is used to make a beep for 1 second. There are two ways to make noise with the APPLE. One is to PEEK memory address −16336 within a FOR/NEXT loop, and the other is to CALL −1052. The PEEK version makes a very short sound and must be executed many times to be noticeable. The CALL −1052 makes a beep for 1/10 of a second. The two sounds are different; you should try both of the instructions to see which one you like.

After the FOR/NEXT instruction is done, line 3290 slowly clears the error message and automatically returns to the calling GOSUB.

This error routine has the advantage of not requiring the operator to respond. It has the disadvantage of lasting a specific length of time and making a noise which may embarrass the operator.

3310   REM ---------------------

3320   REM NUMERIC EDIT

3330   REM SPACES OR NUMBERS ONLY

The NUMERIC EDIT ROUTINE checks GBANSWER$ and returns a code of Y if GBANSWER$ contains all spaces or all numbers. If GBANSWER$ does not pass the edit test, a code of N is returned. The routine consists of three FOR/NEXT loops.

3340   N2 = LEN (GBANSWER$)

3350   X1$ = "Y"

3360   FOR N1 = 1 TO N2

3370   IF MID$ (GBANSWER$,N1,1) < > " " THEN X1$ = "N": N1 = N2

3380   NEXT

3390   IF X1$ = "Y" THEN 3460

3400   X1$ = "Y"

The routine starts off by finding the length GBANSWER$ and initializing the switch to a starting value of Y. Then the first FOR/NEXT loop tests every character of GBANSWER$ for spaces. If a nonblank character is found, X1$ is set equal to N and the FOR/NEXT statement is terminated.

If the GBANSWER$ contains only spaces, logic flow exits the routine (see line 3390). If a nonblank character is found, the switch is reset to Y and the second FOR/NEXT instruction is executed.

3410   FOR N1 = 1 TO N2

3420   IF MID$ (GBANSWER$,N1,1) < "0" OR MID$ (GBANSWER$,N1,1) > "9" THEN X1$ = "N": N1 = N2

3430   NEXT

3440   IF X1$ = "Y" THEN 3460

3450   FOR N1 = 1 TO 30: N2 = PEEK (− 16336): NEXT

3460   RETURN

After the second FOR/NEXT instruction is finished, the switch is tested, and logic flow either exits the routine or falls through to line 3450.

Line 3450 provides a second example of how to make noise with the APPLE. The PEEK (− 16336) instruction is used within the FOR/NEXT instruction to generate a short sound with the speaker.

3470   REM --------------------

3480   REM FREE MEMORY ROUTINE
For an explanation of the FREE MEMORY ROUTINE, see the sequential UPDATE
program.

3570   REM --------------------

3580   REM BEGINNING ROUTINE
....

3690   PRINT D$;"OPEN ";F1FILEID$;",L8,D";FDRIVE

3700   FOR REC = 0 TO 99

3710   VTAB 12: HTAB 15: PRINT "REC = ";REC

3720   PRINT D$;"READ ";F1FILEID$;",R";REC

3730   INPUT INDEX$(REC)

3740   PRINT D$

3750   NEXT
The BEGINNING ROUTINE is responsible for reading the INDEX FILE and placing
each record into the INDEX$ table. During this process, line 3710 displays the
relative record number of each record placed in the table. Displaying the record
number lets the user sees what is going on and how fast the computer is working.

3780   REM --------------------

3790   REM PRINT SCREEN IMAGE
....

4010   REM --------------------

4020   REM ENDING ROUTINE
The PRINT SCREEN IMAGE ROUTINE and the ENDING ROUTINE do not present
any new ideas. See the sequential file UPDATE program for a detailed explanation.

The Index File LIST Program

Program Name   IND ADDR LIST PROG

Program Objective   To provide the user with a method of listing all the records in the address file on the screen or printer.

This example follows the same format as the RAN ADDR LIST PROG except that the file is listed by the index value rather than by the entire last name. The IND ADDR LIST PROGram

1. Sorts the records into ascending sequence by the index value, which should be the first five characters of the client's last name.
2. Allows the user either to display the records on the screen or to print a hard copy of each record.
3. Does not use the DRIVE ROUTINE as in previous examples. The coding still uses modules and limits the use of the GOTO instruction, but because of the nature of the program, logic flow is allowed to simply fall through each module as it is executed.

The IND ADDR LIST PROGram displays one record per screen or prints three records per page. When displaying the records, the program pauses after displaying each screen and waits for a response from the operator. When printing records, the program does not pause.

The one record screen format is as follows:

```
INDEX     = (      )
RECORD #  = (   )

NAME      = (                          )
ADDRESS   = (                          )
CITY      = (                )
STATE     = (   )
ZIP CODE  = (       )
PHONE     = (    -    -       )

COMMENT#1 = (                  )
COMMENT#2 = (                  )


PRESS  Q   TO QUIT PROCESSING
PRESS  C   TO CONTINUE
```

Instructions for Running the Program

Run the program by entering

RUN IND ADDR HELLO PROG <RETURN>

After the menu is displayed, enter a 2 to start execution of the listing program.

After the listing program has started, the screen will be cleared and a message displayed as follows:

```
READING FILE & LOADING TABLE

        REC = ##
```

The IND ADDR LIST PROGram only needs to load the index values from the INDEX FILE into a table, so the message is not on the screen very long.

After all the index values have been read and placed into the table, the values are sorted. The length of time it takes the program to sort the indexes depends on how many index values were found. If only a few indexes were loaded into the table, the sort executes so fast you do not even know it has taken place. But if every record on the file contains data, it takes around a minute to sequence the indexes.

While the records are being sorted, the following screen is displayed:

```
        SORTING TABLE ENTRIES

- TAKES ONE MINUTE IF FILE IS FULL -

        PASS ## OF ##

SORT DONE - PRESS SPACE BAR TO CONT.
```

During the sorting process, two numbers are displayed. The last number indicates the total number of passes needed to sort the table, while the first number indicates which pass the computer is currently working on.

After the sort is done, the operator must press the space bar to continue. The pause is put in so the operator has a chance to see the screen and know what is going on.

After the sort is done and the operator has responded, the next screen is displayed. The screen allows the operator to enter either D to display the records on the screen or P to print the records.

```
ENTER D TO DISPLAY THE NAMES

ENTER P TO PRINT    THE NAMES

RESPONSE = [
```

If the operator chooses to display the records, then the display process is started. If the operator wants to print the records, another screen is displayed, and the program pauses to give the operator time to make sure the printer is ready.

```
PRESS SPACE BAR WHEN:

    1. PRINTER IS TURNED ON.

    2. FORMS ARE ALIGNED.
```

Program Listing

```
1000 REM IND ADDR LIST PROG
1010 REM ---------------------
1020 REM BEGINNING ROUTINE
1030 TEXT : NORMAL : HOME : SPEED= 255
1040 D$ = CHR$ (4)
1050 FDRIVE = 1:PDRIVE = 1
1060 F1FILEID$ = "INDEX FILE"
1070 F2FILEID$ = "IND ADDR FILE"
1080 REM L$ = TO-TOP-OF-PAGE
1090 L$ = CHR$ (12)
1100 DIM INDEX$ (99)
1110 VTAB 10: HTAB 5: PRINT "READING FILE & LOADING TABLE"
1120 PRINT D$
1130 PRINT D$;"OPEN ";F1FILEID$;",L8,D";FDRIVE
1140 REM
1150 FOR REC = 0 TO 99
1160 VTAB 12: HTAB 17: PRINT "REC = ";REC
1170 PRINT D $;"READ ";F1FILEID$;",R"REC
```

```
1180 INPUT X1$
1190 IF LEFT$ (X1$,5) = "....." THEN 1220
1200 INDEX$(N1) = X1$
1210 N1 = N1 + 1
1220 NEXT
1230 N3 = N1 - 1: REM N3 = EXACT NUMBER OF ENTRIES IN TABLE
1240 PRINT D$;"CLOSE ";F1FILEID$
1250 PRINT D$;"OPEN ";F2FILEID$;",L125,D";FDRIVE
1260 PRINT D$
1270 IF N3 < 1 THEN 1480
1280 REM
1290 REM ------------------------
1300 REM SORT INDEX TABLE
1310 HOME : VTAB 8 : HTAB 8
1320 PRINT "SORTING TABLE ENTRIES"
1330 VTAB 10
1340 PRINT "- TAKES ONE MINUTE IF FILE IS FULL -"
1350 FOR N1 = 0 TO N3 - 1
1360 :: VTAB 12: HTAB 14: PRINT "PASS "N1 + 1" OF "N3
1370 :: FOR N2 = N1 + 1 TO N3
1380 :::: IF INDEX$(N1) < INDEX$(N2) THEN 1420
1390 :::: X1$ = INDEX$(N1)
1400 :::: INDEX$(N1) = INDEX$(N2)
1410 :::: INDEX$(N2) = X1$
1420 :: NEXT
1430 NEXT
1440 VTAB 14: PRINT " SORT DONE - PRESS SPACE BAR TO CONT. ";
1450 GET X1$: IF X1$ < " " THEN 1450
1460 REM
1470 REM ------------------------
1480 REM SELECT DEVICE
1490 HOME
1500 PRINT : PRINT
1510 PRINT "ENTER D TO DISPLAY THE NAMES"
1520 PRINT
1530 PRINT "ENTER P TO PRINT   THE NAMES"
1540 PRINT
1550 PRINT "      RESPONSE = ";: GET X2$: PRINT X2$
1560 IF X2$ = "D" THEN HOME : GOTO 1730
1570 IF X2$ = "P" THEN 1600
1580 GOTO 1490
1590 REM
1600 HOME
1610 PRINT "PRESS SPACE BAR WHEN:"
1620 PRINT
1630 PRINT "  1. PRINTER IS TURNED ON."
1640 PRINT
1650 PRINT "  2. FORMS ARE ALIGNED.";
1660 GET X1$; IF X1$ < > " " THEN 1660
1670 HOME
1680 PRINT D$
1690 PRINT D$,"PR#1"
1700 REM
1710 REM ------------------------
```

```
1720 REM PRINT TABLE ENTRIES
1730 FOR N1 = 0 TO N3
1740 REC$ = RIGHT$ (INDEX$(N1),2)
1750 REC = VAL (REC$)
1760 INDEX$ = LEFT$ (INDEX$(N1),5)
1770 GOSUB 1910: REM READ DISK
1780 GOSUB 2070: REM WRITE PRT
1790 IF X1$ = "Q" THEN 1850
1800 NEXT
1810 REM
1820 IF X2$ = "D" THEN 1860
1830 PRINT L$: REM EJECT ONE PAGE
1840 IF LINE > 0 THEN PRINT L$: REM EJECT SECOND PAGE IF NEEDED
1850 PRINT D$: PRINT D$;"PR#0"
1860 PRINT D$: PRINT D$;"CLOSE"
1870 PRINT D$;"RUN IND ADDR HELLO PROG.D"PDRIVE
1880 REM
1890 REM --------------------
1900 REM READ DISK
1910 PRINT D$
1920 PRINT D$;"READ ";F2FILEID$;",R";REC
1930 INPUT A1ADDR$
1940 PRINT D$
1950 AANAME$ = LEFT$ (A1ADDR$,25)
1960 ABADDR$ = MID$ (A1ADDR$,26,25)
1970 ACCITY$ = MID$ (A1ADDR$,51,15)
1980 ADSTE$ = MID$ (A1ADDR$,66,2)
1990 AEZIP$ = MID$ (A1ADDR$,68,5)
2000 AFPHNE$ = MID$ (A1ADDR$,73,10)
2010 AGCOM1$ = MID$ (A1ADDR$,83,21)
2020 AHCOM2$ = RIGHT$ (A1ADDR$,21)
2030 RETURN
2040 REM
2050 REM --------------------
2060 REM PRINT SCREEN IMAGE
2070 PRINT
2080 PRINT "INDEX    =("INDEX$")"
2090 PRINT "RECORD # =("REC$")"
2100 PRINT
2110 PRINT "NAME     =("AANAME$")"
2120 PRINT "ADDRESS  =("ABADDR$")"
2130 PRINT "CITY     =("ACCITY$")"
2140 PRINT "STATE    =("ADSTE$")"
2150 PRINT "ZIP CODE =("AEZIP$")"
2160 PRINT "PHONE    =("LEFT$ (AFPHNE$,3)"-" MID$ (AFPHNE$,4
     ,3)"-" RIGHT$ (AFPHNE$,4)")"
2170 PRINT
2180 PRINT "COMMENT#1=("AGCOM1$")"
2190 PRINT "COMMENT#2=("AHCOM2$")"
2200 PRINT
2210 REM
2220 REM --------------------
2230 IF X3$ = "D" THEN 2290
2240 LINE = LINE + 1
```

```
2250 IF LINE > 3 THEN PRINT L$: LINE = 0
2260 RETURN
2270 REM
2280 REM ----------------------
2290 PRINT "PRESS  Q  TO QUIT PROCESSING"
2300 PRINT "PRESS  C  TO CONTINUE:;
2310 GET X1$
2320 IF X1$ = "Q" OR X1$ = "C" THEN 2340
2330 GOTO 2310
2340 HOME
2350 RETURN
2360 REM
2370 REM ----------------------
```

Cross Reference Listing

Variable names used with the address record:

A1$ 1930, 1950, 1960, 1970, 1980, 1990, 2000, 2010, 2020
AA$ 1950, 2110
AB$ 1960, 2120
AC$ 1970, 2130
AD$ 1980, 2140
AE$ 1990, 2150
AF$ 2000, 2160
AG$ 2010, 2180
AH$ 2020, 2190

Variable names used with the disk commands:

D$ 1040, 1120, 1130, 1170, 1240, 1250, 1260, 1680, 1690, 1850, 1860, 1870, 1910, 1920, 2940
F1$ 1060, 1130, 1170, 1240
F2$ 1070, 1250, 1920
FD 1050, 1130, 1250
PD 1050, 1870

Variable names used with index table

IN$ 1760, 2080
IN$(1100, 1200, 1380, 1390, 1400, 1410, 1740, 1760

Other general purpose variable names:

L$ 1090, 1830, 1840, 2250
LI 1840, 2240, 2250

N1 1200, 1210, 1230, 1350, 1360, 1370, 1380, 1390, 1400, 1730, 1740, 1760
N2 1370, 1380, 1400, 1410
N3 1230, 1270, 1350, 1360, 1370, 1730
RE 1150, 1160, 1170, 1750, 1920
RE$ 1740, 1750, 2090
X1$ 1180, 1190, 1200, 1390, 1410, 1450, 1660, 1790, 2310, 2320
X2$ 1550, 1560, 1570, 1820, 2230

Explanation by Line Number   Detailed explanations by line number follow.

1000   REM IND ADDR LIST PROG

1010   REM --------------------

....

1080   REM L$ = TO-TOP-OF-PAGE

1090   L$ = CHR$ (12)
For any printer which uses the standard ASCII control characters the symbol represented by the value 12 is used to cause the printer to skip to the top of a new page. That is, by printing this character (sending the character to the printer) the printer automatically advances the form.

1100   The DIMension instruction defines a table of 100 elements 0 through 99. The table is used to store the entire INDEX FILE in memory during execution of the program. After the file is loaded into the table the entries will be sorted into ascending sequence.

1130   The OPEN instruction provides DOS with the length of each record on the file and the number of the disk drive on which the file is located.

1150   FOR REC = 0 TO 99

1160   VTAB 12: HTAB 17: PRINT "REC = ";REC

1170   PRINT D$;"READ ";F1FILEID$;",R"REC

1180   INPUT X1$

1190   IF LEFT$ (X1$,5) = "....." THEN 1220

1200   INDEX$(N1) = X1$

1210   N1 = N1 + 1

1220   NEXT
Lines 1150 through 1220 load the INDEX$ table with the records from the INDEX FILE. Each of the 100 records in the file is read and examined to see if it contains a dummy value. If the record contains five periods, it is ignored. If the record contains an index, it is placed in the INDEX$ table. The value of N1 is incremented after each entry is put in the table. When the sort is done, N1 is 1 greater than the number of entries in the table.

1230   N3 = N1 - 1: REM N3 = EXACT NUMBER OF ENTRIES IN TABLE
....

1270   IF N3 < 1 THEN 1480
After the INDEX FILE has been read into the INDEX$ table, lines 1230 through 1270 finish up the housekeeping job related to loading the file. Line 1230 sets N3 equal to 1 less than the numeric value of N1 at the time the load process ended. Since N1 always points to the next empty table location, N3 now points to the last entry loaded into the table.

    The sort cannot work with fewer than two entries in the table. Line 1270 checks N3 and makes sure there are at least two or more entries to sort. If only one entry is in the table, then logic flow bypasses the sort routine.

    Note: There is an error in the logic. If the file is empty, the program still displays one dummy record. No test is made for an empty file.

1290   REM --------------------

1300   REM SORT INDEX TABLE
Lines 1290 through 1450 make up the logic for sorting the table into ascending order. The sort is exactly the same as the one used in the RAN ADDR LIST PROG, but you may want to go through it one more time just for review.

    Basically, the sort consists of two FOR/NEXT loops. The inner loop is responsible for doing the comparisons and switching the values, while the outer loop resets the counters and determines how many times the inner loop is executed.

```
1350 FOR N1 = 0 TO N3 − 1
1360 :: VTAB 12: HTAB 14: PRINT "PASS "N1 + 1" OF "N3
1370 :: FOR N2 = N1 + 1 TO N3
1380 :::: IF INDEX$(N1) < INDEX$(N2) THEN 1420
1390 :::: X1$ = INDEX$(N1)
```

```
1400 :::: INDEX$(N1) = INDEX$(N2)
1410 :::: INDEX$(N2) = X1$
1420 :: NEXT
1430 NEXT
```

To help explain the logic, let's use the following table values:

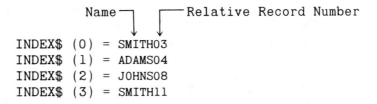

```
            Name ─┐   ┌─ Relative Record Number
                  ↓   ↓
INDEX$ (0) = SMITH03
INDEX$ (1) = ADAMS04
INDEX$ (2) = JOHNS08
INDEX$ (3) = SMITH11
```

The value in INDEX$ (0) is compared with the value in INDEX$ (1) (see line 1380). If the value in INDEX$ (0) is greater than the value in INDEX$ (1), the two names (including record numbers) are flipped (see lines 1390 to 1410). The flipping process is accomplished by setting X1$ equal to INDEX$ (0) in order to prevent it from being lost. INDEX$ (1) is then placed into INDEX (0). After the second value has been moved, the first value, which was saved in X1$, is placed into INDEX (1).

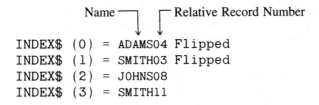

```
            Name ─┐   ┌─ Relative Record Number
                  ↓   ↓
INDEX$ (0) = ADAMS04 Flipped
INDEX$ (1) = SMITH03 Flipped
INDEX$ (2) = JOHNS08
INDEX$ (3) = SMITH11
```

The value in INDEX$ (0) is then compared with the value in INDEX$ (2). If the value in INDEX$ (0) is greater than the value in INDEX$ (2), the two table entries are flipped.

The process is repeated until the value in INDEX$ (0) has been compared with all the values in the table. After the first iteration of the inner loop is completed, the lowest value is in the first entry of the table, INDEX$ (0).

After the first entry has been compared with all the other entries in the table, the outer FOR/NEXT instruction sets N1 up by 1 and the inner FOR/NEXT instructions are executed again in order to compare the second entry with all the other table entries. If you follow the inner loop, you will see that during the second execution, two flips take place. First, SMITH and JOHNSON are flipped.

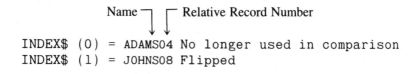

```
            Name ─┐   ┌─ Relative Record Number
                  ↓   ↓
INDEX$ (0) = ADAMS04 No longer used in comparison
INDEX$ (1) = JOHNS08 Flipped
```

```
INDEX$ (2) = SMITH03 Flipped
INDEX$ (3) = BOOTH11
```

Then, when JOHNS is compared with BOOTH, the names are flipped.

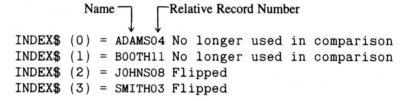

```
INDEX$ (0) = ADAMS04 No longer used in comparison
INDEX$ (1) = BOOTH11 Flipped
INDEX$ (2) = SMITH03
INDEX$ (3) = JOHNS08 Flipped
```

Once the value in INDEX$ (1) has been compared with all the other entries in the table, the outer loop sets N1 up by 1 and the process of comparing the third entry with all the other table entries is carried out. If you follow the inner loop one more time, you will see that during the third execution, one flip occurs. SMITH is compared with JOHNS, causing the names to be exchanged.

```
          Name ⌐        ⌐Relative Record Number
                ↓        ↓
INDEX$ (0) = ADAMS04 No longer used in comparison
INDEX$ (1) = BOOTH11 No longer used in comparison
INDEX$ (2) = JOHNS08 Flipped
INDEX$ (3) = SMITH03 Flipped
```

Since there are only four entries in the table, N1 is now equal to 1 less than the number of entries, and the sort is done.

Look through the code again and see how the sorting takes place. The outer loop of the replacement sort takes one less pass (execution) than the number of entries in the table (4 − 1 = 3). The number of times the inner loop is executed may be computed by the following formula:

Number of table entries * (number of table entries − 1) / 2

For the example the inner loop is executed six times.

4 * (4 − 1) / 2 = 6

If the table contained 100 entries, the inner loop would be executed 4950 times:
100 * (100 − 1) / 2 = 4950

1470   REM --------------------

1480   REM SELECT DEVICE

The operator is given a chance to either display the records on the screen (D) or print the records on the printer (P). If the operator enters P, a second screen is displayed in order to give the operator a chance to align the forms and make sure the printer is ready.

1710   REM ---------------------

1720   REM PRINT TABLE ENTRIES

1730   FOR N1 = 0 TO N3

1740   REC$ = RIGHT$ (INDEX$(N1),2)

1750   REC = VAL (REC$)

1760   INDEX$ = LEFT$ (INDEX$(N1),5)

1770   GOSUB 1910: REM READ DISK

1780   GOSUB 2070: REM WRITE PRT

1790   IF X1$ = "Q" THEN 1850

1800   NEXT

Lines 1710 through 1800 make up the code for displaying the records. The FOR/NEXT loop is executed from 0 to N3 times, where N3 contains the exact number of sorted entries.

Line 1740 extracts the record number from the right part of the table entry and puts the two digit number in REC$. REC$ is used whenever printing or displaying the relative record number. Line 1750 converts the string REC$ to numeric format. REC is used in the DOS READ and WRITE instructions to indicate the relative record number to be accessed.

Line 1790 is important only if the operator selects to display the records. It gives the operator a chance to quit before all the records are displayed on the screen. (see related line 2320).

1820   IF X2$ = "D" THEN 1860

1830   PRINT L$: REM EJECT ONE PAGE

1840   IF LINE > 0 THEN PRINT L$: REM EJECT SECOND PAGE IF NEEDED

1850   PRINT D$: PRINT D$;"PR#0"

1860   PRINT D$: PRINT D$;"CLOSE"

1870   PRINT D$;"RUN IND ADDR HELLO PROG,D"PDRIVE
Lines 1830 through 1850 are executed only if the data is being printed. When the data is printed, two situations can occur.

1.   The program can end in the middle of a page after printing either the first, the second, or the third record.

Top of page   →   First

                         Second

                         Third
Printer
positioned here →

2.   Or the program can end after just printing the fourth entry of a page and ejecting to a new page (see line 2250).

                         Fourth entry
Bottom of page →

Top of next page →   Printer positioned
                     at top of page

If the printer is in the middle of the page, then two ejects are necessary in order to position the paper to make it easy for the operator to tear off the report. If the printer is already at the top of a new page, only one eject is needed to correctly position the paper.

Line 1830 prints one CONTROL-L no matter where the printer is located. Line 1840 prints the second CONTROL-L only if LINE is greater than zero, indicating that a new page has been started.

This is an improved version of the same code as presented in the RAN ADDR LIST PROG. In the random version, two CONTROL-Ls are printed no matter where the printer is positioned. This can result in wasting two sheets of paper rather than one (big deal).

```
1890    REM --------------------

1900    REM READ DISK
        For an explanation of the READ DISK ROUTINE see the SEQ ADDR UPDATE PROG.

2050    REM --------------------

2060    REM PRINT SCREEN IMAGE
. . . . . . . . . . . . . . . .
2220    REM --------------------

2230    IF X3$ = "D" THEN 2290

2240    LINE = LINE + 1

2250    IF LINE > 3 THEN PRINT L$: LINE = 0

2260    RETURN

2270    REM

2280    REM --------------------

2290    PRINT "PRESS Q TO QUIT PROCESSING"

2300    PRINT "PRESS C TO CONTINUE:;

2310    GET X1$

2320    IF X1$ = "Q" OR X1$ = "C" THEN 2340

2330    GOTO 2310

2340    HOME

2350    RETURN
```

The first part of the PRINT SCREEN IMAGE ROUTINE is executed when displaying or printing the data. The end of the routine is split into two segments. The first segment contains the instruction for handling records which are being printed. The second segment contains the instructions for handling records which are being displayed.

Lines 2240 and 2250 are important. Each time a record is printed, LINE is incremented by 1. If four records have been printed (0, 1, 2, and 3), then a CONTROL-L is printed to start a new page. After a new page is started, make sure you reset the line or record counter to 0.

Lines 2290 through 2320 pause to give the operator a chance to view the data and to quit before all the records are displayed. Notice that the program does not end (quit) immediately. The value of X1$ is returned to the calling GOSUB and tested in that module (see line 1790). By letting logic flow go back to the calling module, there is only one ending routine whether the data is being printed or displayed.

The Index File SEARCH Program

Program Name   IND ADDR SEARCH PROG

Program Objective

To provide the user with a method of scanning the file for a specific index value or scanning the file for index values which start with a specific set of characters.

If the file is large, the user will not want to list all the records in sequence just to find one or two individuals. In order to make the system more usable, this program allows the operator to enter all or part of the index. After the search characters are entered, the program searches the entire file for any records which match the characters entered.

The screen design is basically the same as that for the IND ADDR LISTING PROG except that there is a chance that no matching record will be found. If no record is found with a matching last name, an appropriate message is displayed, and the operator is given another chance to search the file.

Instructions for Running the Program

Run the program by entering

RUN IND ADDR HELLO PROG <RETURN>

After the menu is displayed, enter a 3 to start execution of the search program.

The first screen will let you know that the program is reading and loading the table. After the index table is loaded, a second screen will be displayed, requesting that you enter from one to five characters to be used in searching the index file.

```
ENTER FROM 1 TO 5 CHARACTERS TO SEARCH
FOR A MATCH.

SEARCH VALUE = (      )
```

After receiving the value to be used during the search process, the program will search quickly through the index table and then read and display any records which match the characters entered.

The IND ADDR SEARCH PROG works much faster than the SEQ ADDR SEARCH PROG because the search is all done in memory, and only the matching records must be read.

```
MATCH NUMBER 01 OF 04

INDEX     = (JO   )
RECORD #  = (01)

NAME      = (MARY JONES             )
ADDRESS   = (4321 FIRST STREET      )

CITY      = (MODEL TOWN   )
STATE     = (CA)
ZIP CODE  = (98765)
PHONE     = (444-333-2222)

COMMENT#1 = (GOOD BASIC PROGRAMMER)
COMMENT#2 = (KNOWS PASCAL/COBOL/AS)

PRESS  Q   TO QUIT LIST OPERATION
PRESS  C   TO CONTINUE
```

Only one record is shown per screen, but the first line of the screen indicates how many matches were found. The relative record number is displayed on the line following the record index. Normally you do not display the relative record number for the operator. It is provided in this example to emphasize that although the operator retrieves the record by the index value, the program must associate the index with a relative record number before being able to read the file.

If no matches are found, a message is displayed as follows, and the computer pauses in order for the operator to read the message. Once the operator is done, C is entered to continue.

```
            NO MATCHES FOUND


    PRESS  Q  TO QUIT PROCESSING

    PRESS  C  TO CONTINUE
```

If no matches are found, or after all the matches have been displayed, the operator is given a chance to either quit and return to the HELLO menu or enter a new search value.

Program Listing

```
1000 REM IND ADDR SEARCH PROG
1010 REM -----------------------
1020 CLEAR :G1 = PEEK (116) * 256 + PEEK (115) - 40 :GA$ = "
     12345678901234567890" + "12345678901234567890"
1030 REM
1040 REM -----------------------
1050 REM DRIVE ROUTINE
1060 GOSUB 1120: REM BEGINNING
1070 GOSUB 1410: REM MAIN MOD
1080 GOTO 2440: REM END MODULE
1090 REM
1100 REM -----------------------
1110 REM BEGINNING ROUTINE
1120 TEXT : NORMAL : HOME : SPEED= 255
1130 D$ = CHR$ (4)
1140 FDRIVE = 1:PDRIVE = 1
1150 F1FILEID$ = "INDEX FILE"
1160 F2FILEID$ = "IND ADDR FILE"
1170 REM
1180 DIM INDEX$ (99),MTCH$(99)
1190 REM
1200 VTAB 8: HTAB 8
1210 PRINT "READING FILE & LOADING TABLE"
1220 PRINT D$
1230 PRINT D$;"OPEN ";F1FILEID$;",L8,D";FDRIVE
1240 FOR REC = 0 TO 99
1250 PRINT D$;"READ ";F1FILEID$;",R";REC
1260 VTAB 10: HTAB 17: PRINT "REC = ";REC
1270 INPUT X1$
1280 PRINT D$
1290 IF LEFT$ (X1$,5) = "....." THEN 1320
1300 INDEX$(N1) = X1$
1310 N1 = N1 + 1
1320 NEXT
1330 N3 = N1 - 1: REM N3 = EXACT NUMBER OF ENTRIES IN TABLE
1340 PRINT D$
1350 PRINT D$;"OPEN ";F2FILEID$;",L125,D";FDRIVE
```

```
1360 PRINT D$
1370 RETURN
1380 REM
1390 REM ----------------------
1400 REM MAIN ROUTINE
1410 GOSUB 1720: REM ENTER SEARCH VALUE
1420 GOSUB 1660: REM SEARCH INDEX
1430 IF N2 = 0 THEN HOME : VTAB 8: PRINT "NO MATCHES FOUND":
     PRINT : GOTO 1570
1440 REM
1450 FOR N1 = 0 TO N2 - 1
1460 REC$ = RIGHT$ (MTCH$(N1),2)
1470 REC = VAL (REC$)
1480 GOSUB 2080: REM READ DISK
1490 GOSUB 2240: REM WRITE SCREEN
1500 PRINT "PRESS  Q  TO QUIT LIST OPERATION"
1510 PRINT "PRESS  C  TO CONTINUE";
1520 GET X1$: IF X1$ = "Q" THEN N1 = N2
1530 IF X1$ < > "C" THEN 1520
1540 NEXT
1550 REM
1560 HOME : VTAB 10
1570 PRINT "PRESS  Q  TO QUIT PROCESSING"
1580 PRINT
1590 PRINT "PRESS  C  TO CONTINUE";
1600 GET X1$: IF X1$ = "C" THEN 1410
1610 IF X1$ < > "Q" THEN 1600
1620 RETURN
1630 REM
1640 REM ----------------------
1650 REM SEARCH INDEXES
1660 N2 = 0
1670 FOR N1 = 0 TO N3
1680 IF LEFT$ (INDEX$(N1),SIZE) = INDEX$ THEN MTCH$(N2) =
     INDEX$(N1): N2 = N2 + 1
1690 NEXT
1700 RETURN
1710 REM ----------------------
1720 REM ENTER SEARCH VALUE
1730 HOME : VTAB 10
1740 PRINT "ENTER FROM 1 TO 5 CHARACTERS TO SEARCH"
1750 PRINT "FOR A MATCH."
1760 PRINT
1770 PRINT "SEARCH VALUE = (     )"
1780 VTAB 13: HTAB 17
1790 GALEGTH = 5: GOSUB 1890
1800 INDEX$ = GBANSWER$
1810 SIZE = GCCHAR
1820 IF SIZE = 0 THEN 1730
1830 INDEX$ = LEFT$ (INDEX$,SIZE)
1840 HOME
1850 RETURN
1860 REM
1870 REM ----------------------
```

```
1880 REM GET SUBROUTINE
1890 IF G3 = 0 THEN GOSUB 2040
1900 G3 = G1 + GA - 1: FOR G2 = G1 TO G3: POKE G2,32: NEXT : G2 = G1
1910 CALL 768:GB = PEEK (775) - 128: IF GB = 08 THEN 1980
1920 IF GB = 13 THEN 2000
1930 IF GB = 21 THEN PRINT CHR$ ( PEEK (G2));: GOTO 1960
1940 IF GB = 44 OR GB = 58 OR GB < 32 THEN 1910
1950 PRINT CHR$ (GB);: POKE G2,GB
1960 G2 = G2 + 1: IF G2 > G3 THEN 2030
1970 GOTO 1910
1980 G2 = G2 - 1: IF G2 < G1 THEN G2 = G1: GOTO 1910
1990 PRINT CHR$ (8);: GOTO 1910
2000 IF G1 = G2 THEN 2020
2010 FOR GC = G2 TO G3: PRINT " ";: NEXT
2020 FOR GC = G2 TO G3: POKE GC,32: NEXT
2030 GB$ = LEFT$ (GA$,GA):GC = G2 - G1: RETURN
2040 POKE 768,32: POKE 769,12: POKE 770,253: POKE 771,141:
     POKE 772,07: POKE 773,03: POKE 774,96: RETURN
2050 REM
2060 REM --------------------------
2070 REM READ DISK
2080 PRINT D$
2090 PRINT D$;"READ ";F2FILEID$;",R";REC
2100 INPUT A1ADDR$
2110 PRINT D$
2120 AANAME$ = LEFT$ (A1ADDR$,25)
2130 ABADDR$ = MID$ (A1ADDR$,26,25)
2140 ACCITY$ = MID$ (A1ADDR$,51,15)
2150 ADSTE$ = MID$ (A1ADDR$,66,2)
2160 AEZIP$ = MID$ (A1ADDR$,68,5)
2170 AFPHNE$ = MID$ (A1ADDR$,73,10)
2180 AGCOM1$ = MID$ (A1ADDR$,83,21)
2190 AHCOM2$ = RIGHT$ (A1ADDR$,21)
2200 RETURN
2210 REM
2220 REM --------------------------
2230 REM PRINT SCREEN IMAGE
2240 HOME : PRINT
2250 PRINT "MATCH NUMBER "N1 + 1" OF "N2
2260 PRINT
2270 PRINT "INDEX    =("LEFT$ (MTCH$(N1),5)")"
2280 PRINT "RECORD # =("REC$")"
2290 PRINT
2300 PRINT "NAME     =("AANAME$")"
2310 PRINT "ADDRESS  =("ABADDR$")"
2320 PRINT "CITY     =("ACCITY$")"
2330 PRINT "STATE    =("ADSTE$")"
2340 PRINT "ZIP CODE =("AEZIP$")"
2350 PRINT "PHONE    =("LEFT$ (AFPHNE$,3)"-" MID$ (AFPHNE$,4
     ,3)"-" RIGHT$ (AFPHNE$,4)")"
2360 PRINT
2370 PRINT "COMMENT#1=("AGCOM1$")"
2380 PRINT "COMMENT#2=("AHCOM2$")"
2390 PRINT
```

```
2400 RETURN
2410 REM
2420 REM ------------------------
2430 REM ENDING ROUTINE
2440 HOME
2450 PRINT D$
2460 PRINT D$;"CLOSE"
2470 PRINT D$;"RUN IND ADDR HELLO PROG,D"PDRIVE
2480 REM
2490 REM ------------------------
```

Cross Reference Listing

Variable names used with the address record:

A1$ 2100, 2120, 2130, 2140, 2150, 2160, 2170, 2180, 2190
AA$ 2120, 2300
AB$ 2130, 2310
AC$ 2140, 2320
AD$ 2150, 2330
AE$ 2160, 2340
AF$ 2170, 2350
AG$ 2180, 2370
AH$ 2190, 2380

Variable names used with the disk commands:

D$ 1130, 1220, 1230, 1250, 1280, 1340, 1350, 1360, 2080, 2090, 2110, 2450,
    2460, 2470
F1$ 1150, 1230, 1250
F2$ 1160, 1350, 2090
FD 1140, 1230, 1350
PD 1140, 2470

Variable names used with the index table:

IN$ 1680, 1800, 1830
IN$(1180, 1300, 1680
MT$(1180, 1460, 1680, 2270

Other general purpose variable names:

N1 1300, 1310, 1330, 1450, 1460, 1520, 1670, 1680, 2250, 2270
N2 1430, 1450, 1520, 1660, 1680, 2250
N3 1330, 1670
RE 1240, 1250, 1260, 1470, 2090

RE$ 1460, 1470, 2280
SI   1680, 1810, 1820, 1830
X1$ 1270, 1290, 1300, 1520, 1530, 1600, 1610

Explanation by
Line Number

Detailed explanations by line number follow.

1100   REM --------------------
....

1110   REM BEGINNING ROUTINE

1180   DIM INDEX$ (99),MTCH$(99)
Two tables are defined. The first table stores the index values read in from the disk, while the second table is used to store any matches found during the search.

Here comes another "Do as I say and not as I do." Notice that the constant 99 is used to define the tables. The value (99) is hard coded all through the program. A much better approach is to use a variable thoughout the program. If a variable is used and the program needs to be changed, only one line is affected.

Yes: 1175 T1 = 99
        1180 DIM INDEX$(T1),MTCH$(T1)
        ....
        1240 FOR REC = 0 TO T1

No: 1180 DIM INDEX$(99),MTCH$(99)
        ....
        1240 FOR REC = 0 TO 99

If a constant is used, every line in the program must be examined and the lines using the constant changed. Most likely you will miss one line or make a mistake while changing a line. Try to make it a practice always to use variables and to initialize them to their starting values in the BEGINNING ROUTINE.

1240   FOR REC = 0 TO 99
....

1290   IF LEFT$ (X1$,5) = "....." THEN 1320

1300   INDEX$(N1) = X1$

1310   N1 = N1 + 1

1320   NEXT

1330   N3 = N1 - 1: REM N3 = EXACT NUMBER OF ENTRIES IN TABLE
The routine for reading the index varies from that used in the UPDATE program in
that any index which contains dummy periods is not loaded into the table. When
only active index values are loaded, the SEARCH executes faster (depending on the
number of active entries).

1390   REM --------------------

1400   REM MAIN ROUTINE

1410   GOSUB 1720: REM ENTER SEARCH VALUE

1420   GOSUB 1660: REM SEARCH INDEX

1430   IF N2 = 0 THEN HOME : VTAB 8: PRINT "NO MATCHES FOUND": PRINT :
GOTO 1570
The MAIN ROUTINE requests the operator to enter a value to be used in searching
the index (line 1410). After a search value has been entered the INDEX$ table is
searched for matches, and any matching value is placed in the table MTCH$ (line
1420). If no matches are found, a message is displayed, and the operator is given a
chance to enter another value or quit processing.

1450   FOR N1 = 0 TO N2 − 1
The entries are printed out with a FOR/NEXT loop. The loop is executed one less
time than the value in N2. If you look at the SEARCH ROUTINE, you will find that
N2 is always 1 greater than the number of matches.

1460   REC$ = RIGHT$ (MTCH$(N1),2)

1470   REC = VAL (REC$)
Lines 1460 and 1470 extract the record number from the index record. Remember,
REC$ is used for printing, while the numeric variable REC is used in the disk READ
instruction. The RIGHT$ function may appear rather complex, so let's break it down
into parts to see what is happening.

            MTCH$(N1)   = A table entry
RIGHT$(MTCH$(N1),2) = The right two characters of the table entry

A table entry is just like any other variable, but you must remember to use the correct number of parentheses.

1520   GET X1$: IF X1$ = "Q" THEN N1 = N2

Line 1520 tests to see if the operator wants to quit. If the operator wants to quit, the variable used in the FOR/NEXT loop (N1) is set to a number equal to or greater than the number of times the loop is to be executed. This is a way to terminate the FOR/NEXT loop without a GOTO instruction.

1640   REM --------------------

1650   REM SEARCH INDEXES

1660   N2 = 0

1670   FOR N1 = 0 TO N3

1680   IF LEFT$ (INDEX$(N1),SIZE) = INDEX$ THEN MTCH$(N2) = IN
DEX$(N1): N2 = N2 + 1

1690   NEXT

The search is basically the same as earlier search versions, except that since the operator can search the table more than once, the program must reset any variable used in the routine. Line 1660 sets N2 equal to zero each time the SEARCH ROUTINE is executed. The second part of the code to look at is on line 1680. Notice that the variable SIZE is used with the LEFT$ function to make sure only the left portion of the index is compared with the index value entered by the operator. Remember when comparing string variables to always compare equal length variables.

1710   REM --------------------

1720   REM ENTER SEARCH VALUE
....

1810   SIZE = GCCHAR

Line 1810 places the size of the variable into a more descriptive variable name. Remember, the GET subroutine returns the number of characters keyed in by the operator in the variable GCCHAR. By limiting the size of the search to the specific number of characters entered, the program allows the operator to test only a leading portion of the indexes.

1820   IF SIZE = 0 THEN 1730

Line 1820 makes sure the operator entered at least one character to be used in searching the index table. If the operator did not enter a character, then logic flow starts back at the first line of the routine.

1830   INDEX$ = LEFT$ (INDEX$,SIZE)

Since the GET subroutine returns trailing blanks, line 1830 truncates the value of INDEX$ to the exact number of characters entered.

2220   REM ----------------------

2230   REM PRINT SCREEN IMAGE

2240   HOME : PRINT

2250   PRINT "MATCH NUMBER "N1 + 1" OF "N2

2260   PRINT

2270   PRINT "INDEX   =("LEFT$ (MTCH$(N1),5)")"

2280   PRINT "RECORD # =("REC$")"

The PRINT SCREEN IMAGE ROUTINE presents no new coding, but there are several lines which should be touched on. First, line 2250 is a nice feature for the operator. By looking at the first line of the screen, the operator knows immediately how many matches were found and how many screens will be displayed.

If I were rewriting the program, I would change the logic to allow the operator to go through the screens more than once. It is not unlikely that an operator would go through the screens looking at all the matches and then would want to go back and see them again. This would be easy to allow by just putting a message on the last screen displayed asking if the operator wanted to see the matches again (Y or N). If the operator entered a Y, logic flow would branch back to line 1720 to redisplay the records.

ASCII Character, Binary, and Decimal Table

Bit Pattern	Decimal Number	Keying Symbol	Bit Pattern	Decimal Number	Keying Symbol
0000000	000	CTRL-@	0101110	046	.
0000001	001	CTRL-A	0101111	047	/
0000010	002	CTRL-B	0110000	048	0
0000011	003	CTRL-C	0110001	049	1
0000100	004	CTRL-D	0110010	050	2
0000101	005	CTRL-E	0110011	051	3
0000110	006	CTRL-F	0110100	052	4
0000111	007	CTRL-G	0110101	053	5
0001000	008	CTRL-H	0110110	054	6
0001001	009	CTRL-I	0110111	055	7
0001010	010	CTRL-J	0111000	056	8
0001011	011	CTRL-K	0111001	057	9
0001100	012	CTRL-L	0111010	058	:
0001101	013	CTRL-M	0111011	059	;
0001110	014	CTRL-N	0111100	060	<
0001111	015	CTRL-O	0111101	061	=
0010000	016	CTRL-P	0111110	062	>
0010001	017	CTRL-Q	0111111	063	?
0010010	018	CTRL-R	1000000	064	@
0010011	019	CTRL-S	1000001	065	A
0010100	020	CTRL-T	1000010	066	B
0010101	021	CTRL-U	1000011	067	C
0010110	022	CTRL-V	1000100	068	D
0010111	023	CTRL-W	1000101	069	E
0011000	024	CTRL-X	1000110	070	F
0011001	025	CTRL-Y	1000111	071	G
0011010	026	CTRL-Z	1001000	072	H
0011011	027	ESC	1001001	073	I
0011100	028	CTRL-Y	1001010	074	J
0011101	029	CTRL-SHIFT-M	1001011	075	K
0011110	030	CTRL-SHIFT-N	1001100	076	L
0011111	031	CTRL-DASH	1001101	077	M
0100000	032	space	1001110	078	N
0100001	033	!	1001111	079	O

Bit Pattern	Decimal Number	Keying Symbol	Bit Pattern	Decimal Number	Keying Symbol
0100010	034	"	1010000	080	P
0100011	035	#	1010001	081	Q
0100100	036	$	1010010	082	R
0100101	037	%	1010011	083	S
0100110	038	&	1010100	084	T
0100111	039	'	1010101	085	U
0101000	040	(	1010110	086	V
0101001	041	)	1010111	087	W
0101010	042	*	1011000	088	X
0101011	043	+	1011001	089	Y
0101100	044	,	1011010	090	Z
0101101	045	-	1011011	091	[

Index

ABS function, 139
Alphanumeric constant, 57, 130
Alphanumeric variable, 53, 57
APPEND instruction, 258, 266, 269, 298
APPLE IIe, 5
APPLE II +, 5
Applesoft BASIC, 12, 15, 16
Application, 300, 309
Arrays, 202, 424
Arrays, memory usage, 204
Arithmetic expression, 175
Argument, 242
ASC function, 140
ASCII, 128, 140
Automatic tab function, 84

Backup copies, 11, 299, 334, 355, 357, 398
Backward GOTO, 96
Backward slash \, 262, 391
Binary file, 12, 16
Bit pattern, 172
BLOAD command, 24
Booting, 9
BRUN command, 25
BSAVE command, 24
Buffer, 255, 280, 283
Byte, 58

CALL instruction, 241
CALL -868, 111, 168
CALL -958, 168
Carriage return character, 82, 105
Catalog, 253, 255
CATALOG command, 14
CHR$ function, 152, 162
CLEAR instruction, 245
CLOSE instruction, 259, 280
Comma
    automatic tab function, 84

disk usage, 268, 270
disk instructions, 277
embedded, 71
field separator, 44
PRINT instruction, 80, 84
READ instruction, 277
variable separator, 71
WRITE instruction, 272
Colon, instruction separation, 102
Colon, use of, 27
Column 40, problems with using, 105
Concantenation, 128
Conditional GOTO, 96
Constant, 57
CONT instruction, 228
Control function, 162
CONTROL key, 5
Control program, 9
CONTROL-C, 35, 37, 51
CONTROL-D, 141, 164, 263, 267, 307
CONTROL-L, 164, 425
CONTROL-RESET, 35, 197, 198, 260
CONTROL-S, 35, 37
CONTROL-X, 187
COPYA program, 12
CRT (Cathode Ray Tube), 80
CTRL key, 5
Current copy, 355

Data file, 12, 438
Data name, 48, 56
Data name dictionary, 45, 48
Default tab settings, 84
DEF FN instruction, 244
DEL instruction, 42
DELETE command, 23, 259
Dependent code, 326
DIM instruction, 202
Direct access, 379
Directory, 253

511